THE LATIN CLERK

Frontispiece: Adrian Fortescue at Letchworth: probably the last photograph taken of him; circulated after his death by his executrix, Ethel Elmes.

THE LATIN CLERK

The Life, Work, and Travels of Adrian Fortescue

Aidan Nichols, O.P.

The Lutterworth Press

The Lutterworth Press
P.O. Box 60
Cambridge
CB1 2NT
United Kingdom

www.lutterworth.com
publishing@lutterworth.com

ISBN: 978 0 7188 9274 6

British Library Cataloguing in Publication Data
A record is available from the British Library

Contents

List of Illustrations

Preface

I had long admired Adrian Fortescue, dedicating to his memory in 1992 the first, Edinburgh, edition of my *Rome and the Eastern Churches. A Study in Schism* (and the dedication of course remained in the second, San Francisco, edition of 2010). But the idea of writing something about him came to me when reading Janet Martin Soskice's page-turner, *Sisters of Sinai. How Two Lady Adventurers found the Hidden Gospels* (London: Chatto and Windus, 2009). I realised that some of the same elements found in her book were likely to be present in a study of Fortescue.

Firstly, here was someone fascinated by the Christian East and closely acquainted with it through travel. As a commentator on matters Oriental Fortescue combined romantic enthusiasm with political savvy and theological insight, a rather rare but (to me) attractive combination. Secondly, there was a Cambridge connexion — I liked that, as a resident of the city for twenty-five years — for as his diaries show, Fortescue was often in Cambridge, whether to meet dons, shop at Heffer's, or make a sacramental confession. Letchworth Garden City, his home for the larger part of his priestly life, was on the Cambridge to King's Cross railway, and still is, if you catch a stopping train. It is appropriate that perhaps the largest single cache of his letters is preserved in the Cambridge University Library. Thirdly, like Janet Soskice's 'Sisters of Sinai', Fortescue had a passionate concern with Christian antiquity. Listen to what he says — and the undertone of *pietas* in what he says — in so apparently unlikely a source as a Catholic Truth Society pamphlet on vestments. (He is speaking of the old Latin Mass, now celebrated under the somewhat exotic title, the 'Extraordinary Form'.)

> If Ambrose or Augustine or Leo came back now they would find hardly a thing in our world intelligible. Our language, dress, manners, even food would be utterly barbarous and strange to them. And then, if they wandered into a Catholic church, there and there alone would they be at home. They would see the sacrifice they offered still shown forth in the same way. They

would recognize the prayers and understand the language that they used. And as they gazed from the barbarous clothes of the congregation to the altar they would see at least one man dressed as they were. They would recognize the *tunica talaris* [the alb] girt, the *lorum* [the stole], the *mappula* [maniple] on his left arm, and I think — I hope — that they would recognize that he wore over all a *planeta* [chasuble], as they had done. So the ghosts of the mighty men who spread the name of Christ throughout the dying Empire would know that, in spite of all changes, their Church still stands, after sixteen long centuries.

That reminds me of a fourth and last reason for wanting to write about Fortescue. Whereas Professor Soskice's 'Lady Adventurers' were Presbyterians, the relics of Anglican clergymen, and rather enjoyed conversational opportunities to share with the Orthodox indignation at the enormities of Rome, this was a thoroughly Catholic subject, likely to be of use in my own lifetime theological project of accessing and making more available to others the riches of the Catholic tradition. Fortescue's attempts to show people — in both theory and practice — the best of the Church's liturgical patrimony is a good example of that. His love of the Christian East was strong enough for him to consider transferring, as a priest, to the Byzantine Rite (in later parlance, the Byzantine 'ritual church'), but he remained what he called himself: 'The Latin Clerk'.

It was never likely that the drama of Professor Soskice's narrative would be reproduced in my materials. Still, Adrian Fortescue's literary panache might, I thought, make up for the absence of so strong a story-line. I think so still, and he knew a great deal more about Christian history, Liturgy, and the contemporary condition of the Eastern churches than did the 'Sisters of Sinai', as well as surpassing them as a linguist. Syriac, which the ladies (or at any rate one of them) made their *forte*, was among his accomplishments, as bear witness citations — admittedly, these are brief — in that language from the *Chronicle of Edessa* and the *Hymn of the Apostle Judas Thomas* in his teaching notes from St Edmund's College, Ware. It seems to have been rather a Johnny-come-lately among his various tongues: a Notebook preserved in the Westminster Diocesan Archives claims assiduous study of Syriac in the last two years of the First World War, though he must have had an elementary knowledge before that date, for he discusses how best to render Syriac orthography in the preface to his *The Lesser Eastern Churches*, which dates from 1913. More conspicuously, Hebrew and Arabic were constituent elements in the *doctoratus completus* that gave him his sobriquet 'the Doctor' among the Westminster clergy, and he was able to practice a Syrian form of Arabic during his stay in the Middle East in 1906–1907. At that time he was still hopeful he might be considered a candidate for a chair of Oriental Languages at Vienna.

In its zest and many-sidedness, Fortescue's example of a priestly life is inspirational. His life was not without its difficulties: early bereavement, uncongenial postings, self-questioning as a pastoral priest, serious irritation at what he considered the excessive caution of Church authority in its attitude to scholarship, and, signalled poignantly at one point, the breakdown of friendship. And finally there was the cancer that took him to a premature death. But as the king (Fortescue would have considered him, rather, the Elector of Hanover) remarks to the queen in Alan Bennett's *The Madness of George III*: no life is without its regrets, and none without its consolations.

For the help received in looking at original documents I am very grateful to Dom Aidan Bellenger, the Abbot of Downside; Father Nicholas Schofield, the Archivist of the Westminster Archdiocesan Archives, together with his assistants Claire Muller and Peter Kent, and to Nicholas Robinson of the Fitzwilliam Museum, Cambridge, who located for me the Fortescue letters in the manuscripts collection of the Cambridge University Library. Alan Robinson of St Edmund's College, Ware, put into my hands a copy of a privately printed book, *Adrian*, by the late Mgr John R. McCarthy of East Cleveland, Ohio, which assembles a mass of materials — invaluable for Fortescue's family background — in a rather disorganized and altogether non-paginated way. He also allowed me to see, and handle, the wonderful Fortescue vestments and frontals, saved from decomposition at Letchworth by the efforts of Duncan Gallie, also of St Edmund's, Ware. It is excellent to see how well they are now cared for in the place where Fortescue taught seminarians in the last years of his life. Fergal Martin of the Catholic Truth Society kindly arranged for me to look at rare copies of Fortescue pamphlets published by the Society in the early years of the twentieth century, and the staff of the Society's headquarters in Vauxhall — Carlo Boi, Pier Paolo Finaldi, and Eddie O'Brien — went to considerable trouble to help me in my search. And I must thank too, of course, Professor Soskice for the stimulus provided by her delightful book. Finally, the author and publisher are extremely grateful to Josh Tidy, Curator of the First Garden City Museum at Letchworth, for permission to use photographic images made in connexion with the Museum's special exhibition about the life and work of Adrian Fortescue, which was mounted in 2008.

Blackfriars, Cambridge,
Ash Wednesday, 2011.

1. Background and Boyhood

Paternal inheritance

Adrian Fortescue belonged to a gentry family with strong clerical connexions in the Anglican establishment. His father, Edward Bowles Knottesford Fortescue (1816–1877), was born at Stoke-by-Nayland in Suffolk, the son of Francis Fortescue and Maria Fortescue, née Downing (her father, George Downing, was rector of Ovington and a prebendary of Ely cathedral). [1] Francis Fortescue (1772–1859) had taken Orders in the Church of England, as would his son. But thanks to the testamentary arrangements of his godfather he became a very wealthy man. A condition of the inheritance was adding 'Knottesford', the surname of his benefactor, to his own, and in due course it was passed down to the subject of this book. In 1823, the couple moved with (at that point) their two small sons, George and Edward, to the family estate, Alveston Manor,[2] then on the outskirts of Stratford on Avon, where Francis lived as a 'squarson', acting as rector of the parish of Billesley, some five miles from their home.[3] Educated at home and then at Wadham College, Oxford, Edward Fortescue married, when 22, Frances Anne Spooner, the daughter of Archdeacon William Spooner, the rector of Elmdon (like Billesley, Elmdon was a Warwickshire village).[4] The wedding, solemnized by his father, brought Edward valuable connexions. The bride's aunt, Barbara Spooner, from a Birmingham mercantile family of Evangelical

---

1. T. Fortescue, Lord Clermont, *A History of the Family of Fortescue in All its Branches* (London: Ellis and White, 1880, 2nd edition), p. 23.

2. Now, one regrets to say, the Macdonald Alveston Manor Hotel.

3. For most of my information about Fortescue's father and grandfather, I am reliant on J.R. McCarthy, *Adrian. Adrian Fortescue, Cleric of the Roman Rite. A Biography* (East Cleveland, OH: McCarthy, 1999). As mentioned in the Preface, this book has not been provided with pagination. For indications of how his data were acquired, the author refers the reader to his unpublished dissertation of 1972 from Case Western Reserve University, Cleveland, Ohio.

4 T. Fortescue, Lord Clermont, *A History of the Family of Fortescue in All its Branches*, op. cit., p. 23. The elder William Spooner was Archdeacon of Coventry.

propensities, was the wife of William Wilberforce (1759–1833), the hero of the campaign for abolition of the slave trade.[5] Frances's sister would marry Archibald Campbell Tait (1811–1882), who reached the pinnacle of Anglican achievement as archbishop of Canterbury. Her brother, William Archibald Spooner (1844–1930), Warden of New College, Oxford, was the hapless inventor of the 'spoonerism'.[6] Among Frances's cousins was Samuel Wilberforce (1805–1873), later bishop in turn of Oxford and Winchester. In turn, Samuel Wilberforce was related by marriage to Henry Edward Manning (1808–1892), sometime archdeacon of Chichester and later to be archbishop of Westminster (their wives were sisters). Edward Fortescue was thoroughly wired in to the English Establishment. Possibly, given Tait's Caledonian origin, one should write 'British'.

He was made a deacon in 1838, the year he wed, and a priest the year following. Perhaps predictably, he served his title as curate to his father, who gave him responsibility for building a chapel of ease at nearby Wilmcote, hitherto a stronghold of Nonconformity and known to the history of English literature as the birthplace of Mary Arden, Shakespeare's mother. Edward, strongly influenced when at Wadham by the Oxford Movement, made sure the new congregation was Tractarian in allegiance, but he was not to remain a Warwickshire curate for ever. In 1850, owing to the 'powerful recommendations of Lord Forbes and the Honourable Mr Boyle, Banker and Heir to the Earl of Glasgow' (so his father explained to the President of Magdalen College, Oxford, Martin Routh, a Tractarian sympathizer, 1755–1854)[7] — Edward Fortescue was elected Provost of the newly founded Scots Episcopal cathedral of St Ninian at Perth (the first cathedral to be built by the Episcopalians, the foundation stone had been laid the previous year). The terms of the communication leave a strong impression that the canon-electors were swayed not least by the realization that the successful candidate was wealthy enough not to require remuneration. Though the proud father told Routh that Scottish Episcopalianism remained 'the most

---

5   R. Furneaux, *William Wilberforce* (London: Hamish Hamilton, 1974), pp. 161–171.

6   R. Hayter, *Spooner. A Biography* (London: W. H. Allen, 1977), pp. 18–19.

7   A search for this letter (cited by McCarthy) among the Routh Papers at Magdalen College, Oxford, by the Archivist, Dr Robin Darwall-Smith, has proved fruitless. But Routh had a well-documented interest in the fortunes of the Scottish Episcopal Church, see R.D. Middleton, *Dr Routh* (London and New York: Oxford University Press, 1938), pp. 65–75. It is pertinent to the terms in which Francis Fortescue wrote to know that Routh had been the dedicatee of Newman's 1837 *Lectures on the Prophetical Office of the Church*, the classic statement of the Anglican 'via media' between Protestantism and Rome, in R.D. Middleton, *Dr Routh*, op. cit., pp. xi, 138–139.

powerful bulwark and most effective testimony against the errors and corruptions of the Church of Rome', in 1857 his son became chairman of the Association for Promoting the Unity of Christendom, the aim of which was precisely to reconcile the Anglican and Catholic Churches — though the bishops of the Church of England shunned it, and in time the participation of Catholics would be forbidden. In July 1871 Edward Fortescue resigned as Provost of Perth, re-married at Marylebone Parish Church (his first wife had died in 1868), and in 1872, along with his new spouse, Gertrude Robins, was received into full communion with the Catholic Church. He had evidently met with travails in post.

> [A]t Perth . . . Dr. Charles Wordsworth, Bishop of S. Andrew's, Dunkeln, and Dunblane, refused to worship in his own cathedral because he objected to the very mild ceremonial which had been introduced by Provost Fortescue and the Precentor, Mr. Henry Humble.[8]

More fundamentally, however, his change of religious allegiance had been prompted by the ringing clarity of the teaching on Church authority offered by the First Vatican Council (1869–1870) which defined the universal jurisdiction and doctrinal infallibility of the pope.

Conversion

The Provost's conversion was just the sort of thing Cardinal Manning of Westminster, an architect of the Ultramontane triumph at the Council, rather expected — and in the event was by no means wholly disappointed. '[A]fter a lull between 1855 and 1868 the stream of conversions began again. The peak period of this . . . movement lasted from 1869 to 1874 but a gradual flow continued throughout the century.'[9] On the analysis offered by the historian of post-Reformation English Catholicism David Mathew, a sharp contrast pertains between 'Newman's converted disciples' and 'Manning's converts'. The former, 'drawn partly by affection for the Master', were, typically, dons and learned clergymen. The latter, 'assisted towards the Church by Dr Manning's clear rather arid arguments and forceful piety', were more likely to be members of the secular professions (unless they were hereditary peers or, even more abundantly, peeresses).[10] If Mathew is correct in his generalisations, then Fortescue senior was something of a sport in his generation, a throwback to the 'Oakeley–Faber

---

8   P. Anson, *Fashions in Church Furnishing, 1840–1940* (London: Studio Vista, 1965, 2nd edition), p. 184.

9   D. Mathew, *Catholicism in England, 1535–1935. Portrait of a Minority: its Culture and Tradition* (London: Longmans, Green, 1936), p. 210.

10 Ibid.

period'[11]. The son of this belated Tractarian convert was born on 14 January 1874, to a rather elderly father but a very definitely Catholic one.

In the period, the question of the possible (re-)ordination of married Anglican clergy simply did not arise. Instead, Edward Fortescue served his new Communion as an educator, becoming Principal of the school attached to the church of the Sacred Heart in Holloway (north London), where he also taught Latin and Greek. His closest Catholic associations, however, were with the Dominican friars at Haverstock Hill, only a mile or two from the school (both districts fringed Hampstead Heath). The Dominicans evidently appreciated their gifted (and wealthy) friend, responding with full liturgical honours — Solemn Vespers of the Dead, Matins of the Dead, a celebration of High Mass — to his sudden demise in August 1877 at the age of sixty-one. Apart from four sons and a daughter from his first marriage, he had left a young widow and three small children: Clara Mary Katherine, aged 5; Adrian Henry, aged 3, and Gertrude Raphael, aged ten months.

Mother and school

His widow, Gertrude Mary Fortescue, née Robins (1839–1886), came from a similar background to her husband.[12] The daughter of a clergyman, the Revd Sanderson Robins (his literary remains include an 1855 broadside *The Whole Evidence against the Claims of the Roman Church*), her grandmother, Lady Caroline Barham, had been the youngest daughter of the eighth Earl of Thanet. Like her husband to be, Gertrude Robins had gravitated towards the Anglo-Catholic movement in the Church of England — not perhaps in its healthiest form, since she was for a while the prioress of a Benedictine sisterhood founded by the distinctly unbalanced Father Ignatius of Llanthony, otherwise Joseph Leycester Lyne (1837–1908).[13] After breaking with her monastic mentor she moved for a time to a Scottish Episcopal sisterhood, the Community of St Mary and St John

---

11 Ibid., p. 209. The reference is to two Tractarian converts both named 'Frederick': Frederick Oakeley (1802–1880), on whom see P. Galloway, *A Passionate Humility: Frederick Oakeley and the Oxford Movement* (Leominster: Gracewing, 1999), and Frederick William Faber (1814–1863), on whom see M.J. Wilkinson, *Frederick William Faber. A Great Servant of God* (Leominster: Gracewing, 2007).

12 Once again, the writer is indebted for the broad lines of Mrs Fortescue's life to John McCarthy's popularly presented summary in *Adrian* of his earlier research.

13 A. Calder-Marshall, *the Enthusiast. An Enquiry into the Life, Beliefs and Character of the Rev. Joseph Leycester Lyne, alias Father Ignatius OSB, Abbot of Elm Hill, Norwich, and Llanthony, Wales* (London: Faber and Faber, 1962).

– also known as the Scottish Society of Reparation – which had its origins in an orphanage run by the widow of a Tractarian clergyman in Leith. In due course, the foundress, Elizabeth Ann McDowal White, transferred her foundation to Perth where she was assured of support from Edward Fortescue, who acted as its Warden.[14] In addition to its laudable practical aims (the care of homeless children, Christian education, assistance to the parochial clergy), the Society took as its distinctive spiritual aim the 'offering of reparative Adoration to our Lord in the Blessed Sacrament on the Altar',[15] a sign of extremely 'advanced' opinions on Mrs White's part. The historian of Anglican Religious life, Peter Anson, suggests the Warden may have got the idea of a community of 'Adoration and Reparation' while on holiday in France.[16] In any case, there seems little doubt that, unlikely as it seems, this is how Adrian Fortescue's parents met.

Mrs Fortescue was by no means poorly off. Already provided for in Edward Fortescue's will, in 1878 she inherited the estate of the last Earl of Thanet. She moved to Maitland Park, Haverstock Hill, an address which lay within the bounds of the parish (as it would become[17]) attached to the Dominican priory of Our Lady of the Rosary and St Dominic, in Southampton Road, where a memorial chapel to her husband was eventually erected. The question of a Catholic education for her son naturally presented itself to his surviving parent. Despite her Dominican connexions (the English Province's 'apostolic school', then at Hinckley in Leicestershire, was not, in this period, outstanding), Mrs Fortescue sent her only boy to the Jesuit preparatory school at Boulogne-sur-mer from 1883 to 1885, transferring him in that year to the school established by Cardinal Manning's 'Oblates of St Charles' in Bayswater.

A matriarchal regime

Mrs Fortescue did not live long to enjoy her inheritance, dying at the age of 47 at Boulogne where she had taken a house, no doubt, in the first instance, to be near her son. Adrian, now 12, was taken into the household

---

14 P. Anson, *The Call of the Cloister. Religious Communities and Kindred Bodies in the Anglican Communion* (London: Society for Promoting Christian Knowledge, 1955), pp. 446–449.

15 Ibid., p. 447.

16 Ibid., p. 448, footnote 1.

17 The parish system proper was only introduced into the post-Reformation Catholic Church in England in 1918. Earlier, there were 'missions', with missionary rectors rather than parish priests: M.V. Sweeney, 'Diocesan Organization and Administration', in G.A. Beck, A.A, *The English Catholics, 1850–1950* (London: Burns and Oates, 1950), pp. 116–150, and especially at pp. 119–122.

of an aunt, sited not too inconveniently so far as his schooling was concerned in the south of London, at Wimbledon. Katherine Robins had been an Anglican nun at Clewer, near Windsor, the mother house of the Community of St John the Baptist, founded 1852, one of the most successful examples of Catholic-minded Anglicans heeding the 'call of the cloister'.[18] She had left the sisterhood and become a Roman Catholic, and was now looking after her elderly mother, across the road from the Jesuit church.

It does not sound like an ideal environment for a young lad. Oscar Wilde's remarks in *The Importance of Being Ernest* notwithstanding, the loss of both parents before one's teenage years must count as a misfortune rather than carelessness. The exclusively female nature and (one suspects) unremittingly devout tone of the Wimbledon household must have produced at times its *longueurs*. Perhaps Adrian Fortescue's decision to present himself for the priesthood was partly a desire to find a substitute parent in the Church — a Church which, though describing itself as 'Holy Mother', was very definitely patriarchal, rather than matriarchal, in structure. True, he did not give the impression of someone who had suffered serious emotional damage. But it may be significant that, by the demanding standards of priestly obedience in the period, his resilience in uncongenial situations was comparatively low.

The next stage

In October 1891, though a candidate for Manning's archdiocese (it was the last year of the Cardinal's life), Adrian Fortescue entered the Scots College at Rome.[19] It seems an unusual choice. Perhaps there was no room

---

18   P. Anson, *The Call of the Cloister*, op. cit., pp. 304–317.

19   The principal biographical details are given in J.G. Vance and J.W. Fortescue, *Adrian Fortescue. A Memoir* (London: Burns, Oates, and Washbourne, 1924). Downside Archives, IX AF, Box B, 'Notebook', contains a chronology based on Fortescue's correspondence with 'Mrs Squire', presumably his sister Clara Fortescue, who married George Frederick Squire in 1902, though I note that his master of ceremonies at Letchworth was named F.G. Squire. Westminster Diocesan Archives, Series 20, Box 22, includes a Notebook containing year by year summaries of his life and work, based, presumably, on the diaries but including material from the otherwise missing exercise-book notes on his extended Oriental journey of 1906–1907. A useful chronological table is provided in M. Davies (ed.), *The Wisdom of Adrian Fortescue* (Fort Collins, CO: Roman Catholic Books, 1999), pp. 78–85. Davies's book is a collection of Fortescue's articles on the Liturgy (prescinding from those on non-Western rites) as published in the *Catholic Encyclopaedia* (but shorn of much of their scholarly apparatus), preceded by an essay that is substantial but, like McCarthy's book, unprovided with references on Fortescue's life and work.

at the Venerable English College when he applied, or possibly it was thought appropriate for the son of a former clergyman of the Scottish Church, even if Edward Fortescue *had* been an English import to a Protestant cathedral. His son would show no subsequent interest in Scotland – but an absorbing interest in a priestly life, and in everything that was beautiful in the culture of the Catholic Church.

2. The Formative Years

Beginning at the Scots College

The Pontifical Scots College in Rome had been founded in 1600 to educate students for the Catholic priesthood disabled by the sweeping acts of the 1560 Reformation Parliament from training at home.[1] It was centrally located in the Via delle Quattro Fontane, not far from St Mary Major, in a newish building, supposedly the work of the distinguished architect of the reconstructed basilica of St Paul outside the Walls, Luigi Poletti (1792–1869). It seems more likely, however, that Poletti did a rough sketch of the façade and left the rest to minions in his office.[2] From the beginning, its students attended the Collegio Romano (later the *Gregorianum* or 'Gregorian University'), which was in easy walking distance. This continued to be the case even after the Society of Jesus ceased to be responsible for running the College, at the time of the Society's temporary suppression by Pope Clement XIV in 1773. All in all, it must have been, for a seventeen year old Englishman, an unusual experience — Italy, the Scots, papal Rome, all three factors utterly new to him. Fortunately for the historian, Fortescue decided to keep a diary.

The diaries — mostly in Latin when Fortescue is in Rome or England, chiefly in German when, in 1894, he moved to Austria, occasionally straying into Greek, and periodically returning to English, with the odd dash of Arabic — are an invaluable resource for his formative years as an ecclesiastical student. (They are no less useful for his early years as a curate or priest-in-charge of missions whose 'rectors' were, for whatever reason, otherwise engaged, and likewise, if more patchily, for his time as parish priest of Letchworth, which is when he really made his mark). Squeezed into the intervals of a non-negotiable study schedule (so the diaries attest), Fortescue's time at the Scots College was sensibly divided

---

1   Its history is told in the essays collected in R. McCluskey (ed.), *The Scots College, Rome, 1600-2000* (Edinburgh: John Donald, 2000).

2   R. McCluskey, 'Tribulations, 1820–1922', in ibid., pp. 67–107, where McCluskey wrote laconically: 'Indubitably the building could never be acclaimed an architectural wonder', p. 85.

between music-making, familiarizing himself with the Roman churches, attending some of the great ceremonies, and making excursions to local beauty spots: the Pincio, the Borghese gardens, Lake Albano, Tivoli, as well as exploring the Roman catacombs. It was a healthy mix for a well-rounded yet ecclesiastically strongly committed young man who was also a keen and often humorous observer.

Rhythm of Roman life

The diary for 1892 gives us a typical picture, and rather more fully than some of its successors. In January 1892 he heard Mass on St Agnes's day at Sant'Agnese in the Piazza Navona ('music ghastly'), and was intrigued by the blessing of lambs' wool for the weaving of metropolitans' pallia. '[A]t the end of Mass they put two lambs in baskets on the altar, incensed them (which made them cough), blessed them and sent them on their way'[3]. On the day following, 22 January, he attended Cardinal Manning's Requiem, which was celebrated by the bishop of Portsmouth at San Silvestro, the 'English-speaking' church (Manning had died on 14 January), and on 3 March, the anniversary of the Pope's coronation, he watched Leo XIII, wearing the tiara, processing through the Sala Ducale. Despite these spectacles, he was not much affected by *Romanità*. In his Innsbruck years, possibly under the influence of the prevailing sentiment in the Dual Monarchy, he was inclined to think the post-Revolutionary expansion of the role of Pope and Curia to be on balance a bad thing. Discussing with his fellow Innsbruck student Karel Mosterts, a Westphalian a good deal more Ultramontane than himself, he could not agree with him on the advantages of 'the growth of my Lord Pope's power'.[4] (We shall hear more of this theme in due course.)

By contrast with these solemn ceremonies, 11 March records a visit to a cakeshop, while on 17 March he is playing rounders in the Borghese gardens (strenuous outdoor activities play a big part in the diaries). On 5 April, sketching, he notes the flora of the Roman spring, and a fortnight or so later, the 'glorious views' obtained from riding on mule-back in the neighbourhood of Rocca di Papa, in the Alban hills.[5] His strongly developed visual aesthetic sense would in due time be put to good use as a parish priest in the planning of his church, St Hugh at Letchworth, including such telling details as the calligraphy of its church notices and the design of vestments and altar fabrics worthy of Catholic worship.

---

3   Downside Archives, IX AF, Box D, 'Agenda 1892', entry for 21 January, 1892.
4   Downside Archives, IX AF, Box D, 'Diary 1899', entry for 20 September, 1899.
5   Downside Archives, IX AF, Box D, 'Agenda 1892', entry for 20 April, 1892.

Adrian Fortescue at the Pontifical Scots College, Rome.

His Oriental interests were already emerging in his first year in Rome. On Holy Saturday, he attended the Armenian liturgy at San Niccolo di Tolentino and 'got much blessed bread',[6] while a couple of months later he was talking to Greeks at the Collegio Greco about their Liturgy (first in Latin, then in French), and learned from them that 'the best liturgical books are those published at Venice by schismatics', i.e. by the Orthodox.[7]

A few days later he has a class on plainsong (a lifelong passion) with the chaplain of the German church, Santa Maria dell'Anima. On 28 June we find him at St Peter's saying a *de profundis* for the last Stuarts at the monument by Canova. Fortescue's Jacobitism was probably exacerbated by the atmosphere of the Scots College, with its tribunes for the exiled royal family, portraits of Cardinal York as Henry IX and I, and occasional requiem Masses for the Stuart kings or pretenders. But it appears to have been in his background, judging by a reference in Newman's correspondence to his grandfather Francis as hailing from a 'nonjuring' family.[8] (The Non-Jurors were High Anglicans who had gone into schism rather than break their canonical oaths of allegiance to James II, dethroned in the 1688 'Glorious Revolution'.) Quite possibly, the embers of a hereditary Jacobitism had been fanned by his father's experience of Scottish Episcopalianism which, as a dissenting body, held no brief for the House of Hanover — or, later, Saxe-Coburg — over against the Stuarts. At any rate, his allegiance emerges clearly in the diaries, where White Rose Day (10 June, anniversary of the birth of the Old Pretender in 1688) is generally marked. The entry for the death of Victoria records (in Latin) the passing of 'an elderly lady commonly taken to be the Queen of England'.[9] The habit of mind persisted. In 1920 he wrote to the typographer Stanley Morison (1889–1967), who was both Pacifist and Socialist, 'I also am a radical. I want the restoration of our lawful dread Sovereign, King Robert I and V; and I am with anyone who is against the descendants of George Elector of Hannover'.[10] In reality, everywhere in England the principal Mass was followed by a sung versicle and prayer for the de facto monarch: this was an obligation in the wake of the first Catholic Relief Act in 1778.

---

6   Ibid., entry for 16 April, 1892.

7   Ibid., entry for 21 June, 1892.

8   F.J. McGrath, FMS (ed.), *Letters and Diaries of John Henry Newman* X (Oxford: Oxford University Press, 2006), p. 313. Newman claimed to Jemima Mozley that Francis Fortescue had been 'taught secretly Catholic doctrine and practice as a child'.

9   Downside Archives, IX AF, Box D, 'Diary 1901', entry for 27 January.

10   Cambridge University Library, MS Add. 9812/D/90, Letter to S. Morison of 29 January, 1920.

Despite his muscular Christianity (the extent of which would only become plain on his Levantine tour in 1907), Fortescue's cocktail of interests, and enthusiasms, might have raised eyebrows among his own contemporaries — not to speak of later periods in English Catholicism, such as that introduced by the Second Vatican Council (1962–1965).

Vacationing

Back in England for the summer vacation, he continued to record a balance of activities. Staying with his Oxford relatives in Bevington Road, a rather grand North Oxford address, he spent a good deal of time rowing and canoeing, but also lunched with the Jesuits at St Aloysius and was 'shriven'. Regular recourse to the sacrament of Penance was obviously important to him (from Letchworth, his only enduring parochial home, there were frequent visits for the purpose to Our Lady and the English Martyrs in Cambridge, across the diocesan border into Northampton). For aesthetic stimulus, he used his Oxford stay to look out the Turner water-colours at the Taylorian Institute.

Fortescue's reading, as noted in the diaries, as well as his choice of what to visit in museums and galleries, show how much he appreciated the eye and mind of both John Ruskin (1819–1900) and J.M.W. Turner (1775–1851). It is a reasonable speculation, from the qualities of his prose descriptions, drawing and painting, and photography, that these writers taught him to observe the cut of stone, the quality of colour, and the composition of a scene. At the end of July 1892 he read Ruskin's *The Seven Lamps of Architecture*,[11] and in mid-August was making headway with the multi-volume *Modern Painters*.[12] His artistic enthusiasms were, however, by no means confined to the closely associated duo of Turner and his loyal critic. Back at his aunt's house in Wimbledon, what he enjoyed on a July visit to the Royal Academy were the large-scale figure paintings, mostly on classical subjects, of Frederic Lord Leighton (1830–1896), one of the Titans of Victorian art, whose work, largely neglected today, was inspired by the masters of the Italian Renaissance. On St Dominic's day (old style, i.e. 4 August), he assisted at Mass at the Dominican priory in

11 Originally published in 1849, this work 'became immensely influential – compulsory reading for young architects and a key element in the Gothic revival', K. Jackson, *The Worlds of John Ruskin* (London: Pallas Athene, 2010), p. 53. The seven 'lamps' were sacrifice, truth, power, beauty, life, memory and obedience: all relevant to Fortescue's ethos.

12 Published in five volumes between 1843 and 1860, it was instrumental in securing Turner's reputation, as the sub-title of the first volume signals: 'Their Superiority in the Art of Landscape Painting to all the Ancient Masters'. In later volumes Ruskin espoused the equally controversial cause of the Pre-Raphaelites.

Haverstock Hill (customarily, as on this occasion, sung by the Franciscans, so he records), and on 16 August was in attendance at the pro-cathedral for the canons' reception of Manning's successor Herbert Vaughan (1832–1903) as archbishop-elect — very properly so, since he was an ordinand of the diocese.

But not all was diversion. In the vacations he had been studying Modern Greek, which would stand him in good stead for subsequent journeys in the Near East and reportage of contemporary Orthodoxy. On returning to Rome in October, via the scenic route over the Simplon Pass, his first act on arrival was to buy a Greek catechism at the bookshop of the College of Propaganda Fide. That must have seemed a far cry from his September stay in his father's old haunts around Alveston Manor, where at one Warwickshire village he 'went over the church with the Vicar; feigned to be Highdutch [sic] and spoke Latin; explained joke to him afterwards'.[13] This is still a boy, then, albeit a highly sophisticated boy.

Towards Austria

Informed by one of the Scots College students that the rector had asked him to look out for a 'private friendship' between another student and Fortescue, he confided to his diary, 'How happy I shall be, when I leave this and all its Jesuit ways'.[14] He would soon have his wish so far as leaving Rome was concerned, though he was not to be out of the hands of Jesuits. Quite early in what, for the Roman faculties, was the new school year, he was required to send a Latin letter from the rector of the Scots College to the 'regens' of the Canisianum, the Jesuit-run theologate at Innsbruck (founded 1858), asking about a place and accommodation for the year that followed. Perhaps realizing how little time he had left in Rome, his visiting and sketching of churches, gardens, architectural monuments, now intensified. The work on the chant was at any rate maintained (he introduced the College to the new Solesmes versions of the Advent tract Attende Domine, and the Benediction hymn O Salutaris). At the same time, he was reading Dante assiduously (another lifetime interest) and giving that reading a context in mediaeval history.

It was noted posthumously in the *Memoir* written by his cousin in collaboration with a priest-colleague:

> Dante had kindled his enthusiastic devotion early in life and Dante, as ever, had led out and beyond the *Divina Commedia* to splendid vistas of history, art, and literature. Dante had led him to Virgil and Plato. Dante, too, had led him to Boethius, to whose *De consolatione philosophiae* he gave the last years of his life.[15]

13 Downside Archives, IX AF, Box D, 'Diary 1892', entry for 15 September, 1892.

14 Ibid., entry for 12 November, 1892.

15 J.G. Vance and J.W. Fortescue, *Adrian Fortescue*, op. cit., p. 19.

An example of Fortescue's fine drawing and composition skills. Bookplate designed for J.G. Vance.

He was also enjoying Kipling, whose stories of the Raj, newly minted,[16] could not have shed much in the way of direct light on the thesis of his philosophical doctorate at the *Gregorianum*, namely: that 'the power of the soul and its essence are really mutually distinguished'.[17] He passed the — far more comprehensive — oral part of the examination on 25 June 1894. On 2 May he had been at the Collegio Greco for its patronal feast, day, fêting St Athanasius the Great on whom he would write in *The Greek Fathers*.

It was his last term in Rome, where life cannot have been altogether easy under a College rector known to be awkward and unpredictable. There was some suggestion that James Campbell's kidnapping by bandits at the College's villa at Marino, when a younger man, had left him a traumatized personality. If so, this was not taken into account in the cruel lampoon by Frederick William Rolfe ('Baron Corvo', 1860–1913) in his evocation of life at the College in the 1904 novel *Hadrian VII*. The gifted but unstable (and subsequently revengeful) Rolfe had been expelled as unsuitable just eighteen months before Fortescue's arrival.[18]

On 19 July he returned to Wimbledon for a summer of walking and drawing in Hampshire and Kent, and visiting the London galleries, before setting out again on 12 September on a leisurely journey of two and a half weeks to Innsbruck via The Hague and Utrecht, Mainz and Munich. His fundamental seriousness was shown, however, by the way the language of the diary transmutes into German as early as 1 October.

The reason for the move was to follow up philosophy at Rome by frequenting Innsbruck for theology, including Hebrew (Latin and ancient Greek, taught at school, were already well in hand). The choice of Innsbruck for English seminarians, though not common, was by no means unknown as late as the mid 1980s.[19] The pattern Fortescue had established for himself was maintained in relocation to the Habsburg lands (where his *Meldungsbuch* issued by the Theological Faculty of the 'kaiserlich und königlich Universität zu Innsbruck' gives his name as 'Adrian Knottesford-Fortescue').[20] There was a great deal of outdoor activity — sledge-riding to

16 *Plain Tales from the Raj*, Kipling's first major work of prose fiction, was published in 1888.

17 Downside Archives, IX AF, Box D, 'Diary 1894', entry for 29 May, 1894.

18 A.J.A. Symons, *The Quest for Corvo. An Experiment in Biography* (Harmondsworth: Penguin, [1934] 1966); A.S. MacWilliam, 'Fr Rolfe and the Scots College, Rome', *Innes Review* 21 (1970), pp. 124–139; B. Sewell, 'Frederick William Rolfe at the Scots College', ibid. 26 (1975), pp. 20–26.

19 Information provided by the Revd Francis Selman, of the Catholic diocese of East Anglia.

20 Westminster Diocesan Archives, Series 20, Box 18, *Meldungsbuch*.

Adrian Fortescue at the Canisianum in Innsbruck, Austria.

Natters, a village south of Innsbruck, in February 1895 on the monthly 'excursion day', as well as what sounds a demanding Eastertide trip through the Bavarian Alps, with accompanying descriptions of weather and mountains.

Ruskinesque diversion and the future apostolate

While in England again for his first summer vacation from Austria, in the summer of 1895, he travelled up to the Lake District, swimming in Derwentwater and rowing on the lake during a stay at Keswick. The summer entries of the diaries of the Innsbruck years show there was much drawing, and matching prose description of architecture, especially on visits to the English and French cathedrals, and, not unconnected with these, more reading of Ruskin (he noted Ruskin's enthusiasm for Amiens, of which the 1897 diary has a long descriptive entry).[21] He discovered the art historian Philip Hamerton's life of Turner.[22] (Given his calligrapher's love of the clear line he probably sympathized with Hamerton's negative animadversions on Turner's innovatively impressionistic paintings from the 1840s: they 'belong not merely to a period of decline but to a state of senile decrepitude'.[23])

But he was also preparing himself for his future apostolate at home, reading for instance, in October 1897, lives of the English martyrs on whom he would later lecture in London; notably the Redemptorist T.E. Bridgett's lives of Fisher and More;[24] Dom Bede Camm's life of the Welsh Benedictine martyr, John Roberts,[25] and, for good measure, John Morris's biography of Becket.[26] He evidently considered this cluster of martyrs who died in conflict with the English crown for the sake of a wider, international, papally centred but not homogenizing Catholicism, to be co-constitutive of

---

21 Downside Archives, IX AF, Box D, 'Diary 1897', entry for 20 September, 1897.

22 P.G. Hamerton, *The Life of J.M.W. Turner* (London: Seeley, 1895, 2nd edition).

23 Cited in J. Lindsay, *J.M.W. Turner. A Critical Biography* (London: Cory, Adams and Mackay, 1966), p. 192.

24 T.E. Bridgett, C.S.R., *Life and Writings of Sir Thomas More, Lord Chancellor of England and Martyr under Henry VIII* (London: Burns and Oates, 1891); idem., *Life of Blessed John Fisher: Bishop of Rochester, Cardinal of the Holy Roman Church and Martyr under Henry VIII* (London: Burns and Oates, 1890).

25 B. Camm, O.S.B., *A Benedictine Martyr in England: Being the Life and Times of the Venerable Servant of God Dom John Roberts, O.S.B.* (London: Bliss, Sands, 1897).

26 J. Morris, *The Life and Martyrdom of St Thomas Becket* (London: Burns and Oates, 1885, 2nd edition).

English Catholic identity, and thus of the version of the Christian Gospel he was to represent to his fellow-countrymen. 'In England', he would later write in a piece of his controversial journalism, 'Catholics are English in the natural order, just as we are Catholics in the supernatural order'. [27] The combination of patriotism and confession, expressed in lucidly rational prose, would become one of his hallmarks.

---

27 'Guests of the Nation', *The Tablet* for 2 October, 1915, p. 427.

3. Ordination and First Steps in Priesthood

Advance to Orders, apologetics, and animadversions of a liturgical kind

Fortescue was of course getting ready for Major Orders. The locations selected for his Ordination are rather surprising: Darmstadt, in the grand duchy of Hessen-Darmstadt, for the diaconate, and the south Tyrolean city of Brixen (now Bressanone, in the Italian region of Alto Adige) for the priesthood. The probable explanation is factors of convenience, based on the circumstance that his fellow-seminarians included candidates for the dioceses concerned. His diaconal ordination took place in July 1897, when he marked the date in Greek with the words *Megalê Hêmera* ('great day!');[1] his priesting followed on Passion Sunday, 1898, which that year fell on 27 March. Home to celebrate his first Mass, he received from his aunt a fine chalice that, having learned the expression from German-speaking Catholics, he called a *Primizgeschenk*.[2] This would doubtless have been used in his first Masses — at the Jesuit church in Wimbledon, his aunt's parish, and in the Fortescue chapel in the Dominican priory on Haverstock Hill.

On a visit to the Oxford Fortescues, he argued with an Anglican Ritualist to whom he presented the choice of *either* the living voice of the Catholic Church *or* private judgment, a foreshadowing of his later polemics, plotted through the pages of various London periodicals, not least the *Tablet*, then in its strongly orthodox phase under the long editorship (1884–1920) of J.G. Snead-Cox (at the time, the weekly was the personal property of two successive archbishops of Westminster).

In May he received faculties from the bishop of Brixen to hear confessions, and, presumably as a 'thank you' for the training and sacramental ordination received, presented to the 'Convict', i.e. the student residence of the *Canisianum*, 'a red chasuble that I have given . . . it is made by Anglican nuns of East Grinstead according to my own design'.[3] Passionate commitment to

---

1   Downside Archives, IX AF, Box D, 'Diary 1897', entry for 22 July, 1897.

2   Downside Archives, IX AF, Box D, 'Diary 1898', entry for 1 April, 1898.

3   Downside Archives, IX AF, Box D, 'Diary 1899', entry for 21 May, 1899.

excellence in everything concerned with the Liturgy of the Church went hand in hand with acerbic criticism of what did not meet his own high standards.

Fortescue's criticisms of much in the setting and the performance of the Liturgy, as he saw it on his travels in Italy, Austria-Hungary and elsewhere, discourage us from thinking all was necessarily well in this period in the worshipping life of these countries, at any rate so far as externals were concerned (and for the liturgical signs, externals count). On holiday in Tuscany in the spring of 1899, he noted of Easter at Fiesole 'all the holy week ceremonies here unspeakably badly done',[4] and as for some of the Baroque churches visited in Hungary in the summer of that year, they were 'full of tawdry, broken and very dirty gild (sic) woodwork'.[5] His diaries themselves are not always a work of literary art (they were not intended for publication), but vivid descriptions of Romany villages in Slavonia show he had not lost the capacity for writing evocative English prose.

Whitechapel, Arts and Crafts, and commitment to scholarship

The usual leisurely summertime return to England (in 1899 via Ulm, Strassburg, still a part of the German Empire, and Paris), and lazy days spent cycling around the Oxfordshire countryside (in many ways, Fortescue's manner of life was that of a moneyed and cultured undergraduate), came to an abrupt if hardly unexpected end when Cardinal Vaughan informed him in the closing days of September of his first appointment in the archdiocese. The first of a number of 'fill-ins', he was to be the chaplain of the German church in Whitechapel (Sankt Bonifatius, in Union Street), until such time as a German priest could be found. Originally linked to the Bavarian embassy, the church was now supported — at any rate in theory — by the German imperial government together with the Austro-Hungarian emperor. It was not a typical charge, but neither was it atypical in facing Fortescue with some of the practical problems of maintaining a church or chapel and a priest's house where, on both counts, things had been allowed to slide. He noted that the dire financial condition of the place (in a letter of 15 February 1900 he reports 'the creditors were about to sell up the mission'[6]) was only equalled by the fearful dirt. It cannot have been a terribly encouraging start to the exercise of priesthood (in more recent years, ecclesiastical superiors have usually given greater thought to immediately post-Ordination assignments), and the entries for the last months of the dying year show a variety of reactions on Fortescue's part.

4   Ibid., entry for Easter, 1899.
5   Ibid., entry for 19 July, 1899.
6   Westminster Diocesan Archives, Box AGD, Letter to Hamilton Macdonald of 15 February 1900.

The first response was a kind of grieving, chiefly for his lost Innsbruck friends. The second (no chronological order, or order of priority, is implied) was prayer, of a kind that would keep alive, in an immigrant setting, his basic apostolic orientation as an English Catholic priest. On St Edward's day he went to Westminster Abbey (where he reported many Catholics as present) in order to make a 'prayer for the conversion of England to the faith, for the Catholic hierarchy in England, and for myself'.[7] The third response to Whitechapel's Germany-in-exile was commitment to creative, or at any rate craftsmanly, work, and something more can be said about this.

Beginning on 10 November 1899, when he attended an evening exhibition about the (rather recent) Arts and Crafts movement,[8] he would devote a good deal of time to skills he considered should be at the service of the contemporary Church as they had been of its mediaeval predecessor. These included calligraphy, design of clothes, and architectural design for modest buildings. These skills not only gave him recreational pleasure. He also built them up against the day when he could deploy them in the service of a parish of his own. At the end of November he records what is apparently his first visit to the London County Council's 'Central School of Arts and Crafts': the School had opened its doors, in Southampton Row, in 1896. He attended along with his friend Douglas Cockerell (1870–1945), who was to be a leader of the associated movement for quality book production. Two weeks later, he enrolled in the writing class of the School's master calligrapher, Edward Johnston (1872–1944).[9] And it is probably no coincidence that in the Christmas Octave we find him reading J.W. Mackail's life of William Morris the hero (1834–1896), along with Ruskin, of 'Arts and Crafts'

---

7   Downside Archives, IX AF, Box D, 'Diary 1899', entry for 13 October, 1899.

8   The term 'Arts and Crafts' had been coined by the book-designer and binder T.J. Cobden-Sanderson (1840–1922). The exhibitions, at the New Gallery in Regent Street, put on by the 'Arts and Crafts Exhibition Society', began in 1888, at first annually, though after 1890 they were held every three or four years. Thus E. Cumming and W. Kaplan, *The Arts and Crafts Movement* (London: Thames and Hudson, 1991), p. 26.

9   P. Holliday, *Edward Johnston, Master Calligrapher* (London: British Library Publishing, 2007). In 1912, Johnston would follow his friend Eric Gill, who shared his passion for lettering, to the Sussex village of Ditchling where Gill co-founded the 'Guild of St Joseph and St Dominic' for Catholic craftsmen, but though he stayed in the village until his death, he never made an approach to the Church: 'Johnston's wife Greta was coldly anti-Catholic and Johnston himself was perhaps a creature too solitary by temperament for organized religion', F. MacCarthy, *Eric Gill* (London: Faber and Faber, 1989), p. 141.

generally.[10] The same day, 29 December, as if to reinforce the suggestion that this advanced hobby of his was solace, he had buried his maternal grandmother, the last living link with his direct family line.

Not that his execution of priestly duties was undermined. Even when a German-born rector was found he was kept busy enough. As he explained to a priest contemporary from Rome and Innsbruck days, '[M]y Rector is the most charming old gentleman on earth; but he speaks no word of the English tongue, so I have to answer all enq[uiry] letters, and either myself travel about London, or lead him whither he would not go. This means doing much of his work as well as mine own.'[11] His diary records pastoral visits to the sick and dying among German-speaking Catholics in London at large, and the care of German Sisters settled at Walthamstow and Hendon, as well as Whitechapel. He lectured to the *Gesellenverein* ('Guild of Associates') on English Reformation history and the lives and deaths of Fisher and More. He made ready to act as a Catholic apologist vis-à-vis a strongly resurgent Church of England, acquiring for the purpose Anglican polemical literature in the SPCK bookshop in Great Victoria Street. In mid February 1900 he was reading a classic of the genre, Bishop Charles Gore's *The Roman Catholic Claims*.[12] He would parry Gore's arguments in the course of his controversial writing — to be considered in this study under the title 'Anglo-Roman debates'.

At Oxford again in June, Fortescue knocked on the door of Pusey House, the Palm Court of Tractarianism' with its well-stocked theological library (Dr Pusey's personal collection had been acquired as its nucleus) and its corps of resident celibate chaplains serving the impressive chapel by Temple Lushington Moore (1856–1920) whom a competent judge has declared 'the best church architect of his generation'.[13] (The justly celebrated altar, baldacchino and east window in the retro-choir, a late work of the unsurpassable Sir John Ninian Comper, were added only after Fortescue's death.) Fortescue found the Principal, Stuckey Coles (1845–1929), 'extraordinarily sympathetic', accepting from him a copy of his Advent meditations.[14] He also called on the

10 J.W. Mackail, *Life of William Morris* (London: Longmans, Green, 1901).

11 Westminster Diocesan Archives, Series 20, Box AGD, Letter to Hamilton Macdonald of 15 February 1900.

12 Downside Archives, IX AF, Box D, 'Diary 1900', entry for 15 February, 1900. Gore's book had appeared in a second edition in 1899.

13 A. Symondson and S. Bucknall, *Sir Ninian Comper. An Introduction to his Life and Work with Complete Gazeteer* (Reading: Spire Books, 2006), p. 171.

14 Downside Archives, IX AF, Box D, 'Diary 1900', entry for 8 June, 1900. Vincent Stuckey Stratton Coles (1845–1929), Principal from 1897 to 1905, made an honorary canon of Christ Church by Gore in 1912, and a noted hymn-writer and Retreat-giver.

distinguished Anglican liturgiologist Frank Edward Brightman (1856–1932), one of the original Pusey 'priest-librarians', and picked his brains about the history of the Liturgy on which he was equipping himself to write.[15] His own liturgical practice at the German church was enhanced by ongoing discovery of the Solesmes school: someone had given him a Solesmes *Liber graduale*, for the Mass chants, in April,[16] and in July he began to read *Les melodies grégoriennes d'après la Tradition* by Dom Joseph Pothier (1935–1923). Pothier emphasized that plainsong rhythm should take its cue from the text the music accompanied. His book was a turning point in persuading musicians, and eventually the Vatican, to abandon the so-called 'measured' chant introduced in the post-mediaeval period to keep abreast of developments in non-Gregorian music.[17] Meanwhile, Fortescue made good use of his membership of the British Museum library, continuing with the Arabic studies which would be necessary for the kind of doctorate — the *doctoratus completus* — he hoped eventually to gain from Innsbruck. (His half-brother George was Keeper of Printed Books.) He also delved into Magyar, Turkish, and Persian: all languages that in one way or another might conceivably be helpful to him as a student of Oriental Christianity, though one suspects he found a delight in comparative grammar for its own sake.

Walthamstow and iron in the soul

At the end of October 1900, the Westminster auxiliary, Bishop Robert Brindle (1937–1916),[18] informed him he would be leaving the German mission for an industrial school — nefarious invention of the nineteenth century Swedes — at Walthamstow, where he was to be chaplain not just to the Brothers who presided over that doubtless Dickensian establishment, but also to Sisters who ran an orphanage at the adjacent 'Walthamstow House'. Oddly, enough, Walthamstow had been the birthplace of Morris, of Arts and Crafts fame, but by the start of the twentieth century what had been Essex countryside at the time of Morris' birth was virtually unrecognizable (Mackail,

---

15 Brightman was already well-known for his *Eastern Liturgies: Being the Texts Original or Translated of the Principal Liturgies of the Church* (Oxford: Clarendon Press, 1896). See on this figure B. Nichols, 'F.E. Brightman', in C. Irvine (ed.), *They Shaped our Worship. Essays on Anglican Liturgists* (London: Society for the Promotion of Christian Knowledge, 1998, pp. 35-41.

16 By 1900 Solesmes had produced two versions of the *Graduale*, 1883 and 1895: presumably this was the latter.

17 J. Pothier, *Les melodies grégoriennes d'après la Tradition* (Tournai: Desclée Lefebvre, 1881).

18 Only briefly in that office (1899–1901): the following year Brindle became Bishop of Nottingham.

his first biographer, was just in time to take a party to Morris's family home, Elm House, before its demolition in 1898).[19] On 10 November, Fortescue's 'new life' began, but it would not prove to be much of a Dantesque *vita nuova*. Already in the January of 1901 there was some inconsequential negotiation with the archdiocese about a possible return to Whitechapel, and by May he was desperate to be relieved of the post. Looking back, he wrote to his (half-) sister-in-law: 'Walthamstow was not a success: my Rector was a raving Irishman of the most offensive type and so towards the end of June I asked for a move'.[20]

In his own mind he sought to mitigate its asperities by referring to it in mock-Latin: his charges were the *Fratres apud S. Joannem in schola dicta industriali*, while Walthamstow itself morphed into *Silvopagium*. As if to transfer into craft the creativity for which he could find no outlet in the pastoral setting, he began to illuminate his diary entries for the great feasts of the Church. For Easter Sunday, he produced a superbly gilded 'S' for the *Surrexit* of the Easter proclamation, against a background of lilies in white, orange, and gold,[21] and continued the practice at Pentecost, when another gold 'S', this time for the opening word of the Introit of the Whitsun Mass, *Spiritus*, was framed by carnations in red and green.[22]

It should not be thought that these strategies were entered upon so as to save himself from an utterly inhuman existence. He retained friends from all periods of his life, and always made more, women (especially) as well as men. And he never rationed himself on holiday. But he needed — more, perhaps, than most people — satisfaction in the circumstances of his work. He communicated his unhappiness to the archdiocesan authorities, asking the vicar-general on 24 May to be moved from a situation he found intolerable.

Ongar: natural beauty and the gift of friendship

On 5 June he was assigned instead to the mission of St Helen's, Chipping Ongar, Essex, where, so it was explained, he could expect to remain for five years (in fact, he would spend scarcely eighteen months in the place soon dubbed *Angrae ad Castrum inter Orientales Saxones*). Church music was not St Helen's strong point (Fortescue suffered from a lady who sang badly while — so he wrote in Latin — 'beating on that kind of instrument whose altogether inappropriate name is "Harmonium"').[23] But the setting was charming.

19 F. MacCarthy, *William Morris. A Life for our Time* (London: Faber and Faber, 1994), p. 4.

20 Westminster Archive, Series 20, Box 22, Letter of 23 July, 1901 to Alice Fortescue.

21 Downside Archives, IX AF, Box D, 'Diary 1901', entry for 7 April, 1901.

22 Ibid., entry for 26 May, 1901.

23 Ibid., entry for 23 June, 1901.

> Ongar has one little irregular street and all around are fields and
> hedges covered with dog roses, huge elm trees and brooms, corn
> and barley up and down the slopes on every side. It is a horrid
> calumny to call Essex flat or dull: Here it is simply ripping. In
> my walks and bicycle rides I find xiii and xiv cent[ury] churches,
> redroofed farms among the trees, gorgeous old manor houses in
> every side. And I have a jolly little George I house with purple
> flowers growing all over the front and behind a long garden
> sloping down to a brook and full of apples, pear and plum trees,
> gooseberries, currants and raspberries, vegetables of every kind
> and a lawn under the limes with banks of great white lilies.[24]

The affection the place aroused in him is patent, as he indicated in expansive
form to Alice Fortescue, explaining how,

> plain living costs me no pang when I can lie in a hammock under
> my lime trees with a pipe and watch the yellow waning light poured
> across field after field, lighting the wavy wheat and gilding the great
> green clouds of elm trees and I see the shadow of hedge and bank
> getting longer, the dark mass of the forest purple against a sky of
> shining gold, broken by torn lines of crimson and scarlet.[25]

The same affection is suggested, if more laconically, in a letter to a fellow
priest — in this case, Harold Burton, author of brief lives of Challenor and
Milner and subsequently a Professor at St Cuthbert's College, Ushaw, who
would in time become a close friend. Fortescue looked forward to a visit from
Burton when 'we shall be able to continue the violent altercations about the
government of our Lord the Pope in the midst of wild rushes at wasps which
you will no doubt remember as the special characteristic of breakfast in the
house with the blue chair'.[26] Contemplation of the abundant wild flowers
in the surrounding meadowland, described in sumptuous Latin, led him to
a Bonaventurian outburst of praise of their Creator as the 'sapient *Artifex*
who infinitely exceeds all created beauty'.[27] He was sufficiently inspired
to take up gardening, a practice which continued, as did the seeking out
of helpful academics – notably, in early 1902, Edward Granville Browne
(1862–1926), a Cambridge professor,[28] whom he consulted on 'Babism',

---

24 Westminster Diocesan Archive, Series 20, Box 22, Letter to Alice Fortescue of
    23 July, 1901.

25 Ibid.

26 Westminster Diocesan Archives, Series 20, Box 22: Letter to Harold Burton of
    17 September, 1901.

27 Downside Archives, IX AF, Box D, 'Diary 1901', entry for 23 June 1901.

28 Fortescue refers to Edward Granville Browne as 'Professor of Persian'. He had
    been University Lecturer in Persian until that year, but was then made the Sir
    Thomas Adams Professor of Arabic.

an early version of the Baha'i faith, later to be one of Fortescue's numerous specialties.[29] Unfortunately, the Ongar stay was too brief for him to see the results of his horticultural labours. Their fruits were to be enjoyed instead by the returning rector, as he complained in a letter to Burton from his next posting: 'alas for the crocuses and daffodils which are now coming up in my Ongar garden — think of their disgust when they come out and find the apocalyptick beast there!'[30]

His Ongar period was notable for the development of the friendship with Burton whose letters from Fortescue constitute by far the most quotable portion of the Westminster Archdiocesan holdings. With Burton he was able to let his humour run riot, to the point of surreality, as in his reference to the local nuns (the 'Little Pink Daughters of the Penitent Thief'), singing Vespers in 'what purports to be the Latin tongue', with a Sister Philipina Cananina (her *titulus devotionis*, as given by Fortescue, was 'of the Way to Jericho') 'wearing a cope and a Roman missal, from which she tells me that she always sings Vespers'. The nuns informed him (so he claimed to Burton) that a framed card of 'Pontifical Blessing' from Leo XIII would confer just such a benediction if suitably approached, and this he described as

> a striking sight which I am naturally anxious to enjoy. Hitherto I have not succeeded in convincing it of my spiritual propriety. I have told it all the things that I think it would like to hear, that I am dead nuts on Encyclicals, that *ubi Petrus ibi* the whole show, that *Roma locuta est* (she never stops), *nulla salus est* (I hope I haven't got this mixed); I have even said polite things about its predecessors of the X and XV centuries: alas, in vain! it hasn't once burst into: *Sit nome*[sic] *Domini benedictumme*[sic].[31]

He wrote to Burton a few months later, 'Ongar has not gone by without leaving what I am always grateful for — the result of the fortunate combination of accidents that led to a friendship which has changed all the lonely and sullen feeling with which I thought of our clergy in England'.[32] And he added in the same letter, 'Please do not ever think me too heretical or undesirable to keep up with', evidently a reference (as the penultimate chapter of this book will show) to Fortescue's sympathy for Liberal Catholicism.

---

29 Babism was a pantheistic Persian sect founded in 1844 by Mirza Ali Muhammad (1819–1850), who called himself the 'Bab', i.e. 'Gate', (to divine truth, q.v.), and was executed as an apostate from Islam. His disciple Mirza Husayn Ali Nuri founded Baha'ism in 1863.

30 Westminster Diocesan Archives, Series 20, Box 22, Letter of 5 March, 1903.

31 Westminster Diocesan Archives, Series 20, Box 22, Letter of 20 September, 1902.

32 Westminster Diocesan Archives, Series 20, Box 22, Letter of 5 March, 1903.

Otherwise the Ongar interlude was chiefly dominated by the start of preparations for the Innsbruck doctorate, which entailed satisfying the examiners in Hebrew and Arabic as well as Church history and canon law. The diaries make it plain that, even before winning his second, theological, doctorate, he was expecting to be made Professor of Church History at St Mary's College, Oscott, the old seminary of the Midland District and, in the wake of its first Rector, Nicholas Wiseman, a real centre of Catholic intellectual life. As if to prepare for this, he had been giving public lectures on Church-historical topics at Brentwood throughout August and September. These hopes were dashed by the announcement on 10 October that another candidate had been selected. He wrote, 'My whole Oscottian scheme is annihilated'.[33] This precipitated another crisis. Three days later he asked the vicar-general for a more suitable posting — more suited, that is, to his particular combination of gifts.

Colchester with clerical clashes, and the German church again

The upshot was not especially encouraging: transfer, at the end of November 1902, to Colchester, for which, as possibly the oldest Roman settlement in Britain, a perfectly good Latin name already existed: *Camulodunum*, but Fortescue signalled what he thought of its backwoods status by adding the phrase 'in the farthest fields of the East Saxons'.[34] His name was becoming known among the metropolitan elite: in January Methuen commissioned from him an edition of the *Imitation of Christ* based on the 1471 Augsburg *editio princeps*. It was, he noted proudly, to be something 'splendid'.[35] Long prepared, *Thomae a Kempis, De Imitatione Christi* would appear only in 1919.[36] Under an unsympathetic parish priest, caricatured in the correspondence to Burton as 'Scroggs', Colchester was the shortest of his curacies, lasting just under four months. Fortescue fantasized to Burton that 'Scroggs' had an unclean spirit named 'Smufkin'. He certainly had a housekeeper, whom Fortescue unchivalrously denominated the 'last surviving Gadarene Swine', promising Burton stories to come concerning the household quartet: Scroggs, Smufkin, Swine and 'the Latin Clerk' (namely, himself, and thus the title of this book).[37]

---

33 Downside Archives, IX AF, Box D, 'Diary 1902', entry for 10 October, 1902.
34 Ibid., entry for 19 November, 1902.
35 Downside Archives, IX AF, Box D, 'Diary 1903', entry for 15 January, 1903.
36 As *Thomae a Kempis, De Imitatione Christi, libri quattuor quos denuo recognouit*, Adrianis a Fortiscuto Presbyter ritus Latini (London: Methuen, 1919).
37 Westminster Diocesan Archives, Series 20, Box 22, Letter of 1 January, 1903.

However much Fortescue may have pestered the diocesan authorities to liberate him from the house of Scroggs, it is only fair to say he was genuinely needed at the German church to where, if briefly, he now returned. He explained to Burton, communicating his news.

> Mr Bernhard Schaefer, my rector, is an ex-Jesuit, the founder of an order (our friends the little pink daughters) and a raving maniack, also a seer of visions and dreamer of dreams, lastly an exceedingly pious person of the modern Gallo-Roman type (the sort who count special devotion to St Joseph and adulation of the illustrious incumbent of the Roman bishoprick as better than ethical righteousness, who don't play the normal game but take endless trouble over extras; e.g. He doesn't fast in Lent but he does scourge his old flesh so that it sounds like carpet-beating all down the passage.

In which letter numerous other instances of Schaefer's lack of judgment followed,[38] yet all in all it was not so bad. '[O]ld Schaefer's lunacy does not really hurt me', while:

> [a]ll day I have schools and clubs and hospitals and sick calls and then far into the night when the roar outside stops I shut myself in my little room (all white like at Ongar) and draw my Morris curtains, light my lamp and sit among my books and pictures and read my work for the next and last exam — about Babylon and Assyria, Marduk the great god and Tigaltapilassara [Tiglath-pileser] the King who swept across Asia like a blazing tornado, and I peg away at Hebrew and Cuneiform, and think of palm trees and the great desert, and Babylon the huge city, Ninive and Sargon's gorgeous palace, and I forget the howling wilderness of slums outside.[39]

As for the slums, he declared he loved them 'and all the German beggars'. 'I tramp down through the slush of Whitechapel Road, and sit in the awful filth of the rooms in which a whole family sleeps and eats and lives (and never a window open) and talk the most beautiful tongue on earth (save Greek) and have a real joy in knowing that I am doing something for Christ'. He found himself interviewing beggars from every nation in (Eastern or Southern) Europe, but best of all he enjoyed encounters with 'the Chosen People', i.e. East End Jews.

> though they are the poorest and dirtiest of all they always have that superb scorn for the Gentile that suggests Mount Zion and the glory of the things that are gone. Even when I give them alms,

---

38 Westminster Diocesan Archives, Series 20, Box 22, Letter of 5 March, 1903.
39 Ibid.

in their souls they know that I am only 'Goyi' [sic] and unclean
(unclean! My word, if you could see them!), but they bless me
with a beautiful Hebrew blessing that again suggests the holy city
and the Dead Sea, Isaiah and Ezekiel and the Waters of Babylon
where their fathers sat and wept — and all the while the roar of
the dray-carts and trams, yelling hawkers and shrieking children
goes on in Whitechapel Road outside.[40]

It need not be supposed that Fortescue's evocation of the poverty of
Whitechapel was exaggerated. It was in Whitechapel in the last quarter of
Victoria's reign that William Booth had hit upon the plan of founding The
Salvation Army to bring religion to the poorest of the poor.

Moving into the light

In the half-year he was back in Whitechapel, Herbert Vaughan died, as did
Leo XIII, and while the Holy See experienced an interregnum of only a fortnight,
Westminster had to wait for two and a half months. By the time Francis Bourne
(1861–1935) of Southwark was appointed, Fortescue was on the move again,
this time with some hopes (soon dashed) of being a rector, at Enfield, or, less
bathetically, *Pratis Oeneis*. (He toyed with an alternative translation, *Oenopratum*.)
Apart from embarking on gymnastic exercises — superfluous had he known
how much cycling he would need to do at his next posting, the main distinctive
feature of the Enfield stay was that for the first time he was able to orchestrate the
great ceremonies as he wished. 'But what', he wondered, 'of next year?'[41]

Inconveniently returning rectors were a feature of this period of his life.
In February 1904, he had confided in a letter: 'Since I have been in England
I have had bad luck in my intercourse with our priests and am more and
more getting suspicious and sulky and generally disinclined to be even civil
to my own kind — all of which is very bad for the character'.[42] Plainly,
the friendship with Burton had not eased all the pain. In the following
month he learned that he was to stand in once again, this time at Witham,
Aquae Separatoriae. This time, however, we do not hear the cry of lament
that sounded from Walthamstow, or even the sardonic tones prompted by
dealings with his immediate ecclesiastical superior at Colchester.

In a happy interlude, and at the request of Bourne, he designed heraldic
arms for the archbishop (he had developed a real gift for this skill, which
requires a fund of knowledge for its correct execution, as well as good taste). He
wrote to Bourne on 8 March, 'I have tried not to make them too mediaeval-

---

40 Ibid.

41 Downside Archives, IX AF, Box D, 'Diary 1903', entry for 25 December.

42 Westminster Diocesan Archives, Box AGD, Letter to Hamilton Macdonald of
     13 February, 1904.

looking. Sham mediaevalism is, I think, as silly and almost as ugly as sham cinque-cento'. Though remarking humbly 'I hardly foresee that I have any use for these little drawings expect perhaps as bookmarkers', he was actually sufficiently confident in their quality to ask if he 'might have the honour of offering you a block made from my drawing — Walker and Cockerell are the right people to do it, I think'.[43] (He would repeat the experiment with other applicants, including, much later in his career, another metropolitan, Frederick William Keating of Liverpool, whom he described as 'in a bit of a hurry. You see, he is already appointed and palliumed and recognized by his brother of Rome, and yet he cannot even excommunicate a Canon till he has the proper note-paper on which to do it'.[44])

Fortescue's own transistion from Enfield to Witham was gentle — he did not begin till 6 April — and the diary illumination for Pentecost strikes an exultant note, with red tulips on a white-starred crimson ground surrounding a golden 'S', the initial for some lines of his own composition: *Splendente aestivo sole*, an evocation of how multi-coloured flowers mirror the dispersed glittering flames of Pentecost as the Son of God renews the face of the earth.[45] It must have helped his spirits that he liked the rector, declaring him (in German) 'a loveable old gentleman' to his priest-friend Hamilton Macdonald who had just become archdiocesan chancellor, an elevation which, jesting, Fortescue describes as leaving him overwhelmed at his own audacity in writing to him at all.[46] In June he had the pleasure of translating Pius X's *motu proprio* on the revival of the Chant, *Tra le sollicitudini*, which vindicated the effort he had put into both learning and teaching this, the preferred music of the Latin church. He was also preparing the outline of a book — it would become in due course three — on the Eastern churches. On 21 September, he was given for the first time a mission entirely his own, as rector of the church of the Assumption, at Maldon (*Meldun*), in Essex.

Fortescue was moving into the sunlight where his great gifts could coruscate at last. In a burst of concentrated effort in the spring, he produced the thesis on the authenticity of St John's Gospel which would be the written component to the coveted degree. He acquired a new organ in time for his first Easter at Maldon, and was pleased with the way the Holy Week ceremonies unfolded under his direction. He learned to deal with trouble-makers in decisive fashion, telling a man who had sought to extract money in compensation for an invented grievance that 'unless he straightway left

43 Ibid., Letter to the Archbishop of Westminster of 8 March, 1904.

44 Cambridge University Library, MSAdd 9812/D/90, Letter to S. Morison of 26 July, 1921.

45 Downside Archives, IX AF, Box D, 'Diary 1904', entry for 22 May, 1904.

46 Westminster Diocesan Archives, Box AGD, Letter to Hamilton Macdonald of 7 June, 1904.

my house, I would do sharp violence to his person, which person I no less accurately than succinctly described as ill-liking and mispleasing. He tarried not at all, but silent went'.[47] On Easter Monday he wrote (in German, as was usual in this correspondence) to Hamilton Macdonald, sharing his joy in the Easter ceremonies — as celebrated at Maldon, finely, so he claimed, and with the music 'entirely Solesmes'.[48] In June he made his way via Basle and Zurich to Innsbruck for the *ultimum rigorosum in doctoratu*, and was rewarded on 10 June with the qualification which made him forever after, in Westminster parlance, 'the Doctor'.

Buying a Turkish grammar in the New Year paved the way for a truly extraordinary sabbatical for it consisted in a Levantine 'grand tour'. Though we have no diary entries for the period concerned, some 'Rough Biographical Notes', possibly in the hand of his executrix, Miss Elmes, record that on 22 October 1906 he left for the University of Beirut, to improve his Arabic and study at first hand the Oriental liturgies.[49] It was to be a landmark in his life.

---

47 Westminster Diocesan Archives, Box AGD, Letter to 'the Chancellor, Archbishop's House, Westminster', of 7 February, 1905.

48 Westminster Diocesan Archives, Box AGD, Letter to Hamilton Macdonald of 16 April, 1906.

49 Downside Archives, IX AF, Box B, 'Notebook'. See footnote 1 above.

4. The Levantine Grand Tour (1906–7) and *The Greek Fathers*

An Oriental expedition

The phrase 'Levantine grand tour' should not be misunderstood. Fortescue's sabbatical, based ostensibly at the Jesuit University of St Joseph at Beirut, bore no relation to the stately progress of English aristocrats along the familiar roads or, later, railroads, of France and Italy. Despite the possibility of travelling on certain stretches of the Berlin-to-Baghdad railway, planned, and partly built, by the German imperial government for their Ottoman allies,[1] his was a high-risk adventure of rural travel of a mostly uncomfortable and — on at least two occasions — mortally dangerous kind which is better compared with the exploits of one of his heroes, Sir Richard Burton (1821–1890), Orientalist, linguist, ethnologist, poet, explorer of Africa and Western Asia.

There is, unfortunately, no diary for the year of the tour. What seems to have been the equivalent, a 'green exercise book' noted as once among his papers, is not to be found with the remaining diaries in the Downside collection. We do possess, however, a chronology, contained in a Notebook, passed onto the Westminster priest-philosopher Mgr John Vance by Fortescue's parishioner Edith Cowell, and this includes two summaries of his journey, one of them reasonably detailed.[2] The Archives, furthermore,

---

1 S. McMeekin, *The Berlin-Baghdad Express: the Ottoman Empire and Germany's Bid for World Power, 1898-1918* (London: Allen Lane, 2010). By the time of Fortescue's journey the section from an existing Anatolian Company railhead at Eskişehir across Anatolia via Konya to a somewhat insignificant town, Bulgurlu, had been built, despite financial and diplomatic obstacles (not to mention the constant threat from brigands) and in June 1907 German engineers had begun surveying for the tunnels through the formidable Taurus range, from stations north at Ereğli and south at Adana, ibid., pp. 32–53. There were also more local French-owned railway lines from Smyrna inland to Kasaba and along the coast from Mersin to Adana.

2 Westminster Diocesan Archives, Series 20, Box 21, 'Note-book'.

hold a couple of letters, one notably graphic, that are also *ad rem*, and then we have in addition the indications he left in his recently re-printed classic, *The Greek Fathers*, the original of which dates from 1908.[3]

Before setting out, Fortescue had asked the Westminster diocesan chancery for a Latin letter of recommendation from archbishop Bourne. He had in mind, so he explained to Macdonald, such possible recipients as the librarian of the Orthodox Patriarchate of Antioch and the inmates of the Athonite monasteries: thus a note to the archdiocesan chancellor the month before his departure.[4] (It was perhaps a trifle naïve of Fortescue to assume that such a document from a 'Frankish' cleric was likely to bear fruit, at any rate on the hyper-Orthodox Holy Mountain, but he seems to have been lucky.) The writing of *The Greek Fathers*, published the year after his return, enabled Fortescue to add to occasional passages in letters, and the (presumably) more detailed account in the lost 'green exercise book', some topographical descriptions, and even directions for future travellers, which clearly derive from personal observation and experience.

The comparison with Burton might be thought far-fetched; however, a folder, mainly of photographs, and entitled, indeed, *Photogrammata locorum inserendo libro* (had he considered writing, at least for his own amusement, a travelogue of his life?), includes a print of a sketch by F. Emery Jackson, showing him in the Arab attire he had adopted for the sake of protective self-concealment on the more sensitive stages of his Near and Middle Eastern expeditions.[5] At the start of the twentieth century, the Ottoman empire was utterly unable to impose the rule of law in its far-flung Arab dominions, from the Hejaz to Mesopotamia. But in this heyday of Orientalism, quite a number of intrepid Europeans took their chances nevertheless.[6]

Fortescue explains his *modus vivendi* in a letter from the Levant to Hamilton Macdonald.

> Since I have been in Syria I have made my headquarters with the Jesuits at Beirut, who are extraordinarily kind and hospitable, and from there I go for expeditions all through the Lebanon, which is a heavenly land, and all over the plain of Damascus

---

3 *The Greek Fathers. Their Lives and Writings* (London: Catholic Truth Society, and St Louis, MO: Herder and Co., 1908; reprinted San Francisco: Ignatius, 2007). Pagination will follow the reprinted version of 2007.

4 Westminster Diocesan Archives, Box AGD, Letter to Hamilton Macdonald of 21 September, 1906. The letter, impressively sealed, survives in the Westminster Diocesan Archives, Series 20, Box 21.

5 *Photogrammata locorum inserendo libro* is included in the collection in the Downside Archives as AC 3008.

6 R. Irwin, *For Lust of Knowing. The Orientalists and their Enemies* (London: Allen Lane, 2006).

and North Syria. In the Spring I mean to set out across the desert to Baghdad; back through Palestine, then to Athos and Constantinople by Asia Minor and home across the Balkans in the autumn.

He adds: 'Meanwhile I am learning Arabic all days and can already talk Syrian dialect enough to get on easily.' And boasting that he had already paid his respects to 'most of the 7 different Patriarchs of Antioch' (perhaps including, then, the Greek Orthodox to whom Bourne's letter was predestined), he announced he was about to 'set out [from Damascus] for Antioch itself, by Palmyra, Aleppo and Emessa; then from Iskenderun by one of the little Greek boats to Rhodes and Cyprus and so back to Beirut.7

The Itinerary

The letter just cited fills in a gap in the Note-book which in other respects can amplify these brief indications. He had left Victoria Station on 8 October for Athens, via Paris, Avignon, Marseilles and Naples, arriving for a 'memorable day', when on 15 October he gained the first impressions he would write up in his cameo portrait of St Basil. The next day he sailed to Smyrna, still predominantly a Greek city, and made his way, via the wonderful antique remains of Ephesus, to Beirut, which he reached on 22 October. After a stay of some few days in Damascus at the end of that month (this, evidently, is the period when he wrote to Macdonald), he began serious study at Beirut on 5 November, with classes in Arabic, Oriental archaeology and Islamic history. The Jesuit University of St Joseph was an admirable choice for deepening his knowledge of the Christian East. As he wrote later, 'The Jesuits have students of all Uniate Churches, who hear the same lectures and then have each their own liturgical practices'.[8] 'In their big church every Sunday morning various liturgies, Byzantine, Maronite, perhaps Armenian, Coptic, and Syrian, may be seen celebrated in various chapels, attended by groups of students'. Such multi-ritualism had the disadvantage, as he registered, that none can enjoy in thorough-going fashion the 'atmosphere' of his own.[9]

The vacations, however, were set aside for strenuous travelling. Christmas was spent on Cyprus, an excellent choice. He sailed on 19 December, walking from the port to Old Larnaka, and making his way to Nicosia where he arrived three days later. On 29 December he took the railway for

7   Westminster Diocesan Archives, Box AGD, Letter to Hamilton Macdonald of 15 December, 1906.

8   *The Uniate Eastern Churches* (London: Burns Oates and Washbourne, 1923), p. 231.

9   Ibid., pp. 231-232, footnote 2.

Famagusta (the Note-book records a good deal of drawing) and was back in Larnaka just in time for the Orthodox Christmas, on 6 January, before returning to Beirut the next day. A three day excursion to Tyre and Sidon in early February was followed by a much more ambitious journey to the Holy Places in March.

He began by taking a boat to Jaffa, and then going on to Jerusalem by rail. It was Holy Week, presumably not by chance. He attended Tenebrae in the Latin chapel at the Church of the Holy Sepulchre (he preferred to use its Greek designation, 'The Anastasis'), spent the morning of Holy Thursday with the Melkites, and had an audience on Good Friday with their patriarch, Cyril VIII. He noted in his *Catholic Encyclopaedia* article on the Rite of Constantinople, published the following year, the excellence of the rendering of the Byzantine chant at the Melkite church and seminary of St Anne where the choirmaster had published a guide to this — to Westerners — little known form of sacred music.[10] The memory of that institution clearly remained green; fifteen years later Fortescue was writing eulogistically about its merits.

> The French professors keep their Roman rite; but all the students are Melkites; the Byzantine rite dominates the whole house. All the ceremonies carried out in the church are Byzantine; the prayers and devotions of the students are scrupulously formed on Byzantine models. They are taught their rite by the Fathers who have become experts in its history and rules. Perhaps nowhere in the East will you see the Byzantine liturgy carried out so carefully and with such reverence as at St Anne's Church, or when the students go to serve and sing at the Patriarchal Church.[11]

I do not think we have to look much furher to find the source of the Byzantine fever which haunted him and made him wonder whether he should consider entering the ranks of the Melkite clergy himself.

Still on Good Friday: Fortescue was at the Dominican church, St Stephen's, for the Creeping to the Cross. Easter Day Mass took him back to the Anastasis (Easter fell on 31 March that year), and on Easter Monday he made a sortie to Bethlehem. On 5 and 6 April he visited Jericho, bathing in the Dead Sea; on 8 April he was at Hebron, where he drew a good deal, and he continued to sketch in and around Jerusalem until 22 April when Beirut beckoned again, with a new class, this time on Arabic calligraphy. The Note-book records he had the opportunity at this juncture to make some revisions to his forthcoming book *The Orthodox Eastern Church*.

10 'Constantinople, The Rite of', art. cit., p. 316; J.B. Rebours, *Traité de psaltique. Théorie et pratique du chant dans l'Eglise grecque* (Paris: Picard, 1906).

11 *The Uniate Eastern Churches* (London: Burns, Oates and Washbourne, 1923), p. 230.

In early June he did justice to Galilee. He rode up Mount Carmel by donkey, over-nighting on the summit; and went on donkey-back again to the Fountain of Elijah. At Acco he stayed with the Franciscans, the official Latin 'custodians' of the Holy Places, and took the opportunity to swim in the Mediterranean. Nazareth was reached by 'carriage' on 9 June. Fortescue hired a horse to get to Mount Thabor and, on the Sea of Galilee itself, Tiberias, taking in an Orthodox monastery and church at Babalhawa on the way. A boat brought him to Capernaum where he could view the remains of the synagogue where the Lord had preached; he commented on how 'excellent' the Franciscans there were. Boat and train returned him to Haifa on 13 June. More drawing and painting preceded a Samaritan expedition, to Shechem and Nablus. He took in the Samaritan synagogue, Mount Gerizim (the holy mountain of the Samaritan version of Israel's religion), and the traditional site of Jacob's well (though he was not at all sure he had actually found it in its ostensible location in the Orthodox church). A horse was acquired to carry him to Sebastiyeh for the church and tomb of St John the Baptist, from where he went on to Jenin which furnished highly paintable views of the Vale of Esdraelon. On the afternoon of 23 June he crossed by carriage the Plain of Jezreel (described in the Note-book as 'horrible'), though at least there was chance to draw the mountains of Gilboa en route. Back in Haifa he could dip in the sea again before leaving for Beirut on 27 June.

In July he used Beirut as a base for a number of sea excursions with friends: back to Larnaka; to Tarsus; and to Alexandretta (Iskenderun) from where they drove for a day in order to reach Antioch, where Capuchin Franciscans gave them shelter. The next days were chiefly in the saddle — to Seleucia, Adana, Aleppo. A glance at the atlas will show these are enormous distances for travel by horseback. On the last lap, so he records, he could hardly keep his saddle for sleepiness. It proved possible to recover, however, by means of a Turkish bath. A fever kept him in bed from 11 to 13 July, and he wisely decided to do the Ba'albek leg of his itinerary by train (presumably a stage of the Aleppo to Damascus railway, a separate venture from the partly constructed, partly projected, Berlin-to-Baghdad line).

On 16 July he was safely ensconced again in Jesuit quarters at Beirut. On 20 July he left by a tortuous and exceedingly protracted route for home. He coasted Cyprus and Asia Minor, landing at Rhodes and Smyrna where he changed boats. From Smyrna he sailed to Athens, whence he used the railway to reach Kalabaka, before changing to horse-back for the ride up to Meteora, those amazing monasteries perched on high pinnacles of rock, far above the plain of Thessaly. Drawing could be counterpointed by the study of the grammar of Modern Greek, as he made his way via Salonica through the Dardanelles and the Sea of Marmora to Constantinople which, delightfully, he reached at sun-rise. The Note-book records laconically 'great days there', which occupied the week between 16 and 25 August. After excursions into Asia Minor from the Ottoman capital, Fortescue took the Austrian-Lloyd line ship 'Salzburg' for Patras, on the west coast of the Peloponnese. From there he could easily reach the delicious island of Corfu prior to picking up another vessel of the same line bound for Trieste. By 11 September he was at Venice, whence he returned via Florence, Milan and Paris to England.

The book on the Greek Fathers

The plan of combining some travel notes with concise studies of a septet of the Eastern Fathers is not likely to have occurred to many, and to be sure, the project, so understood, could not be carried through consistently, insofar as Athanasius the Great and Cyril of Alexandria, two of the Fathers chosen for treatment (and without considerable imbalance they could hardly have been omitted) had their ministry in Egypt, which did not form part of Fortescue's itinerary. But the fortunes of the controversies in which Church and empire were caught up took both Athanasius and Cyril farther afield, and notably to the ecumenical councils held in the cities of Asia Minor, where Fortescue, thanks to personal acquaintance with the topography, could follow them.

Fortescue had began work on the first figure he wanted to present (Athanasius of Alexandria) soon after his initial Christmas at Letchworth, when he was still settling in and establishing the rhythm of life that would be his until his death some fifteen years on.[12] In the early pages of *The Greek Fathers* the apologetic caste of Athanasius's divinity (he was, after all, the defender par excellence of the divinity of Christ) exemplified Fortescue's simple and handy definition of a Church Father. 'Any saint . . . who wrote in defence of the Catholic faith between the first and the eighth centuries and whose works are still extant is a Father of the Church'.[13] The 'great' Fathers of the fourth and fifth centuries are called such, he added, because 'their works are so much more voluminous' contrasting the early 'Apostolic Fathers' whose combined efforts, as we have them, are smaller in quantity than the New Testament, with the literary output of St Augustine which 'fills sixteen volumes of Migne' (the mid-nineteenth century French editor of all the known ecclesiastical writers, in Latin or Greek, of ancient and mediaeval times).[14]

As he took pains to make clear, Fortescue's emphasis was going to lie on the Fathers as 'great figures in the Church history of their time'.[15] He

12   Downside Archives, IX AF, Box E, 'Diary 1908', entry for 11 January, 1908.
13   *The Greek Fathers*, op. cit., pp. xviii-xix.
14   Ibid., p. xix.
15   Ibid., p. xx.

feared that an attempt to lay out their 'theological systems' might prove too burdensome for the 'laymen' for whom he is writing. Still, since much of patristic history is concerned precisely with struggles over doctrine, it was inevitable that he had to sketch out for readers some at least of the intellectual issues of the day in which these figures (all of them, except Damascene, bishops) became so embroiled. It was a weakness in him that he does not seem fully to have realised how exciting the engaged exposition of theological doctrine can be. He had chosen to write about the Greek Fathers (rather than the Latin who, he implies, are already well enough known) because, he says, Catholics would be convicted of ingratitude should their achievements fall into oblivion among Western Christians in communion with Rome. But the question of orthodoxy — right belief and hence right worship — was central to the service they performed.

Athanasius

After a lengthy introduction which sets the scene for the Arian crisis, Fortescue structured his narrative around the five exiles of the saint. He makes plain enough the doctrinal issues at stake in Arianism, the radical Subordinationism for which the Son was only 'God' in a highly analogous sense, being as he was the most exalted of creatures, indeed the first-born of creatures, through whom all other things were made, and thus a kind of demiurge used by the Divinity who would otherwise have been defiled by immediacy of contact with the material world. In Fortescue's view — and present-day patristic scholars are likely to concur — Athanasius was basically a biblical theologian, steeped in the Scriptures, though he also credits Gregory Nazianzen's statement that Athanasius was 'very learned in both the Christian faith and profane letters'. [16] Fortescue ascribes to him not only a sophisticated grasp of Greek philosophy but also (and here he has the support of Socrates' *Ecclesiastical History*) a knowledge of Roman law which served him in exposing the technical flaws of the case against him at the (335) Council of Tyre. Athanasius needed these skills because Arius was tricky. The heresiarch 'wandered about Syria and Asia Minor making converts', and 'explained his ideas speciously enough, declared that of course he taught the Divinity of Christ — in a wider sense . . . ' (Fortescue possibly has in mind the contemporary 'Latitudinarian' Anglicans of the Modern Churchmen's Union, who were notoriously unreliable in Christological questions).[17]

Nor was the emperor very supportive. In fact, reports Fortescue, Constantine was 'immeasurably annoyed'.[18] 'He was braving the anger of

---

16   Ibid., p. 9, citing Gregory of Nazianzus, *Oratio* 21, 6.
17   *The Greek Fathers*, op. cit., p. 11.
18   Ibid., p. 12.

the immortal gods by being friendly to these Christians, and now he found that the Christians had two parties and, whichever he defended, he would have the other for an enemy'.[19] Constantine's solution, in 325, was to bring the bishops together, providing 'carriages and horses' for their journey and 'hospitality' when they arrived. The city whither they made their way (and Fortescue evidently enjoyed combining in rolling sentences the sonorous names of both the persons in transit and their places of origin) was Nicaea.

Though it is not stated explicitly, we are left in little doubt Fortescue went there on the 'Levantine grand tour', so that he might echo the 'undying honour' the bishops bestowed upon its name. '[E]ven now the Christian traveller in Asia Minor braves the difficult journey to an unsavoury Turkish village, that at Iznik he may stand by the shattered palace wall and dream of the meeting of the fathers at the first and most famous of all oecumenical synods',[20] among which 'fathers' he does not fail to mention specifically the legates of the pope. Though Fortescue is perfectly well aware, as he shows in a footnote, that the Creed said or sung at the Mass of the Roman rite reflects the amplification of the confession of Nicaea at the (381) First Council of Constantinople,[21] he invites his readers to find in the *Credo* 'the voice of the 318 "holy and divinely inspired fathers" that sounds through our churches till after seventeen centuries'.[22] It was a peal of triumph for the doctrine of the full Godhead of the Son.

The pity was that Constantine's family fluctuated in its attitude towards Arianism, such that, for all practical purposes, Nicaea became more the beginning of a larger crisis than the ending of a lesser one. Government attempts to restore the Arian bishops broke down on the rock of Athanasius's determined resistance, though that did not prevent theological dissent from spreading. Yet, the importance of the church of Alexandria, not only politically and culturally but ecclesially (it was the see of St Mark, the fellow-worker of St Peter), meant that without Athanasius the peace of the Church was well-nigh impossible to attain.

> [W]hether he sat on his throne by the great harbour in the richest and most famous centre of the Hellenic world, or wandered in exile in the west, or the desert, every Catholic looked up to Athanasius as the Lord of the East, who brought to their cause not only his learning and virtues, but the honour of so great a see.[23]

---

19 Ibid., pp. 12-13.
20 Ibid., p. 14.
21 Ibid., p. 15, footnote 17.
22 Ibid., p. 15. The phrase 'the 318 holy and divinely inspired fathers' derives, as Fortescue mentions, from the title of the feast in honour of the Council celebrated by the Orthodox and Melkites on the Sunday after the Ascension.
23 Ibid., p. 16.

Fortescue makes a valiant attempt to identify and categorise the numerous positions on the spectrum which joined — or separated — Arianism and Nicene orthodoxy. The Enlightenment period historian Edmund Gibbon may have mocked patristic Christians for worrying about an iota — the difference in spelling between those who said the Son was 'of the same substance of the Father', the Homoousians, those who said he was 'of like substance to the Father', the Homoiousians. But, replies Fortescue, who is impatient with the Semi-Arians ('We know them in all controversies, the people who tell us that no doubt there is a great deal to be said on both sides'),[24] it is obvious that a single letter can alter the whole sense of a word, citing an example quoted by Newman, the difference between 'personage' and 'parsonage'.[25] Fortescue has no time for those who consider the doctrinal controversies of the age of the Fathers to be mere 'logomachy', fighting about words. 'These passwords were technical forms that stood for very real differences.'[26]

Though Fortescue cannot cope with the Orthodox canonization of Constantine ('The Catholic Church, more difficult in her standards of sanctity, honours Helen only [Constantine's mother, q.v.] as a saint'), he writes with pathos nonetheless of the lying in rest at the church of the Holy Apostles which followed Constantine's death-bed baptism, 'first of the long line of Roman emperors who were buried around him, till in 1463 the Turk cleared away the burial-place of the Caesars to make room for the mosque of Mohammed the Conqueror'.[27]

Fortescue considers Athanasius's appeal for vindication to Pope Julius an outstanding example of recognition, in the early centuries, of the universal appellate jurisdiction of the bishop of Rome. The anti-Nicene objection to Athanasius' action (it was unnecessary because the matter had already been settled by the various post-Nicene councils) reminded Fortescue of 'what we hear in this country' (among Anglicans and Protestants, he means). 'To appeal to councils is a splendid argument, when you are quite sure which councils are the right ones to appeal to.'[28] Fortescue takes the zenith of the crisis to be the 359 Synod of Ariminium which Constantius, the most Arianising of Constantine's sons, forced to accept the fourth creed of Sirmium. (By Fortescue's reckoning, there were at this date eleven distinct creeds in competition with the Creed of Nicaea.) Despite this — echoing Newman's *On Consulting the Faithful in Matters of Doctrine* — the 'simple people kept the faith through all this clash of quarrelling bishops, and they

---

24 Ibid., p. 19.
25 Ibid., p. 20, footnote 25.
26 Ibid., p. 20.
27 Ibid., p. 24.
28 Ibid., p. 26.

looked out toward the hot Libyan desert where the column of the faith
[Athanasius] lay hidden till God should bring him back'.[29]

All the later Fathers, says Fortescue with only slight exaggeration, praise
Athanasius as champion of the faith. All (Christian) Egyptians, he claims,
own him the greatest saint of their country. All four claimants to the throne
of St Mark — the Coptic Monophysite patriarch, the Coptic Uniate
patriarch, the Orthodox patriarch, and the Melkite patriarch — acclaim
him as 'their most glorious predecessor'.[30] Fortescue ends his essay by citing
the collect and sixth Matins reading for his memorial, 2 May, in the Roman
Liturgy to show how this applause is no merely Eastern affair.

Basil and Gregory Nazianzen

With Basil and Gregory Nazianzen, those two great friends who thought
(for much of the time) alike, Fortescue could make more use of his 'grand tour'.
He gives the impression that he had travelled in Pontus, the area of their birth
in the north of what is now Turkey. His description of their youthful arrival in
Athens to study rhetoric is too vivid not to be first hand; he had clearly gone
out of his way to visit the scene of their episcopal activity in Cappadocia, lying
to the south-east of Pontus in a region of Asia Minor with which their names
will forever be associated. Fortescue is less forthcoming about their theological
work than he was with Athanasius. Indeed these chapters correspond much
more closely to his initial statement of intent in The Greek Fathers.

Thus, he might have presented Basil as the doctor of the Godhead
of the Holy Spirit (he recognizes the importance of his Peri tou Hagiou
Pneumatos, 'On the Holy Spirit'),[31] but instead he chose to regard him as
'a great Catholic bishop in a troubled time, as a man of very ascetic life
and as the father of organized eastern monasticism'.[32] Fortescue opens by
describing Basil's background in a family of the senatorial nobility, which
was not, it seems, a barrier to sanctification since his father, mother and
maternal grandmother are all recognized as saints in the Eastern church.[33]
Fortescue, who makes much of the sanctity of Basil's siblings — specifically,
his sister, the nun Macrina, and his younger brother Gregory, later bishop
of Nyssa — only notes at the end of his account these holy forbears, and
somehow manages to leave out Basil's father, St Basil the Elder.[34] This is

29 Ibid., p. 32.
30 Ibid., p. 36.
31 Ibid., p. 77.
32 Ibid., p. 43.

33 H.R. Drobner, The Fathers of the Church. A Comprehensive Introduction
    (Peabody, MA: Hendrickson, 2007), p. 266.
34 The Greek Fathers, op. cit., p. 74.

not out of the desire to paint in darker colours the picture of Basil's pre-monastic life. Indeed, Fortescue describes in idyllic terms the life they lived in a great household set in magnificent countryside, Basil and his three brothers 'hunting, fishing, riding through the forests along the slopes of the mountains that stretch down toward the Black Sea', a vignette — so one suspects — of a remembered landscape from his own explorations.[35]

Initially, Basil and his brother Gregory had met Gregory Nazianzen (as he later became known) at Caesarea, the Cappadocian capital where, however, rhetorical studies were not first class. They met up again at Athens. Cultural Hellenism was the mark of the civilized man in Victorian England (as in the Germany of the same period) and Fortescue's account breathes its spirit. He treats the appearance of Athens as a veritable epiphany.

> The city of Pallas Athene, crowned with violets, was still ancient Athens. That wonderful vision of gleaming marble and stately orders of columns, the glowing colours of the Parthenon, the shining golden helmet of the virgin goddess, the cool arcades, crowded theatre and the glorious Propyleia — all the splendours that we now try to recall among the piteous ruins of the Acropolis — were then real things. Where we look up from the bay of Salamis and see only broken columns and the split gable of the great temple — even now incomparable in its ruin — there the sailor of the fourth century saw the Parthenon radiant with colour and the mighty statue of Athene lifting her gleaming spear over the wine-dark sea.[36]

But even more important to him was the inner spirit. 'Athens was still the heart of that rich and subtle combination of philosophy, letters and perfect aesthetic taste that make up *Hellenism*.'[37] Basil took the risk that pagan philosophy might subvert his faith for the sake of what he might learn by way of mastering the resources of the Greek language — combining, in the company of Gregory Nazianzen, study and prayer.

He might have remained a professor of rhetoric, and a good one, but on his baptism, influenced, thinks Fortescue, by his sister's example, he decided to become a monk. Fortescue notes Basil's expedition through Palestine-Syria, to Egypt and Mesopotamia in a characteristically efficient study-tour to register ascetic best practice. But he also notes Basil's love of fine scenery, and ascribes to a proto-Romantic impulse the choice of a Pontic location, Annesi, for his first monastery where Basil would establish two inter-related colonies, one on each side of the river Iris, for women and men respectively, with the former containing, among others, his mother and sister. Fortescue makes it obvious to the reader he has been there.

35 Ibid., p. 46.
36 Ibid., p. 49.
37 Ibid. Italics original.

'There is a high mountain, not easy to reach, covered with woods; its green slopes lead down to the clear river; banks of wild flowers cluster around the roots of the trees; birds sing all day in their branches, and the river is full of fish.'[38] Basil was prevailed upon to leave this glorious setting (and Fortescue is not exaggerating, as Basil's Letter 14 indicates), and make a return to public life. The reasons were the pagan reaction under the emperor Julian the Apostate, and the continuing threat, in Cappadocia, of Arianism.

In 364 Basil returned from Annesi to Caesarea. Though this could hardly be guessed today, the capital of Cappadocia was a great metropolitan see ruling much of what is now northern and central Asia Minor, and with jurisdiction over the church of Armenia until the latter rejected Chalcedon and became Monophysite. Fortescue can report: 'It is a dusty little Turkish town now; but of the few people who brave the hideously uncomfortable journey of five days' hard riding from Angora [Ankara] to *Kaisari*', and plainly he was among their number, 'most do so because it was the city of Basil'.[39] Basil proved a wise leader who knew when to conciliate and when to stand firm, although he could not prevent the sub-division of his province by the pro-Homoean (and thus quasi-Arian) emperor Valens. Fortescue offers St Basil his homage:

> proudly conscious of the liberty of the Church against the state, gentle and kind to the poor, courteous, friendly and charming to his friends, best and most entertaining of letter-writers, submitting his difficulties to his rightful chief at Rome [a reference to Basil's Letter 70 to Pope Damasus], from far Cappadocia he has left an example that any bishop in any land may pray to be worthy to follow.[40]

What then of St Gregory? If one failed to remember Fortescue's self-set rule of not over-burdening the layman with difficult ideas, one might have thought he would do St Gregory Nazianzen justice as theologian of the Holy Trinity. He is perfectly well aware that the Greeks call him 'Gregory the Theologian'. Curiously, he rated Gregory's 'Apology for his Flight' (this is, in effect, a treatise on the priesthood), above the *Theological Orations* — for most orthodox students of the Fathers, the crown of his theological work.[41] Since, unlike Basil, Gregory was not entirely successful as a pastor, the effect of marginalising his intellectual labours is to make the cameo-portrait of this theologian-bishop a disappointing appendix to Fortescue's fuller and more appreciative study of his friend. Given the ancient prejudice against the translation of bishops from one see to another, Gregory's highly unwilling consecration as bishop of Sasima, forced on him by Basil, called into question his status as custodian archbishop of Constantinople at the time of the Second Ecumenical Council in 381, and indeed his standing as bishop of

38   Ibid., p. 57.
39   Ibid., p. 62.
40   Ibid., p. 69.
41   Ibid., p. 102.

Nazianzus, his birth-place, the see he administered for a while after the death of his father, who had occupied it previously. (This is a cue for Fortescue to explain to potentially scandalized Catholic readers that not until the 692 'Quinisext' Council was it absolutely forbidden for bishops to be married[42]).

Fortescue declares roundly that 'Basil's ill-considered impulse about Sasima ... ruined [Gregory's] life,'[43] even if a 'want of consistent purpose' should also be laid at Gregory's own door.[44] Granted Gregory's output (four volumes of Migne), and his clear explanation to Basil that his way of serving the Church in the monastic life was as writer and teacher, in the mode pertaining to what later centuries would call 'an intellectual', this seems remarkably harsh. I hazard the suggestion that admiration for sheer thought of a philosophical-theological kind only stole over Fortescue at the very end of his life. Despite his capacious mind which housed so vast a treasury of facts, Fortescue was too strongly marked by the pastoral orientation of the diocesan clergy to treat the notion of a priest-intellectual with favour. Only with his Boethius project, to be described in the last chapter of this study, did he, at the end of his life, gain more insight into how such a priest or, in Gregory's case, bishop (Boethius himself, however, was a layman) might serve the Church's good. This was just as well, since Modernism — like ancient Gnosis, sixteenth century Protestantism and the early modern Enlightenment — cried out for a strenuous (but intelligent) response from the orthodox among the clergy and laity in the West.

John Chrystostom

John Chrysostom fares better at Fortescue's hand, and that is because the nature of his ministry to the believing and worshipping community can so readily be made plain. 'To Catholics as to the Orthodox he remains for all time the great model and patron of preachers.'[45] The setting is plain — the ambo at the Liturgy — and the task, the upbuilding of faith and (especially) morals is almost equally so.

John was from Antioch on the Orontes, the capital of Roman Syria, and for the ancient world a colossal city — Fortescue mentions that the colonnade which crossed Antioch, joining its gates on east and west, was the equivalent of five miles long. As the author of the Acts of the Apostles famously remarks, it was at Antioch that the apostles were 'first called Christians' (Acts 11:26). Christians made up roughly half of the population. The Antiochene theology, so Fortescue reports, was celebrated, though with its Christology of the man Jesus united to the Word (rather

---

42 Ibid., p. 85, footnote 6.
43 Ibid., p. 100.
44 Ibid.
45 Ibid., p. 105.

than, as at Alexandria, the single reality of the Word incarnate) its learning
and Bible interpretation were deemed by some to be 'unsafe'.[46] Alas, the
sands of time have covered up most of its glory, or, in Fortescue's words:
'The splendour of the great Seleucid capital has gone now. You may ride
from the port of Iskanderun to *Antakiye* in a day, and you will find a little
town, half Turkish, half Arab, that does not fill up a tenth of the space
enclosed in the old walls'.

Reporting, evidently, on his own visit, he paints a word-picture of what
the visitor can expect.

> Among the thick olive-woods around it, you will see broken
> columns, by the mosque in the chief street ruins of the old
> colonnade. Going out through the Mohammedan tombs you
> come to the grove of Daphne. Her laurels still tremble in the
> cool winds as if she feared the god, but Apollo has gone long
> ago. Even the Christian memories hardly linger here; of the five
> persons who bear the splendid title of Patriarch of Antioch not
> one now lives here.

A note informs the reader that the

> Orthodox and Melkite patriarchs live at Damascus, the Maronite
> at Bherki in the Lebanon, the Jacobite at Diarbekr on the Tigris,
> the titular Latin patriarch [a hangover from the Crusading
> States: later in the twentieth century the honorific ceased to be
> bestowed] at Rome. . . . From the tombs across the river you see
> the town with its minarets and the great wheels that churn up
> the brown water under the mountains on which you may trace
> the ruins of the old walls against the sky.

Fortescue concludes that only a strenuous effort of imagination can screen
out the intervening Islamic centuries and restore to the mind's eye the
church of Chryostom's early ministry.

> You may try to call up the old glory of the "great and God-
> protected city" in which John Chrysostom preached. While the
> distant wail of the Mu'ezzin tells you that there is no God but
> Allah and Mohammed is the prophet of Allah, you will think
> that here we first got our name of Christians.[47]

In the course of describing Chrystostom's education — an excellent
one, thanks to his good fortune in having as teacher one of the finest of
the philosopher-rhetors of late antiquity, Libanios, who was a pagan —
Fortescue provides a nice contrast between the pagan and Christian world-
pictures of the time. Pagans:

46 Ibid., p. 106.
47 Ibid.

loved Hellas and sunlight, the pleasant old feasts that scattered roses over the steps of temples while the glorious statues gleamed in the clear light. And they wanted the old gods, Apollo and Aphrodite and Artemis, the ideals of perfect beauty, and the dear homely gods of wood and fountain and roadside that were so easily pleased and so content to see their children happy.[48]

Not surprisingly, perhaps, the alternative world-picture of the Christians left them cold. '[T]he mystic glory of the Lord who reigns from the cross, the strange joy of pain for Christ's sake, the silent love of the good Shepherd, were as much beyond them as the awful majesty of the Lord of Hosts reigning alone above the distant heavens'.[49]

Fortescue does justice to the claims of paganism, and he obviously considered Chrysostom did as well, despite the saint's objections to learning oratorical technique for its own sake and his occasional criticisms of Homer. He also notes the entirely positive influence on John of his bishop Meletios of Antioch, against whose episcopal line the see of Rome maintained an unjustified opposition for well over a century, dogged in its refusal to abandon the judgment of Meletios's critic the unhappily named Lucifer of Cagliari to the effect that a bishop originally sponsored by Arians could never be any good. In his study of the making of the schism with the Greeks, Fortescue will cite Rome's mistake over the Meletians as an example of papal mishandling of Eastern affairs.

It was while John was a priest at Antioch, where he was ordained by Meletios's successor Flavian, that he acquired the renown as a preacher that gave him his sobriquet, 'The Golden-mouthed'. Fortescue catalogues the homilies on various biblical books, the Lenten catecheses and the sermons on special occasions which, taken cumulatively, justified the name 'Chrystostom'. Fortescue, whose own preaching manner, except in Passiontide, was rather dry, waxes lyrical about John's Greek style.

His flow of words is amazing; he adorns his speech with every ornament of rhetoric. Sometimes he is majestic and splendid, and then he suddenly comes down to pleasant familiarity. He is indignant, and the sentences roll like thunder; he is pathetic, and it is all tears and woe. Or he argues subtly, persuasively, he pleads tenderly, he threatens awfully. He weaves chains of argument or paints pictures, teaches, exhorts and carries everyone with him up to some crashing climax.[50]

---

48 Ibid., p. 107.
49 Ibid.
50 Ibid., p. 113.

Fortescue adds an interesting sidelight on Orthodox practice as he had observed it in Greek-speaking congregations.

> One is not surprised that every Greek preacher down to our own time tries to model himself on Chrysostom and that still, on the rare occasions when you may hear a sermon in an Orthodox church, you are surprised to notice that the homely language of the preacher suddenly stops, and that under the low cupolas rolls a splendid sentence, pompous and magnificent, that he has learned by heart from Chrysostom.[51]

John Chrysostom was a Nicene Christian, and Fortescue notes that his friendship with Theodore of Mopsuestia, later regarded as a father of Nestorianism, seems to have done him no Christological harm. From the body of his teaching Fortescue isolates two moral motifs — care for the poor and the sanctity of marriage, and one theological one — the Holy Eucharist. All three are well-chosen. Fortescue's notion that they are prominent in Chrysostom's homiletics is not far-fetched. John's social doctrine combined audacity with practical common-sense realism. As Fortescue explains, among other ideas, he wanted rich people to keep on their estates permanent guest-houses for poor travellers, certainly an audacious proposal. But the manner in which Chrysostom commended it was down-to-earth. 'Have at least such a place by your stables. Christ comes to you in the form of the poor. Let Christ, at least, use your stable. You shudder at such an idea. It is still worse not to receive him at all.'[52] There is not a great deal about the social problem of late industrial England in Fortescue's writing, even if personally he was so generous (as well as spendthrift on books, travel, and the adornment of his church) as to imperil his own livelihood. So it is good to have these admiring comments on the *doctor eucharisticus*.

Fortescue's narrative gifts are shown to full effect in his account of Chrysostom's troubled years as archbishop (or as Fortescue writes, admitting the usage at this early date is questionable, 'patriarch') of Constantinople. The clarity of John's ethical judgment and his boldness in exercising it from the ambo led to difficulties first with Eutropius, the eunuch-favourite, later consul, under the emperor Arcadius, and then with the emperor's wife Eudoxia. The fate of the venal Eutropius, who fell from grace and fled into a church to claim the right of sanctuary he earlier had sought to eliminate, and there was protected by his enemy, the archbishop, has, so Fortescue claims, 'taken hold of the imagination of people in those parts': he has 'seen boys at a Greek school playing this scene'.[53]

---

51 Ibid.

52 John Chrysostom, *In epistolam primam ad Corinthios*, 40, quoted in *The Greek Fathers*, op. cit., p. 118.

53 Ibid., p. 127.

As to the empress, who conspired with Theophilus of Alexandria, the rival see, to arrange the two exiles Chrysostom suffered, Fortescue finds the archiepiscopal description of her as another Jezebel, and another Herodias, distinctly plausible. Though painting her face was one of Chrysostom's objections to her, other charges in the background to his first exile were more weighty, including acts of injustice owing to Eudoxia's nefarious influence on government. The second exile, from which Chrysostom did not return alive, was prompted by her erection of a silver statue of herself immediately outside Constantine's church of the Holy Wisdom. The statue became a focal point for riotous behaviour and the archbishop asked the prefect of the City to have it moved further away. The saint was banished, initially to the 'extreme end of Cappadocia, near the Cilician frontier, in little Armenia'.[54] This was an area which, during Fortescue's Levantine grand tour, still had a large Armenian population inherited from the middle ages — indeed, so much so that when the Turkish massacres of Armenians resumed during the First World War few competent men could be found to work on the all-important section of the Berlin-to-Baghdad railway on the western side of the Cilician Gates.[55] The imperial government then ordered Chrysostom to be sent on by route march, to the north of Asia Minor.

He got as far as Komanes in Pontus, too ill to continue. He had collapsed near the tomb of the Diocletianic martyr St Basiliskos, whose voice he seemed to hear in a dream, bidding him take courage since on the morrow they would be together. He vested, celebrated the Liturgy, and died. The dispute caused the Roman see, in the person of Pope Innocent I, to break off relations with Constantinople for a generation. Fortescue movingly describes the act of healing of memories by which Theodosius II made amends, going down to the shore to meet the relics of the saint as they arrived by sea.

> In the evening of January 27, the procession of boats came up the Golden Horn, lit by blazing torches that gleamed from the Bosphorus to the Propontis. The emperor kneeling before the barge on which the body rested "asked forgiveness for his parents and for what they had done in ignorance".[56]

Fortescue contributes his own comment to that report of the historian Theodoret of Cyr:

> The waves of the Golden Horn, lit up by the light of the torches, fllowing out into the Hellespont and into the great sea beyond [the Mediterranean], are a symbol of the glory of the golden-

54 Ibid., p. 133.

55 S. McMeekin, *The Berlin-Baghdad Express: the Ottoman Empire and Germany's Bid for World Power, 1898–1918*, op. cit., p. 254.

56 *The Greek Fathers*, op. cit., p. 136, citing Theodoret of Cyr, *Historia ecclesiastica* V. 36.

mouthed preacher that spread out from his patriarchal city to the ends of the Christian world.[57]

Fortescue completes his vignette of Chrysostom by, in effect, invoking the intercession of St John Chrysostom not only for the ending of the schism between Greek East and Latin West but also for an end to the Muslim domination of Constantinople (at the time of Fortescue's writing, in 1908, the city had a population of which roughly half was non-Turkish, and of those the overwhelming majority were Christian).

> If anything can trouble the peace of the saints, he must be troubled to see his successors rebel against those of Innocent, and to hear the Mu'ezzin cry from the place he would not have defiled by Eudoxia's statue. And if any saint has a special reason to pray to God for the end of these evils, it is John who appealed to old Rome as lawful Bishop of New Rome, who, where Islam is now preached, spoke for the gospel of Christ with his golden mouth.[58]

Cyril of Jerusalem

It is surprising that, writing on St Cyril of Jerusalem, Fortescue does not take the opportunity to interweave his own impressions of the Holy Places. It cannot be because they failed to leave any. In a Christmastide letter from 1909 weather conditions at home conspired with the season to throw back his mind to the two cities of the Incarnation (Bethlehem, Jerusalem). Waiting alone for Christmas Matins to begin and looking out 'over the silent night across the great field (over my fence)', he 'saw again the long white twisting road that goes out from the Jaffa gate of Jerusalem, past Rachel's tomb, to Bethlehem, and the market place, and there the Nativity church and the huddled roofs, and the quiet fields outside where they were keeping the watches of the night by their sheep'.[59] In describing Cyril of Jerusalem there are nothing like the dramatic possibilities of the Chrysostom story, or even that of Basil. Perhaps this is why Fortescue does not linger over a *mis-en-scène*. It is true that, like Chrysostom, Cyril was at times banished from his see. During the Arian crisis (Cyril was born around 315, John a generation later in 344) temporary deprivation was a normal part of the experience of orthodox bishops generally, and no circumstances attended Cyril's banishment so vivid and personal as those that explain the Chrysostom affair.

---

57   *The Greek Fathers*, op. cit., p. 136.
58   Ibid., p. 137.
59   Cited M. Davies, 'Adrian Fortescue – Priest and Scholar', in idem., *The Wisdom of Adrian Fortescue*, op. cit., p. 50.

Cyril was (more or less) a Jerusalemite, born and bred. He served for ten years as a deacon in the church there before Maximos of Jerusalem ordained him priest in 345. Fortescue's account ascribes Cyril's marvellous set of catechetical instructions to the early years of his priesthood and takes the opportunity to explain how the approach to Baptism was managed in the ancient Church, at Rome as well as Jerusalem and Antioch. He explains the *disciplina arcani*, which he thinks applied especially to the Eucharistic mysteries. He feels some scholars are inclined to minimize it (true, it may not have existed as early as Justin Martyr's time, but Augustine is still aware of it in his *Tractates on John*). It is odd that in his *Catecheses* Cyril avoids the term *homoousion*, the keyword of Nicene Christology. Yet he conveys its meaning in equivalent ways, and Fortescue cannot credit those who think Cyril in his early period (even as a bishop) may have inclined to Semi-Arianism. The Second Ecumenical Council, Constantinople I, had no hesitation in deposing Semi-Arian bishops as well as Arian ones, yet Cyril remained unscathed.

The political problem of Cyril's life was that, when the Romans reconstructed Jerusalem (in every sense) as a pagan city, 'Aelia Capitolina', they rather queered the pitch for a Christian bishop there. Until the time of Cyril's successor Juvenal, the bishop of Jerusalem, though esteemed in the counsels of the universal Church, was actually only a suffragan of the metropolitan of Caesarea, and for much of Cyril's episcopate, that worthy was an Arian sympathizer. Thrice Cyril was removed from his see. Ironically, it was by the policy of tolerance adopted by the neo-pagan emperor Julian the Apostate, that in 361 he found himself restored on the second occasion (the third and final time was more predictable, for the emperors, Gratian and Theodosius I, were Catholics).

Not that Julian's accession had been *entirely* good news for Christians in Jerusalem. Because Julian genuinely believed in the national religions as comparable expressions of a single philosophical truth and in order, perhaps, to throw a spanner in the works of Christian progress, the emperor proposed to re-build the Temple cast down in the Roman-Jewish wars — which would thus become a (quasi-)falsification of the prophecy of Christ that not one stone of it would be left on another. It belongs with Fortescue's occasional quirkiness that he had a soft spot for Julian, recommending to readers a recent three volume study in French for furnishing:

> a really scientific, moderate and sympathetic treatment of a man who was almost a genius, always extraordinarily interesting, very ideal in his character and irreproachable in his morals, rather mad and in any case a hopeless failure. If only poor Julian had taken up any less hopeless cause than that of the gods he would have been the greatest emperor since Constantine.[60]

60 *The Greek Fathers*, op. cit., p. 156, fn 53. The work Fortescue recommended is

Somewhat in the manner of *Indiana Jones and the Lost Ark*, Fortescue seems willing, nonetheless, to credit the report of Ammianus Marcellinus that preternatural forces prevented the labourers from getting on with the work. Ammianus Marcellinus was, after all, a 'heathen historian'.[61]

Cyril of Alexandria

Fortescue has told us that the name 'Kyrillos', meaning 'little lord', is a common one in Greek,[62] so we are not too surprised to find a second Cyril figuring in *The Greek Fathers*, and this is Cyril of Alexandria.

Cyril is the only one of these figures for whom Fortescue clearly feels obliged to make a defensive case. The problem is the murder of the Neo-Platonist woman-philosopher Hypatia. Fortescue writes in what seems at first a damaging, not to say, damning, admission, that 'the chief work of [Cyril's] life was not murdering Hypatia, but fighting for the person of Christ and the honour of the Mother of God against the Nestorians'.[63] Does this wording imply that 'murdering Hypatia' *was* a 'work' of Cyril's life? Not at all, but Fortescue understands why people have regarded Cyril as complicit in this horrible crime. Cyril came from a family with the arrogant spirit of those who consider themselves born to rule — the high-handed action of his uncle, the previous patriarch, Theophilos, in helping to secure the first deposition of Chrysostom had already been noted in the pages of *The Greek Fathers*. There was a strong local reason why Cyril might have wanted to deal a stunning public blow to the pagan party: the governor, Orestes, though nominally a Christian, was inclined to favour them. The main actors in the tragedy were a cleric under Cyril's authority in the shape of a lector, Peter, and a group within the church of Alexandria, the *Parabolanoi*, whose task in theory was to tend the sick, notably plague-victims, though in fallow periods for nursing care they had developed a regrettable tendency to become the bully-boys of the bishop. The doctrinal controversy of Cyril with Nestorius and the Antiochene school does not give the impression of a figure loth to polarize situations by ruthless action.

Nevertheless, Fortescue finds the charge incredible.

> [I]f ever a man had bitter enemies, it was Cyril. Wilful murder was considered just as unsuitable conduct for bishops in the fifth century as it is now. Why, during all the fierce conflict with the Nestorians, when they brought every possible charge against him, did no one think of calling him Hypatia's murderer?[64]

P. Allard, *Julien l'apostat* (Paris: Lecoffre, 1900).

61   *The Greek Fathers*, op. cit., p. 156.

62   Ibid., p. 143.

63   Ibid., p. 163.

64   Ibid., p. 166.

Fortescue finds that, while there is an insinuation of this kind in a pagan source (considerably later than the events), it had no currency until in the mid nineteenth century the Anglican Broad Churchman Charles Kingsley opted to revive it in his 'singularly silly novel' *Hypatia*.[65] Furthermore, through the good offices of a German scholar, Fortescue found a text in the Theodosian Code which records a request of Alexandrian citizens to the emperor to suppress the *Parabolanoi*, a petition which, inter alia, pleads for Cyril to remain in the city as part of the solution, rather than part of the problem.[66] Orestes had wanted to expel him.

As Fortescue says, not a quarrel with a magistrate but a struggle with a major heresy was the fulcrum of Cyril's life: a task worthy of his 'restless energy' and 'high spirit'.[67] There follows an excellent account of the Nestorian issue, though Fortescue's conviction that lay readers will not be able to tolerate too much theology is in evidence when he declares 'we *may as well* understand' what the concepts of 'nature' and 'person' mean.[68] Indeed, we had better or we shall understand nothing of the debate at all. If the union between the divine and human natures at the Incarnation is not hypostatic — that is, if it is not brought about in the person of the Word, such that the Mother of Jesus is really and truly Mother of One who is God, the *Theotokos*, then the only alternative is 'some close moral connexion, some indwelling of the Divinity that did not affect his person, but made that person its temple'.[69] For Fortescue, Cyril was not in fact precipitate. Antiochene radicals in episcopal orders triggered the crisis. At first Cyril confined himself to counselling monastics and others in his own patriarchate — through a paschal letter, which was the normal way of treating concerns that arose in a given year. The title *Theotokos* which had come under attack had excellent precedents, as well as theological justice on its side. Only when Nestorius complained of Cyril's interference (it was nothing of the sort — as yet) did Cyril write a letter of theological remonstrance.

In 430 a Roman synod under Pope Celestine required Nestorius to take back into communion the 'Theotokians' i.e. orthodox believers he had excommunicated and threatened the archbishop of Constantinople with excommunication himself if he did not retract his heresy. In a letter to Cyril

---

65   Ibid. The reference is to C. Kingsley, *Hypatia, or New Foes with an Old Face* (London: J.W. Parker, 1853, 2 vols.).

66   Theodosius, *Codex Legis,* 'On Bishops', XVI. 2. Fortescue had come across this text in J. Kopallik, *Cyrillus von Alexandrien, eine Biographie* (Mainz: Kirchheim, 1881).

67   *The Greek Fathers*, op. cit., p. 167.

68   Ibid., p. 177, footnote 37. Italics added.

69   Ibid., p. 169.

accompanying a copy of the synodal acts, Celestine made him his legate at the forthcoming Council, called by Theodosius II to resolve the matter, a gathering which opened at Ephesus at Pentecost 431. On the basis of his own experience, Fortescue tells travellers how to get there. From Smyrna one takes the Aidin railway to the village of Ayasoluk — a Turkish attempt to render the Greek for *hagios theologos*, for this is where the 'holy theologian' par excellence, St John the Evangelist, had been bishop. At Ayasoluk a horse is required for the remainder of the journey, an hour's ride to the plain where the ruins of Ephesus are being excavated by a team of Austrian archaeologists.

> Looking down from the rising ground (*Panayir Dagh*) to the east you see the plain stretch out to the sea between the high mountain (*Bülbül Dagh* — Nightingale hill) and the river Kaystros. A canal brings the water up to the great Ephesian harbour. At your feet lies a glorious and wonderful white Greek city. Standing out from the long grass, the olive trees and the carpet of many-coloured flowers, are the columns of the broad road, the stage of the great library, the curve of the theatre — temples and baths and colonnades, broken and ruined now, but still majestic and splendid in their gleaming white marble and all eloquent of the rich and mighty city that was the capital of Asia.[70]

Clambering over broken walls and pushing a way through thick bushes one finds oneself within the space of the 'double church' of Ephesus where the Council took place. In the early summer of 431 the Antiochene patriarch and his bishops were delayed, thus enabling Cyril to score a clear victory.

Fortescue thinks the 'delay' rather fishy. En route, John told Cyril it was going to take him thirty-five or so days' travelling. Fortescue computes the distance in 'easy horse-stages of 30–40 miles a day' as no more than a fortnight.[71] '[F]rom the beginning there was something not straight about John of Antioch.'[72] The refusal of the Antiochenes to uphold the decisions so far made and the unwillingness of their patriarch to join the original conciliar fathers in continuing session led to the suspension of the Syrians — and a confused period of some two years until first Theodosius and then John of Antioch finally accepted Nestorius' deposition. Such hesitations, whether they were the result of politics or of conscience, did not deter the Ephesian citizenry who, after the first and crucial session of the Council, 'accompanied the fathers back to their lodgings . . . with a great torchlight procession'.[73] The Turkish guides who escorted Fortescue knew the Greek

70 Ibid., p. 179.
71 Ibid., p. 181, footnote 59.
72 Ibid.
73 Ibid., p. 183.

phrase *panagia Theotokos* ('the all-holy Mother of God'), which is how the church that served as council-chamber came to be known, but not the meaning of the word 'Theotokos'. Fortescue was convinced nonetheless that 'the Turkish peasants, who all over the Levant surprise one by their curious memories of local Christian events, have kept a vague consciousness of what was done in the double church'. And he added that 'still as one looks over Ephesus in the evening, one seems to see the gleam of the torches move down the great street among the shadows and the ghosts'.[74]

Wisely, Cyril would spend the remaining three years of his life pacifying the Syrian churchmen, notably through discouraging any attempt by the orthodox to condemn the great Antiochene exegete Theodore of Mopsuestia. Just as Catholics implicitly recall Athanasius when they recite the Nicene Creed, so likewise, says Fortescue, they tacitly remember Cyril when in the Litany they call on our Lady as *Dei genetrix* or in the Hail Mary greet her as 'Mother of God'. Fortescue was irritated by High Anglicans who, in their enthusiasm for all things Eastern and distaste for all things Roman, deemed the Orthodox title 'God-bearer' excellent, but the Roman equivalent 'Mother of God' unacceptable. For Fortescue, the terms are synonymous. It is just that Greek is good at compound words, unlike Latin, and also Arabic, in which tongue, to confound us with linguistic science, he offers the translation of 'Theotokos' as *wâlidat allâh*. And he delivers a resounding smack to the trans-Atlantic translator of the Orthodox services Isabel Hapgood, who rejects 'Mother of God' in favour of 'Birth-giver of God', declaring her version as a whole the 'funniest mixture of Prayer-book English and American slang'.[75]

John Damascene

When writing about St John Damascene, the seventh and last of his 'Greek Fathers', Fortescue who could not claim ever to have set foot in Alexandria, was able to compensate by setting forth his impressions of Damascus. On 15 December 1906 he had sent Hamilton Macdonald a letter addressed from 'Damascus, at the house of Cyril VIII, Melkite Patriarch of Antioch, by the eastern gate of the city and behind the bazaar of the brass-smiths'. The letter provides a thumbnail sketch of the journey to that point, and the future itinerary,

> My expedition has been a very great success so far. On the way out I stopped at Smyrna and made a long ride up Asia Minor. I saw beautiful and gorgeous things, and have so fallen in love with those parts that I am arranging for a still bigger expedition, right

74 Ibid.
75 Ibid., p. 172, fn 39.

> through Cappadocia, on my way back. Of course Asia Minor is
> dirty and uncomfortable, neither the Orthodox monasteries nor
> the Turkish khans at which one has to sleep are pleasant quarters,
> the Christians are not nice and the Turks are brutes.

These disadvantages paled in comparison with the riches unveiled.

> One finds palaces like in a fairy-tale; gorgeous white Greek cities
> forgotten in hidden valleys, Byzantine fortresses and churches,
> wonderful mediaeval mosques. Everyone has left something
> there, Romans and Greeks, Turks and Arabs, back to the
> huge broken walls built by Phoenicians and Assyrians and the
> mysteries of the Hittites.[76]

Oddly enough, he makes no attempt to convey the spirit of the place where
he is writing. For a description of Damascus itself, 'this gleaming white city
by the river, at the head of the caravan roads', we must turn back to the
pages of *The Greek Fathers*.[77]

Fortescue describes the intersections of routes which made Damascus
such a great *entrepôt*, now (that is, in 1908) as well as then (in Damascene's
lifetime, in the eighth century). Fundamentally, there were five such roads:
due east, across the Syrian desert to Baghdad; south, through Palestine
to Mecca; northwest, through Homs, Aleppo and across Asia Minor to
Constantinople; northeast, via Mosul to the Caspian, and due west, across
the Anti-Lebanon to Beirut — a journey which in the modern period,
Fortescue tells readers in a note, can be done in nine hours by the (French-
built) railway, while from Beirut one may take ship to anywhere in the
world. On the edge of desert country, Damascus is excellently supplied
with river-water from the nearby mountains; streams flow round it and
through it in a 'silver network'.

> For seven miles, these rivers flow through gardens and orchards
> around the city. Looking down from the Salihiye height you
> may see the bright green of the apricot groves (rarest sight in
> Syria), a broad girdle around the city whose domes and minarets
> stand up white and palest gold or flushed with the faintest
> red, all iridescent with subtle suggestion of many colours in
> its gleaming whiteness, like a pearl set in emeralds. To come
> back to Damascus from the hideous rocks of the Hauran is like
> going up to the gates of heaven after hell. After the parched sand
> and burning rocks, you walk among green rushes amid showers
> of apricot blossom and hear the water trickling beneath the cool

76 Westminster Diocesan Archives, Box AGD, Letter to Hamilton Macdonald of
    15 December, 1906.
77 *The Greek Fathers*, op. cit., p. 194.

damp banks; and all through the shady bazaars where you look up and see the minarets, pencils of dazzling white against the blue, you hear the fountains plashing in the courts of the houses.[78]

No wonder 'every Arab poet sings of the glories of the City of Syria', *Mâdinat ash-Shâm*.[79] No wonder too that the Muslim Arabs coveted it, taking it so soon in their advance that most people have forgotten it was once a notable Christian city which still houses the head of the holy Precursor and Baptist John, in the mosque of the Ummayads. That dynasty, while not granting parity to Christians (scarcely possible in Koranic law), treated them with notable tolerance.

They were the employers of John Mansur, whom posterity would know as 'Damascene', and eventually his protectors against a rabidly Iconoclast regime in Christian Byzantium. John's father was a wealthy civil servant in Ummayad employ who obtained the services of a learned Sicilian Greek as tutor to his son. These were shared sessions. John's tutorial partner was the future St Cosmas the Melodist (On the basis of the relevant references in the 'Life' by Joannis Hieros, edited under Louis XIV by the learned French Dominican Michel Lequien, Fortescue inclines to think Cosmas was the adopted brother of John.) The tutor knew his stuff. As John's theological works would show, he was well instructed in philosophy. Though Fortescue probably has in mind John's systematic study of Christian truth, the 'Fount of Knowledge', his dialectical gifts were sorely needed early on in his writing career. Before his entry into the monastic life, as a time when, like his father, he was a finance officer in the service of the Damascus Caliph, he began to work out his refutation of the Iconoclast heresy.

Fortescue pauses to note how appalling it would have been had the movement to eliminate sacred art succeeded in the civilization born from the Gospel. He takes the view that for well-instructed biblical monotheists there is no possibility of confusing an image with what it images, while for those who hold that the one God made himself known through incarnation nothing could be more appropriate than a Christian art.

> Everyone who has seen a catacomb has been shown the rude wall-paintings of scenes in our Lord's life, allegorical representations of the holy Eucharist, pictures of the good Shepherd, of the holy Mother with her Child, of the apostles. As soon as the Church was free and more prosperous, naturally these representations became more artistic, richer, more elaborate.[80]

In any case, gestural expressions of interior attitudes, like 'kneeling, standing, lifting up hands', are just as much physical signs as are the painting or

---

78 Ibid., p. 196.
79 Ibid.
80 Ibid., p. 203.

carving of images; both are equally appropriate in Christian worship.[81] To deface or insult visual images detracts from the honour of the persons they represent: 'to honour the real thing involves a delegate honour paid to its picture'.[82] Fortescue takes the view, shared by many modern scholars, that the Iconoclast emperors were influenced by their Islamic neighbours.

The results were deplorable, not only through the suffering and even deaths that followed resistance by Iconophiles, but in the losses to art — at any rate to art with sacred themes, for the secular equivalents were still permitted. 'The great church of the blessed Virgin at Constantinople was stripped of its icons and painted in a new style, which people said made it look like a bird-cage and a fruit-shop'.[83] It took a great deal of passion (in both senses of the word), of political skill, an ecumenical Council, and changes of monarch, before the cult of the icon could be definitively restored, in 843, an event celebrated thereafter as the 'Triumph of Orthodoxy'. Fortescue deplores the way the Orthodox (but not Melkites in union with Rome) have tagged on to the end of the liturgical memorial, references to heresies represented by the Popes. That was in starkest contrast to the original celebration for, in the Iconoclast crisis, 'Rome never swerved, and all the image-worshippers looked to the Pope as their leader (Theodore of Studion especially), while the Patriarchs of Constantinople wavered backward and forwards at the emperor's command'.[84] This was a fair observation.[85] John wrote two treatises 'Against the Destroyers of the Holy Icons' before, to the Caliph's regret, he left Damascus to begin the monastic life at the lavra of St Saba in the Judaean wilderness.

Fortescue evokes the site for the traveller starting from Jerusalem, as he himself had set out from there in the April of 1907.

> From Jerusalem, you cross the valley of the Cedron and take the road toward the Dead Sea. In about three hours, you will have left the green valley and will come out into the burning desert whose barren rocks slope down toward Jericho. And here you find one of the most wonderful sights of Palestine, Mar Saba. The monastery is not well seen from the road, only a great tower and a wall appear. One must go in at the gate, through the court past Saint Saba's miraculous palm-tree, down into the *wadi* and along the bed of the dried-up torrent. Here you pick your way among burning rocks and climb up the other side.[86]

81 Ibid., p. 205.
82 Ibid.
83 Ibid., p. 209.
84 Ibid., p. 211, footnote 50.
85 See E. Lanne, O.S.B., 'Rome and Sacred Images', *One in Christ* XXIII. 1-2 (1987), pp. 1–21.
86 *The Greek Fathers*, op. cit., p. 214.

That is how to position oneself for the panorama.

> Against a sky that is at once deep blue and yet glowing with hot light every tint of white and yellow, from dazzling dead white through pearl grey to warm brown, is piled up in a savage kind of order. Rocks, sand, white earth and cliffs are heaped together like a gigantic fortress, and climbing up the side of the *wadi* is the fortress-monastery. Its walls rise out of the rocks so naturally that you cannot see where they really begin, its terraces are hewn out of the cliff, and its towers mount buttressed in tiers up into the sky. Its balconies are bridged over frightful chasms, and its walls lie in winding curves up and down the ground like monstrous snakes.[87]

The human inmates share in the somewhat scary character of the scene as a whole. At the time of Fortescue's visit, St Saba's was in use as a prison for refractory monks of the Orthodox Church. 'All night the wolves howl and the jackals bark outside; and the wailing chant of the *kalogeroi*, the "good old men", comes from the beautiful church, where they stand under stern Byzantine frescoes and sing their hours'.[88] The monks who receive the visitor do not fail to take him to make the 'great salam' at the tomb of John Mansur. (Fortescue mentions that his hosts had used Greek and Arabic indifferently.)

Damascene's contemporaries in the monastery did not approve of the time he and Cosmas the Melodist gave not only to hymnography but also to study. Fortescue is cutting about Eastern monasticism. 'It is scandalous to do anything at all in a Byzantine laura.'[89] But John's humility in accepting works of penance, together with a vision of the Mother of God who reproved his principal critic, sufficed to let his stream of theological writings continue to flow. Following the *Vita*, Fortescue tells us that John reacted to his priestly ordination at the hands of the patriarch John V of Jerusalem by resolving to remove from his texts all superfluous ornament, as a mark of literary (and not only ascetic) humbleness.

Fortescue praises John's theology for its philosophical thoroughness. It is basically Aristotelean, yet happy to draw elements of truth from anywhere. Patristic scholars would later recognise John's philosophical inheritance as a complex unity of Aristotelean and Neo-Platonist strands,[90] but far from undermining Fortescue's claim that John was proto-Scholastic, this fortifies it — since present day historians of mediaeval thought are likely to say much the same of the High Scholastics themselves! His emphasis on the self-

---

87 Ibid., pp. 214–215.

88 Ibid., p. 215.

89 Ibid., pp. 216–217.

90 See, for instance, A. Louth, *St John Damascene. Tradition and Originality in Byzantine Theology* (Oxford: Oxford University Press, 2002), pp. 42–44.

moved character of the will is striking. His account of the divine attributes anticipates that of Catholic Scholastics, 'demonstrated as in our schools'.[91] 'In all his philosophy, then, we see a faithful reflection of Aristotle, who has become through him the "master of them that know", to Greeks and the Orthodox Church as much as he has to Latins and Catholics through Saint Thomas.'[92] He is exceedingly clear on the Trinity, Christology, grace and the sacraments of Baptism, Chrismation and Eucharist. He understands the Spirit to proceed through the Son. It is a pity he has nothing to say about the place in the Church of the Roman pope. Still, it is 'by a very right comparison that he is called the Aquinas or the Peter Lombard of the eastern Church'.[93]

Last but not least, like Aquinas (and like his foster-brother Cosmas the Melodist, whom he excelled) he was also a great poet in liturgical Greek. John Mason Neale had translated a good deal of Damascene's poems. Fortescue admired Neale enormously as a translator of Latin hymns, but he was critical of these other efforts. 'His metres when compared with the originals seem as a rule, undignified; and his versions are so free that in many cases he has practically written a new poem on the same subject'.[94] Fortescue thought he could do better, and offers extracts from the Golden Canon (for Easter Day), a Canon for the feast of the Annunciation and a more private poem expressive of contrition in short anacreontic verse.

The Iconoclast synod of Hiereia in 754 cursed the name of John Mansur, but the Church in both East and West has blessed it. Fortescue sounds slightly regretful that the name given him by the early Byzantine chronicler Theophanes — 'Chrysorroas', after the chief river of Damascus, for 'in his life and in his teaching gold-gleaming spiritual graces shine' — did not catch on.[95] He was called simply *Damaskênos*, 'Damascene', and it was under that sobriquet that the pope of Fortescue's Roman studies, Leo XIII, declared him a doctor of the Church in 1890.

Valediction

Here is how Fortescue summed up his 'Levantine' experiences to his friend Harold Burton.

---

91   *The Greek Fathers*, op. cit., p. 222, with reference to John Damascene, *De fide orthodoxa*, I. 1–5.

92   *The Greek Fathers*, op. cit., p. 222, with an internal quotation of Dante, *Inferno*, canto IV, line 131.

93   *The Greek Fathers*, op. cit., p. 225.

94   Ibid., p. 226.

95   Theophanes, *Chronographia*, ad annum 734.

> I have just come back from a year spent in Syria, Mesopotamia, Asia Minor and Greece. I saw many and wonderful things. I rode long days across the great Syrian desert, alone among Arabs. I stood among the ruins of strange dead Greek cities in Asia Minor and slept on the bare earth under broken white columns where Diana of the Ephesians had once reigned as a mighty god. And I saw forests and climbed mountains and crept through deep passes in the heart of Asia Minor. I went a-pilgriming to the holy places too, said Mass at the holy sepulchre, spent the night of Maundy Thursday on the Mount of Olives and saw the Easter sun rise above the golden walls of Herod's temple. Then there were Damascus, the slow brown waters of the Euphrates, the orchards of Galilee, Cyprus (a heavenly island), the tawny pillars of the Athenian Acropolis, the fat plains and strange Byzantine monasteries of Thessaly; and — far most glorious of all — the line of domes and minarets, radiant, white, and fretted like ivory against a hot grey-blue sky, that crown imperially Constantine's New Rome by the Bosphorus.[96]

Fortescue described this as a 'purple' time. He says he made a lot of progress with Arabic and Turkish, and the trip had encouraged him to begin Persian, for he wanted to repeat the experience, but this time in Iran. He had 'made a heap of drawings' and learned 'much about Mohammedan ideas'. But there had been a price to pay in terms of discomfort and danger.

> I suffered a great thirst and heat, was under fire from robbers and Bedawin [sic] several times; once I saved my life by flight, leaving all my baggage to the spoiler, once I shot a man dead (a horrid memory); I had my shoulder smashed to bits in a fight near Hebron and lay six weeks sorely sick in the French hospital in Aleppo. Such is the outline.[97]

Fortescue told Burton he must come to Letchworth to hear more. To Letchworth we too must go, but not before we have investigated further what he made of the Churches of the East.

---

96 Westminster Diocesan Archives, series 20, Box 22, Letter of 25th Sunday after Pentecost, 1907.

97 Ibid.

5. Studies of the Eastern Churches, Far and Near

Introduction to the Trilogy

It is difficult to think that clergy sabbaticals were a major pre-occupation of Cardinal Bourne. That Fortescue was increasingly able to pay his own way, and support financially the Letchworth mission *in absentia*, must have made the prospect distinctly more feasible. There was a further consideration in granting permission for extended leave from pastoral duties for the sake of the 'Levantine grand tour'. Fortescue had shown he was no mere dabbler, nor a light-weight, where the intended scope of his year-long journey was concerned. He had been seeing through the press a substantial volume on Orthodoxy, care of the Catholic Truth Society, even if by the time it saw the light of publishing day he had already started for abroad. This was his *The Orthodox Eastern Church*.[1] It will be convenient to consider the book in relation to its two subsequent companion volumes, *The Lesser Eastern Churches*,[2] and the unfinished *The Uniate Eastern Churches* published in the year of, but after, his death.[3] They constitute a trilogy.

Fortescue's journey to the East helped with succeeding writing on the Oriental churches, as might only be expected; not least did it convince him, if further convincing were needed, of the importance of the subject. 'Every one who has travelled eastward of the Adriatic Sea or the River Vistula', he told the Anglo-Russian Literary Society on his return, 'has realized at any rate something of the enormous force of that great body that calls itself the Orthodox Church.'[4]

His observations of the situation on the ground meant he was not starry-eyed. Although, he declared, the Slav is 'as a rule naturally religious; except for the amazing vagaries of Russian dissent, his religious instincts are satisfied by the rites of the Orthodox Church', the Greek, so Fortescue

---

1   *The Orthodox Eastern Church* (London: Catholic Truth Society, 1907).

2   *The Lesser Eastern Churches* (London: Catholic Truth Society, 1913).

3   *The Uniate Eastern Churches* (London: Burns and Oates, 1923).

4   *Rome and Constantinople* (London: Catholic Truth Society, 1908), p. 1. This was the published form of the lecture he gave to the Anglo-Russian Literary Society on 3 March 1908, reprinted from their *Proceedings*.

had found, 'is not religious by nature, nor is the Christian Arab to any great extent. But to both Greeks and Arabs their national church is a national cause; and so political motives make up for piety, and they are as ardently loyal to her as is the Russian'.[5]

This did not destroy his vigorous romanticism of spirit.

> Go to Athos, and bury yourself for a week or so with the 'good old men'. Listen to the clang of the symantron and stand in their church before the tarnished splendour of the ikonostasis, while the cloud of incense hangs around the dim lamps and the strange chant echoes under the low cupolas. . . . Standing in a Byzantine church, listening to the Byzantine chant, you can almost make yourself believe that over there across the Aegean Caesar still reigns in the magic splendour of the Imperial city, that Caesar's gorgeous ships still carry the legions to the far countries, where barbarians dare to lift up their hands against the Roman eagles. You will begin to wonder what is real and what is only a dream — England, London, what is all that? Surely Justinian is building his white dome over the Holy Wisdom, Belisarius is fighting the Goths, and there is trouble because the monks will not sign the Three Chapters.[6]

At the same time, Fortescue was acutely aware of the political significance of Orthodoxy. The Orthodox Church

> is the most actively alive body in the Levant. If you consider the tangled question of Balkan politics, at every step you are brought face to face with the Orthodox Church. . . . Every political question is reflected in [Levantines'] ecclesiastical affairs; or rather ecclesiastical politics are the form that civil and national disputes inevitably take.[7]

Unless we are to allow something for exaggeration when addressing a religiously mixed audience likely to contain not a few Orthodox, he made it plain that, on the grand tour, he had only been encouraged by hospitality received. He had become an ecumenical optimist so far as the Christian East was concerned.

> Somehow or other, the old mutual hatred is dying out, and we no longer want to call each other by offensive names. I have stayed in Orthodox monasteries and have been treated always and everywhere with every possible courtesy and kindness by Orthodox monks. I have had the honour of audiences with various Orthodox patriarchs, and have found them always more

5   Ibid.
6   Ibid., p. 2.
7   Ibid., pp. 2-3.

than anxious to be friendly. If I have been embarrassed in their presence, it was chiefly because I was not always ready with an answer to their first question, "How is the health of the most blessed Lord Pope?"[8]

I have given this chapter the title 'Studies of the Eastern Churches, Far and Near', and must explain what is meant by the latter phrase. The 'Lesser Eastern Churches', conventionally called 'Nestorian' and 'Monophysite', though these terms are, at the present day, rather out of favour (for reasons both good and bad), were 'far' when compared with 'The Orthodox Eastern Church' which itself was as much European, in Belgrade or St Petersburg, as it was Asiatic, in Jerusalem or Harbin. The 'Uniate Eastern Churches', even if some of them were clones of the 'Lesser' and thus 'farther' bodies, can also be called 'near' if one has in mind their co-belonging, with the Latin or Western Church, to the same (Roman) Catholic Communion. Geographically far away does not necessarily mean ecclesially distant in the unique topology of the Mystical Body of Christ.

I. The Orthodox

I turn first to the Chalcedonian Orthodox not in union with Rome. The delightful thing about Fortescue's *The Orthodox Eastern Church* is not just the painless way it introduces the reader to so much in the history and theology of Orthodoxy. After all, a great deal of the information provided under this head can be found equally well elsewhere. What is more striking is the good luck whereby the moment of his writing enabled him to paint a picture of the Orthodox Church on the very eve of the two great transformations which were to change its position for ever — for good or for ill. Although Fortescue had no inkling of this, the first decade of the twentieth century was also the last decade in which Orthodoxy in much of Eastern Europe and the Near East lived out its life on terms that had remained constant for some hundreds of years. In the course of the First World War and its immediate aftermath, both the Russian and the Turkish empires would be swept away, and with them the crucial institutions that had framed Orthodox life over vast swathes of the earth's surface — the Tsardom and the Ottoman Porte. Those years would also see the end of Austria-Hungary. Fortescue was never one to conceal his pro-Habsburg sympathies. He thought the Orthodox living under the Danubian monarchy should count themselves fortunate in their fate. The Habsburg polity had guaranteed them protection without intervention, which was more than could be said for the Tsar.

In the attached 'Note' which prefaces the third edition of his study, from 1911, Fortescue tells the reader that since the first edition in 1907 much has happened in Europe and the Near East that affects the Orthodox. The most

---

8   Ibid., p. 23.

notable development he has to record concerns the advent to power of the Young Turks in the Ottoman empire. Their policy was to 'Turkify' public life in a multi-ethnic empire and privatize religion in an Islamic polity where other religions received civic recognition and backing under the *millet* system. Neither plank was acceptable to the Phanar, the standing synod of the ecumenical patriarch. Moving rapidly northwards: in Russia, the Holy Synod had been concerned to reform the monasteries and nip in the bud any tendency on the part of former Uniates in the West of the Russian empire ('Ruthenians') to revert to communion with Rome. Fortescue reported on the movement to revive the Moscow Patriarchate (which would indeed happen at the *Sobor* of 1917, following the fall of the Tsardom). But much of the rest of the introductory updating of his book is rather small beer.

The Roumanians of Macedonia had been excommunicated for using their own tongue in the Liturgy. In Roumania itself a metropolitan, incensed by patriarchal support for a government scheme to give a greater role in the Church to the lower clergy, had accused the patriarch of heresy, fornication, and obtaining his degree by plagiarizing the writings of a Jesuit. The Albanians were seeking ecclesiastical autonomy. The Orthodox in Crete had transferred their allegiance from Constantinople to Athens. The (Greek) patriarch of Alexandria had planted six bishops in Abyssinia. Various patriarchs had survived attempts to unseat them by their synods, notably Joachim III at the Phanar (his reign of ten years, so Fortescue claimed, was a 'modern record' there),[9] Damianos I at Jerusalem, and Gregory IV at Antioch, while to the annoyance of the Phanar the candidate supported by Alexandria (but not by 'New Rome') was now Archbishop of Nea Justiniana and All Cyprus. It all illustrated what he termed in the body of the book 'the fact that, in spite of their inter-communion, the dominant note of these sixteen bodies in our time [the autocephalous Orthodox churches of the period] is their extreme quarrelsomeness. The thing is too patent to be ignored.'[10]

Ecclesiastical equivalents of news flashes from Reuter's Correspondent were to pale in comparison with the world-shaking events that would soon overtake the Orthodox: the seizure of power by the Bolsheviks in Russia in 1917 and in 1918 the dismemberment of the Ottoman Empire by the victorious allies, together with Atatürk's abolition of the Muslim Caliphate in 1922. In the preface to the third edition, as more widely in the main body of his book, Fortescue occasionally poked fun at the Orthodox, or, rather, at their hierarchs, but he used the opportunity of the third edition of *The Orthodox Eastern Church* to make amends.

9   *The Orthodox Eastern Church* (London: Catholic Truth Society, 1911), 3rd edition), p. x (all page references are to the 1911 edition). This was correct: no ecumenical patriarch had managed to remain in office for more than a decade since Jeremias I (1522–1545), nor would another do so until Athenagoras I (1948–1972).

10 Ibid., p. 273.

I want to assure my Orthodox friends that I would not say a word of disrespect about their venerable Church, as such. It is not the Orthodox Church, it is the political Phanar that is so preposterous. For the great Church herself, the humble priests and people throughout the Levant who love Christ and find comfort in His holy mysteries, who among Moslems keep His faith in silence while their leaders shriek and quarrel about politics, for those silent millions we Latins have nothing but honour, affection — and regret that the shadow of Cerularius still lies between us. For, after all, what was Cerularius but one big Phanariote?[11]

Curiously, he makes no mention of his hostility to the Tsardom — which was also, after all, an Orthodox institution. As we shall see, a remarkable turn-about of his views on this subject was forced on him by the alliance between England the Russia in the First World War. Still, it is the schism between the sees of Constantinople and Rome that is most crucial to the story Fortescue tells.

Fortescue opens *The Orthodox Eastern Church* with a very clear account of the emergence of the five patristic patriarchates (Rome, Alexandria, Antioch, Jerusalem, Constantinople) of which Alexandria and Antioch, owing to their roles in the genesis of the Monophysite (Alexandria and Antioch) and Nestorian (Antioch) schisms will also be pertinent to his successor study, *The Lesser Eastern Churches*. Fortescue's animus against the — as he held, historically unjustified — claim of the see of Constantinople to apostolic origin, and the trajectory on which the patronage of the East Roman emperors launched that somewhat parvenu body, is made clear from the outset.

The 'Note' which serves the third edition as preface was not an afterthought to the whole.

It was . . . this ambition of the bishops of the Imperial City that far more than anything caused and fostered friction with Rome, so that, if one looks for the deeper causes of the schism, one realizes that it was not the Filioque in the Creed, not the question of leaven or unleavened bread, not the rights of Ignatius the Patriarch [in the ninth century] that really drove a wedge between the two halves of the Christian Church. It was, long before the 9th century, the slowly climbing ambition of Constantinople that bred mutual jealousy and hatred; the thin end of the wedge was when, in 381, the Bishop of Constantinople was given the "precedence of honour after the Bishop of Rome".[12]

---

11 Ibid., p. xiii.
12 Ibid., pp. 28-29.

Byzantium had been a small city ecclesiastically subject to the metropolitan of Heraclea, who was the exarch of Thrace. But, re-founded by Constantine and chosen as the seat of empire, it had a great future before it.

Fortescue's presentation is plausible, in terms of psychology — 'socio-psychology' might be a better term.

> Might not Caesar's own bishop — the honoured chaplain of his Court, who stood side by side with the highest ministers of the Empire before their master, the bishop of the city that was now the centre of the Roman world — might not even he hope to be counted as great as that distant Patriarch, left alone among the ruins by the Tiber?[13]

Fortescue thinks that the title 'ecumenical' adopted by the Byzantine patriarchs from the time of John the Faster (582–595) possibly *means* 'imperial'.

He does not like the upshot. '[N]owhere is there a more degrading example of subjection to the civil government than the mingled contempt and furtherance that these bishops received from the Emperor'.[14] At first, not only Rome but Alexandria and Antioch objected to Canon 3 of the Second Ecumenical Council (Constantinople I, in 381) which legitimized the new state of affairs by giving the church of the imperial city a place second in honour only to Rome's. The churches of the chief cities of Egypt and Syria could claim a Petrine origin (Alexandria through Mark, the co-worker of Peter), and both had been supremely active in the evangelization of the surrounding regions. So far as the West is concerned, Fortescue contributes the useful information that the disputed canon entered the Latin canonical tradition only with the eleventh century legist Gratian's 'Concordance of Discordant Canons'. But the damage was done well before that. Canon 28 of the Fourth Ecumenical Council (Chalcedon, in 451) not only gives Constantinople a place immediately after Rome but ascribes Rome's own primacy to the civil status of the city ('the Fathers wisely gave the Primacy to the see of the Elder Rome, because that city was the ruler').[15] If the ruling city is now New Rome, that cannot but imply a certain rivalry. As Fortescue remarks, 'a certain animus against Old Rome shows in the contrast between their frigid reference to "the see of the Elder Rome" and the rapturous "most holy See of the most holy Church of Constantinople"'.[16] Fortescue does not consider the suggestion that 'the Fathers' mentioned in this canon

---

13 Ibid., p. 30.

14 Ibid.

15 The text as thus rendered is Fortescue's own translation of the canon from the Greek of F. Lauchert, *Die Kanones der wichtigen altkirchlichen Concilien nebst den apostolischen Kanones* (Freiburg: Mohr, 1896).

16 *The Orthodox Eastern Church*, op. cit., p. 39, footnote 3.

might perhaps be the apostles Peter and Paul — though that interpretation has found some scholarly support in modern times. The more natural implication of the way Canon 28 of Chalcedon refers comparatively to Canon 3 of Chalcedon ('the 150 most God-beloved bishops') is that the three-hundred and eighteen bishops of the First Ecumenical Council (Nicaea I, in 325) are the real 'Fathers' in view.

Fortescue does not fail to add that, owing to the sustained protest of the popes against the new legislation — which prejudiced the actual position of Alexandria and Antioch (not to mention the nascent claims of Jerusalem, original seat of the Twelve and the guardian of the Holy Places), at least as much as it threatened the theological position of Rome — the canon is found in no Greek collection until the time of the troubles with the patriarch Ignatius and his opponent Photius in the ninth century. Only the *civil* law of Byzantium recognized it: for instance, in the codex of the emperor Justinian (527–565). For although not every church of apostolic origin could claim patriarchal status (there were, after all, as Fortescue comments, 'numberless Pauline Churches'[17]), could a church be patriarchal without being apostolically founded?

Yet eventually the Roman church accepted not, to be sure, the secular explanation of her own universal primacy found in Canon 28 but nonetheless the fact of Constantinople's regional primacy in the East. This was so certainly by the time of the Council of Florence in 1439, though even at the Fourth Lateran Council in 1215 the Latin patriarch of Constantinople was set on the pope's immediate right. (There was a much earlier instance which Fortescue seems to have overlooked: the twenty-first canon of the Eighth Ecumenical Council, Constantinople IV, in 869, having spoken of the honour due to the patriarchs, runs, 'This applies in the first place to the most holy pope of old Rome, *secondly to the patriarch of Constantinople*, and then to the patriarchs of Alexandria, Antioch, and Jerusalem'.[18])

Fortescue has an explanation of this seeming *volte-face*. 'Rome has often accepted a *fait accompli*, as long as it does not injure faith or morals, even if it begins by an injustice against which she had protested.' And he adds as examples, though these must have stuck in his craw as a Legitimist, 'She eventually acknowledged Napoleon Buonaparte and the Protestant succession in England.'[19] The bizarre aspect of the rise of the church of Constantinople in Fortescue's eyes is that, with the Ottoman capture of the city in 1453, its entire ecclesial *raison d'etre* evaporated.[20] This has gone unnoticed by the Greeks — though not by the Russians.

---

17 Ibid., p. 48.

18 N.P. Tanner (ed.), *Decrees of the Ecumenical Councils* (Washington, D.C.: Georgetown University Press, 1990), I., p. 182. Italics are, of course, added.

19 *The Orthodox Eastern Church*, op. cit., p. 44, footnote 2.

20 Ibid., p. 39, footnote 2.

Admitting it does not make for the most riveting reading, Fortescue offers a catena of texts which illustrate the positive attitude of Greek Fathers and early Byzantine theologians towards the claim that the place of St Peter among the apostles is now embodied in the place of the bishop of Rome among the bishops of the Church at large. The Eastern church did not differ from the Western in holding that '[t]he foundation stone must last as long as the building that rests on it, and therefore it could not have died with St Peter. It must still *exist in his successors*'.[21] As Fortescue says, to students of early Church history many of the pertinent texts are well-known — which is not to say that he never adds any that are less familiar, citing, for instance, examples of Byzantine liturgical texts of the kind collected by the learned Solesmes Orientalist Cardinal Jean-Baptiste Pitra, or, again, by Fortescue's own contemporaries, the Byzantine-rite 'Augustinians of the Assumption' in their scholarly journal, *Echos d'Orient*.[22] His own reading in German monographs as well as the standard patristic editions of Jacques-Paul Migne (for the Fathers) and Giovanni Domenico Mansi (for the ancient Councils) enabled him to uncover the occasional hidden gem, such as a letter from 'Syrian archimandrites and monks' to Pope Hormisdas (514–523), who (the monastics say) 'holds the see of the Prince of the Apostles ... whom Christ our God has set up as Chief Shepherd and Teacher and Physican of souls'.[23] The evidence Fortescue amasses makes a strong case that, before the Photian crisis, the East accepted a primacy of Rome in teaching (not least through the hearing of appeals on disputed matters of faith). That the same texts give expression to a primacy of Rome in 'cases of Church government' (his phrase) might well be disputed (unless it is specifically appellate jurisdiction Fortescue has in mind).[24]

He is surely right, however, to stress one curious fact. Recognition of Roman primacy is clearest and most eloquent in the Dyothelite theologians (especially St Maximus Confessor) and the Iconophile doctors (notably St Theodore the Studite) who were the Fathers closest in time to the Photian schism. Fortescue is also on safe ground when making much of the 'Formula' or 'Little Book' (*Libellus*) signed by many Eastern bishops and others, including the emperor Justinian, at the end of the ill-fated attempt to construct a union between the Great Church and the Monophysites under Zeno (emperor 474–491). The *Libellus* would re-appear, signed by Latins and Byzantines at what Catholics reckon the Eighth Ecumenical Council (Constantinople IV, in 869). Rightly discerning its

---

21 Ibid., pp. 54–55. Italics original.

22 J.B. Pitra, *Hymnographie de l'Eglise grecque* (Rome: Civiltà cattolica, 1867); 'Les titres glorieux de l'Apôtre Saint Pierre dans l'hymnographie grecque', *Echos d'Orient* 1 (1897), pp. 307–309.

23 Quoted in *The Orthodox Eastern Church*, op. cit., p. 71.

24 *Ibid.*, p. 57.

significance, Fortescue would make it the subject of a free-standing short but thorough study in 1919.[25] Signatories acknowledged that 'in the Apostolic See the Catholic religion is always kept immaculate'; expressed the hope that they might 'deserve to be with you [the Pope] in that one Communion taught by the Apostolic See, in which Communion is the whole, perfect and real solidity of the Christian Religion', and promised that for the future they would not 'say in the Holy Mysteries the names of those who are banished from the Communion of the Catholic Church, that is, who do not agree with the Apostolic See'.[26]

On the Ecumenical Councils, Fortescue makes the best case he can for the role of papal mandates and legates in what were for the most part (and in the case of the Second Council, exclusively) East Roman gatherings. His most palpable hit comes when he asserts that the Papacy was at any rate the organ of reception of Councils, since the wider claim that a Council can be termed authoritative *only if it is received in the Church at large* is vacuous.

> [T]here has always been a party (often a large party) which rejected these councils. The test of orthodoxy is to accept them; those Christians are orthodox who agree with the general councils. If, then, we say that those councils are general with which the orthodox agree, we have a perfect example of a vicious circle.[27]

Naturally, he has to explain how, against this background, an eventual schism was possible. He cites a number of long term factors. The Eastern churches, unlike many of those in the West, were in no sense founded from Rome. Moreover, they had their own patriarchs. Again, the Latin language fell into total desuetude at Byzantium. For their part, the popes had access to Greek translators (for example, at Grottaferrata) but they did not learn Greek themselves, not even when, like Gregory the Great, they had been envoys at Constantinople. Furthermore, for reasons connected with the Trinitarian and Christological controversies of the early centuries (on points where the Orthodox would now agree with Catholics that Rome, as it happened, was right), Constantinople had been periodically out of communion with Rome for — on Fortescue's calculation — two-hundred and three out of five-hundred and twenty-nine years between 323 and 852 (the year when Photius became patriarch) and had become, in effect, semi-accustomed to that state of affairs.

---

25 *The Reunion Formula of Hormisdas* (London: Catholic Truth Society, 1919). Compare the words of a modern writer, 'The "Formula of Hormisdas" was one of the strongest acknowledgements of the authority of the Bishop of Rome ever accepted by the East', W. Henn, OFM Cap., *The Honour of My Brothers. A Brief History of the Relationship between the Pope and the Bishops* (New York: Herder and Herder, 2000), p. 89.

26 Quoted in *The Orthodox Eastern Church*, op. cit., pp. 85, 86.

27 Ibid., p. 74.

A predisposing cause of schism where Fortescue was inclined to the Byzantine side was the popes' gradual withdrawal of allegiance to an Eastern emperor powerless to aid them against barbarians (or Muslims), so that they looked instead to the Franks. Here family pride and a Legitimist instinct struggled with each other for mastery in Fortescue's breast.

> [H]owever much loyalty one feels as a Frank and a Latin to the long and splendid line of Western Emperors that lasted for just over a thousand years, from Charles the Great (800) to Francis I (1804), one must also sympathize with the feeling of the Court of Byzantium. After all, they had the direct line of continuity.[28]

Presumably Fortescue calls himself a 'Frank' because his eponymous ancestor whose 'Brave Shield' ('Fort Escu'), so the family legend ran, saved the life of Duke William at the Battle of Hastings, hailed from Normandy. As to 'Latin', he was, of course, despite hankerings after the Byzantine Liturgy, a 'Latin Clerk'.

Supremely, however, 'the chief cause of all ill-feeling was the ambition of Constantinople' — what we can call Fortescue's anti-Phanariot obsession.[29] So we are not surprised when the Council of Trullo of 692 (meeting in a domed room in the imperial palace — hence its name — but sometimes called the 'Quinisext Council', since it provided canons for the Fifth and Sixth Ecumenical Councils which had left none) began to legislate in terms that were not only independent of the West but hostile to its traditions. Hostile towards priestly celibacy, against the validity of the marriage of the orthodox with heretics, against the pre-Sunday Latin fast on Saturdays, and renewing the claim that Pope Honorius, signatory of a compromise formula in the Monothelite crisis, had been condemned as a heretic — whereas Rome did not accept the statement to this effect in the Acts of the Sixth Ecumenical Council (Constantinople III, in 681), Pope Leo II (682–683) condemning Honorius only insofar as 'he had not crushed out the flame of heresy at once, as behoved his Apostolic authority, but rather fostered it by his negligence'.[30]

By the confluence of these various factors, the scene was set for the Photian schism.

Doctrine and worship, piety and art

Set in a church that for its faith and rites warmed the cockles of Fortescue's heart; he explains how the faith and worship of the 'Orthodox Eastern Church' before the schism beautifully cohered with that of the Catholic Church. That is so even if Fortescue's eyebrows rise at some of the saints canonized in Byzantium (emperors and patriarchs whom he finds

---

28 Ibid., p. 94.
29 Ibid., p. 89.
30 Cited ibid., p. 80 from G.D. Mansi, *Concilia* XI, col. 1050; J.P. Migne (ed.), *Patrologia Latina* XCVII, col. 683.

somewhat questionable figures). It is so even if, furthermore, looking back, later Orthodox spokesmen identified the seeds of problems to come in attitudes to Purgatory and predestination as well as to what Catholics call the Immaculate Conception of the Mother of the Lord.

As to Purgatory, the Greeks objected at the second Reunion Council (at Ferrara-Florence) to the notion of purging by fire but were assured the Latins had never defined it. For Fortescue, the Catholic faith concerning Purgatory includes only two points: that the redeemed dead may 'still keep some stain of sin', and that such stain must be penally 'expiated' before the departed enter their bliss.[31] The most one can say for difference here is that the Eastern 'state of mind' is somewhat 'vaguer' on the point.[32]

A degree of vagueness is also Fortescue's explanation for any tensions with Latin theology about grace and predestination.

> [T]he subtle system explained by St. Augustine in his *de Dono perseverantiae* and *de Praedestinatione sanctorum*, the great field of discussion that he left to his Church, the endless controversy that has gone on amongst us ever since about the fine line between antecedent reprobation on the one hand and semi-Pelagianism on the other — all these things have never troubled Easterners at all.[33]

Whether for good or ill, says Fortescue, the Greeks have never had a Scholastic period — we should note that this judgment may be accepted if the emphasis is laid upon *period*. There were certainly individual Byzantine Scholastics and not all of them were pro-Latin: Gennadios Scholarios, the first man to be ecumenical patriarch after the Ottoman conquest, is a good example.[34]

With regard to the Immaculate Conception, Fortescue notes how the confession of the spotlessness of the Blessed Virgin Mary entered the Latin West from, precisely, Byzantium. He mentions the group of doctors of the seventh and eighth centuries sometimes called collectively the *Philotheotokoi* or 'lovers of the Mother of God', and surmises that 'the Eastern theologians, never behindhand in giving honour to the all-holy Theotokos, taught her Immaculate Conception more and more plainly, till the influence of Protestants produced an opposing school and at last the fact that the Pope defined the doctrine was a sufficient reason for altogether denying it'.[35]

---

31 *The Orthodox Eastern Church*, op. cit., p. 105.

32 Ibid., p. 107.

33 Ibid., p. 109.

34 H.C. Barbour, *The Byzantine Thomism of Gennadios Scholarios, and his translation of the commentary of Armandus de Bellovisu on the 'De ente et essentia' of Thomas Aquinas* (Vatican City: Libreria editrice vaticana, 1993, Studi tomistici, 53)

35 *The Orthodox Eastern Church*, op. cit., p. 108.

As to worship in the East, in ancient times the Oriental churches belonged to distinct liturgical families, Syrian, Egyptian, and Byzantine, though gradually, with the advent of the schisms of the Nestorians and Monophysites when the Orthodox patriarchates at Antioch and Alexandria shrank to shadows of their former selves, the Byzantine rite became the exclusive diet of Eastern Orthodox public devotion. True, the Liturgy of St John Chrysostom was varied on certain days by the use of a Liturgy of St Basil (with some affinities to Syrian practice), just as it was on fasting days by a 'Liturgy of the Pre-Sanctified' ascribed to the Roman pope Gregory Dialogos (St Gregory the Great). Fortescue is inclined to think the staple Byzantine Liturgy did not develop significantly after Justinian (later scholarship would correct him here), such that 'any Orthodox church today will show almost exactly the same vestments, ceremonies and rites as those that Justinian knew'.[36] Naturally, there is some wiggle-room provided in that commodious phrase 'almost exactly'.

Fortescue's imagination was stimulated by references to the sometimes curious phenomena of Byzantine piety and the always beautiful evidence of Byzantine architecture and art. On the question of customs (especially 'sacramentals'), he noted how the category of lustral water comprised not only water blessed on the Epiphany (in the West this was done at Easter) but also water poured into a Eucharistic chalice and out again as well as water used for personal ablutions by some 'specially holy monk' — which unhygienic custom was familiar, he tells his readers, among their own Muslim contemporaries in the East. He notes how in the Sudanese uprising which brought General Gordon to his end followers of the Mahdi had drunk his washing water as a prophylactic against disease.[37]

On the topic of Byzantine art and architecture, Fortescue does not really commit himself to any one of the schools of thought about its genesis which in his time divided the world of German-speaking scholarship, though he sets out their characteristic theses for the reader to consider. Broadly speaking, there were two questions involved. Was Byzantine art the result of an 'Asiatic' invasion of Greco-Roman art or, rather, an internal development of the latter once placed in a Christian environment; were the artists who worked in the Byzantine manner necessarily Easterners, or could they be — at Ravenna, say — Italians (with the possible implication that, for theological reasons, stylistic change came about independently at different centres at roughly the same epoch)?

---

36 Ibid., p. 119. *The Byzantine Rite. A Short History* (Collegeville, MN: Liturgical Press, 1992) by Robert F. Taft, S.J., recounts a post-Justinianic history in terms of two waves of liturgical reform emanating from monastic centres in the Jerusalem patriarchate.

37 *The Orthodox Eastern Church*, p. 119.

For Fortescue the most important thing is that the word 'Byzantine' really does name a common style. Of that style Justinian's church of the Holy Wisdom at Constantinople is, for him, the paragon. In Fortescue's day it was still an active mosque (in ours, unless some pro-European Union Turkish government decide otherwise, it is a museum), with the names of the 'four Khalifahs' covering up the mosaics of the saints, and the 'Mihrab pointing to Mecca behind the place where the old altar stood'.[38] These brief indications of its alien captivity do not subvert but on the contrary enhance Fortescue's loving evocation of the church's glories. His precise description of its architectural structure (a wonderful combination of cupolas, arches, and walls that make a wellnigh perfect square) is complemented by a glowing description of its coloured marbles, goldwork, and use of precious stones. It is also crucial to his story of the Byzantine schism, yet to come.

> Here Ignatius refused communion to Bardas; the Synod of 869 deposed Photius; the three Legates in 1054 said, "Let God see to it and judge", as they laid the Bull of Excommunication on the altar. It was at the old altar under the dome of the Holy Wisdom that, in 1054, the Latin Mass announced to the angry Byzantines that they must now obey a Latin lord, and that, fifty-seven years later, the Greek Liturgy told them that their own Emperor was restored. Here Constantine XII received Holy Communion on the morning of May 29, 1453, before he went out to die for his city and his Empire, and now, in a column in the church, you may still see the blood-red mark of Mohammed the Conqueror's hand.[39]

Fortescue cannot tear himself away from the subject of the art of the Byzantines till he has mentioned San Vitale in Ravenna with its mosaic figures of Justinian and Theodora, with their retinues, bringing up the offertory for the Eucharistic Mysteries.

> Very rich and sumptuous, standing as calm and as stately as the palm trees between them, these figures still show the image of that court by the Bosphorus, where the Roman name still lingered, that was lifted above the new world our fathers were hewing out of its lost provinces by the unapproachable majesty of its memories.[40]

Today the 'King of Hungary' — he means the Austro-Hungarian emperor in his capacity as *rex apostolicus* — still 'wears a gorgeous piece of Byzantine jewellery with Byzantine enamels as the crown of St. Stephen and the symbol of the Apostolic kingdom', while 'above the fields of Essex' (how

---

38 Ibid., p. 128.
39 Ibid.
40 Ibid., p. 130.

well Fortescue knew them, from Ongar and Colchester!) 'you may go into Copford Church and see above the altar the figure of the Byzantine Christ in glory, with his court of Saints and the signs of the zodiac, who has come all this way from the Church of the Holy Wisdom'.[41]

The story of the Eastern schism

Fortescue's retelling of the stories of the Photian and Cerularian schisms makes excellent reading. The drama of the first lies in the contrast he draws between, on the one hand, the unimpeachably worthy and upright but unexciting patriarch Ignatius, whose cause, after his illegal deposition by the imperial authority, was always steadfastly maintained at Rome and, on the other hand, Photius who was, in effect, a usurper, but, in Fortescue's words, 'one of the most wonderful men of all the middle ages. Had he not given his name to the great schism, he would always be remembered as the greatest scholar of his time, and as, in every way, the greatest man in the Byzantine Church'.[42] Fortescue thinks his learning wonderful, his personal moral life — as distinct from the actions he undertook to forward the pretentions of his see — beyond reproach.

Ignatius, who was Photius's predecessor on the throne of the imperial city, was deposed for his perfectly just criticisms of the Court — the Caesar Bardas, living incestuously with his daughter-in-law, expected nonetheless to receive the Eucharistic sacrament from the patriarch; an attempt was made, indefensibly, to send the empress Theodora to a nunnery against her will. Photius was then intruded by government fiat into a see that was not vacant, with an excommunicated archbishop to ordain him and to do so, moreover, without reference to the 'Interstices', the intervals between receiving Major Orders that were canonically required. For Photius was a layman. Though Ignatius managed to convey his protests to Rome, the legates sent to look into the matter were weak and venal. Only after Pope Nicholas I was independently apprised of the real situation did he act to vindicate the deprived patriarch and in so doing unwittingly precipitated a full-scale crisis.

Fortescue, who depends on the best German scholarship of the period, and very good it was,[43] finds nothing to mitigate Photius's share in the blame for what happened next.

---

41 Ibid. Fortescue is referring to the church of St Michael and All Saints, Copford Green. The frescoes, uncovered in the nineteenth century, would presumably be more commonly described as Romanesque.

42 Ibid., p. 138.

43 Notably J. Hergenröther, *Photius, Patriarch von Constantinopel* (Regensburg: Manz, 1867, 3 vols.) which remains today, despite its age, an indispensable work.

Ignatius was kept chained in prison. The Papal letters were
not allowed to be published; he insisted to the tyrants of the
Government that this was their affair, they had put him in the
place he held, the Roman Patriarch was trying to rule over their
heads in their own land, the Ignatians were traitors for trying
to protect themselves by the authority of this foreigner. It is the
typical attitude of the schismatic who betrays the Church to the
State rather than obey the Pope.[44]

It must be admitted that the contemporary competition of the Latin
and Greek churches for the privilege of evangelizing the Bulgarians — a
Turanian people who had settled in the ancient Illyricum, long an apple of
discord between Rome and Byzantium — certainly did not help. Photius
had already removed Pope Nicholas's name from the diptychs. Now in
his 867 encyclical letter to the other Eastern patriarchs he sought the
excommunication of the rest of the Latin church likewise.

His *gravamina* were, judges Fortescue, quite unfair. Among the Latins,

[n]o one has ever tried to make Easterns fast on Saturday,
eat cheese in Quinquagesima week, be celibate, stop priestly
Confirmation, or say the Filioque in the Creed. The only
quarrel against [the Byzantines] was the iniquitous usurpation
of Photius. In trying to turn his personal quarrel into a general
dispute between the two great Churches he can find nothing
better to say than to complain of some differences of custom,
that were in no way his business, and on the strength of them
to excommunicate all of us, over whom he had no pretence of
jurisdiction, as well as our Patriarch, who was his own overlord
as well.[45]

The questionable element in this statement is the view that the *Filioque* can
be considered merely a custom — for surely, apart from the liturgical usage
entailed, it is a doctrine as well. Fortescue must play down the significance
of the doctrine of the procession of the Spirit from Father and Son if he
is to persuade his readers that the list of Greek objections to the Latins
was a trumped affair. '[T]his very remote speculation, that either way has
certainly never for a moment affected the Trinitarian faith or piety of any
single human being, has become to [Easterners] a standard of anti-Latin
orthodoxy, and they cherish and value it accordingly.'[46]

---

44 *The Orthodox Eastern Church*, op. cit., p. 150.

45 Ibid., p. 153.

46 Ibid., p. 154. Where negative repercussions of the Filioque doctrine may
     perhaps be detected is not in 'faith and piety' so much as in systematic
     theology. 'It has often been signalled that the Filioque makes the Holy Spirit

Only the murder of the emperor Michael III (whom Fortescue presents as usually inebriated) by the future Basil I reversed the tables: the pro-Michaeline Photius was removed, and, since his popularity had never faded in some quarters, Ignatius was brought back. The 869 Council, reckoned by Catholics as the Eighth Ecumenical Council, otherwise 'Constantinople IV', regularized Latin-Byzantine relations. That Council would later be important in the mediaeval West for the canons it passed prohibiting the installation of hierarchs by act of the temporal power. For Fortescue its real importance is, rather, the role played there by the Formula of Hormisdas, with its clear acceptance of the Petrine authority of the Roman bishop. Such acceptance was, after 869, in no way merely partial or local: the ecumenicity of the council by the criterion of 'pentarchy' (presence of all five patriarchs, at any rate in their delegates) saw to that. Though at length Ignatius disappointed the Romans in the matter of Bulgaria, and storm-clouds were gathering at the end of his life, Fortescue bids his readers remember him as 'one of the best bishops who ever sat on the soul-endangering throne of New Rome'.[47] That is certainly arguable.

Fortescue's text needs correction, however, in his account of the 879 'Pseudosynodus Photiana' which so far from leading to a second schism by Photius was in fact an eirenic 'Council of Union' between the Roman see and a Photius now legitimately ensconced on the throne of St Andrew and accepted as such in Catholic eyes. So Francis Dvornik, a mid-twentieth century Czech successor to the German giants of later nineteenth century Byzantine studies, was able convincingly to show.[48] Though it is credible that, between the schisms of Photius and Cerularius an anti-papal party survived in Byzantium, feeding on Photius's critique, Fortescue is more inclined to lay weight on the career of St Nilos, the tenth century (hence post-Photian) Greek founder of the monastery of Grottaferrata outside Rome.

---

more strictly dependent on the Word, and thus also ties his action more to determinations, to instituted forms. All this throws some light on how, outside the chapter on the Holy Spirit in Trinitarian theology, Catholic theology, with the particular development of the question of the Filioque, has scarcely reunited in a formal treatise all that concerns the Holy Spirit as a person who is sent and operative. In reality, all that is very present in Catholic theology, but it remains dispersed through all the treatises. Certain affirmations, in themselves very rich, have scarcely been made the object of a proper development', Y. Congar, O.P., 'La Pneumatologie dans la théologie catholique', *Recherches des sciences philosophiques et théologiques* 51 (1967), pp. 250–258, and here at pp. 251–252.

47 *The Orthodox Eastern Church*, op. cit., p. 161.

48 F. Dvornik, *The Photian Schism. History and Legend* (Cambridge: Cambridge University Press, 1970 [1948]).

Nilos had fled from the Saracens, but he elected to live among Latins, fearing too eager veneration of his merits as a confessor by the Greeks.

> And out there in the Campagna, at Grottaferrata (*kryptopherê*) St. Nilos at last built a home for his wandering monks, and there he died, looking out towards Rome. Through all the changes that have taken place since, Grottaferrata [Fortescue provides conveniently a drawing of his own] has stood unchanged; not only has no Pope ever tried to destroy it or Latinize it, it has always been a point of honour with them to endow it and to protect it. Still, after ten centuries, it stands within sight of the Roman walls, and still its monks sing out their Greek office in the very heart of the Latin patriarchate, while outside the Latin olives shelter its grey Byzantine walls.[49]

The Cerularian schism fits Fortescue's template well. It too exemplifies what we might call 'proto-Phanariotism': that is, the tendency of Byzantine patriarchs to consider themselves quasi-popes. In the Turkish period, and more specifically in 1603 when the patriarch took up residence within this quarter (near an old lighthouse — hence its name — on the bank of the Golden Horn), 'The Phanar' became the equivalent of the *palazzo apostolico* of the popes. Released from the reunion efforts of the later East Roman emperors, the inhabitants of the Phanar came to see themselves as a sort of Oriental Vatican; however, the mid-eleventh century crisis over Cerularius's headstrong attempt to homogenize with Byzantine usage the practices of the churches of foreigners in Constantinople fitted in perhaps too well with Fortescue's interpretive scheme. He might have considered the possibility that calling these events 'the final rupture' was a step too far.[50] True, the calling in 1274 of the first Reunion Council — known to the West as Lyons II — implies that by that date there were two halves to be reunited. But 1054 was not necessarily *the* moment when the golden bowl was broken. Strictly speaking, the reciprocal excommunications of that year concerned persons not churches, and the process of ecclesial disaffection was precisely that — a process, a protracted affair.

The clash pitted a pope typical of the Gregorian reform, Leo IX, not a man to minimize the Roman claims, against a patriarch of senatorial and court background, with a temperament (here Fortescue relies on the characterization by the Byzantine historian Michael Psellos, a political bellwether) that brooked no opposition. Cerularius might have been restrained by the imperial hand, but his master, if not exactly a cipher, was a vacillator: in Fortescue's phrase 'weak and paralytic'.[51] It is curious

---

49 *The Orthodox Eastern Church*, op. cit., p. 170.

50 Ibid., p. 172.

51 Ibid., p. 177.

— not least from the standpoint of later Orthodox polemics — that little if anything was made of the *Filioque* dispute in the amassment of Latin malpractices.[52] Fortescue remarks elsewhere of the latter, 'If anyone wants to see how silly a heated controversialist can become, he should read that list of grievances.'[53] At first the question of the Saturday fast figured prominently. Fortescue explains how at this time in much of the West the entire period of Christ's being in the tomb — thus, Friday through Saturday — was seen as appropriately remembered by fasting and abstinence (adding that by the pontificate of the mid-eighteenth century Benedict XIV the custom had largely disappeared, except in Italy, such that most modern Catholics will never have heard of it).

Anti-Latins in Byzantium smelled Judaising, as though this were a form of Sabbatarianism. But the focus of ill-feeling soon transferred itself to another topic. And this was the use of unleavened bread, 'azymes', in the Western Mass, which not unreasonably *could* be described as a matter of continuity between Jewish and Latin Christian practice. This was the cause, or at any rate, the pretext for Michael Cerularius's closure of Latin churches and chapels at Constantinople until such time as they should agree to the use of leavened bread for the Holy Eucharist and adopt the Byzantine rite. Judging by the papal reaction, Michael had made much of his title 'ecumenical' patriarch, which Leo understood to mean 'universal' patriarch — a natural misreading since, apparently, Michael had offered that if the pope gave suitable honour to his name at Rome, he would oblige by performing the same service for Leo 'in the whole world'. Though no doubt a great game was being played, there could also have been, one suspects, incomprehension through ambivalence; 'ecumenical' may also mean 'within the bounds of the empire'. As is well-known, the behaviour of the legates Leo sent to Constantinople confirmed the breach.

Fortescue exonerates them. As papal legates they shared in the primacy of governance of the frst patriarch whose legates they were. They were right to carry their episcopal crosiers in Michael's presence. They were justified in refusing to make the customary and expected prostration, but if so, their 'body language' gave Cerularius the excuse he seems to have desired. He removed the pope's name from the diptychs, the 'tablets' containing

---

52 The question of the procession of the Spirit surfaced briefly in the post-excommunication efforts of Cerularius to win round his brother patriarch at Antioch to his way of thinking, ibid., p. 191.

53 *The Mass. A Study of the Roman Liturgy* (London: Longmans, Green, 1955, 2nd edition), pp. 270–271, footnote 6, in which Fortescue refers readers to C. Will, *Acta et Scripta de controversiis ecclesiae graecae et latinae* (Leipzig–Marburg, Elwert: 1861), pp. 122–123.

the names of the chief persons with whom the church of Constantinople communicated. That Leo IX died as the negotiations were coming to their disastrous conclusion did not alter, for Fortescue, this salient fact. The excommunication of Cerularius by the legates followed inevitably. As Fortescue rightly notes,

> this is the only sentence that the Roman Church pronounced against the Eastern Communion. She has never excommunicated it as such, nor the other patriarchs. If they lost her communion it was because they too, following Cerularius's example, struck the Pope's name from their diptychs.[54]

Fortescue's overall interpretation of Cerularius (and he ascribes to him not only conscious mendacity in dealings with Peter of Antioch but the intention of securing the imprisonment or even death of the papal legates) is that he aimed at a theocracy of his own invention, in which the emperor would be the civil arm of the ecumenical patriarch, and the other patriarchs his vicars. If so, it was a vision of the world in which the Papacy could have no place.[55]

Despite the catastrophism with which Fortescue sees the events of 1054, he insists that the Orthodox are, after all — unlike Protestants — simply schismatics. '[W]e pray for the conversion of Protestants and for the reunion of the Eastern Churches.'[56] For Fortescue Protestants included Anglicans. The (realistic) Ratzingerian notion of *Anglicanorum coetibus* did not figure on Fortescue's ecclesial horizon, much less the (more spectral) Malines Conversations Anglican body 'united yet not absorbed'. Unfortunately, as time went on, Latin spokesmen began to speak foolishly about Byzantine customs as Church-separating in exactly the way Cerularians spoke about Latin ways. In his comments on the two Reunion Councils, Lyons II in 1274 and Ferrara-Florence in 1438–1439, Fortescue is surely right that the basic problem lay in the deficient enthusiasm of Byzantine people.

> Already it was the enemies of the union who could pose as the conservative party, and the intensely conservative instinct of all Easterns in Church matters made that position a stronger one as each century passed, strengthening the schism merely by making it older.[57]

To which it must be added that the experience of the Crusades ('there are few so great disillusionments in history')[58], climactically of the Fourth Crusade, 1204, which Fortescue does not scruple to call 'abominable', [59]

---

54 *The Orthodox Eastern Church*, op. cit., p. 185.
55 Ibid., pp. 192-195.
56 Ibid., p. 202.
57 Ibid., p. 208.
58 Ibid., p. 221.
59 Ibid., p. 225.

'unpardonable',[60] confirmed the worst fears such theological conservatism could nourish. Though Fortescue has the admiration for the pluck of the Crusading host which his own identification with martial valour might lead us to expect (compare his escapades on the Levantine grand tour), he frankly admits that '[o]n the whole, the Orthodox were distinctly worse off under the Crusaders than under the Moslems'.[61]

The drama of the making and the ending of the union of the Council of Florence deeply stirred Fortescue. In terms of attendance (which included the emperor, John VIII Palaeologos), no council since Nicaea, 'ever had such a clear case to be considered ecumenical', and he traced thereto the especially negative animus with which the Orthodox sought to justify its rejection. The pope, Eugenius IV, did what he could to succour the beleaguered Byzantines in its wake (two galleys and three hundred soldiers), and the Republic of Genoa, to its eternal credit, did likewise (five ships and seven hundred men). Mohammed the Conqueror did not want the Christians he ruled to be friendly with Western princes. '[T]he people of the city, now as wildly fanatical and intolerant as the last remnant of a lost cause always is (witness the Jews of Jerusalem during the siege), had said: Rather the Sultan's turban than the Pope's tiara; and they have had their wish'.[62] The body of the last emperor, Constantine XI Palaeologos, who had died defending the city was found, recognized by the golden eagles on its shoes, and the Sultan let him be buried near the Mosque of Suleyman where a lamp burns. Fortescue reports, surely, from his own visit: 'As far as they dare, the Greeks still make the grave of the last Autocrat of the Romans a place of pilgrimage'.[63]

He adds musingly, 'But they have not canonized him. Is it because he was a Catholic?' Fortescue concludes that Constantine,

> does not need the doubtful honour of Byzantine canonization. Saint and hero he rests in peace in the city he guarded till death, and all over the Christian world his glorious memory is honoured. *In pace Christi quiescas Auguste Caesar* [May you rest in peace, august Caesar].[64]

The reference to the 'doubtful honour' should not be supposed to mean Fortescue belittled the sanctity possible to post-Conquest (and thus post-Union) Orthodox in the Ottoman empire. On the contrary, he writes that 'there have been many confessors of the faith on the patriarchal throne down to the martyr-patriarch Gregory V'(hanged during the Greek War of Independence to which he had given no encouragement);[65] and more widely:

---

60 Ibid., p. 228.
61 Ibid., p. 224.
62 Ibid., pp. 217–218.
63 Ibid., p. 232, footnote 2.
64 Ibid.
65 Ibid., p. 244.

we, who have never had to sit under the shadow of the Sultan's blood-stained throne, if we remember the ugly story of their fathers' schism must also remember how valiantly the Eastern Christians have stood for Christ ever since, and how in the days of her trial the Byzantine Church, once so foolish and obstinate, has sent that long procession of her children to join the white-robed army of martyrs.[66]

Fortescue offers a brief overall characterization of the post–1453 position of the Orthodox under Islam, and this we may as well deal with here. A Christian was, in a Turkish loan-word, a 'rayah', one of a protected but also severely restricted subject-people (the better known Arabic equivalent is *dhimmi*.)

[T]o be a subject-nation governed by a foreign race is a position with which no civilized people can be finally satisfied. So there have been endless revolts among the Rayahs, and after a revolt the Turks has no mercy. That is why, in spite of the tolerance of Moslem law, the history of the Ottoman Empire in Europe has been one long, monotonous story of the shedding of Christian blood.[67]

Under the *millet* ('nation') system, all Orthodox rayahs in the Empire came under the authority of the ecumenical patriarch (until 1856 in various civil matters also).[68] What surprised Fortescue was that, under the disadvantageous conditions in which Orthodoxy now found itself, the Church managed to preserve some means for fostering a theological culture (initially at Venice and Kercyra, and then in the eighteenth century at Constantinople itself, Smyrna, Janina, Athos and Bucharest), albeit disproportionately organized in the service of anti-Catholic polemic. Orthodox controversial literature attracted Protestant interest, at first Lutheran, then Non-Juror and finally mainstream Anglican, in the forlorn hope of 'building up a great united anti-papal Church to rival and balance the Catholic body'.[69] Fortescue is speaking about the Mediterranean world and its extensions. When he comes to survey the Orthodox Church on the ground he has to admit that a far more significant intellectual life flourished in the early modern and modern period in Russia.

---

66 Ibid., p. 238.

67 Ibid., p. 237.

68 Fortescue takes the opportunity to note that the Gregorian, i.e. non-Uniate Armenian patriarch holds a corresponding position for Monophysites, and his Uniate counterpart for Eastern Catholics, though shortly before the time of writing *The Orthodox Eastern Church* the other Uniate patriarchs had secured a comparable status, ibid., p. 239.

69 Ibid., p. 252. Surprisingly, Fortescue scarcely mentions the Old Catholics in this connexion.

Contemporary Orthodoxy

Fortescue's general survey of contemporary attitudes in the various Orthodox jurisdictions draws on a wide variety of sources. These range from major scholarly syntheses of the late nineteenth and early twentieth centuries, such as the (Lutheran) Ferdinand Kattenbusch, *Lehrbuch der vergleichenden Konfessionskunde. I. Die orthodoxe anatolische Kirche* and the (Catholic) Isidor Silbernagl, *Verfassung und gegenwärtiger Bestand sämtlicher Kirches des Orients*,[70] through specialist monographs like Dimitar Mishev's, *La Macédoine et sa population chrétienne*,[71] to his own scanning of such newspapers as *Ekklêsiastikê alêtheia*, the journal of the ecumenical patriarchate, the Athenian *Astu* and the *Nea êmera* of Trieste which he regarded as the best of the Greek-language newspapers. His evaluation, based on such wide-reading together with a disposition to make sharp judgments, remains of value to historians of Eastern Christianity whose period of study is the beginning of the twentieth and the former part of the nineteenth centuries.

Fortescue's overall description of the Church in the Balkans emphasizes the animosity that pits Greek against Slav, and indeed Bulgars, Serbs and Roumans against each other. He stresses that the quarrel is principally of ethnicities, not of States, for the boundaries of the former do not correspond to those of the latter (and probably could not, given the Balkan, and especially Macedonian, kaleidoscope).

> When they rose against the Turks, the Great Powers felt they must give them some result for their fighting: on the other hand, if they had all been made free there would have been no Turkey left. So bits were cut off where these populations were supposed to be thickest and made into the kingdoms of Greece, Servia, Roumania, and the princedom of Bulgaria. The people of Montenegro, who have always been free, are Serbs. But these four races went on as before, scattering all over the Balkans and overflowing into Hungary.[72]

Fortescue thinks it is owing to accumulated resentment against the way Phanariot bishops were imposed on largely non-Greek speaking communities that nowadays 'as soon as ever a Balkan State gets independent of the Sultan it makes its Church independent of the Patriarch'.[73]

---

70 F. Kattenbusch, *Lehrbuch der vergleichenden Konfessionskunde. I. Die orthodoxe anatolische Kirche* (Frieburg: Mohr, 1892); I. Silbernagl, *Verfassung und gegenwärtiger Bestand sämtlicher Kirches des Orients* (Regensburg: Manz, 1904, 2nd edition).

71 D.M. Brancoff, *La Macédoine et sa population chrétienne* (Paris: Plon, 1905). Mishev wrote under the pseudonym 'D.M. Brancoff'.

72 *The Orthodox Eastern Church*, op. cit., p. 275.

73 Ibid., pp. 276–277.

The ancient Byzantine notion that the governance of the Church should mirror the civil polity, an idea once invoked against Old Rome and its Petrine claim, is now turned against the Phanar which in 1872 held a synod to declare 'Phyletism' — in Fortescue's definition, 'the love of one's race in ecclesiastical matters', the 'latest and most poisonous heresy'.[74] For Fortescue Phyletism is only poetic justice reaped by Phanariot hubris. Even within the 'poor remnant' of the Constantinopolitan patriarchate, once the Balkan national churches are removed, there is agitation for accession to the new Phyletist bodies by Serbian and Roumanian-speaking congregations while the Bulgars — excommunicated at the time of the first edition of *The Orthodox Eastern Church* — have set up an 'exarch' (one stop short of a patriarch) to enjoy jurisdiction wherever in the remaining territories of the Great Church Bulgarian-speakers are to be found. Fortescue's anti-Phanariotism was not lessened by his awareness of its proneness to the rivalries of the ambitious — in 1897, he pointed out, there were simultaneously four ex-patriarchs all living in hope of re-election[75] — nor by the somewhat brutal response made in 1895 by Anthimos VII to Pope Leo XIII's graciously worded appeal to the separated East in his 1894 encyclical *Praeclara* (but two years later Anthimos had become one of the quartet of deposed ever-hopefuls). Fundamentally, however, Fortescue's *parti pris* was based on two factors: his reading of the genesis of the Byzantine schism and his observation of contemporary Balkan affairs.

None of the trials suffered by the see of Constantinople were as hard, so Fortescue opined, as the pressure it underwent from the other side of the Black Sea.[76] Fortescue's analysis finds the Russian menace to the Phanar to be a two-pronged weapon: in the Balkans, and in Asia. The generalization which covers his more particular remarks runs, '[W]here the Russian Government wants a sphere of influence there is the Orthodox Russian faith preached'.[77] This maxim leads him to enquire, what spheres of influence *does* St Petersburg seek? In answer, Fortescue ascribes to Russia a policy goal of complete dominance over the Balkan States; the intention to bring within her orbit Persia as a whole, as far as the Gulf;[78] and (no doubt the most controversial element in his analysis) the desire to acquire a belt of territory from the Caucasus to the Syrian littoral. The latter 'would cut the

---

74 Ibid., p. 277.
75 Ibid., p. 343.
76 Ibid., p. 278.
77 Ibid., p. 279.
78 Fortescue interpreted the attempts of Russian missionaries to convert Persian Nestorians to the Russian Orthodox Church as in service of the mother country's geo-political goal. But Nestorians are not relevant to Eastern *Orthodoxy*.

Mohammedan world in two, greatly hasten the day on which the Russian eagle is to fly over Constantinople, and it would secure Jerusalem, the Holy City of all Christendom, for the Czar.'[79] Hence the pincer movement with which the patriarch is faced. In the Balkan peninsula, Russia 'always takes up the cause of the Slavs against the Phanar, she made the Sultan constitute the Bulgarian Church, and, in spite of the schism, the Russian Church remains in communion with it'.[80]

In the Middle East, where Fortescue finds the Russian Church 'infinitely active',[81] 'she has [he tells us] two objects — to convert all Christians there to the Orthodox faith, and to make that faith synonymous with the Russian national Church'.[82] Fortescue gives a figure (sixty-four) for the number of Russian schools for Arab children in Syro-Palestine, describes the higher schools for future priests destined for the Russian academies, and lists the other institutions — hospitals, pilgrim hostels, consulates, monasteries — Russia plants wherever she can. Russian influence has put an end to the state of affairs where Phanariot Greeks could assume their inevitable appointment to the metropolitan sees in Syria and the Holy Land — and above all to the two patriarchal sees of Antioch and Jerusalem. Some Orthodox are saying it would be better if Russia directed Orthodoxy generally (Fortescue reckoned the Russian element in the world-wide Church to be between four-fifths and nine-tenths.)[83] But 'all this is gall and wormwood to the Phanar'.[84]

Fortescue enters a protest that some commentators should consider Austria-Hungary no less imperialistic in the Catholic cause than is Russia in the Orthodox. 'Doubtless Austria-Hungary has interests in the Balkans, but it does not make a ray of difference to the statesmen in Vienna whether the Balkan peoples are Catholic or Orthodox or Mohammedan.'[85] In a footnote, indeed, Fortescue recommended Albania, Macedonia and Thrace to petition for government by the Dual Monarchy, a 'tolerant and civilized Government', claiming that in Bosnia-Hercegovina (then under Austrian administration) even Turks recognized they were better off than with the Sublime Porte.[86]

Writing on the three other historic patriarchates, with their relatively small populations (especially Alexandria), and the church of Cyprus (which, like Alexandria, Antioch and Jerusalem can claim genuine apostolic origin), Fortescue pursues his analysis further, arguing that power-relations

---

79 *The Orthodox Eastern Church*, op. cit., p. 179.
80 Ibid., p. 280.
81 Ibid., p. 279.
82 Ibid.
83 Ibid., p. 293.
84 Ibid., p. 280.
85 Ibid., p. 282.
86 Ibid., p. 282, footnote 2.

between the Phanar and Russia, complicated by the ethnic aspirations of locals, explain the sometimes bewildering speed with which office-holders in these churches change.

As to the Russian Church itself, Fortescue's hostility to its Erastianism soon emerges, compounded with a negative view of the Tsardom as such. 'The Czar's Empire contains about 130 million victims of his government.'[87] After outlining the Church's history and its present organizational strength, Fortescue adds some lines on its missionary work in Syria, Persia, Manchuria, China, Alaska, and Japan. The trouble is that 'Russian missions, enormously subsidized by the Government, are always and everywhere the thin end of the wedge for Russian conquest', and more mordantly still: 'Russia and her ecclesiastical arrangements are the common enemy of the rest of Christendom'.[88] One obvious source of Fortescue's anxiety is the well-founded conviction that Russian advance inevitably spelled the end of freedom of action for Catholic missions (Manchuria, until the reverses suffered by the Tsardom in the Russo-Japanese War of 1902, was a case in point). 'Russia, even when it has only a protectorate, means at once intolerance and persecution of every other form of Christanity'.[89]

In the Old Believer schism the same State arrogance was directed to her own children; the subsequent sects, some stranger than fiction in 'a wild anarchy of mad opinions and mutual cursing', fared, unsurprisingly, no better.[90] That does not mean, he insists, that there are in Russia no village priests who are admirable pastors and liturgists for their people. He expects there to be thousands of such, especially among the married clergy who are mercifully exempt from the careerism of monks. In a footnote, he recognizes that the Revolution of 1904 has brought a degree of greater tolerance, but in the body of the text he points out how the tiny flame of expectation can soon be doused, as in the case of the Georgians who were longing to recover some of their ancient liberties of their church.[91]

During the Great War Fortescue underwent a remarkable change of temper when writing about Russia — for which the only possible explanation is the presence of the Tsardom on the side of England (and France). In his 1915 essay 'Russia and the Catholic Church', originally written for the Irish Jesuit journal *Studies*, Fortescue confronted the probable prospect that, in the event of a victory of the Entente over the Central Powers, some two and a quarter million Ruthenian Uniates would pass from Habsburg to Romanov rule.[92]

---

87   Ibid., p. 297.
88   Ibid., p. 298.
89   Ibid.
90   Ibid., p. 301.
91   Ibid., footnote 3; cf. p. 305.
92   'Russia and the Catholic Church', *Studies* IV. 14 (1915), pp. 184–205.

At the present time, Fortescue noted, the Russians, advancing into Habsburg territory, were doing everything they could to push the Eastern Catholics of Galicia into the Orthodox Church (they had confiscated churches and exiled the metropolitan of Lemberg — Lviv — the outstandingly gifted Andrew Sheptycky). The solution was for Russia to come into line with the practice of other civilized communities in matters of religious liberty.

Was this whistling in the wind? Fortescue consoled himself with the thought that a restoration of the patriarchate was likely: 'there is in fact a large and influential party in Russia, perhaps we might say that it contains practically all the best and really religious elements, which desires this'.[93] He thought, optimistically, that the recovery of patriarchal government might produce a Romeward movement. Competition with the Phanar could incline an independent Russian church to look towards the Tiber. He claimed (on what basis, one wonders) that 'there is in Russia, among the Russian clergy, many a soul *naturaliter catholica*'.[94] Fortescue was aware of the Russian-rite Catholic parish at Petersburg, founded by a high society *grande dame*, Natalya Sergeievna Utčakova (the fact that the curate had been an Old Believer enabled her to skirt the legal prohibitions).[95]

Surely if two and a half million Uniates were in communion with the handful worshipping in that chapel, it should be possible for the Orthodox under a renewed Moscow patriarchate to see how

> it is possible to be Russian, to keep the venerable liturgy of their fathers in the language they know, and yet to be no longer in that disastrous state of schism from the Patriarch whom they themselves, still in theory, acknowledge to be the first bishop and chief of all Patriarchs.[96]

Naturally, the Bolshevik revolution and the Peace of Brest-Litovsk put an end to these speculations, though had Fortescue lived to see the eventual forcible incorporation of the Byzantine-Slav Uniates into the Moscow patriarchate under Stalin he would have been obliged to consume a considerable helping of humble pie.

Fortescue deals with the (at the time) sixteen bodies that make up the Orthodox Church in the strict chronological order of their attaining either de jure or de facto autocephaly. But it will be more instructive to continue with his catalogue by grouping together some of its entries. Thus we can bring together under one heading what he has to say about the Orthodox in the Austro-Hungarian Empire to which, as already noted, he was favourably inclined. In

---

93   Ibid., p. 198.

94   Ibid., p. 200.

95   See for the story P. Mailleux, *Entre Rome et Moscou: l'Exarque Léonide Féodoroff* (Brussels: 1966).

96   'Russia and the Catholic Church', art. cit., p. 205.

the Habsburg dominions were four Orthodox jurisdictions, the 'Church of Carlovitz', the 'Church of Hermannstadt', the 'Church of Czernovitz', and the 'Church of Hercegovina and Bosnia'. These groupings received their due canonical independence at dates ranging from 1765 to 1880.

The first of them, based at Karlocza, a Danubian city in Slavonia, Fortescue describes as representing the mediaeval Serbian metropolitanate of Ipek around which the Serbian patriarchate of the middle ages was organized (initially, the metropolitan of Carlovitz called himself 'exarch of the throne of Ipek' until that throne was no more). In 1765 the Porte accepted the Phanar's argument that a continuing ecclesiastical autonomy for Serbians was a mistake, and suppressed the Church of Ipek — except where Ottoman authority met its political limits: in Montenegro (which thus left as a complementary successor to Ipek 'The Church of Czernagora') and in the Austrian empire. When with the constitutional and administrative reforms of the late 1860s and early 1870s Slavonia fell into the Transleithian or Hungarian portion of the Dual Monarchy, the Hungarian government, Fortescue avers, always acted with the greatest propriety towards the Orthodox. It salaried the Orthodox bishops, created seats for them in the Hungarian Upper House, and encouraged them to arrange their own affairs via a 'Congress'.

The same was true for greater Hungary's Roumanian Orthodox bishops who, at their own request, were organized separately from the Serbs as the Church of Nagy-Szeben (Hermannstadt), so named for its metropolitan see in southern Transylvania. (That Fortescue gives the place-name in Magyar and German but not in Roumanian is indicative, however, of the very subordinate position occupied by the Roumanian language in Habsburg Hungary.) The Church of Czernovitz, the third of these jurisdictions, existed for the sake of Orthodox of diverse backgrounds in the Cisleithian portion of Austria-Hungary — linked, then, not to Budapest but to Vienna. It had a trio of dioceses: Zara and Cattaro (with eleven monasteries), chiefly Serbian, in Dalmatia, and Czernovitz itself (with three monasteries), in the Bukovina, which was largely Roumanian. Again, as with the jurisdictions on the Hungarian side of the River Leith, the Austrian government saw to the financial needs of the bishops and seated them in the upper house of Parliament. Finally, the 'Church of Hercegovina and Bosnia' existed in the territories that since the 1878 Berlin Congress, Austria administered on, nominally, the Sultan's behalf (analogously, so Fortescue points out, with British rule in Egypt in the Sultan's name).

Fortescue took it for granted that Austria would eventually annex Bosnia-Hercegovina outright. He thought its inhabitants fortunate in their likely destiny. He expected that when the present transitional arrangements came to an end the metropolitan of Sarajevo would constitute himself as Exarch. Meanwhile that worthy was *primus inter pares* among four bishops, the other three having their sees at Zvrnik in Bosnia, and Hersek (resident at Mostar) and Banjaluka in Hercegovina. No doubt when the provinces were fully incorporated in the empire the bishops of the Church of Hercegovina and Bosnia would receive senatorial places like their episcopal brothers in the Churches of Carlovitz, Hermannstadt and Czernovitz. Meanwhile, the Habsburg emperor appointed the bishops, informing the Phanar of his choice via the Austro-Hungarian ambassador to the Porte. To compensate the patriarch for his loss of clerical taxes from Bosnia and Hercegovina, the Austrian government sent him an annual sum in compensation.

Fortescue reports that the Orthodox in question 'are all Serbs, and so have no regrets whatever for their former dependence on the Phanar'.[97] A footnote deplores the Russian allegations of Austrian misrule in Hercegovina and Bosnia,[98] and directs readers to a chronicle of improvements in good governance (in German).[99] Alas, there runs the trail of powder that led to the explosion of the keg in August 1914.

Fortescue must say something, however brief, about the miniscule Church of Sinai. Fortescue explains that the abbot-archbishop lives at the Sinaitic metochion (daughter-house) in Cairo and rules over only his monastery and its fourteen metochia, his authority limited by a council of monks. The then incumbent, Porphyrios Logothetes, had been the Orthodox chaplain in Paris. Fortescue regretted that at his consecration in Jerusalem in 1904 he had spoken bitterly against Catholics, which was widely considered ungracious since a number of the latter had been invited to the ceremony.

That left him still to deal with the modern national churches of the Balkans: the Greek, autocephalous in 1850; the Bulgarian exarchate, established in 1870, the Serbian, autocephalous in 1879; and the Roumanian whose canonical independence was agreed in 1885. As to the Church of Greece, Fortescue points out that the troubles with the ecumenical patriarch which attended its declaration of autocephaly are no more, since 'in face of the common Slav danger, the Free Greeks and the Phanar have forgotten their differences and have become firm allies'.[100] Though Constantinople protested when in 1866, upon the British cession to Greece of the Ionian islands, the Greek government separated the newly acquired territories ecclesiastically from the patriarchate, it did not bother to do so when in 1881 Thessaly and part of Epirus were added to Greece and the same thing happened. The Greek Church, Fortescue maintains, is quite as Erastian as the Church of

---

97 Ibid., p. 335.
98 Ibid., p. 336, footnote 1.
99 J.V. Asboth, *Bosnien und die Herzegowina* (Vienna: Hölder, 1888).
100 *The Orthodox Eastern Church*, op. cit., p. 314.

Russia with 'this exception, that, instead of being at the mercy of an autocrat, it has to submit to the even worse rule of a Balkan Parliament'.[101] He has to admit that it is nonetheless a well organised and flourishing body.

Bulgarian Church affairs were rather messier. The mid-eighteenth century Phanar had played the same trick on the Bulgarians as it had on the Serbs: it persuaded the Porte that the Bulgarians would be better off without the substantial ecclesiastical autonomy still attaching to their Church whose primate was the metropolitan of Achrida (otherwise 'Ochrid'), now in Macedonia, to which see it had been transferred from the original Prejslau (in the modern-day Bulgaria, between Tirnovo and Varna). In 1767:

> all Bulgars were made members of the Roman nation under the Oecumenical Patriarch, just like Greeks, Serbs, and Vlachs. From that time began the persecution of which the Bulgars so bitterly complained. Of all the rivalries between the Balkan Christians, that between the Greeks and the Bulgars has always been by far the most bitter. The Greeks hate a Serb, a Vlach, an Albanian — any one who has a nationality to oppose to their dream of a great Hellas covering all the Balkan peninsula, but they hate a Bulgar far the most of all. The Bulgars are the most numerous, active and generally dangerous of their rivals.[102]

The events which precipitated the declaration of an Exarchate for Bulgarians throughout Turkey were almost novelistic in character. Bulgar leaders approached the Catholic Church through the Uniate Armenian patriarch in Constantinople, contacts which led Pius IX to consecrate a Bulgarian archimandrite as archbishop of a Byzantine-rite Church — whereupon the *neo-consecratus* was kidnapped by Russian emissaries and taken to Kiev until such time as he return to Orthodoxy. The Tsar pressured the Porte into granting the Bulgarians *millet* status within the Ottoman empire, whereupon Anthimos VI of Constantinople excommunicated the Exarch and his followers, whom he declared guilty of not only schism but the (new) heresy of Phyletism.[103]

---

101 Ibid., p. 315. Elsewhere Fortescue made it plain that his objection to the idea of 'Most Holy Directing Synods' was not restricted to their subjection to a State apparatus. The whole idea of gatherings which legislate by majority vote is for him a transgression of the proper authority of patriarchs, metropolitans and individual bishops: the historic Byzantine *synodos endêmousa*, which survived under the Ottomans until 1856, was no precedent, for it was 'simply a consulting body, itself entirely subject to the monarchical patriarch': thus 'Holy Synod', *Catholic Encyclopaedia* VII (1910), pp. 428–432 and here at p. 429.

102 Ibid., pp. 317–318.

103 See T.A. Meininger, *Ignatiev and the Establishment of the Bulgarian Exarchate,*

When in 1878 the Berlin Congress set up a quasi-sovereign principality of Bulgaria, and in 1885 Eastern Roumelia was incorporated by the same, the religion of the State was deemed to be the Orthodox Church *in communion with the Bulgarian Exarch*. Worse still, from the viewpoint of the Phanar, the Exarchate was not limited to independent Bulgaria but existed wherever ethnic Bulgarians were to be found. That meant: throughout Ottoman Macedonia. As Fortescue writes,

> [T]he cause of the revolutionary committees in Macedonia is practically identified with that of the Exarchate. The Greeks . . . hate the Exarchist schismatics and the revolutionary committees so much that, pending the realization of the great idea, they always side with the Turkish soldiers in hunting down the insurgents.[104]

Fortescue notes that while the Phanar has a long list of grievances against Russia, topping the list is 'Russian patronage of the Bulgarian schism'.[105]

In contrast, the Serbian church had achieved a peaceful *modus vivendi* with Constantinople. In 1810 a tiny Serbia came into existence, broke away ecclesiastically from Constantinople, and put its people under the jurisdiction of the Church of Carlovitz. By 1830 Serbia was a small principality under an independent metropolitan at Belgrade. When in 1879, as a consequence of the increase in its territory after the Berlin Congress, the Serbs declared autocephaly, the Phanar, taught by the Bulgarian example, decided to admit graciously the *fait accompli*. Where there have been difficulties is, again, in Macedonia. Northern Macedonia, defined by the latitude of Skopia (modern Skopje, to which Fortescue also gives the Turkish name Uskub), is the region called by Serbs 'Old Servia', and here the Serbian Orthodox wavered between siding with Bulgars against Greeks or vice versa. After prolonged intrigues, the Serbs succeeded in gaining control of the two sees of Skopia and Prizren, whose Serbian population the Porte had recognized as a new *millet* separate from the 'Roman nation'. The price to be paid was Greek discontent. The Greeks of northern Macedonia then began sending their ordinands to be priested at Thessalonica (in southern Macedonia), with the patriarch's connivance.

The Roumanian church is Fortescue's last port-of-call. A people with a Latin-based language living in Eastern Europe are never going to be typical, but at least 'the Vlachs' (the term once customary for Roumanians as yet politically unorganized) had the same basic gravamina to complain of vis-à-vis the Phanar as did the Bulgars and Serbs. They too had once had a mediaeval version of autocephaly, even if of a less ethnically clear-cut kind. As Fortescue

---

1864–1872. A Study in Personal Diplomacy (Madison, WI: University of Wisconsin Press, 1970).

104 *The Orthodox Eastern Church*, op. cit., p. 321.

105 Ibid., p. 322.

explains, after the Bulgarian empire, with Achrida as its ecclesiastical capital, was laid low by the Byzantine emperor Basil II, a joint Bulgaro-Vlach polity emerged towards the end of the twelfth century. Until the competitive rise of the Serbian kingdom of Stephen Dushan put paid to its pretensions, this was, for much of the thirteenth century, the predominant power in the Balkans, but the combined efforts of Serbs, Byzantines and eventually Turks swept it away. While it existed, its ecclesiastical capital — chiefly Vlach, so Fortescue insists — was Tirnovo, reunited to the patriarchate in 1396 (much earlier, then, than the comparable Constantinopolitan absorption of Ipek and Achrida in the eighteenth century), such that by the modern period 'the only thing left of it was the vague memory of the Vlachs that they, too, had once had a Church and been a nation'.[106] Phanariot policy was far more successful among the Vlachs (who, he claims, have less of the fighting spirit) than with the Bulgars or Serbs.

> When Greeks publish statistics of Macedonia, nearly all the people they brazenly write as "Hellenes" are really these half-Hellenized Vlachs, men who talk Greek abroad, who sometimes even call themselves Greeks, but who around their own fireside always fall back into the beautiful Romance tongue of their fathers.[107]

What altered the situation at the heart of the Balkans was the early nineteenth century revolt, further north and east, of the Roumans of the provinces of Wallachia and Moldavia against the Turks. The Roumanian kingdom as constituted in 1885 consisted of those very provinces, and its church, by Fortescue's time well provided with monasteries, seminaries and its theological faculty at Bucharest, was autocephalous. The Phanar could live with this, but not with a Roumanian policy of intervening in Macedonia, paying for the building of Vlach schools, salarying Vlach priests and — according to hostile Greek report — 'bribing peasants to learn Roumanian and call themselves Vlachs'.[108] As Fortescue explained, 'The Phanar knows that if all the Vlachs go there will be, indeed, nothing but a slender remnant of its Roman nation left to work for the "Great Idea" in Macedonia.'[109] But a Vlach *millet* is precisely what was now asked and what the Porte was inclined to provide. So Fortescue foresaw yet another autocephalous Church — for Roumanians in Macedonia — on the near horizon. He had relied for some of his analysis of the Macedonian situation on the work of a member of the Macedonian Relief Committee during the winter of 1903 to 1904, Henry Noel Brailsford (1873–1958). 'His book is admirably temperate in tone, and he writes of the things he himself saw.'[110]

106 Ibid., p. 328.
107 Ibid., pp. 328-329.
108 Ibid., p. 332.
109 Ibid., p. 332.
110 H.N. Brailsford, *Macedonia: its races and their future* (London: Methuen,

Prospects for reunion with Orthodoxy

Fortescue ended his study on an eirenic note, with a contribution on the prospects of reunion. Writing about the faith of the Orthodox, he had already remarked,

> Let it . . . be said at once that the pious Orthodox layman lives in the same religious atmosphere as we do. His Church stands in every way nearer to the Catholic Church than any other religious body. The Orthodox use the Nicene Creed, and understand every word of it (but for one fatal clause) just as we do.

He went on to admit that, so far, as the same could be said for Trinitarian Protestants. But there was more.

> It is in the points about which Protestants disagree that we see how near the Orthodox Church is to us. The Orthodox believe in a visible Church with authority to declare the true faith and to make laws. They have a hierarchy against which our only complaint is that it has lost the topmost branch; they accept the Deuterocanonical books of Scripture as equal to the others, they believe in and use the same seven Sacraments as we do, they honour and pray to Saints, have a great cult of holy pictures and relics, and look with unbounded reverence towards the all-holy Mother of God.[111]

In this encomium, a characteristically Fortescue-esque touch followed. 'Their sumptuous ritual, gorgeous vestments and elaborate ceremonies, their blessings and sacramentals, all make their Church seem what she so easily might once more become – the honoured sister of the great Latin Patriarchate.'[112]

What divides the Orthodox doctrinally from Catholics, in Fortescue's opinion, is not only the disputed topics of an historic agenda. The latter would include the issues of the primacy, the *Filioque*, the azymes and Purgatory, though Fortescue, invoking the criterion of early twentieth century controversial theology, eliminates the azymes from that list and in their place adds two alternative Eucharistic themes, transubstantiation and the epiclesis, and a Marian motif, the Immaculate Conception of the Mother of the Lord. More important, because determining the entire stand the Orthodox take, is the tacit theological criteriology for which the 'Byzantine Period' provides the benchmark of both orthodoxy and orthopraxy. Orthodoxy, he thinks, is fixed in the amber of Byzantium. 'And

---

1906).

111 *The Orthodox Eastern Church*, op. cit., pp. 361–362.

112 Ibid., p. 362.

they stay there, satisfying neither the need of continuous development that is the mark of a living Church, nor the rival ideal of unchanged primitive observance.'[113]

Yet he could not find it in him to regard the doctrinally dividing issues as conclusive — even against this wider background. Was the *Filioque* really so important? Surely the Orthodox would not truly want to diminish the honour of the Mother of God? Must they not realize, in their heart of hearts, that if God genuinely guides his Church he would not let the first patriarch teach heresy? Fortescue deeply wanted to see reunion as a possibility. It would help the Orthodox themselves. 'Never yet have the Eastern bishops stood so much in need of their natural arbitrator as now.'[114] It would also help Catholics, by bringing them a more deeply liturgical piety and a devotional life that was less specifically modern (and, by implication, comparatively shallow).

> Their love of the liturgy and dislike of innovations has something to teach our people. If we regret the way in which new devotions spread amongst us, the gradual divorce of the people from the real rites of the Church, the slight regard paid to her seasons, the exaggeration of pious fancies above the old and essential things, the abuses in such matters as indulgences, privileges, and special favours against which the Council of Trent spoke, we should find the remedy of all these things in the solid piety and the unchanging loyalty towards the customs of their fathers among Eastern Christians.[115]

Alas, he saw little prospect of significant advance towards unity. In a conservative Church, the schismatic party, though at some time innovators, will inevitably appear with the passing of time as the true conservatives, and therefore the soul of the Church as a whole.

It has to be said that Fortescue's willingness to recognize the fully ecclesial character of Orthodoxy (as of the other separated Eastern Churches) did not go down well in absolutely all quarters. An admiring letter from a New York lawyer, deeply read in Eastern Christian matters, and a close observer of Eastern Christians (both 'United' and Orthodox) in the United States — an article in the *Catholic Encyclopaedia* on the Uniate churches planted there by immigration, is from his hand[116] — praised 'the tone and spirit in which

---

113 Ibid., p. 394.

114 Ibid., p. 430.

115 Ibid., p. 431.

116 A.J. Shipman, 'Rites in the United States, *The Catholic Encyclopaedia* XIII (New York: Robert Appleton, and London: Caxton, 1912), pp. 78–87. Shipman's essay somewhat exceeds its remit by giving historical and liturgical information provided elsewhere in the *Encyclopaedia*, not least by Fortescue. But its report on the condition of the Eastern Catholic communities in

your work is written', while also recommending major works of reference in Russian not noticed by Fortescue and pointing out that the Russian cross on the cover of the book had accidentally been printed in reverse.[117] Andrew Shipman's judgment was not, however, universally echoed.

The generosity of Fortescue's ecclesiology was unappealing to rigorists, though its foundations were, by historic Catholic criteria, perfectly sound. Without at first mentioning Fortescue by name, a correspondent in *The Tablet* objected, 'As nothing is a Church in the proper sense of the word which is outside of holy unity, the various bodies of Oriental separatists are not properly called Churches, but sects only'.[118] This commentator, also writing, as it happened, from the United States, argued that, where there was no recognition (at least tacit) of the 'Petrine Commission', the high-sounding titles of Eastern hierarchs were fraudulent. He excoriated those 'semi-Protestants in Holy Church . . . who treat the Oriental sects as if they really represented the ancient Churches of the Orient, and their officers as if they were really prelates, and in every way glorify them, thus confirming them in their errors.[119]

The omission was especially pernicious when subsequently discovered by Episcopalians who were emboldened thereby in their separation from Catholic unity.

When Fortescue wrote in to criticize the critic, the latter replied with delight that the 'coryphaeus of the whole school against which I am contending' had been summoned out of his lair.[120] Fortescue's usage, he declared, was contrary to reason, contrary to catholicity and 'inimical to the most vital interest of the Church of God'.[121] But Fortescue's practice where the separated Eastern churches were concerned would be sanctioned by the Decree on Ecumenism, *Unitatis redintegratio*, of the Second Vatican Council (1962–1965).

For Fortescue, the 'only theological differences that count are the Pope's position and the Filioque in the Creed', the first of which has 'got bigger since the schism'. Yet he did not abandon hope that 'even here things might be arranged'.[122] What in the ecumenical movement of the later 1960s and 1970s was termed the 'dialogue of charity' recommended itself because 'to me this position seems obvious: The schism was caused first by a long

---

America at a high point of immigration is well worth having.

117 Westminster Diocesan Archives, Series 20, Box 21, Letter to Fortescue of Andrew Shipman from 37 Wall Street, New York, 10 February 1908.

118 Letter of M. Porter Snell, *The Tablet*, 15 February, 1913, p. 264.

119 Ibid.

120 Letter of M. Porter Snell, *The Tablet*, 12 April 1913, p. 583.

121 Ibid., p. 584.

122 *Rome and Constantinople*, op. cit., p. 23.

period of friction and mutual bad feeling'. Naturally, as a Latin Catholic he was not prepared to say it was all the fault of the West, or of the pope. No more would people

> expect an Orthodox priest to say it is caused by Orthodox wickedness. And yet somehow we might perhaps come to some sort of understanding about it; a really candid attempt to understand what our opponents have to say would perhaps leave us on both sides with the same impression — that it was all a great pity, that it is a disastrous misfortune for both Catholics and Orthodox, and that we both have something to regret.[123]

II. The Non-Ephesian and Non-Chalcedonian Eastern Churches

Fortescue explains at the outset of *The Lesser Eastern Churches* that the bodies he will be describing come either from Nestorianism or from Monophysitism. In modern ecumenical parlance (after his death) the latter were customarily referred to as 'Non-Chalcedonian' (or sometimes 'Pre-Chalcedonian') Orthodox Churches. Monophysites reject the Council of Chalcedon. I have never seen the expression 'Non-Ephesian' (or indeed 'Pre-Ephesian' for that matter), but patently it performs the same role and is coined in analogous form and with the same courteous intent. Nestorians reject the Council of Ephesus.

Fortescue belonged to a more forthright age.

> All the people of this volume are heretics and schismatics. These are harsh words, which one uses unwillingly of pious and God-fearing Christians. But we must be clear on this point. It is, of course, true inevitably from the Catholic point of view. And they too, equally logically from their point of view, say that we are heretics and schismatics. Indeed, we are a very bad kind of heretic. We are Creed-tamperers, Papolaters, gross disturbers of the peace by our shameless way of sending missionaries who compass the land and sea to make one proselyte. We understand all that, and like them the better for being consistent. But they should also understand our attitude: we stand for our own position, on either side, and there is no malice.[124]

That is not to say that Fortescue never uses any other terms, for he needs to distinguish between national or regional examples of these two very different sorts of Church-life, and he also has to find linguistic space for their Uniate counterparts, which sometimes involves some further tweaking of terms.

---

123 Ibid., p. 4.
124 *The Lesser Eastern Churches*, op. cit., pp. 4-5.

Nomenclature apart, Fortescue used his introduction to ask some well-formulated questions. Is it true that they stand closer to the Orthodox than to Catholics? Following the learned German student of 'comparative Confessions-knowledge' Ferdinand Kattenbusch, who had called the Lesser Eastern Churches *Nebenkirchen* (Fortescue translates this 'bye-churches') of the Orthodox, he was inclined to answer, Yes.

> When they broke away they left the Eastern half of Christendom. The "Orthodox" Church in our technical sense did not yet exist, or (if one likes) the Orthodox were then Catholics. But they always had their own customs, rites, and in many points their own ideas. It was these that the lesser Eastern Churches took with them. And since then, since the schism of the Orthodox, that Church has been their great neighbour. Rome is far away; most Nestorians and Monophysites have been too poor, too ignorant, to know much about her. The great rival at hand was always the Church of the Eastern Empire.[125]

How do they relate to the rest of the Church? Do they, like the Orthodox — and like Catholics — claim they *are* the Church, from which all other communities have fallen away? Fortescue admits he can only attempt to answer this question by either anecdotal information or sheer speculation. But he is inclined to think the Lesser Eastern Churches, whether Nestorian or Monophysite, *do* adhere to something like the 'Branch Theory' which both Catholics and Orthodox reject (but of which High Anglicans in the England of his time made a very great deal). 'Has . . . the Branch Theory adherents in the Highlands of Kurdistan, the Egyptian desert and the wilds of Abyssinia? I am not sure; it is a difficult point; but I believe it has.'[126]

The Nestorians

The vivacity of Fortescue's historical imagination ensures that he does not leave the reader unenlightened as to the romance of the Nestorian church. 'The stranger who passes the Turkish-Persian frontier near Lake Urmi, the stranger who goes to delve among the ruins of Nineveh, will perhaps wonder to find in these parts buildings which are plainly Christian churches.'[127] On enquiry, he or she will find that those who worship there are the 'last tragic remnant of a Church whose history is as glorious as any in Christendom'.[128] The people Fortescue proposes to study in the first four substantive chapters

---

125 Ibid., p. 12.
126 Ibid., p. 13.
127 Ibid., p. 17.
128 Ibid.

of his book have been, both in antiquity and since, bandied about by great powers, but essentially 'they remain just the same Semitic Syriac-speaking native population of Mesopotamia and Eastern Syria'.[129]

After a rattlingly readable background history of eastern Syria and Persia from Alexander to the Tatars, Fortescue turns his attention to the pre-history of the Nestorian schism. As he points out, much in the life of the Nestorian church is simply the pre-Nestorian liturgy, customs, canons, of the church of Edessa (the capital, originally, of a Bedawin kingdom, Osrhoene, uneasily perched between Rome and Parthia), and the missionary daughter of Edessa, the church of Persia. Fortescue seems inclined to accept the thesis of the Cambridge scholar Francis Crawford Burkitt (1864–1935), to the effect that a strongly Jewish Christianity in the earliest generation at Edessa was fused after the Roman conquest (in 216) with a more obviously Catholic type of Gentile Christianity stemming from Antioch.[130] (Fortescue adds his own home-based comparison: rather like the ancient British Church fusing with the mission of Augustine of Canterbury[131]).

Edessa belonged to the patriarchate of Antioch, but separation by geography and language rendered the tie somewhat theoretical.

> '[T]he East Syrian liturgy, though one might classify it remotely as Antiochene, was celebrated so far from its original source, was so little confronted with the later use of Jerusalem-Antioch, that it developed into a special rite, hardly recognizable as having any connection with that of West Syria.'[132]

In legend (the *Acta Maris*, a Syriac work of the sixth century), the Edessene apostle Addai (one of the seventy-two disciples of Jesus's ministry) sends his own disciple Mari to Nisibis, from where Mari travels down the Tigris, preaches the Gospel at Nineveh, and ordains the first bishop of the Persian capital, Seleucia-Ctesiphon.

Fortescue's modern authorities were dubious, though he wishes to hold on to the notion of a very ancient Christianity at Nisibis (not least because St Ephrem, whose historicity is scarcely dubitable, hailed from there). It is the bishops of Seleucia who emerge as primates of Persia, notably at the moment, after the great persecution under Shapir II, when a synod in the city accepts the decrees of Nicaea, including its Creed. The Seleucian bishop takes the title *Katholikos* (at any rate, Fortescue offers this as an Anglo-Greek rendering of the cognate Syriac word), and this step was of greater moment than ecclesiastical nicety. 'No doubt its suggestion of the

---

129 Ibid., p. 19.
130 F.C. Burkitt, *Early Eastern Christianity* (London: Murray, 1904), chapter 1.
131 *The Lesser Eastern Churches*, op. cit., p. 33, fn 3.
132 Ibid., p. 37.

name of the Church in the Creeds made it seem a suitable form for the chief bishop of a vast semi-independent local Church. It was meant to imply the next thing to a Patriarch.'[133]

Though the *see* of Seleucia waned, the office of the *Katholikos* waxed. At a synod in 424 to settle various internal affairs, the name of the office was changed, unblushingly, to that of 'Patriarch' and, spectacularly, it was decreed that 'Easterns shall not complain of their Patriarch to the Western Patriarchs [i.e. of Antioch and beyond]: every case that cannot be settled by him shall await the tribunal of Christ'.[134] Fortescue finds that already a schismatic act – though by the time Edessa and Antioch have heard of it they are already caught up in the whirlpool of Nestorianism. That is another way of saying the road is open for schism to be followed by heresy.

Fortescue stresses that Nestorius was a Greek-speaking Antiochene who preached his Christological errors at Constantinople. There is no reason to think the founder of Nestorianism knew a word of Syriac. Nor will Fortescue accept notions of some arcane predisposition towards a bi-personal Christianity in the East Syrian mind. His explanation of events is quite straightforward: 'The acceptance of Nestorianism in the East and in Persia was very largely a corollary of its rejection by the Empire'; and 'Monophysism, the extreme contrary heresy, began almost as soon as Nestorianism. A great deal of East Syrian Nestorianism is at first only a vehement denial of Monophysism.'[135]

Fortescue's line in Christology is simple. The doctrine of Chalcedon reflects the witness of the New Testament, and is the only possible logical outcome of reflection on its content. Jesus Christ is a divine person acting in two natures, human and divine, both of which he possesses perfectly.

The two false solutions, Nestorianism, Monophysitism, 'together make up one story', and at its head stands the figure of Apollinaris of Laodicea who was unfortunate enough to pose the problem in a way that distracted minds from the obvious (i.e. Chalcedonian) solution.[136] Nestorianism is anti-Apollinarist zeal *à l'outrance*; Monophysitism is Apollinarianism *après la lettre*. In his article 'Apollinarism' in the Hastings Encyclopaedia, Fortescue described Apollinaris (died c. 390) as 'a sort of forerunner of Eutyches', the standard-bearer of radical or extreme Monophysitism.[137] As a zealous defender of Homoousianism against the Arians (he was a friend of Athanasius), Apollinaris felt obliged to offer an answer to the question:

---

133 Ibid., p. 49.

134 Cited at ibid., p. 51, from J.B. Chabot, *Synodicon Orientale, ou Recuil de Synodes nestoriens* (Paris: Académie des Inscription et des Belles-Lettres, 1902).

135 *The Lesser Eastern Churches*, op. cit., p. 54.

136 Ibid., p. 55.

137 'Apollinarism', in J. Hastings (ed.), *Encyclopaedia of Religion and Ethics, I* (Edinburgh: T. and T. Clark, 1908), pp. 606–608, and here at p. 606.

how could the Logos be joined with human nature?' Apollinaris' solution, in which his heresy consisted, was an attempt to save the unity of Christ's Person at the expense of His human nature.'[138]

The Antiochene exegetes who emphasized the full integrity of the man who had been joined to the Word were nothing if not anti-Apollinarian. In the decrees of Ephesus the theologians of Edessa and Nisibis saw an attack on their revered masters Diodore of Tarsus and Theodore of Mopsuestia, 'The Interpreter'. For Fortescue, who is thoroughly Cyrilline in his understanding of Chalcedon, those judges were not mistaken. He rehearsed the story of Cyril's confrontation with Nestorius much as he had earlier laid it out in *The Greek Fathers*. He also added something more: a vindication of the Ephesian condemnation of Nestorius against Nestorius's modern defenders.

Foremost among these was the Anglican James Franklin Bethune-Baker who, basing himself on an English translation of extracts of the newly discovered Syriac text *The Book of Heracleides*, written at the end of Nestorius' long life, declared the fifth century archbishop a much misunderstood man.[139] Fortescue had access to the Syriac text and a French translation and notes of the whole and disagreed (though he also took a favourable *moral* impression from his reading).[140]

> Nestorius is a heretic, not because he speaks of two hypostases, or even of two prosopa, in Christ, but because he explains this language in such a way as to make clear that he means just what we mean by two persons, two Christs — namely, Jesus Son of Mary, and the Word of God who dwelt in him.[141]

The point for the future of the Nestorian church is that, even after the Antiochene patriarch John was reconciled with Cyril of Alexandria in the aftermath of Ephesus, there were 'Syrian anti-theotokians' (Fortescue also calls them, ironically this time, 'the old guard of incorruptibles'), who 'held Nestorius for an injured saint, still denied our Lady's title, still clung to the theology of Diodore and Theodore'.[142] These are they whose story, and present fortunes, he means now to present.

---

138 Ibid. Fortescue claims that Apollinarism considered as a sect 'seems to have been gradually absorbed by the far more important Monophysite movement . . . the movement gradually disappears as its place is taken by Syrian Monophysitism', ibid., p. 607.

139 J.F. Bethune-Baker, *Nestorius and his Teaching. A Fresh Examination of the Evidence* (Cambridge: Cambridge University Press, 1908).

140 P. Bejān, *Le livre d'Héraclide de Damas* (Paris: Harrassowitz, 1910); F. Nau, *Nestorius: le livre d'Héraclide de Damas* (Paris: Letouzey et Ané, 1910).

141 *The Lesser Eastern Churches*, op. cit., pp. 67–68.

142 Ibid., p. 75.

The school of Edessa was, despite its highly Cyrilline bishop, Rabbula, the first centre of self-conscious theological Nestorianism, but the emperor Zeno soon put a stop to that (in 489), and the theologians of Edessa transferred their activities across to Persian border to Nisibis, which became the real diffusion point for the banished Christology. Gradually, the Persian church committed itself ever more clearly to Nestorianism, *pari passu* with its rejection of clerical celibacy, even for bishops. Fortescue does not attempt an exploration of the possible connexion but notes the fact, as when he comments on the *Katholikos* Babai II (in office 497–502), 'This man marks almost the lowest degradation of the Persian Church. He could not even read, and he had a wife'.[143] This is one of those pithy sentences where it is hard to tell how tongue-in-cheek Fortescue wishes to be.

Like Ephesus, the Council of Chalcedon too was rejected — or, speaking guardedly, Fortescue declares it truer to say it was never accepted. Yet, as he points out, the maxim according to which the branch that does not remain on the vine withers was scarcely verified at once in the Nestorian case. Fortescue does justice to Nestorian learning, Nestorian proficiency in the professions (highly useful to their Mazdaean and, later, Muslim masters), and, above all, Nestorian zeal in foreign missions. These last were principally directed to India, Turkestan, and China, although, granted the indifference of the Caliphs to the anti-Nestorian legislation in the East Roman empire, Nestorians were also able to found communities in Syro-Palestine, Cyprus, and even Egypt, 'the very home of Monophysism'.[144] A curiosity in whose defence Fortescue could appeal for support to a distinguished Tibetologist is the claim that Lamaist practices, introduced into Tibet in the mid-seventh century, derive from Nestorian ceremonial custom. 'At the source of the Lamaist ritual which so surprises the modern explorer stand a Nestorian monastery and a Nestorian bishop celebrating his liturgy.'[145] (After the initial wave of enthusiasm for matrimony, Nestorian monasticism was recreated in the sixth century by Abraham of Kashkar, called the Great, though Fortescue can speak of no extant monasteries in the 'Church of the East', but only 'a few wandering monks'.[146])

All in all, and taking the thirteenth century as the probable period of the Church's maximum extent, Fortescue estimates the number of Nestorian sees as somewhere between two hundred and two hundred and

---

143 Ibid., p. 82.

144 Ibid., p. 104.

145 Ibid., p. 109. Fortescue appeals here to L.A. Waddell, *The Buddhism of Tibet, or Lamaism, with its mystic cults, symbolism and mythology, and in its relation to Indian Buddhism* (London: W.H. Allen, 1895), pp. 421–422.

146 *The Lesser Eastern Churches*, op. cit., p. 113.

fifty. There was some excuse, then, when John Mason Neale claimed 'it may be doubted whether Innocent III possessed more spiritual power than the Patriarch in the city of the Caliphs'.[147] And Fortescue offers his own accolade.

> Those forgotten Nestorian missionaries, they were not Catholics but they were Christians. Braving long journeys, braving heathen tyrants and horrible danger, they brought the name of Christ north to Lake Baikal, south to Ceylon, and east right into the heart of China. They must have baptized thousands, and they taught the wild men of Tartary to worship one God, to serve Christ even if they did think him two hypostases, to love his mother, even if they did not call her Theotókos. Let that be remembered to their honour.[148]

What of Fortescue's own day? In the mediaeval West the Nestorians were almost forgotten, as the comedy of errors of an envoy from the Patriarch Yaballâhâ III to the Roman curia suggests,[149] even if by the time of the later Renaissance, the popes were more savvy and even established a Uniate 'Chaldaean' patriarchal line. But the ignorance in England (and America) could hardly have been more total. It began to be dissipated through the accident that Nestorians lived around the ruins of the great buildings of the first Assyrian empire. Fortescue thinks the first substantial account of modern Nestorians in English may well be the Assyriologist A.H. Layard's *Nineveh and its Remains*.[150] The suggestion that Nestorians might be the 'Protestants of the East' attracted religious sympathy in Anglo-America, while their sufferings at the hands of Kurdish tribesmen aroused humanitarian concern. Fortescue comments:

> It may be noted that this is the normal state of the Turkish Empire. All its more mountainous and wilder parts are practically independent and at the mercy of the strongest tribe that dwells there. The authority of the Government obtains in the towns

---

147 J.M. Neale, *A History of the Holy Eastern Church*, I. (London: Masters, 1850), p. 143, cited *The Lesser Eastern Churches*, op. cit., p. 108.

148 Ibid., pp. 109–110.

149 Fortescue gives a brilliant characterisation of this episode, based on Jean-Baptiste Chabot's *Histoire de Mar Jab-Alaha, Patriarche, et de Raban Sauma* (Paris: Ernest Léoux, 1895, 2nd edition).

150 A.H. Layard, *Nineveh and its Remains: a narrative of an expedition to Assyria during the years 1845, 1846 and 1847* (London: John Murray, 1849, two volumes). An abridged edition of this work was published under the same title, with an introduction and notes by W.F. Saggs (London: Routledge and Kegan Paul, 1970).

where there is a garrison, and as far round as the energy of the local Wali cares to enforce it. If he neglects his duty (most Walis do), there may be anarchy within sight of the gates.[151]

Though Chaldaean Catholics, and their co-religionists from elsewhere, had been active in the remote places of Kurdistan for several centuries, the place was now discovered by Presbyterian missionaries from the United States and also by Anglicans — who soon created the 'Archbishop of Canterbury's Mission to the Assyrian Church'.[152] The archbishop in question was originally Dr Tait, who, it may be remembered, was brother-in-law to Fortescue's father by his (Edward Fortescue's) first wife. This was certainly no imposition, for the request for help came from the then Nestorian patriarch Mâr Shim'un. There were also Danish and Norwegian Lutherans, Baptists, and, not least, the Russian Orthodox at work. '[T]he Nestorians, once themselves so great missioners, now know what it is to be the objects of copious missionizing.'[153]

In point of fact, Fortescue had great admiration for the Anglican effort among the Assyrians, though he does not claim to understand its theological basis.

> The Anglicans print books for use in Nestorian churches, they educate future Nestorian clergy, and teach their pupils the duty of obeying Mâr Shim'un. They are always at hand to counsel, encourage and support the Patriarch. Naturally this attitude is pleasant to the Nestorians; the Anglicans are on the best possible terms with Mâr Shim'un and his clergy. Only — how is it possible thus to co-operate with a heretical sect? If they thought the Nestorians one more branch of the Catholic Church, a branch long neglected, so now backward and in need of reform, their attitude would be most natural and right. But how can they think this? The Nestorians formally reject the fourth general council and honour Nestorius among the saints. If that does not make a body heretical, what does?[154]

---

151 *The Lesser Eastern Churches*, op. cit., p. 117, footnote 1.

152 Fortescue had read Athelstan Riley's *Report on the Foundation of the Archbishop's Mission to the Assyrian Church* (London: Richard Clay, 1886), which Riley would follow up in subsequent publications based in part on his own visits to Kurdistan and Persia. See on the whole remarkable project: J.F. Coakley, *The Church of the East and the Church of England: A History of the Archbishop of Canterbury's Assyrian Mission* (Oxford: Clarendon Press, 1992).

153 *The Lesser Eastern Churches*, op. cit., p. 119.

154 Ibid., p. 123. 'Fourth' here is presumably a slip for 'third', unless Fortescue is counting the (apostolic) council of Jerusalem as the first. Anglicans claimed to have the blessing of the Orthodox patriarch of Antioch return to whose obedience by Nestorians they were assisting. But for Fortescue 'the Patriarch of Antioch can no more make cooperation with a heretical sect lawful than can

The intolerance that the Anglican visitors displayed toward the Chaldaean Uniates compounded Fortescue's bafflement.

> The Chaldee abjures Nestorius, accepts Ephesus, and (on Anglican principles) leaves a heretical sect to enter the Catholic Church, in its largest branch. Is not this a good thing for him? When we consider further that the Chaldees have the original Patriarchal line, that Mâr Shim'un represents merely an (originally Romanist) schismatical line, the Anglican talk about Chaldees as schismatics becomes quite unintelligible. Except, of course, on the basis (so often assumed by Protestants of all kinds) that you had better be anything, even a Nestorian heretic, than be in union with the Pope of Rome.[155]

The Nestorians of Fortescue's day (since then there has been considerable emigration, especially to the Americas) lived, as he explains, in a 'triangle between Lake Van, Lake Urmi and almost down to Mosul', which meant that civilly they were divided between Turkey and Persia.[156] The plains further south, around Mosul and Baghdad, were more likely to be home to Chaldaeans, though the distinction was by no means cast-iron. At the time of writing (1913), the patriarch was twenty-seven; he had been seventeen when appointed, and the nephew of his predecessor, as had become their custom. Though bishops must be celibate, priests, notes Fortescue regretfully, may marry several wives in succession, including after Ordination. Rather charmingly, the Nestorians claim that their hierarchy corresponds to that of the angels, conceived according to the following format: patriarch, a cherub; metropolitan, a seraph; bishop, a throne; archpriest, a domination; chorepiscopus, a virtue; priest, a power; deacon, a principality; subdeacon, an archangel; reader, an angel. No doubt rightly, Fortescue thought they were hazy about the distinction between a full sacrament and a mere sacramental, and he suspected their rite for the hallowing of a bishop as patriarch to be nothing short of re-ordination. In general, he found their doctrine cloudy, and their practice somewhat wayward (their avoidance of sacred images, apart from the Cross, was perhaps a consequence of Moslem influence). They themselves, he reported, 'divide Christendom into three sects, the Monophysites, Melkites (including Franks), and the "Easterns" (themselves), who alone "never changed their faith, but kept it as they received it from the Apostles"'.[157] He adds:

---

anyone else', ibid., p. 124.

155 Ibid., p. 125.

156 Ibid., p. 127.

157 Ibid., p. 139, with an internal citation of the Nestorian text called the 'Jewel' or 'Pearl' of Ebedjesu of Nisibis, taken from G.P. Badger, *The Nestorians and their Rituals*, ed. J.M.W. Neale (London: Masters, 1852), II., pp. 399–401.

Needless to say, Nestorians entirely reject the universal primacy and infallibility of the Pope, though they acknowledge him as first of the Patriarchs. If they were consistent they could not give him even this honour, since he is steeped in Ephesian and monohypostatic error, being himself a mighty leader of Ephesian heretics.[158]

Fortescue, however, cannot withhold his admiration for their rare and exotic liturgy, even if, so far as its written forms are concerned, it is in a condition of some confusion (the Chaldaean books, printed by Dominicans and the Lazarist missionaries and corrected at Rome, were, he gathered, in a better state). But lack of user-friendly Syriac texts did not necessarily worry the worshippers: cantors knew vast quantities of liturgical material by heart. Fortescue's nearly twenty-page description of their worship is largely indebted, as he admits, to Anglican guides: Maclean and Browne's *The Catholicos of the East*,[159] though the style and commentary are quintessentially his own. It is a good thing Fortescue had been complimentary about Anglican altruism if not Anglican consistency, because here he was drawing on the 'work and travels' of Churchmen in harsh places, not on efforts of his own. One notes with interest his remark on the absence of words of institution in their 'Liturgy of Addai and Mari': 'if one accepts the idea of consecration by the whole *barahah* [here he refers to his own study *The Mass*], valid consecration without the words of institution explicitly might perhaps be defended'.[160]

Alternatively, it has been suggested by apologists for this ancient and unusual Anaphora that the words *are* to be found but scattered through the Prayer.[161] The issue would re-surface in the context of ecumenical outreach to the 'Church of the East' by Catholics around the turn of the twenty-first century.[162]

---

158 *The Lesser Eastern Churches*, op. cit., p. 139.

159 A.J. Maclean and W.H. Browne, *The Catholicos of the East and his People: being the impression of five years' work in the 'Archbishop of Canterbury's Mission'. An account of the religious and secular life and opinions of the Eastern Syrian Christians of Kurdistan and Northern Persia [known also as Nestorians]* (London: Society for the Promotion of Christian Knowledge, and New York: E. and J.B. Young, 1892).

160 Ibid., p. 155, footnote 3. The reference is to *The Mass. A Study of the Roman Liturgy* (London: Longmans, Green, 1914), p. 405.

161 The 'Anaphora' is the crucial consecratory section of the Liturgy, the 'Canon of the Mass' or 'Eucharistic Prayer'.

162 A. Nichols, O.P., *Rome and the Eastern Churches* (San Francisco: Ignatius, 2010), pp. 78–79.

The Monophysites

It is time now to turn to the much larger body of Christians who can be found in the historic churches of the Copts and Abyssinians of Africa, the Syrians of the Levant and India, and the Armenians of the Caucasus. As Fortescue introduces the topic, with his accustomed briskness, 'Monophysism made an appalling disturbance throughout the whole Eastern Empire for about two centuries, and then settled down in not one but four great national Churches'.[163] He explains that Monophysitism has no eponymous ancestor after whom it is named. Rather is it a response, of an overwrought kind, to the heresy of Nestorius. It is an extreme example of emphasis on the unity of Christ: 'in all things, personality, hypostasis, even nature (*phusis*), he is one'.[164] In so saying, these ardent opponents of the two-persons doctrine that emerged from the Antiochene school recreated something very like the older Apollinarianism — and even (writes Fortescue, somewhat harshly) an echo of the yet more ancient Docetism, for did not they 'make our Lord's humanity, his birth, life, and death, a mere appearance and a useless mystification'?[165]

Now Fortescue was a one hundred per cent supporter of Cyril of Alexandria — from whom the characteristic emphasis of Monophysite Christology on the unity of Christ descended. So as to distance his hero from Cyril's unruly children, Fortescue locates the origin of the doctrine in Alexandrian opposition to Cyril's formula of concord with John of Antioch, made in 433, two years after the deposition of Nestorius at Ephesus. Rightly, Fortescue distinguishes the 'wild' theories put forward at Constantinople by the archimandrite Eutyches — opponent *à l'outrance* of the Antiochenes — from the position of more moderate Monophysites elsewhere.

> Starting as the great champion of Ephesine doctrine, of which the dogma that Mary is Mother of God is the very essence, [Eutyches] came to a conclusion which (were he logical) denied that dogma. A channel through which a totally disconnected being passes, a person who is merely the *place* in which a pre-existent body is combined with the eternal nature of that being, is in no possible sense his mother.[166]

---

163 *The Lesser Eastern Churches*, op. cit., p. 163.

164 Ibid., p. 164.

165 Ibid. To make this connexion, Fortescue appealed to his own article, 'Docetism', in J. Hastings, *Encyclopaedia of Religion and Ethics, IV* (Edinburgh: T. and T. Clark, 1912), pp. 832–835, while modestly concealing his authorship.

166 *The Lesser Eastern Churches*, op. cit., p. 168.

Whereas early twenty-first century ecumenists would probably draw that same contrast (radicals versus moderates) in order to declare the quarrel of the orthodox with moderate Monophysites sheer *logomachia*, Fortescue warns, 'We must remember that a man or a national Church is by no means proved innocent of Monophysism because of a declaration against Eutyches'.[167]

After a careful yet colourful narration of the 449 'Robbers' Synod' of Ephesus and the 451 Council of Chalcedon which 'has made the name of that obscure suburb so famous', Fortescue draws his principal theological conclusion. 'A Catholic is (as far as the Christological question is concened) one who accepts the dogmatic decree of the fifth session of Chalcedon; a Monophysite is not a man who accepts all Eutyches' ideas, but one who rejects this.'[168] He only regrets that the bishops had not left the Asiatic suburb of the City straightaway, for, lingering, they promulgated the canons, of which the twenty-eighth proved in time so lethal to the union of the Latin and Greek churches. But that was an inner-Chalcedonian dispute.

The Monophysite churches take their rise from the large numbers of people in Egypt and Syria to whom the Chalcedonian definition and its practical corollary, the deposition of archbishop Dioscorus, Cyril's successor on the patriarchal throne of Alexandria, were wholly unacceptable. Why so? Noting that both Egypt and Syria had been imperfectly hellenised, Fortescue anticipated the thesis of some modern historians whereby political passions, especially in Egypt, played a large part in this.[169] Seeking, rather in the spirit of the English philosopher of history R.G. Collingwood, to imagine for himself the contemporary Egyptian Monophysite mind-set, Fortescue wrote:

> It was an appalling, an unheard-of outrage on Egypt that its Patriarch, its "ecclesiastical Pharoah", should stand as a culprit before Byzantine bishops, should be deposed, excommunicated, banished. So Egypt rose to defend its Pharoah, to defend the cause of Ephesus and Cyril, which was the cause of the old Fatherland by the Nile. It was Egyptians who first persuaded people in Syria and Palestine to join them in the common cause against the Emperor and his Government.[170]

---

167 Ibid., p. 169.

168 Ibid., p. 179.

169 See especially W.H.C. Frend, *The Rise of the Monophysite Movement* (Cambridge: Cambridge University Press, 1972). But see for a *sed contra* A.H.M. Jones,'Were the Ancient Heresies National or Social Movements in Disguise?', *Journal of Theological Studies*, New Series 11 (1959), pp. 280–298.

170 *The Lesser Eastern Churches*, op. cit., p. 183.

While Fortescue writes unsympathetically of the various imperial attempts, lasting until the late seventh century, to find forms of words that would conciliate Monophysites doctrinally and hence reconcile them politically, he does note one interesting phenomenon — which, so far as it goes, supports the eirenicism of contemporary ecumenical commentators today.

Towards the end of the sixth century, the Alexandrian philosopher Stephen Niobes proposed that, if Monophysites like himself allowed any difference between divine and human attributes in the Word incarnate, they would be obliged in logic to admit two natures in Christ. Accordingly, Stephen's appeal was for the recognition of no differences *at all*. Fortescue describes the great German historian of the Council Karl Josef von Hefele (1809–1893) as commenting 'aptly' that if the 'Monophysites who excommunicated Niobists really admitted distinct Divine and human attributes in our Lord, there could have been little but a mere verbal difference between them and Chalcedon, in spite of their formula, "one nature only"'.[171]

In any case, by then it was, on the wider scene, for Egypt (and not only for her) too late. In the 'hot desert of Arabia' the 'little cloud which was to burst over the richest province of the empire' had arisen.[172] After a confused period when Byzantine authority was in effect limited to the hellenised cities of the Nile Delta (and Fortescue does a sterling job of tracing the lines of Monophysite and Orthodox patriarchs at Alexandria, making use chiefly of Arabic chronicles in the *Patrologia Orientalis* and its companion collection the *Corpus Scriptorum Christianorum Orientalium*),[173] a spell of Persian occupation in the years 616–628 presaged the disaster to come. After a decade defined by the last effort at imperial compromise with Monophysitism (Monothelitism, the doctrine of the single will of the two-natured Redeemer), a definitive turning-point ensued.

In 639, militant Islam arrived *en masse*. 'Now from the churches for which these sects quarrelled and fought the altars have been taken away; from their towers the mu'eddin proclaims that Mohammed is the Apostle of God.'[174] That cannot of course be *entirely* the case — or else Fortescue would not be able, after this patristic preliminary, to write of the non-

---

171 Ibid., p. 208. Fortescue cites Hefele's *Conciliengeschichte* in the extended version published in eleven volumes in French by Dom Henri Leclerq of Farnborough: *Histoire des Conciles* (Paris: Leyouzey et Ané, 1907–1952), II (2), p. 878.

172 *The Lesser Eastern Churches*, op. cit., p. 182.

173 Ibid., pp. 214–223. The work he put in would be more useful to him than he knew at the time: for the invitation to complete Jean Maspero's study of the history of the Alexandrian patriarchs, see page 136.

174 Ibid., p. 182.

Chalcedonian churches of Egypt and Syro-Palestine (with the latter's extension in India) as well as of Abyssinia and Armenia. But this is what he now proceeds to do.

The Copts

The Christian population in Egypt was so overwhelmingly estranged from Chalcedonianism that, in Fortescue's explanation, '[a]s a matter of historical continuity, the old Church of Egypt, the Church of Athanasius and Cyril, is now represented by the Monophysite Copts. They are the old Church, fallen into heresy and schism.'[175] And with a sly dig at those Eastern Orthodox who may be inclined to treat Latin Catholics as wholly out of place in such parts of the world: 'The Orthodox in Egypt, with their foreign rite and foreign language [i.e. Greek], are just as much foreigners as the Latins.'[176] Part of the reason for the alien, and minute, character of Orthodoxy in Egypt lies in the nature of the Arab conquest. Naturally, the new rulers showed especial animus against those Christians who were aligned with their principal enemy, the East Roman empire. When the rules of 'dhimmitude' were followed by Muslim governors in Egypt, Copts did relatively well — for instance, they were granted many churches previously used by the Orthodox and, thanks to the educational attainments of the Coptic elite, often served as professional auxiliaries to the Muslim governing class. With an allusion to the contemporary East, which so often illuminate Fortescue's historical analysis, he notes that '[t]he Coptic *kātib* [secretary] became a recognized institution; even now in Egyptian books and plays he appears, generally as a comic character, an ingenious rascal, whose astuteness is finally defeated by True Believing honesty'.[177]

Unfortunately, playing by the rules could not guarantee safety. Copts were subject to periodic persecution, sometimes of a horrendous kind. Fortescue chronicles them selectively, under successive regimes, whether Sunni (Abbasid) or Shi'ah (Fatimid), up to the time of the Crusades, referring the reader for a fuller account to Stanley Lane-Poole's *History of Egypt in the Middle Ages*.[178] Occasionally he pauses for an inspirational vignette, as with the Coptic patriarch Christodoulos (in office 1047 to

---

175 Ibid., p. 214.

176 Ibid. But Fortescue records that in the mid-eighth century the Orthodox succeeded in obtaining recognition as a 'millah' (milet) from the Amīr. 'Some at least of their churches were given back to them; so from now the Melkites [i.e. Orthodox] have a fairly regular succession and reappear as a small group of *dimmis*, by the side of the Copts', ibid., p. 231.

177 Ibid., p. 227.

178 S. Lane-Poole, *History of Egypt in the Middle Ages* (London: Methuen, 1901).

1077), the first to reside in Cairo, from the lintel of whose front door the government erased the inscription 'In the name of the Father and of the Son and of the Holy Ghost, one God'. 'The Patriarch had to let them do so; but he said: "You cannot erase the words from my heart"'.[179]

In the crusading period, the advent of the Kurd Saladin, as sultan of Egypt under the nominal suzerainty of the Abbasid Caliph, did not bring for Christians the relief the polite dealings of this figure with Richard I of England might suggest. Fortescue cannot justify the arrogance of Latin knights towards Eastern Christians, and his musings as to alternative policies the Westerners might have adopted (a general proclamation that they came as champions of all Christians; deliberate abstention from intervention in theological matters; profession of respect for the ecclesiastical status quo) end inconclusively. Probably Oriental Christians were too cowed by Moslem overlordship to be capable of galvanization, and they were too hostile to each other, along the lines of their various divisions, readily to accept the novel concept — had it been presented to them — that the Latins could be friends of all. The situation continued (with, however, fewer historiographical sources for its depiction) under the Aiyūbid Sultans and the Mamluks, after whom the arrival of the Ottomans in 1517 can be considered a distinct improvement — though Fortescue notes that, curiously, the Turks tended to give preference to the Orthodox. His explanation for that is a simple one. The Porte had become used to dealing with them at Constantinople.

Fortescue does not give much space to the displacement of the Turkish Pashas by the Albanian adventurer Mohammed Ali, which produced an ongoing line of Khedives in token subordination to the Ottoman empire. As a development, it was far less significant than the protectorate declared by Great Britain in 1882 which 'differs from governing the country only in theory'.[180] Though Copts complained that the British favoured Muslims — this was the gravamen of Kyriakhos Mikhail's *Copts and Moslems under British Control in Egypt* to whose case Fortescue draws attention,[181] they could no longer say they suffered persecution or lacked 'decent' conditions of life.[182]

Fortescue was fascinated by Coptic Christianity. 'The Copts are wonderfully primitive'.[183] Their development was arrested in 639, such that should Christians wish to see with their own eyes the 'days of Athanasius' it is to them they must look, rather than to the Orthodox and other

179 *The Lesser Eastern Churches*, op. cit., p. 236.

180 Ibid., p. 250.

181 K. Mikhail's *Copts and Moslems under British Control* (London: Simpkin and Marshall, 1911).

182 *The Lesser Eastern Churches*, op. cit., p. 250.

183 Ibid., p. 252.

Monophysite Christians do so look to them for leadership, that is (with the possible exception of the Armenians who 'in many ways stand apart').[184] Rich merchants at Cairo and Alexandria, they are peasants in Upper Egypt where in many villages in Fortescue's time they were majoritarian.

Their cohesion as a community must in part be explained by the relation all Coptic Christians enjoy with the patriarch, the formidable character of whose primacy Fortescue underlines: he cannot be deposed; he chooses and ordains all bishops; only he can consecrate chrism. Chosen by lot, he is now always a monk of the monastery of St Anthony by the Red Sea (in our own period, 'general bishops' — vicars-general of the patriarch for this or that area of Church life — can be candidates, but not diocesans). In a typical aside, Fortescue notes that, in any case, historically: 'The Patriarch had to lead an exceedingly abstemious life; so the dignity was not much coveted'.[185]

Though the literacy of the parochial clergy left, Fortescue believed, much to be desired, a recent movement for Church reform was demanding better education for priests as well as certain lay rights of control, notably in finance. He was inclined to agree with conservative critics who ascribed some of the reforming zeal to the influence of 'Anglicized Semi-Protestants' (the Church Missionary Society had been active in Egypt, as had American Presbyterians).[186] Fortescue records that 'it has been proposed that the Archbishop of York should do for the Copts what Canterbury is doing for the Nestorians'.[187]

This draws a characteristic reaction. Pointing out the 'plain Monophysism' in the Arabic text of the 1912 Coptic Catechism, Fortescue draws attention to some difficulties for 'High Church missionary effort' in this regard.

[I]n spite of the modern craze for denying that heretical bodies really hold the heresy of which they are accused, I have not yet found anyone who claims that the Copts are not Monophysites. That may come. The people who so hotly maintain that Nestorians are not Nestorians may quite as well take up the defence of Monophysism. This then is plain. Ignorant sympathizers with this ancient and venerable Church, who see no reason why Anglicans should not join in communion with it, must first make up their minds about the Council of Chalcedon. Reunion with Copts is only possible if Anglicans turn Monophysite, or succeeding in converting Copts to Chalcedon. This last case may be ruled out at once.[188]

---

184 Ibid.
185 Ibid., p. 254.
186 Ibid., p. 258.
187 Ibid., footnote 3.
188 Ibid., pp. 260-261.

Tongue in cheek, Fortescue complains that though, when urged, Monophysites will say in so many words they are the true Church of Christ, they nevertheless 'make no effort to convert the millions of Diophysite heretics who surround them'.[189] 'In vain have I tried to make Coptic clergy see that they ought to missionize us and to set up a proper Monophysite patriarch of Rome'.[190] (We must assume, I think, that these semi-serious conversations took place while Fortescue was in Jerusalem.) Apart from their distinctive Christological doctrine, which does not occupy 'nearly as large a place in their consciousness now as it did in that of Dioscor and the Cat',[191] and possibly their attitude to the *Filioque* — 'adding a slightly darker shade to people who are already black with Chalcedonianism',[192] what for Copts is important is 'the existence of their National Church, their customs and traditions', and by way of corollary a rejection of the universalistic claims of the pope of Rome.[193] But their Canon of Scripture includes the Epistle of Barnabas, Hermas, Clement of Rome and various apocrypha. (A better way to put this may be that they bind these other texts together with Scripture so that they may be read in church.)

Fortescue makes it plain that, despite his allegiance to the Dyophysite pontiff Pius X, he regards those traditions and customs with enormous sympathy, giving a vivid, and often moving, account of their churches, vestments, service-books, music, ceremonial and calendar.

> [T]he memories of the old Church of Egypt give it a dignity not shared by many larger and more prosperous Churches in the West . . . Perhaps nowhere in the world can you imagine yourself back in so remote an age as when you are in a Coptic church. You go into a strange dark building. At first the European needs an effort to realize that it is a church at all, it looks so different from our usual associations. It is enormously older than the clustered columns, moulded arches and glowing clerestory, than the regular aisles and balanced chapels to which we are accustomed. In a Coptic church you come into low dark spaces, a labyrinth of irregular openings. There is little light from the narrow windows. Dimly you see strange rich colours, all mellowed by dirt. In loops from the

---

189 Ibid., p. 262.

190 Ibid.

191 Ibid., p. 265. Timothy Aelurus ('The Cat') was Dioscorus's successor as Monophysite patriarch at Alexandria.

192 Ibid., p. 261.

193 Ibid., p. 265.

vault above hang the white ostrich eggs and lamps sparkle in the gloom. Before you is the exquisite carving, inlay in delicate patterns, of the haikal screen. All around you see, dusty and confused, wonderful pieces of wood carving. Behind the screen looms the curve of the apse; on thick columns and along the walls under the low cupolas are inscriptions in exquisite lettering — Coptic and Arabic. The impression is a confusion of dark misty colour, out of which gleam patches of crimson and blue from the paintings — S. George's cloak and our Lady's mantle.[194]

Fortescue invites the reader not only into a church waiting for prayer but one that is actually praying.

If you assist at a liturgy you see the clergy moving in and out of the haikal door in their shabby, gaudy vestments; the incense fills the dark vault with clouds of blue smoke, and the strange wailing goes on with clashing cymbals and jangling bells. They sing chant after chant in the ancient tongue which they do not understand themselves; but the ghosts of their fathers know it, Rameses II would know it, and the heavenly powers whom they address know it.[195]

Never is he more eloquent than in his closing peroration in the chapter entitled 'The Copts in our Time'.

So here among the dirt and the incense smoke, while Coptic and Greek roll around the haikal screen, you may dream of the mighty men who once lived here, Pachomius and Pambo, Antony star of the desert, and Paul, the first hermit, Athanasius fleeing from the sword of Constantius. For the sake of these glorious memories, for the sake, too, of the long line of their martyrs under Islam, we can feel nothing but respect, wish nothing but good to the people of Christ in Egypt. They have stood for his name so faithfully during the long, dark centuries now past. May they stand for it always in happier ages to come. May they confess it (honouring the all-holy Lady Theotókos) no longer, please God, in unhappy isolation, but joined again to the Church which acknowledges him throughout all the world, the evil done to them by Dioscor and the Cat being at last undone.[196]

---

194 Ibid., pp. 288-289.
195 Ibid., p. 289.
196 Ibid.

The Abyssinians

Still dependent on the Coptic patriarch of Alexandria in Fortescue's period was the Church of Abyssinia, a term he treats as more or less interchangeable with 'Ethiopia', which, as he knows, is the proper Amharic name for the ancient Christian kingdom in the Horn of Africa.[197] The British punitive incursion of 1867, which produced the battle of Magdala, the suicide of the Negus Theodore, and a remarkable haul of books, paintings, vessels and fabrics for the British Museum, was recent enough history for Fortescue to assume a basic familiarity with the country on his readers' part (that familiarity will no doubt have received a boost from newspaper coverage of the spectacularly unsuccessful Italian invasion attempt in 1895).

There are certainly some curious features in Ethiopian Christianity, but Fortescue is not inclined to indulge them. The Church of Abyssinia was founded under 'happy auspices', he writes, when Athanasius consecrated Frumentius to be metropolitan of Aksum, but the close connexion with Egypt which gave the Ethiopians a Monophysite Christology did not bring them effective parity with the mother-church at any level.

> The Copts themselves do not hold a very enlightened form of Christianity; we can imagine what a backward dependent of their Church must be, we can conceive how little culture, theology and spirituality there is in a body which looks to the Coptic Patriarch as its highest standard, conscious that it lags some way behind that exalted ideal.[198]

Fortescue assumes, possibly incorrectly, that the (fifth or sixth century) 'Nine Saints' treated as secondary apostles of Ethiopia were Monophysite monks, but in any case, as he says, the adherence of the country to heresy was inevitable given the tradition that the ruling bishop, the *Abūna*, must be a Copt sent from Alexandria.

This 'small highland state, surrounded by Islam on all sides',[199] was lost to European view until the arrival of the Portuguese in the sixteenth century, whence follows a flood of information and a disastrous attempt at union with Rome. The lasting legacy was 'a great distrust and fear of Europeans and European missionaries'.[200] In the nineteenth century, English and Swiss Protestant missions foundered, but a tiny Catholic presence endured, with a seminary for indigenous

---

197 'More or less' insofar as Western geographers had begun to reserve 'Abyssinia' for the polity ruled by the Negus, 'Ethiopia' for the highland zone which was the historic heart of the State.

198 *The Lesser Eastern Churches*, op. cit., pp. 296–297.

199 Ibid., p. 299.

200 Ibid., p. 303.

vocations. Fortescue saw the principal danger to Ethiopian Christianity in the menace of Islam which, he reports, has recently taken great strides in Tigray (the northern region of the country), though, with his robust (and not altogether unjustified) Russophobia he also predicted a Russian attempt to detach the Ethiopians from the Copts and attach them to Orthodoxy.

That sounds a trifle far-fetched, and his basis for claiming there *was* a Russian policy of this kind is circumstantial. It turns on two sorts of evidence: first, Russian interest in the deterioration of relations between Menelik II and the Coptic patriarch over the question of ownership of the Coptic (or was it Abyssinian?) monastery near the Holy Sepulchre, and secondly, the interventions of Russians in the theological controversies of the Ethiopian church about the moment and manner of the union between divine and human in the incarnate Word.[201]

The interest of Fortescue's account is in part his reportage of the situation which pertained in the first three decades of the twentieth century: before the Italian occupation, prior to the post-War adjustments which gave the Church its independence, and, before, likewise, the Marxist officers' plot that overthrew the Abyssinian monarchy. That the *Abūna* was always Egyptian, and in general if not in every case ignorant of both the sacred tongue (Ge'ez) and the civil language (Amharic), created a gulf between metropolitan and people, which in turn was filled by a married clergy close to the peasantry thanks to its own agrarian lifestyle and low educational level. That the senior abbot of Ethiopia, the *'Itshāgē*, was, by contrast, native, gave him a cachet which rivalled that of the *Abūna,* not least since he was, by office, a close counsellor of the Negus.

Neither of these asseverations hold good today, when Ethiopia has its own indigenous patriarch and the 'Lion of Judah' is no more. The present writer, who has spent some time in Ethiopia, can state with confidence, however, that the life of the Ethiopian church in her liturgical and devotional round continues much as Fortescue describes it, basing himself on published sources (which for the texts of the Liturgy could only be incomplete) and personal inspection of the so-called 'church of Paradise' which, some few years before, the Ethiopians had built just outside Jerusalem (as well as of their other establishments in the vicinity of 'The Anastasis', Fortescue's preferred name for the church of the Holy Sepulchre).

He mentions the calendrical curiosity of recurring monthly feasts – the birth of Christ, the Virgin Mary, the archangel Michael, and the patriarchs Abraham, Isaac and Jacob, the latter celebrated as a trio. He discusses with his usual intelligence the *tābōt* kept on the altar of every church where the Ge'ez Liturgy is celebrated, coming to the conclusion that this highly venerated object, whose contents an Abyssinian priest, he says, refused to disclose to

---

201 Fortescue attempts a delineation of this tripartite controversy on pp. 318–319.

him,[202] is in reality an empty box which originally contained, or possibly was joined to, the altar-board, from where it drew its original significance. (That hypothesis is corroborated by its role as a stand for the chalice during the Holy Eucharist.) The legend which connects the *tābōt* with the Ark of the Jerusalem Temple (via the aboriginal bejewelled *tābōt* in the church of St Mary at Aksum) should be regarded as merely another expression of the Judaizing tendencies among traditional Ethiopian Christians.

Eschewing the thesis of Jewish influence on early Christianity in the highlands, Fortescue offers by way of explanation of those tendencies, the following sagacious comment:

> A backward and isolated people, who receive the Old Testament as the word of God, an Eastern people surrounded (like the Jews) by unbelievers, to whom much of the Mosaic Law must seem natural, might easily evolve the idea that it applies to them too. They know nothing of the anti-Jewish struggle which forms a chapter in our early Church history, and they set great store by King Solomon and the Queen of Sheba; the Negus thinks the Kings of Israel his own glorious ancestors. I doubt if we need look further than this for the origin of their Judaizing practices.

He adds, with a twinkle, 'But they count St. Paul (and Hebrews) among the canonical books; they read St. Paul in their liturgy. Apparently in Ethiopia, as in some other places, he has not succeeded in making himself understood.'[203] Fortescue downplays the negative judgments of European travellers on the devotional practices and other life-style choices of Ethiopians. 'If a man is an African he is an African. In any case they are Christians.'[204]

The Jacobites

The Jacobites are of course, not the supporters of the House of Stuart among whose number Fortescue never ceased to count himself. They are, rather, 'the Monophysites of Syria'.[205] (In a footnote, Fortescue takes pleasure in the fact that the seventeenth century French Orientalist Eusèbe Renaudot was asked by Louis XIV to help the English exiles at the court of St Germain: 'so he had to do with Jacobites in both senses of the word'.[206]) Unlike Copts and Abyssinians, Syrian Monophysites were highly

---

202 Ibid., p. 315, footnote 2.

203 Ibid., p. 321.

204 Ibid.

205 Ibid., p. 323.

206 Ibid., p. 336, footnote 2. Fortescue had made use of his work as a guide to the history of the Alexandrian patriarchs: E. Renaudot, *Historia patriarcharum Alexandrinorum* (Pars: Fournier, 1713).

minoritarian on their native heath. Fortescue reports them as currently concentrated around Diyārbakr (a city earlier known as Amida), but with communities in most Syrian towns. The Jacobites take their name from James Baradai (his surname was actually a nickname meaning 'horse-cloth', he wore a ragged cloak) who travelled widely through Syria, and indeed the entire Levant, ordaining bishops who could in turn ordain priests to preserve and transmit the Monophysite cause. James consecrated the two patriarchs of Antioch who succeeded the theologian-patriarch Severus of Antioch, and thus stood at the fountain-head of the Syrian Monophysite church understood as at last definitively separated from its Chalcedonian rival (something not fully the case in Severus's lifetime).

Jacobitism was never a national cause, if only because Syria, without natural frontiers and with a large Greek-speaking population, was not easily described as a nation. But while Jacobites let go the succession at Jerusalem (Fortescue finds that odd, for they had Jerusalemite supporters), they kept hold of the claim to Antioch, and this was so even though, owing to the predominance of the Orthodox there, the patriarch did not live in his titular city. In fact, as Fortescue describes, the entire orientation of Syrian Monophysites was precisely that — a movement *ad Orientem,* to the east, where, despite competition with Nestorians, they no longer had unfriendly Orthodox to cope with.

As with the Assyrians, the Jacobites were often distinguished in the arts and sciences, especially, thinks Fortescue, in the twelfth century — in which judgment he is reflecting the discovery, not long before the writing of *The Lesser Eastern Churches,* of the Chronicle of the Patriarch Michael I (in office 1166–1199).[207] Their mediaeval literature includes liturgiological treatises so rich that 'we know more about the history of the Jacobite rite than of any other'.[208] They were, however, dogged by internal schisms, with at one stage a foursome of patriarchal lines: at Mardīn, Sis (in Cilicia), Tur 'Abdīn and the monastery of Mâr Bar Saumâ. This self-harm was the more regrettable in that from the fourteenth century onwards (the time of the schisms) Muslim pressure meant their numbers were falling dramatically. In the modern period, while embryonic schemes of Anglican assistance to the Jacobites have not come to birth, American Presbyterians and Congregationalists have been active with what Fortescue terms the 'usual' results. '[T]hey began with the idea, not of making converts, but of educating and spiritualizing, then quarrelled with the hierarchy, and now have small sects of ex-Jacobite Protestants.'[209]

---

207 The text of Michael's Chronicle was edited in Syriac and French by Jean-Baptiste Chabot, and published at Paris in four volumes between 1899 and 1910.

208 *The Lesser Eastern Churches,* op. cit., p. 331.

209 Ibid., p. 336.

Fortescue writes sharply of the (then) current condition of the Syrian Monophysites — Arabic-speaking, except in the thirty to forty villages where Syriac was retained, around Tur 'Abdīn — and under a patriarch, Ignatius 'Abdullah Sattuf, of whom he disapproved, chiefly on the ground that Ignatius' high dignity appeared to have been won by bribery and corruption. Owing to the lack of any equivalent to the rich sociological detail of the Anglican sources tapped for the Assyrians, his account of their common life could only be schematic (it depends largely on academic German sources). At least he provides some useful information about the organization of the Jacobite hierarchy — and particularly, the change of definition which overcame the 'maphrianate', the most original of the Syrian Monophysite institutions. Intended as a kind of catholicate for Jacobites in the lands beyond the Tigris, this office subsequently metamorphosed into that of resident assistant to the patriarch, with, in effect, right of succession to the patriarchal throne. Technically, the maphrian bore the title 'metropolitan of Jerusalem' (an auxiliary bishop represented him there), but Fortescue had the impression the role was losing its significance, not least because it was not always filled. We are fed some curious tit-bits of information: the Jacobites have 'innumerable deacons, ordained in crowds';[210] monasteries that contain the tomb of a patriarch or a maphrian are autonomous; all clergy shave their heads entirely, even though they wear beards.

Fortescue had come across Syrian church-buildings on his tour (at Beirut, for example); they held none of the interest for him of their Coptic counterparts. He found them 'much affected by Orthodox and Byzantine influence',[211] and hence less interestingly *sui generis*. He was disappointed by the lack of liturgical grace, and even knowledge, on the part of their clergy, awarding higher marks in these respects to the Uniate Syrians whose current patriarch, he tells readers, is a 'great scholar'.[212]

The Malabar Christians

Before moving on to the fourth of the great blocs of which, historically speaking, Monophysite Christians are composed, Fortescue inserts an interlude on the Indian Christians of the Malabar Coast who, originally, were just one of the many missions of the East Syrian church (and thus, in time, Nestorians). Likewise, in the modern epoch, after the fiasco of Portuguese Latinisation, when disaffected Orientals had recourse to the Monophysite representatives of 'Antioch', they were 'simply Jacobites in India'.[213] 'In no case

210 Ibid., p. 341.
211 Ibid., p. 344.
212 Ibid., p. 351.
213 Ibid., p. 353.

has Malabar itself anything to justify our reckoning it as a special Church, except its geographical position.'[214] In any case, most Malabar Christians are Uniates, and thereby constitute a topic to be covered elsewhere.

Some of the recent German scholarship read by Fortescue was favourable to the traditional notion that at the origin of the Malabar church lay the preaching of the apostle Thomas.[215] The most he himself will admit is the possible historicity of a mission by Thomas to Parthia and, beyond that, to a state in North India. He thinks the real origin of Malabar Christianity lies in a migration of Persian Christians during the persecutions of the fourth century. Moving down the west coast of India they found refuge in the territories of the more tolerant Hindu kings.[216] To call this a 'Nestorian' implantation would be premature; these were Christians of East Syrian tradition who in time accepted Nestorianism. The language in which their successors worshipped remained the Syriac tongue, their Katholikos, resident at Angamale, was a Syrian or Persian sent out by the Patriarch (the parallel with the Abyssinians and Alexandria leaps to the eye). Probably the Indian Christians sat lightly to the Christology of their Syrian brethren. In the sixth and seventh centuries they were not averse to asking Monophysites for bishops.[217]

This was a strange anticipation of what actually transpired when the Latinizing zeal of Western missionaries (by 1502, Vasco da Gama had conquered the coast for the crown of Portugal) drove some of them to ecclesiastical revolt. Cannily, the Portuguese had blocked the routes to Mesopotamia; the relapsed schismatics appealed, accordingly, to the Copts, showing, as Fortescue writes, how little they 'cared … about the Council of Ephesus'.[218] In fact not till 1665, by which time the Dutch had replaced the Portuguese as masters of the coast, did a Monophysite metropolitan, Gregory of Jerusalem, reach the descendants of these petitioners.

> Here, then, occurs of the most astonishing transformations in Church history. The Uniate majority were not, of course, affected. But the schismatical Christians of Malabar, who had been Nestorian, now became Jacobite. Thomas [their leader] accepted the Jacobite rite and was in communion with the Jacobite patriarch of Antioch. That is still the state of a great part of the schismatical body.[219]

---

214 Ibid.

215 Notably J. Dahlmann, S.J., *Die Thomas-Legende* (Freiburg: Herder, 1912).

216 For evidence, Fortescue refers the reader to W. Germann, *Die Kirche der Thomaschristen* (Gütersloh: Bertelsmann, 1877), pp. 82-83.

217 Ibid., pp. 148–149.

218 *The Lesser Eastern Churches*, op. cit., p. 364.

219 Ibid., p. 365.

This *volte-face* did not prevent the Nestorian church seeking later to recover its own — nor, in the British period, the incursion of Protestant missionaries, mainly Low Church Anglicans from the Church Missionary Society who 'taught justification by faith alone and an unsacramental theology'.[220] More recently, says Fortescue, who rarely misses an opportunity to slap the Church of England around the head, 'High Church clergymen have travelled in Malabar' — that was easy because Travancore was under the direct rule of the Raj, while Cochin, a princely state to the north, would have had, of course, its British 'Resident' — 'and have shown these people that there are different kinds of Anglicanism'.[221]

Indeed Anglican interventions increased the confusion, not to say chaos, of non-Uniate Eastern Christianity along the Pepper Coast, adding two more bodies (the Mâr Thomas Christians, a reform movement that broke with Jacobitism, and 'Church of England Syrians', directly under the Anglican clergy[222]) to the already existing patchwork of patriarchalist and non-patriarchalist Jacobites and the returned Nestorians.

The Armenians

On this topic, Fortescue could have used his half-brother's Edward's writings,[223] but he preferred to refer to more recent literature, in German and (especially) French.[224] He explains that, while most readers will be conscious of Armenians as a diaspora, 'there is, or was, a country, Armenia, the original home, still the nucleus of their nation'.[225] They are an Aryan people who arrived in the area of historic Armenia around

---

220 Ibid., p. 366.

221 Ibid., p. 367. But he is very laudatory about G.B. Howard's *The Christians of St Thomas and their Liturgies* (Oxford: Parker, 1864), on which he depends for his account of the Malabar Jacobites' faith and rites, describing the author as 'a most sympathetic Anglican clergyman . . . He is not very High Church; but he cannot stand the ways of the C[hurch]. M[issionary]. S[ociety]. He does not like Rome either', *The Lesser Eastern Churches*, op. cit., p. 378, fn 10.

222 Three if one bears in mind that the counterpart to the Mâr Thomas Christians in British Malabar was the 'Church of Anjur': see ibid., pp. 374–375 for Fortescue's listing.

223 E.F.K. Fortescue, *The Armenian Church, founded by St Gregory the Illuminator; being a skcetch of the history, liturgy, doctrine, and ceremonies of this ancient national church.* (London: Hayes, 1892; reprinted New York: AMS Press, 1970).

224 Notably T.F. Tournebize, *Histoire politique et religieuse de l'Arménie* (Paris: Picard, 1910).

225 *The Lesser Eastern Churches*, op. cit., p. 383.

the sixth century before Christ, their language highly distinctive, having 'the most amazing combination of consonants; except for its inflections, the build of its grammar and one or two words, it would hardly seem Aryan at all'.[226] Fortescue thinks Christianity reached Armenia from Edessa in the second or third century, even before, then, the mission of St Gregory the Illuminator, born c. 255, and baptized in Cappadocia (in Fortescue's conjecture, Gregory's family were among the Armenians who crossed into the Roman empire to escape the Persians). He has no time for the dream-vision, ascribed to Gregory, which depicts Christ descending to earth bearing a golden hammer at what became the ecclesiastical capital of the country: 'a late invention, after the schism with Caesarea, to glorify the office of Katholikos, to represent the national Church as founded by an independent commission of our Lord, and to exalt the later centre Etshmiadzin'.[227] On the other hand, he agreed that, as a consequence of Gregory's apostolic labours, Armenia officially accepted Christianity before the Roman empire did (if not long before, perhaps twenty years).

Fortescue's account of the subsequent history is not especially easy to follow because he tells it twice, once as civil history and then over again as the history of the Church. Some civil history is necessary in order to show how historic or 'Greater' Armenia ceased to be a political unit, thanks to the invasions of Persians, Romans (including Byzantines), Tatars, and Turks. Armenians became a diaspora people in mediaeval times, not modern: wandering, yet maintaining their own communities, from Anatolia to Poland; with good reason can they be called the Jews of the Christian world. Fortescue likewise needed to fill in the background to the emergence of a 'new Armenia' — his term for 'Lesser Armenia' — in Cilicia and the Taurus (in the south of Asia Minor, then),[228] where a principality, already established at the end of the eleventh century, made common cause with Crusading Franks and endured for some three hundred years.

In modern times, much of historic Armenia passed from Ottoman to Russian rule after the Russo-Turkish war of 1828–1829, though in Fortescue's opinion 'on the whole, Orthodox Russia has treated the heretical Armenians almost as badly as the Turks did'.[229] Fortescue writes 'did' rather than 'does' because he is aware that, towards the end of the nineteenth century, for those Armenians who remained within the geographical limits of the Ottoman empire the disabilities they had

226 Ibid., p. 384.
227 Ibid., p. 399.
228 Ibid., p. 388.
229 Ibid., p. 391.

suffered for centuries were transformed into something far more terrible. Though Fortescue describes the Armenian massacres as too 'fresh in everyone's memory' to be recounted again, he has no such inhibition when it comes to describing their fundamental character. 'The point to remember', he holds, is that this was not a 'case of a lawless mob attacking Armenians on their own initiative'.[230] No doubt Kurds were ready to slay their Armenian neighbours. But Ottoman soldiers helped them to do so. 'The massacres were done in obedience to secret (not even very secret) orders from the Yildiz Kiöshk', i.e. from the heart of the Sultan of Turkey's government.'[231] Why?

Fortescue suggests three explanations. 'Abd-ul Hamid II feared the growing national consciousness among Armenians who were imbibing Western ideas and, at least abroad, forming societies dedicated to the restoration of their independence.' Alternatively (or additionally), 'in some characteristically tortuous way', he hoped to provoke European intervention and gain something from it.[232] For the third analysis offered, which was perhaps the most plausible, Fortescue was indebted to Sir Charles Eliot whose *Turkey in Europe* had appeared in 1908.[233] According to Eliot, and Fortescue registered this in a footnote a further distinct possibility, the aim was to so reduce the Armenian population that nowhere in the Sultan's realm could Armenians be regarded as 'the predominating element in any distinct'.[234] In the years 1890–1896, 'enormous numbers' perished wherever a significant Armenian population could be found, including six thousand deaths at Constantinople 'under the eyes of the Diplomatic Corps'.[235] In 1909 another twenty-thousand died in Cilicia. When Fortescue added, 'It seems that under the Turk there is no hope for this ill-fated race',[236] he spoke prophetically. The Armenian genocide which effectively eliminated this commercially prosperous but often unpopular element in the Ottoman empire began, under cover of the First World War, two years after his book was published.

---

230 Ibid., p. 393.

231 Ibid.

232 Ibid.

233 Sir Charles Norton Edgcumbe Eliot (1862–1931), political analyst and marine biologist, had been a British diplomat in Turkey from 1893–1899. A formidable linguist (he wrote grammars for both Finnish and Swahili), the British Government sent him to Russia in 1918 to investigate the facts about the death of the imperial family.

234 C. Eliot, *Turkey in Europe* (London: Arnold, 1908), p. 408, cited in *The Lesser Eastern Churches*, op. cit., p. 393, footnote 2.

235 Ibid., p. 394.

236 Ibid.

The elements of general history Fortescue provides make possible an understanding not only of the importance of the Church to Armenians — '[u]ndoubtedly, the national Church (which in the truest sense is their "nation") has been the main factor in their preservation' — but also its peculiar shape and identity.[237] Dependent at first on the Cappadocian mother-church of Caesarea, the chief bishop of the Armenians, as was not unusual in missionary churches, bore the title 'Katholikos'. But he had no fixed see. The letters of St Basil throw light on the break with Caesarea, which arose from the ambition of an especially unpleasant ruler in the short period of Armenian independence.[238] The Katholikos now acquired the title 'Patriarch'; at the same time the first Armenian literature came to be written (in an alphabet based partly on Greek letters), and the Armenian Liturgy formed (from the Byzantine rite).

This was symbolically apt, for the civilization coming into existence would be 'mostly Greek with a less prevailing Syriac influence'.[239] The subsequent division of the country between the Roman Empire and Persia produced two Patriarchs (both itinerant: only in the Cilician Armenia of the eleventh century would a fixed seat emerge for the first time, at Sis), and that is also a harbinger of things to come. 'Armenian Church history is full of rival Patriarchs, domestic schisms and disputed successions — faithful echo of the distracted state of the nation'.[240] As to Monophysitism, though linguistic difficulties in expressing the nature-hypostasis distinction in Armenian played a part, Fortescue considers the adherence of the Armenian church to anti-Chalcedonianism to be largely political in inspiration.

> Like the Copts and Jacobites, the Armenians would not become Melkites — Emperor's men. Oddly enough, the Persian persecutor who then dominated Armenia saw the political advantage to himself of such a schism, encouraged it, and the Armenians listened for once to their greatest enemy.[241]

They took with them into schism Caspian Albania, but not their other ecclesiastical dependency, Georgia (otherwise 'Iberia'), whose own Katholikos accepted Chalcedon and was duly anathematized.

The disturbed situation of life in a country conquered and re-conquered by a succession of occupying powers; the fluctuating alliances with Byzantine Orthodox and Latin Catholics; the lack of an agreed primatial see until the fifteenth century emergence of Etshmiadzin: all of these made for considerable confusion in Church life — and explain the at first

---

237 Ibid., p. 391.
238 Basil the Great, *Letters* 120, 121, 122.
239 *The Lesser Eastern Churches*, op. cit., p. 409.
240 Ibid.
241 Ibid., p. 412.

The 'Mother Church of St. Etchmiadzin' in Russian Armenia: an example of Fortescue's illustrations in his Eastern Churches trilogy.

sight bewildering state of affairs whereby 'Gregorian' (i.e. non-Uniate) Armenians acknowledge in all five Patriarchs, though giving supreme honour to the Etshmiadzin line, whose holder bears the title 'Supreme Katholikos' or 'Katholikos of all the Armenians'. This nomenclature is a curious comment on a history little understood by Armenians themselves, for in the patristic period when these titles originated, 'Katholikos' implied a senior metropolitan himself dependent on a patriarch, not, as with the Armenian Monophysites, a super-patriarch of sorts. Fortescue notes that the patriarchs of Sis and Agthamar (near Lake Van) also claim the title 'Katholikos', though the latter is really only a titular patriarch with a single bishopric under him, but the Armenian patriarchs of Jerusalem and Constantinople do not, though in reality, owing to the (then) size of the Armenian population in the Ottoman empire, the latter must be accounted the 'second greatest prelate in the Church'.[242]

Looking at Russian Armenia (which included Etshmiadzin, and thus, by the nineteenth century, the pinnacle of Church office), Fortescue muses that, had the Tsardom treated the Armenian church with more respect, nothing would have been more likely than a reunion of Gregorian Armenians with Orthodoxy. But 'the stupid bullying of Russia' — whose government had taken control of Church property, claimed a right of veto over the appointment of the Katholikos, and forbidden all conversion to the Armenian church — 'makes Armenians cling to their Monophysism as the one principle which preserves their nation'.[243] The

242 Ibid., p. 430.
243 Ibid., p. 421.

consequence was that the Supreme Katholikos had lost all authority beyond Russian Armenia: 'to those in Turkey he is too much the creature of the Russian Government to count'.[244] In a striking observation which, characteristically enough, combines specialized knowledge with acerbity of judgment, Fortescue remarks: 'Over his vestments he wears a diamond pectoral cross given to him by the Czar. He would gladly give up this ornament to be free.'[245]

Fortescue had first-hand knowledge of the Armenians from the Levantine grand tour, and especially from Jerusalem. When he came to describe an Armenian church-building, Armenian vestments, the Armenian Liturgy, he did not always have his head in books. Through their contacts with Latins in the middle ages, Armenian Monophysites had taken some Western customs; Fortescue could not approve what they had made of them.

> The *mensa* of the altar is a narrow shelf. All is covered with gaudy cloths and white altar-cloths with lace. Then they pile on their altar and retable a very curious collection of objects. There are many candles, books showing their ornamental bindings, the liturgical fans with bells, relics, the chalice-veil, perhaps a huge mitre. All these show their gilding and finery, so that one wonders where the celebrant can find room to celebrate. The impression of the whole is like that of a Baroc [sic] Latin altar, but more full of bad ornament. Sometimes there is a tabernacle on the altar, but they do not make much of it.[246]

Fortescue was not flattering about the Armenian Liturgy, yet he saw a symbolic providence in it.

> I do not think it possible to share the natural enthusiasm of Armenians for their liturgy. It is late in type, and this mixture of foreign elements is not attractive to a liturgist. But it has the advantage of representing very well the character of their Church. Greek in essence, looking towards Syria, and much Latinized. If she is less attractive to a student from this mixture, she may through it be destined to act as a connecting-link between East and West, Greece and Syria. If Armenia could help to heal our lamentable breaches, the thanks of a united Christendom would bring her more honour than would a pure rite; and her survival during so long a martyrdom would not have been in vain.[247]

---

244 Ibid., p. 422.

245 Ibid., p. 430.

246 Ibid., pp. 433–434. He describes Armenian mitres, adopted from the Roman rite, as 'worse decorated than the worst 18th century mitres in the West', ibid., p. 436, footnote 1.

247 Ibid., p. 437.

The hope of reunion with the 'lesser' Eastern Churches

Crediting the rumour that Gregorian Armenians were better disposed towards the Catholic Church than were the members of any other of the separated Eastern Churches, this devout, if implausible, wish brought Fortescue rather smoothly to the end of his study, which concerns the 'hope of reunion'.

Fortescue considered that reunion with Orthodoxy should be the principal ecumenical aspiration of the Catholic Church, but he does not want to write off the prospects of unions with these 'lesser' Churches. After all, 'in some way they may be nearer to us than are the Orthodox. They went out so early that all that bitter later strife against the Papacy did not affect them.'[248] In purely pragmatic terms, these bodies could have only profited by help from the Catholic Church in terms of education, library facilities, the training of the clergy and other (unspecified) means of succour. 'I think no one who knows the Levant will dispute that the Uniate clergy are intellectually and morally above the others.'[249] Whatever a rational calculator might determine, he does not think the prospect likely for all that. The national principle is against it, yet these separated Christians may come to realize that 'nationalism and religion belong to different orders';[250] and they may notice that Uniate Catholics manage to combine perfectly happily the 'national and Catholic ideals'.[251]

Optimistically (and not altogether coherently in the light of these last words), Fortescue thought he saw among separated Orientals the 'growth of the Catholic ideal, as opposed to nationalism', discerning in them 'an increasing conviction that things are not right as they are, that what Christ founded was one visible united body of all his followers'.[252] Despite his rumbustiousness towards Anglicans at home, in the way he expressed himself at the close of *The Lesser Eastern Churches*, Fortescue was a genuine ecumenical pioneer.[253] 'These other Christians too are children of God, baptized as we are . . . Shall we call them heretics and schismatics? They are martyrs and sons of martyrs.'[254]

---

248 Ibid., p. 447.

249 Ibid., footnote 1.

250 Ibid., p. 448.

251 Ibid.

252 Ibid., p. 447.

253 This is the perspective on him adopted in Anthony Dragani's study, *Adrian Fortescue and the Eastern Christian Churches* (Piscataway, NJ: Gorgias Press, 2007), work which gives a very faithful, and judiciously assessed, account of Fortescue's views in the light, not least, of modern ecumenical dialogue.

254 *The Lesser Eastern Churches*, op. cit., p. 449.

Fortescue evaluated with supernatural realism, he did not write revisionist theology. 'The long blood-stain which is their history, must atone, more than atone, for their errors about Ephesus and Chalcedon. For who can doubt that when the end comes, when all men are judged, their glorious confession shall weigh heavier than their schism.'[255] And again, 'There is a promise to which these Eastern Christians have more right than we who sit in comfort under tolerant governments.'[256] The promise in question, given in the form in which it appears in the Vulgate Bible, ran: the one who confesses the Son of Man before men, the Son of Man will himself confess before his Father (Matthew 10:32).

Fortescue considered his *The Lesser Eastern Churches* to be, from a scholarly point of view, his most worthwhile book. He told Stanley Morison, '[T]he best work I have done so far is *The Lesser Eastern Churches*. There is quite a lot of solid stuff in that never before published'.[257] The section on the Copts was pertinent to a later commission. The widow of a noted French Orientalist, Jean Maspero, had been searching for someone to complete an unfinished work left by her husband at his death. Her British contact was Walter Ewing Crum (1865–1944), compiler of the 1905 *Catalogue of the Coptic Manuscripts in the British Museum* (he would go on to edit the Oxford Coptic dictionary of 1939).

Crum must have known Fortescue through the Museum, whose records include a letter of late 1919 in which Fortescue promises to undertake the work involved.[258] He reported to Morison it was hard going but rewarding:

> a difficult job, finding the references for another man's book, finishing up his chapters, joining together his loose paragraps and unfinished sentences. But I had got into it. It is a good book. I am becoming quite keen about it, am full of it all day and far into the night. I have found hundreds of references at the Brit[ish] Mus[eum].[259]

Fortescue had two helpers, Gaston Wiet and (for the assembling of the appendices) Eugène Tisserant, who went on to become Prefect of the (Roman) Congregation for the Oriental Churches. The book appeared in

255 Ibid.

256 Ibid., p. 450.

257 Cambridge University Library, MS Add. 9812/D/90, Letter to S. Morison of 25 May, 1920.

258 British Museum, Additional Manuscripts 45684. f. 10, Letter to W. E. Crum of 7 November, 1919.

259 Cambridge University Library, MS Add. 9812/D/90, Letter to S. Morison of 20 May, 1920.

1923 as *Histoire des patriarches d'Alexandrie depuis la mort de l'empéreur Anastase jusqu'à la réconciliation des Eglise jacobites (518–610)* under the auspices of the prestigious *Bibliothèque de l'Ecole des Hautes Etudes*, an official organ of the French State.[260]

III. The Catholic Eastern Churches

Because Fortescue left his book on the Uniate churches in a radically incomplete state, it is good that we have the pages in his brief essay *The Eastern Churches* where he gives in tiny compass the overview death prevented him from writing, no doubt much more compendiously, in the last book of his Oriental trilogy. He describes shortly the Chaldean Catholic Church, with its patriarch at Mosul, where the Dominicans were responsible for printing the liturgical books of the Chaldaean rite books and ran a college for the training of the clergy, and highlights its three monasteries of Rabban Hormuzd (near Mosul), Alkosh and St George on the Tigris (also near Mosul). On the Copts, he explains that the patriarch resides at Cairo where the Jesuits take care of a college for the education of the priests of the Coptic Catholic Church, though students, he reports, also go to Beirut and Rome. He notes the smallness of the Abyssinian Uniate body, still under a Latin vicar apostolic at Keren and using the Roman rite in Ge'ez until the Oriental rite can be 'restored', at which point, he thinks 'there should be a Uniate Abuna under the Uniate Coptic Patriarch'.[261] (One wonders in what sense the Ethiopian Catholic Church of this date can be regarded as including *Eastern* Catholics at all.)

As for the Syrian Uniates, the patriarch, who lives at Beirut, has, Fortescue records, eight suffragan sees and several monasteries within his remit, while the Uniate Armenians are gathered under the patriarch of Cilicia, resident at Constantinople, since, 'for a long time the Catholic Armenian Patriarchs officially represented all the other Uniate churches before the Turkish government'.[262] A relatively numerous body (Fortescue estimates one-hundred and thirty-thousand Armenian Uniates in Turkey, Persia and Egypt), their Church included, in canonical independence of its patriarch, the Armenian communities of Austria-Hungary and the Russian empire.

Fortescue tells of the Malabar Uniates that their liturgical practice consists of the Chaldaean rite in Syriac, considerably romanised. The disadvantages

---

260 J. Maspero, *Histoire des patriarches d'Alexandrie depuis la mort de l'empereur Anastase jusqu'à la réconciliation des Eglise jacobites (518–610)*. Ouvrage revu et publié après la mort de l'auteur par le R. Adrien Fortescue, D.D., D.Ph., et Gaston Weit (Paris: Edouard Champion, 1923).

261 *Eastern Churches* (London: Catholic Truth Society, 1909), p. 26.

262 Ibid., p. 30.

under which they laboured jurisdictionally are indicated in their mode of governance: they were in the pastoral care of two Latin vicars-apostolic who, however, dealt with them via vicars-general of their own tradition. On the Maronites, while venturing no judgment on the disputed question, Do they constitute, on Mount Lebanon, a distinct ethnicity?, Fortescue is in no way undecided about the possible link between the Maronites of the ancient Church and Monothelitism. 'In spite of their own vehement assertion of perpetual catholicity there is no doubt that they were once Monotheletes [sic] and that their separate organization is the relic of what was once a schismatical Monothelete church'.[263] But, he finds, '[t]here is, of course, no trace of their former heresy among them now; their splendid fidelity to the Catholic faith and to Catholic unity amidst Moslems and schismatics has long atoned for their original schism.'[264] The Maronite patriarch, we hear, has the title 'Patriarch of Antioch and all the East', even though 'he in no sense represents the old line', which did not, however, prevent him from always taking the name 'Peter' (St Peter had his chair at Antioch before he moved to Rome) and living in a 'great palace in the Lebanon'.[265] Though Fortescue again reports a certain Latinization of a Syrian liturgy, he notes the interesting practice whereby the Maronite liturgical books print their rubrics in Arabic, in a Syriac script, a combination called (apparently) 'Karshuni'.[266]

That Maronites are all in Roman communion does not make them the largest of the Eastern Catholic churches for this honour falls to the Uniates of Byzantine rite, in their various sub-divisions which, writing in 1909, he lists as: Melkite (using, liturgically, Arabic interspersed with Greek), Greek ('scattered about Turkey and in Greece'),[267] Georgian (at Constantinople), Ruthenian (in Austra-Hungary and 'hidden still in corners of Russia'), Bulgarian, Roumanian (in Roumania and Transylvania), and Italo-Greek (in southern Italy and Sicily, with their monastery at Grottaferrata, and colonies at Livorno ('Leghorn'), Malta, Algiers, Marseilles, and on Corsica.

Through the accident that Fortescue began the unfinished *Uniate Eastern Churches* with the latter, we have much more from his pen on the Italo-Greeks than on any of the rest. Though before his untimely death Fortescue managed to write the chapter on the Melkites, no *disjecta membra* were left for an editor to assemble, so as to describe the Uniate bodies that correspond to the Nestorian and Monophysite communions treated in *The Lesser Eastern Churches* or indeed to report in depth on the Maronites, a substantial account

---

263 Ibid., p. 27.
264 Ibid., p. 28.
265 Ibid., p. 29.
266 Ibid., p. 29.
267 Ibid., p. 31.

of whom Fortescue had planned for the fourth and final part of the new book.[268] Hence the sub-title given editorially to the torso that appeared in 1923, 'The Byzantine Rite in Italy, Sicily, Syria and Egypt'.

The Italo-Greeks

Fortescue was familiar enough with the Italo-Greeks from visits to the much-loved monastery at Grottaferrata, of which an encomium had already appeared in *The Orthodox Eastern Church*. Now he had the opportunity to re-visit (in reflection and writing), and to place it in a wider setting. The Italo-Greeks are the 'original Greek-speaking inhabitants of Lower Italy and Sicily' who, considerably Latinised by the fifteenth century, were subsequently 'fortified, almost, one might say, revived' in their liturgical identity by 'an immigration of Albanians'.[269]

Fortescue stresses how close the eastern cities of southern Italy are to Greece; indeed, even Sicily is closer to Athens than is Cyprus. It is hardly surprising that the Greek tongue, and the Greek liturgical tradition, should flourish there, yet the situation was complex. There was Latin influence, yes, but it was not necessarily Roman, as the late sixth century Neapolitan lectionary evidence attests — even if, at any rate in Lower Italy, the bishops were subject to the pope not only as patriarch but even as metropolitan. Then the Greek rites in use could hardly have been, in early centuries, 'Byzantine', since the Byzantine rite was as yet unformed. Fortescue thinks they were probably akin to those of Antioch.

> Because of the close connection of Greater Greece with Constantinople, no doubt these rites developed in much the same direction as that of Constantinople. There would naturally be constant Byzantine influence over bishops who had so much to do with the capital. But the formal imposition of the Byzantine rite is part of the work of the Emperors from the eighth century.[270]

The attempt to remove Sicily, Calabria and Apulia from Roman ecclesiastical governance and replace it with Constantinopolitan (ongoing in the eighth to the eleventh centuries) failed, and while the Norman kings made no attempt to extirpate the Byzantine liturgy as such, '[t]he general trend after the Norman conquest was that the Byzantine bishops were succeeded by Latins'.[271] This did not mean, however, that the Greek

---

268 For the scheme, see the 'Editor's Preface' (by G.D. Smith), in *The Uniate Eastern Churches* (London: Burns Oates and Washbourne, 1923).

269 Ibid., p. 47.

270 Ibid., p. 75.

271 Ibid., p. 98.

patrimony disappeared. 'Under the Latin bishops there remained Byzantine churches, Byzantine priests, monasteries, and institutions of various kinds, all through the Middle Ages.'[272] These areas remained 'channels of Greek learning for the West'.[273] It was in the monasteries that islands of Byzantine Christianity could best flourish in a Latin sea. 'The parish clergy, under a Latin bishop, easily forsook the foreign rite for his; but the monasteries were closed corporations, much less liable to such influence.'[274]

Fortescue was convinced by evidence amassed by the eighteenth century Italian historian Pietro Pompilio Rodotà,[275] and a contemporary French successor, Fortescue's friend Cyril Karalevsky (Charon),[276] that by the early modern period — even for the monks — the situation was dire. Immigration (chiefly Albanian but also Cretan), of Byzantine-rite Christians fleeing from the Turks came in the nick of time to save the Italo-Greek world. So when turning to the contemporary state of affairs, Fortescue can state, in all simplicity, 'There are still Italo-Greeks, though now they are all Albanian'.[277]

Among their institutions he gives pride of place to 'the dear monastery of the Mother of God at Grottaferrata'.[278] He praises the monks of Grottaferrata in lyrical terms for the perfection of their liturgy, the excellence of their scholarship, and even the grove of trees they have planted around the (ceremonially employed) fountain outside their monastery — as 'ought to be at every monastery of the rite'.[279] The warmth of his writing is explained when he tells us in a note,

> Years ago, when I was a student at Rome, it was at Grottaferrata that I first learned to be interested in the Byzantine liturgy. It was from a Grottaferrata monk that I learned to speak Greek. After nineteen years, on Sunday, February 9, 1913, I stood again in that church and heard the heavenly music of the Trisagion, the Cherubikon, *Eis hagios, eis hagios, Iêsous Christos eis doxan Theou*

---

272 Ibid., p. 99.

273 Ibid., p. 101.

274 Ibid., p. 129.

275 P.P. Rodotà, *Dell' origine, progresso e stato presente del Rito Greco in Italia* (Rome: salomoni, 1758–1763, 3 vols). Fortescue's use of Rodotà's work enabled him to present a mass of circumstantial material about a variety of localities, including the Greek Uniate communities at Venice, Ancona and Bibbona (in Tuscany), all of which were extinct by Fortescue's day.

276 C. Karalevsky, *Documenit inediti per servire alla storia delle chiese italo-greche* (Rome: Bretschneider, 1911).

277 *The Uniate Eastern Churches*, op. cit., p. 146.

278 Ibid.

279 Ibid., p. 149.

Patros, before the Ikonostasion. So I thought of the days when I had stood there, a boy in my purple cassock, and I thanked God for all Grottaferrata had given me.[280]

The Greek College in Rome, which was far less ancient — its bull of erection is dated 1577, whereas Grottaferrata is tenth century — did not engage his affections in the same way. It produced some fine priests, bishops and scholars (some of whom, as he notes, reverted to Orthodoxy), but he finds it inexplicable that at the beginning the College used habitually the Roman liturgy and only occasionally the Greek, and regrettable that its direction was entrusted to Jesuits who often sought to persuade the students to enter the Society. '[T]he money spent on the education of these boys was certainly not intended to provide a nursery for future Jesuits.'[281] Fortunately, Leo XIII transformed the situation in both respects (exclusively Byzantine worship, and no more Jesuits), but a church can hardly consist of monks and clerics but no people. So Fortescue's last pages on the Italo-Greeks are devoted to a description of their village life in Calabria and Sicily (and at Livorno, which he calls by the old English name 'Leghorn', and on Corsica as well).

Melkites

As Fortescue points out, the term 'Melkite' (often also spelled in English 'Melchite') originally denoted the Chalcedonian Orthodox in Syro-Palestine and Egypt. The Antiochene patriarchs, despite the quarrels with the Holy See of their Constantinopolitan brothers, had been in at any rate fluctuating union with Rome. By the time he was writing *The Uniate Eastern Churches* Fortescue had a more nuanced account of how the Eastern schism took hold south of Constantinople. In accents that are new compared with his stance in *The Orthodox Eastern Church* he calls the schism a 'gradual, a very gradual, parting of the ways', and adds by way of description of the outcome: 'The Melkites represent the tendency, never quite extinct, towards union with Rome, now crystallized in one Church; the Orthodox represent the other tendency towards Constantinople crystallized in another'.[282] But by contrast with his pre-War writings, in the posthumously published study he identified a precise point for the introduction of the term 'Melkite' in its present-day acceptation — namely for Byzantine Christians of the

---

280 Ibid., p. 150, footnote 4. 'One is holy, one is holy, Jesus Christ, to the glory of God the Father'.

281 Ibid., p. 157.

282 Ibid., p. 190. He thinks something analogous was the case at Alexandria as well, ibid., pp. 194–197. Fortescue had little information about Jerusalem, ibid. p. 197.

Antiochene patriarchate in union with Rome. It was, he now claimed, by a deliberate act of the first patriarch of the *continuous* Uniate line, Cyril VI — who in 1724 'left the more common name [Orthodox] to his rivals and annexed "Melkite" for his flock'.[283]

That was a change of mind since contributing 'Melkites' to the (1911) tenth volume of the *Catholic Encyclopaedia* when he had thought it by some inexplicable shift of idiom that the term became restricted in the early modern period to those Antiochene Chalcedonians who were in union not with Constantinople but with Rome.[284] It is an example of how Fortescue was constantly updating his knowledge of *Orientalia*. In the case of the Melkites he paid especial homage to a French Catholic priest of the Byzantine rite, Cyril Charon (mentioned briefly above), whom he had met on the Levantine grand tour and whose exhaustive *Histoire des Patriarchats melkites,* which began publication in Paris in 1911, he regarded as the *ne plus ultra* for a scientific history of an Eastern Catholic Church.[285]

Fortescue rehearses the difficulties of the patriarchal succession among the Melkite (i.e. Uniate) portion of the Syrian, Palestinian and Egyptian Orthodox. That the Porte recognized only an Orthodox *millet* for Byzantine Christians enabled the schismatic authorities to meddle with impunity in Melkite affairs, which were themselves complicated by a curious sympathy with the papally condemned Synod of Pistoia (1786). One might have thought that was because Pistoia's Jansenist notions of liturgy and Church governance were seen as closer to Eastern models. Fortescue is inclined to find the explanation, rather, in biography — specifically, in the friendship between the Melkite theologian Germanos Ādam, who in 1777 became metropolitan of Aleppo, his native city, and Scipio Ricci, the bishop of Pistoia. Under Maximus III (in office 1833 to 1855), 'Melkite Gallicanism', as Fortescue calls it, waned,[286] though this was not through any false modesty on the part of the occupant of the patriarchal throne. In 1838 the latter obtained from the Holy See the right to add the titles of Alexandria and Jerusalem to that of Antioch, on the ground that he and his predecessors had long administered the small Melkite communities beyond Syria. Fortescue describes this as a personal honour, rather than a heritable title, citing the *Annuario pontificio* for 1915 as evidence that any ongoing claim goes unrecognized at Rome.

To complete the cup of Melkite satisfaction, there is another see whose name might (but to Orthodox fury) be added to the rest. As Fortescue reports, 'I have heard it whispered in Syria that Cyril VIII [with whom

283 Ibid., p. 186.

284 'Melkites (Melchites)', *Catholic Encylopaedia* X (1911), pp. 157–161, and here at p. 158.

285 *The Uniate Eastern Churches*, op. cit., p. 185, fn 1.

286 *The Uniate Eastern Churches*, op. cit., p. 211.

he had stayed in Damascus] had vague dreams of being Oecumenical Patriarch,' commenting indulgently on this potentially damaging velleity, 'People in the East love titles'.[287] To do Cyril VIII justice, Fortescue noted that the 'present custom is for the Patriarch to divide his time between Cairo and Damascus, at both of which he has houses', though he adds, 'He is rarely at Jerusalem, where his flock is very small'.[288] This at least indicates a modicum of ministerial *disponibilité*.

Fortescue noted how Melkite patriarchs are elected by the bishops of their Church, but confirmed by Rome: the 'modern' system of seeking confirmation by telegraph, so Fortescue implies, avoids any delay which might give an unfortunate appearance of Roman foot-dragging.[289] Fortescue also records that the enthronement of the patriarch does not actually wait upon the arrival of news from Rome.[290] Then as now Melkites were touchy about their rights.

Conclusion on the Eastern Churches

Fortescue was an impassioned spokesman for the Uniate churches — and a defender of the adjective *unitus* which, as he says, is simply a technical condensation of the phrase *Orientales uniti sanctae sedi*, 'Easterners united to the Holy See', or *Ecclesia unita ecclesiae romanae*, 'a church united to the Roman church'. (Incidentally, he claims the English word originates from the Russian: there is no Latin adjective *uniatus*.)[291] He finds Uniates 'from every point of view . . . the aristocracy of Eastern Christians. It may not be a very splendid aristocracy, but, compared with the others, it is a real aristocracy, intellectual and moral'.[292] This judgment may, of course, be queried, but it cannot be said it was made without a determined attempt — via the Levantine grand tour — to assess the situation on the ground.

Eastern Catholics mattered enormously to Fortescue as an apologist for the Roman Catholic Church. 'They are an exceedingly important factor in our concept of the universal Church; they are our great palpable argument that the primacy of Rome is more than Patriarchal rights over part of the Church. Indeed, in some ways, it is just the Uniates who save the whole situation, from our point of view.'[293] Though they have, he thinks, when

---

287 Ibid., p. 224.
288 Ibid., p. 225.
289 'Melkites (Melchites),', art. cit., p. 160.
290 *The Uniate Eastern Churches*, op. cit., p. 223.
291 Ibid., p. 1.
292 Ibid., p. 27.
293 Ibid.

faced with lingering abuses, 'that salutary fear of Rome and what Rome will say, to repress the *animalis homo*,'[294] more fundamentally he divined in them a similar attitude to the see of Rome (and the Roman curia) as his own.

> The really wonderful thing about the Uniates is not that occasionally they have grumbled; it is, in spite of that, in spite of blunders made by the West towards them, their magnificent loyalty to the Catholic ideal. It is the right sort of loyalty, to an ideal, not to persons. They have no more personal devotion towards Italian Cardinals and the Monsignori of the Roman congregations than we have in the North. What they care for is the one united Church of Christ throughout the world, and the Holy See as guarding that unity. They see around them the same process of erosion among the schismatics as we see among the Protestants; and they, too, understand that the bond of union among Catholics is our common loyalty to the primate-see.[295]

It is, for Fortescue, 'not their fault, nor ours, that [the Uniates] are now much smaller than the Western branch. If some day the schismatics come back to union with Rome, then they will all be Uniates and it will be impossible for any one to make what is always a ludicrous mistake by saying that all Catholics are Latins, use the Roman rite, have a celibate clergy, and so on. Meanwhile, whether they are great or small bodies, Uniates have as much right to their own liturgies, customs, and laws as we have to ours [he means, in the Latin West]'.[296] For 'Uniates represent exactly the old eastern churches as they were before the schism cut them off. They have absolutely the same right to the name Catholic that we have'.[297] He gives the impression he would almost like to say they have more right, calling on Latins to 'revere with special honour those who stand by this ideal under the greatest difficulties'.[298]

---

294 Ibid., p. 26.

295 Ibid., p. 23.

296 *Eastern Churches*, op. cit., pp. 23–24.

297 Ibid., p. 23.

298 *The Uniate Eastern Churches*, op. cit., p. 29.

6. Letchworth and Beyond

Arrival at Letchworth

The death of Fortescue's aunt during his Near-Eastern stay (appropriately enough, for an unmarried Edwardian lady, she succumbed in Florence, and had been buried at San Miniato) left him without a home in England. On appointment to the first English 'Garden City', Letchworth, with responsibility for building a church for the needs of the Catholic community, he wisely decided he would make it into the home he had lost.[1] Increasingly resigned, and if sometimes regretful, or at least wistful, when considering what might have been, he was not for all that unhappy. That is because he was able to pour all his talents into the various aspects of what, in the judgment of many, could serve as a model of a well-catechised and liturgically exemplary parish life.

It is difficult to agree with Michael Davies's opinion that a parish 'less suited to [Fortescue's] talents and his temperament could hardly be imagined'.[2] Whoever among the authorities of the Archdiocese of Westminster took the decision that Letchworth would be right for Fortescue deserves full marks for sensitivity and imagination. The place perfectly suited his Morrisian enthusiasms, as did many of its first inhabitants. Under the direction of the creator of the Garden City concept, Letchworth was planned by two architects with strong Morris connexions, Raymond Unwin, a supporter of Morris's Socialist League and Barry Parker, who was much involved in the Arts and Crafts Movement.

Davies was perhaps thinking of the absolute beginnings of Fortescue's mission, when, *faute de mieux*, he was obliged to organize worship in a 'shed' — one of the wooden buildings thrown up by the Letchworth Corporation to house workers for the new town. In 1907, so Davies reports, the Arden Press moved to Letchworth bringing with it a number

---

1   R. Beevers, *The Garden City Utopia. A Critical Biography of Ebenezer Howard* (London: Macmillan, 1988). Howard originated the term 'Garden City', and much of the concept, though it has roots in the thinking of Ruskin and Morris.

2   M. Davies, 'Adrian Fortescue Priest and Scholar', in idem., *The Wisdom of Adrian Fortescue*, op. cit., p. 34.

of Catholic employees (Bernard Newdigate, the son of the Press's founder, figures later in this story).[3] Fortescue celebrated his first public Mass in the shed in question on the First Sunday of Advent, 1907, describing its condition in a visitation report for the diocese.

> The shed is partitioned in two — one half used as an infant school. There are broken windows and the children have kicked holes in the partition. The building is mean and ragged and against one wall there is a poor altar. The Blessed Sacrament is not reserved except on Sundays. A bedraggled curtain across one corner serves as a confessional. There are a dozen or more broken chairs, two or three benches. And a number of deal boards, resting on bricks. There are twenty men, twenty-seven women and fifty-four children in the parish.[4]

The children were, of course, the hope for the future. It was only four years, after all, since the limited dividend company 'First Garden City' had been formed to develop an estate of some three-thousand eight-hundred acres between Hitchin and Baldock. The Church had done quite well to get in on the act so soon. Fortescue was energetic in capitalizing on what he found in place.

Parochial — but in no pejorative sense

Catechising children, instructing converts, and the careful celebration of the Liturgy and such para-liturgical ceremonies as Rosary and Benediction, were, along with visiting the sick, the staple of Adrian Fortescue's priestly life. A useful sidelight on how he saw the first of these duties is contained in a letter to Hamilton Macdonald who had consulted him about catechetical materials. Fortescue thought no one book satisfactory, either through lack of proportion or through 'adding things that are not part of the faith' or by virtue (or, rather, vice) of being 'rather mawkish'. He recommended the thripenny Catechism (originally the 'Penny Catechism') supplemented by talks, which would amplify that succinct text in three areas: the Liturgy, the main epochs of Church history, and the lives of the saints — he especially recommended the latter, since hagiology could incorporate, in painless fashion, a good deal of history, dogma and morals. 'I found that worked very well with quite rough boys once — they remember the story because it hangs round one figure (make it all vivid and dramatic) and they get very enthusiastic about the heroes — and that is always good for them'.[5]

---

3   Ibid., p. 35.
4   Cited ibid.
5   Westminster Archdiocesan Archives, Box AGD, Letter to Hamilton Macdonald of 12 November 1907.

Parochial duties aside, he found — and intended to find — plenty of time not only for entertaining, and being entertained by, parishioners and friends but for reading and research, writing and the attending of London lectures as well. In the first half of 1908 that meant: writing up his patristic and travel notes in *The Greek Fathers*; researching Persian Christianity and the reception of Nestorius' theology at the British Museum; attending lectures on the folksong tradition of Montenegro at the Anglo-Russian Society — where on 3 March he would deliver the lecture on the Eastern Schism noted in the last chapter, and listen to a lecture by the Blake scholar Joseph Wicksteed on the 'Marriage of Heaven and Hell' (was Blake a Nietzschean avant la lettre, he wondered?). Fortescue was producing articles on such diverse topics as the Byzantine Liturgy, Heinrich Denzinger (the late nineteenth century compiler of the standard collection of dogmatic texts), and the Use of Durham, all for the *Catholic Encyclopaedia*;[6] and reading on matters liturgical two of the premier French Catholic students of ancient Christianity, Dom Fernand Cabrol (1855–1937),[7] and Mgr Louis Duchesne (1843–1922).[8]

There was much to do in starting up a new mission, or, as he put it in a letter of November 1907, to begin 'a new place *ab ovo*'.

> I must hire a cottage, buy furniture and crockery, find a housekeeper, get a tabernacle, wine, azyme bread, vestments — every mortal thing, down to a sanctuary bell and altar cards . . . I hope that we shall really have a decent and creditable little church for once. Spooner [the architect Sir Charles Sydney Spooner, 1862–1938, Fortescue's cousin] is designing everything — crucifix, tabernacle, candlesticks and we are going to have a royal time getting it all right — really right and no cheap brass-ware from the wholesale people!

6   'Constantinople, The Rite of', in C.G. Herbermann et al. (ed.), *The Catholic Encyclopaedia. An International Work of Reference on the Constitution, Doctrine, Discipline, and History of the Catholic Church IV* (London: Caxton, and New York: Robert Appleton, 1908), pp. 312–320; 'Denzinger, Heinrich Joseph Dominicus', ibid., pp. 736–737; 'Durham Rite', ibid., V, pp. 213–214. The first and third of these articles will be discussed in Chapter 7 below. On the second, it is characteristic that Fortescue draws attention to Denzinger's little known Oriental interests as expressed in his *Ritus Orientalium, Coptorum, Syrorum et Armenorum* (Würzburg: Stahelianis, 1863–1864, 2 vols.)

7   Cabrol was abbot (from 1903) of St Michael's Abbey, Farnborough, Hampshire, then a monastery of the French Benedictine Congregation.

8   Duchesne had become rector of the *Ecole française* at Rome in 1897; his *Origines du Culte chrétien: Etude sur la liturgie latine avant Charlemagne* (Paris: Thorin, 1899) had long been a classic; he was currently engaged on the early volumes of his *Histoire ancienne de l'Eglise* (Paris: Fontemoing, 1906–1910).

And he added, 'Please God the outward rightness of things we hope to get for the church will be a right symbol of the more important things that one does not see', describing the whole project as one of 'building up a little branch of the great vine and clothing the hidden beauty of the sacraments and the unseen presence with something of the *decor domus tuae* that it hurts one so often to miss'.[9]

The work proceeded quickly, and, under Fortescue's direction, in a unconventional manner. In the summer of 1908 a Letchworth newspaper produced a report on the result under the headline, 'Opening of New Catholic Church'.

> It is only twelve months since a small body of Catholics assembled at Ashley Cottage, Black Road, the residence of Mr B. Newdigate to hear the first Mass said in Letchworth since the Reformation, the celebrant being the Rev. Charles Newdigate, S.J. Arrangements were subsequently made whereby one of the sheds which had been built for the unemployed who helped to make some of the roads in Letchworth, were utilized for Divine Service. At the end of November last year the Rev. Adrian Fortescue, D.D., was appointed to take charge of the Catholic Mission of Letchworth. On Sunday last the new church was solemnly blessed and opened by the Most Rev. Patrick Fenton, Bishop of Amycla, auxiliary of Westminster. The event was of more than ordinary significance owing to the fact that it was the first time in the history of the Catholic Church in England that the liturgies of the Orient and Occident have been celebrated at the opening of a church.

The report noted that Fortescue had sung the responses to the Byzantine liturgy in Greek and Arabic, while at the luncheon following in the Letchworth Hall Hotel the visiting bishop had spoken of him in 'very eulogistic terms': 'Dr Fortescue was worthy of a Chair in a University, but he was like the humble violet, he bloomed and shed his fragrance in Letchworth.'[10]

The metaphor was apt, for Fortescue allowed his knowledge and artistic skills to be widely tapped by the inhabitants. It was noted after his death:

> His services were at the disposal of everyone. I doubt if anyone who asked him to give a lecture, or translate a letter, or clear up a difficulty, went away disappointed. If the book club wanted a Dante lecture, or the dramatic society wanted help in their

9   Westminster Diocesan Archive, Box AGD, Letter to Hamilton Macdonald of 27 November 1907.

10 Text as cited from the Letchworth newspaper, *The Citizen*, in J.R. McCarthy, *Adrian*, op. cit.

St Hugh's Catholic Church, Letchworth: an unpretentious building that Fortescue
considered all glorious within.

costumes for *Everyman*, or the golf club wanted an illuminated
address, they all knew their way to the presbytery, and Dr.
Fortescue always found time somehow to do what they wanted.[11]

The Eucharistic Congress

On 15 July Fortescue received a visit from Cardinal Bourne on a matter
which would occupy him for much of the rest of the year and gain him
a deal of publicity. Bourne brought an invitation; he wanted Fortescue
to arrange a celebration of the Byzantine Liturgy for the forthcoming
Eucharistic Congress, an international event in modern Catholicism, as
of 1881, when the first such gathering took place in Lille, in northern
France. The 1908 Congress was to be held in London, where the eyes of the
Catholic world would, accordingly, for a brief space be turned.

Just back from the Levant and currently engaged in incorporating visual
memories into the text of *The Greek Fathers*, the request was appropriately
timed. It was a unique opportunity to make better known among Catholics
a liturgy which had become, for the Orthodox, the worshipping form of
the Eastern patristic tradition as a whole. Fortescue accepted, and there
began a flurry of activity: designing vestments, preparing the Byzantine
chant, in collaboration with the director of the Russian choir in London

11 E. Cowell, 'Adrian Fortescue', *Blackfriars* IV. 41 (1923), pp. 1029–1034, and
here at p. 1034.

and with R.R. Terry (Richard Runciman Terry, 1865–1938), the master of music at Westminster Cathedral, and producing his own translation of the Greek text, with an introduction, to enable the intelligent assistance of those who would attend.[12]

Fortescue's orchestration of the celebration of the Liturgy of St John Chrysostom at the 1908 Eucharistic Congress was certainly a high-point of his public life as a priest. The official report claimed that the Byzantine Liturgy had never before been celebrated by Uniates in England. (Strictly speaking, that could hardly be correct, since, as we have just seen, Fortescue had arranged for a celebration in connexion with the consecration of the new church at Letchworth.) The archimandrite who officiated had been brought over from the Melkite parish in Paris, S. Julien-le-Pauvre, but even with a celebrant thoroughly accustomed to the rite, entrusting its performance, so far as deacon, acolytes, and choir were concerned, to Latin Christians in a building designed for the Western Liturgy and a context of intense public scrutiny, must have made for some anxiety on the part of the Congress organizers.

The author of the report, who paid tribute to Fortescue — 'the Revd Dr Fortescue, who superintended the arrangements in all their details' — found the rite 'impressive and wonderful'.[13] But he could not forbear to note the drawback to full participation represented by the iconostasis, which had been erected for the occasion in the sanctuary of Westminster Cathedral, declaring with breathtaking arrogance: '[I]n this, as in all things, Rome [i.e. the Roman rite] points the better way, to the open sanctuary and the closer union of Christ with his brethren'.[14] Fortescue was hardly responsible for this brutally naked statement of opinion. The simplistic mind-set about the inter-relation of liturgy and architecture which had raised up so much opposition to A.W.N. Pugin's revival of the classic mediaeval English choir-screen was obviously still alive and well in the early twentieth century Catholic Church.[15]

One wonders whether this unique celebration of the Byzantine Liturgy was noticed by the 'No Popery' brigade whose protests led Herbert Asquith, the Liberal Prime Minister, to pressurise Bourne into abandoning the

---

12 *The Divine Liturgy of Our Father among the Saints, John Chrysostom*, translated by Adrian Fortescue (London: Catholic Truth Society, 1908).

13 *Report of the Nineteenth Eucharistic Congress held at Westminster from 9ᵗʰ to 13ᵗʰ September 1908* (London and Edinburgh: Sands and Company, 1909), pp. 449–451, and here at p. 451.

14 Ibid., p. 450.

15 'A screen, partially veiling the sanctuary, attracts the gaze and at the same time resists it, emphasizing both the centrality and the impenetrable mystery of the Mass', R. Hill, *Pugin and the Building of Romantic Britain* (London: Allen Lane, 2007), p. 210.

proposed procession through London streets with the Blessed Sacrament.[16] Byzantine worship, carried out by those in union with Rome, showed the Catholic Church to be more than its Western patriarchate, and certainly more that the Italianate style favoured by many nineteenth century Neo-Ultramontanes. Despite his attachment to the Roman rite well celebrated, this corresponded precisely to Fortescue's intentions. One of the reasons for thinking Fortescue a worthy object of study by Catholics of later generations is precisely the fullness of his catholicity. (It will also become apparent below that he had considered transferring to the Byzantine rite.)

A round of activities — and self-doubt

Though there could hardly be a repetition of the 'great day' at the Cathedral (a 'one-off' event on 12 September), in other respects the pattern of the first year at Letchworth would persist. In 1909–10, for instance, we find Fortescue working on various short articles on Armenian and Byzantine topics for the *Catholic Encyclopaedia*, looking at Ambrosian and Mozarabic missals in the British Museum for more data on the Western rites, and gathering materials for an essay on the *Cherubikon*, the hymn at the Great Entrance in the Greek Liturgy. The essay was destined for a contribution to Dom Cabrol's highly prestigious *Dictionnaire d'Archéologie et de liturgie* (1907–1953), co-edited with his fellow monk of Farnborough, Dom Henri Leclerq (with whom Fortescue had to stay in Letchworth in the early spring of 1909).[17] We find him at Caxton Hall, to attend a meeting of Joseph Wicksteed's London Society for the Study of Religion; penning journalistic pieces for *The Tablet* (in June 1909, for instance, he was reporting the 'English Church Pageant', a 'history of the English Church as conceived by Ritualists' — held in the grounds of Fulham Palace, the residence of the Bishop of London, the pageant included an appearance of G.K. Chesterton as Dr Johnson),[18] and in the following year speaking at Cambridge on the text known as the 'Apostolic Constitutions' (in the presence of Dom Hugh Connolly of Downside, 1873–1948, warden of Benet House, the Downside Hostel in Lady Margaret Road, from 1904–1916), a rather temerarious act as

---

16 T. Harwood, 'Public Opinion and the 1908 Eucharistic Congress', *Recusant History* 25 (2000), pp. 120–133.

17 Downside Archive, IX AF, Box E, 'Diary 1909–1910', entry for 9 March 1909. For Leclerq, see T. Klauser, '*Henri Leclerq, 1869-1945. Vom Autodidakten zum Kompilator grossen Stils* (Münster: 1977, Jahrbuch für Antike und Christentum, Ergänzungsband 5).

18 Downside Archive, IX AF, Box E, 'Diary 1909–1910', entry for 15 June, 1909.

subsequent events would show.[19] He enjoyed the liturgical extravaganza of the consecration of Westminster Cathedral on the Vigil of SS Peter and Paul, 1910, where he was Master of Ceremonies to Bishop Francis Mostyn of Menevia at the hallowing of the altar in the Cathedral's chapel of St George and the Martyrs of England.[20] He also contributed an account of the Eastern ceremonies for consecrating a church to the commemorative book prepared for the occasion.[21]

More prosaically, he read Ada Earland's *Ruskin and his Circle*,[22] and, in the build-up to Christmas 1910, went off on a book-buying expedition to Heffer's in Cambridge. 1910 was the year he began at Letchworth a reading class in Dante (in Italian) which he continued right up to his death.[23] It was not a monotonous life, then, yet Fortescue was easily bored by the duller aspects of a parochial charge. In August 1908, he penned an impatient note to Mrs Courtenay Crickmer, the wife of one of the architectural team working on the Garden City and (through the circumstance that Fortescue had been at school with her brother-in-law) among his earliest Letchworth contacts.

It belongs with a series of letters made available to John R. McCarthy; by a process of elimination from among the acknowledgements in his book, these may be assumed to be the 'copies of Adrian's letter to her mother' given him by Mrs J.E.T. Cruse.[24]

> Today I have a letter from the ladies' committee asking for a scheme for decorating the hall. I have just written them a beast of a letter saying I know they will hang up garlands and tissue-paper roses and calico banners and that I will have no truck with all their infectious filth.

He made clear he was already — only two months after his church had opened — the victim of *Wanderlust*.

> Think of Tirol now and lying on the long grass under the white peaks and hearing cowbells where the meadows slope down to the hurrying water, and think of Rhineland, where the wine is nearly ripe now. And I think of Umbria and the tawny cities that crown the hills – the white road to Assisi . . . I want to go away so bad. This

19 Ibid., entry for 10 March, 1910. For Connolly's criticism of Fortescue see pages 201–203.

20 Ibid., entry for 28 June, 1910.

21 'The Rite of Consecration in the East', in Abbot Bergh (ed.), *The Official Handbook of the Consecration of Westminster Cathedral* (London: Burns and Oates, 1910), pp. 68–78.

22 A. Earland, *Ruskin and his Circle* (London: Hutchinson, 1910).

23 C.B. Purdom, *Life over Again* (London: Dent, 1951), p. 245.

24 J.R. McCarthy, *Adrian*, op. cit., 'Preface'.

day last year I sat at Qadi'koy [Kadiköy, otherwise Chalcedon] and heard the mu'ezzin call as I looked across as the Golden Horn and saw the great ships ploughing up from the Black Sea.[25]

Wanting to 'go away to a Christian country so bad' could, it seems, include taking an Islamic country easily enough in its stride.

It has to be admitted it was not the sort of gritty priestly existence presumed by Fortescue's first bishop, Herbert Vaughan. Formed in the school of Manning, Vaughan's principal preoccupations for the clergy at large were the celebration of the sacraments, social relief, and (a specialty of his own as founder of the St Joseph's Missionary Society at Mill Hill) foreign missions.[26] He manifested, according to David Mathew, 'an entire absence of interest in anything concerned with literature and the arts', though Mathew adds a possibly saving clause, 'except in so far as they bore upon religion'.[27] Vaughan's successor, Francis Bourne, was a less driven if also more reticent character, but that is not to say his ideas of priestly work and life-style differed *toto caelo* from those of his predecessor.

Certain feelings of guilt come to the surface in a letter Fortescue wrote on 2 August 1909, when describing his participation in a preached archdiocesan Retreat.[28] 'In my heart I am not really a bit keen about poor people and working up a thriving parish, and young men's clubs and schools. Of course I wish I were.'[29] He considered (in the letter) two possibilities. One was remaining as priest of the diocese, but with a mandate to write:

> I am sure there is room for a few student-priests among us —
> there will never be more than very few. So if I am to go on as a
> secular priest it would seem more reasonable that I should do
> the kind of work that I am naturally good at (that is wanted too)
> than what I should never do as well as heaps of other men.[30]

But, at a deeper level, he feared this was not sufficiently a priestly life — at any rate in the way he was already living it (in effect) at that time. 'My soul is going to sleep and rotting till the end comes.'[31] In that perspective, 'tea-

---

25 Letter to Mrs Courtenay Crickmer of 8 August 1908, cited in ibid.

26 R.O'Neil, M.H.M., *Cardinal Herbert Vaughan. Archbishop of Westminster, Bishop of Salford, Founder of the Mill Hill Missionaries* (London: Burns and Oates, 1995).

27 D. Mathew, *Catholicism in England*, op. cit., p. 220.

28 Downside Archives, IX AF, Box A, (photocopied) Letter of 2 August 1909, from which the name of the recipient has been elided. Evidently, it was Mrs Courtenay Crickmer, on whom see below. The letter has pagination.

29 Ibid., p. 3.

30 Ibid., pp. 3-4.

31 Ibid., p. 4.

parties and photography make me sick'.[32] He explained he had long since abandoned any hope that he might have an academic career, or become a bishop and have some wider influence.

He now proposed an alternative. On his summer journey to the Continent, he would ask at Melk — historic Benedictine abbey on the Danube, some forty miles west of Vienna — what might be the likelihood of abbot and community allowing him to try his vocation in the monastery. This would have been a radical solution, which his fluent German and years of residence in Austria made more plausible. The diary for 1909 shows he turned back at Salzburg. The reader of the diaries will naturally assume he had thought better of the plan — this was not in fact the case, as a (further)[33] letter to Mrs Courtenay Crickmer shows. Writing on 10 September 1909, from the Park Hotel, Salzburg, Fortescue explains he had met with the abbot of Melk that same day, since the monastery had a daughter house in the city.

The abbot was concerned that Fortescue's request was only *ein plötzlicher Einfall*, 'a sudden whim'.

> The abbot said I had better say nothing about it to my bishop yet, but go on for the present as if I were never going to leave my diocese. He thinks, I am sure, that I shall really go on here [i.e. in Letchworth] and that all this idea will fizzle out. I suppose that is what will be, it was written. I have tried again and God will not have me. And this was the last chance. Everything I have ever wanted to do has fallen though — the old professorship, the Melchites [transfer to the Byzantine rite, q.v.] and now the Benedictines. All was written. It is the *vas contumeliae* ['vessel of affliction'] like poor Esau who was hated before he was born.

It seems not to have occurred to him, at any rate when writing these despondent letters, that the sort of apostolic approach he could offer, and very effectively, was actually well-suited to the situation of an early twentieth century Garden City with a higher than average proportion of 'arty and crafty' people seeking like himself to acquire and use well-designed things within a simple, economical, but gracious way of life.[34] At any rate, the old life was resumed, and not without fruit for the Church. But the discontent still gnawed.

On 30 November 1908 he wrote again to Mrs Crickmer:

> [T]oday I tramped to Hitchin through the horrible mud and fog (and Cyprus lies out there shining gold in hot clear light in the middle of the radiant purple sea; and Damascus, while I was

---

32 Ibid.

33 See above, footnote 173.

34 E. Cumming and W. Kaplan, *The Arts and Crafts Movement*, op. cit., pp. 58–64.

ploughing through muddy dusk, was glowing in evening light
amid its apricot orchards; and flaming torn lines of scarlet behind
Constantinople) — and I . . . saw visions of white minarets and
dark cypresses, and quiet blue-green waves rolling up to tawny
rocks and the hot silent desert all along the dismal black Hitchin
road. It calls to me all day now; and I have to sit in a poky
room by a stupid fire all alone; with fog and damp and the *petite
bourgeoisie anglaise* outside (*Dieu! comme ils m'embâtent*).[35]

He took refuge in writing an Arabic poem for the Melkite patriarch
about how he was 'shut up in a distant island under cloudy skies' while
his soul was 'back in the land of Syria under the apricot trees, where
the waters of Barada splash in the fountains under the hot sky, and the
camels growl by the shady vaults of the gates'. Fortescue had undergone
a crisis of vocational identity, but he soon showed he had picked up the
pieces.

In peace and war

In 1911 Fortescue could be found, inter alia, attending a lecture series
by Philip Henry Wicksteed on his beloved Dante. This is worthy of note
since it can be considered an ecumenical gesture, *avant la lettre*. Wicksteed
(1844–1922), though a sympathetic student of Dante and Aquinas, the
translator of Dante's Italian and Latin works in the Temple Classics series,
and much in demand as a University 'Extension' lecturer on the topic,
had been minister of Little Portland Street Unitarian chapel and warden of
Toynbee Hall, mecca of liberal theology, and, according to his son Joseph
Wicksteed, could be termed a theist only in some rather Pickwickian
sense.[36] That did not prevent his last essay on Dante, *From Vita Nuova to
Paradiso* (1921), attempting to bring all Dante's work into relation with the
vision of God in the *Commedia*'s closing canto. One can see why Fortescue
found him sympathetic.

More robustly, Fortescue was controverting that same year with the
Anglican High Churchman Thomas Alexander Lacey (1853–1931);[37]
that debate will enter the chapter on his polemics with Anglicans, to be
considered below. He was also reading yet another life of Burton (the

---

35 Cited in J.R. McCarthy, *Adrian*, op. cit..

36 C.H. Herford, *Philip Henry Wicksteed, his Life and Work, with a Foreword and
     Appreciation by J. H. Wicksteed* (London: Dent, 1931), pp. xx-xxi.

37 A doughty apologist for Anglo-Catholicism, as in *Catholicity: conciones ad
     clerum* (London: Mowbray, 1914); *Unity and Schism* (London: Mowbray,
     1917); and the earlier *The Unity of the Church, as Treated by English Theologians*
     (London: Society for the Promotion of Christian Knowledge, 1898).

blockbuster two volume affair by Wright),[38] and preparing his article on 'Docetism' for the Hastings' *Encyclopaedia of Religion and Ethics*, a sign, along with Cabrol's invitations, of scholarly recognition at a high level.[39]

In 1912 the diary shows him correcting the proofs of the first edition of his book on the Mass, writing what became *The Lesser Eastern Churches*, and dipping into E.T. Cook's life of Ruskin, which had just appeared,[40] as well as more of the seemingly endless *Modern Painters*. In 1913 he was at Moscow Road, to assist at a Liturgy in the Greek Cathedral, and worked on a corrected edition of *The Mass*.

The same year he published his translation of a number of the hymns of the Latin Liturgy,[41] and this prompted a sharp little exchange in *The Tablet* with the sculptor and type-designer Eric Gill (1882–1940) on the topic of Latin letters. Fortescue held that that the vernacular Romance distinction between 'u' and 'v' should not be carried over into present-day Latin inscriptions, and in his translations, originally privately printed, he put this conviction into typographical practice. Gill wrote in to dissent in characteristically pugnacious vein. 'Pedantry is deservedly discredited as a kind of intellectual priggishness. A usage based on common practice is in this latter, as in all human things, a better thing than one resting on the authority of an individual, however learned.'[42] Fortescue replied that the letter 'u', printed with a rounded bottom, was an ugly letter, and he ascribed Gill's negative reaction to unfamiliarity with historic inscriptions.[43] This was why Gill found a return to sound practice 'queer and "artistic"'. Gill retorted that he certainly found Fortescue 'queer and "artistic" in thinking the round U ugly'.[44]

The remark seems to have rankled. Some years later he would recount the story for a figure who bears comparison with Gill in the history of print, Stanley Morison.

38   T. Wright, *The Life of Sir Richard Burton* (London: Everett, 1906).

39   The 'Docetism' article in Volume IV, from 1912, joined a contribution to Volume I, from 1910, on 'Apollinarianism', the early Christological heresy touched on in *The Greek Fathers*, and it would be succeeded by four others: two on Enlightenment period ecclesiological and theological movements in the Catholic Church ('Febronianism' in Volume V, also in 1912, 'Hermesianism' in Volume VI, in 1914) and 'Iconoclasm' and 'Law' in Volume VII, from 1915. These are substantial essays amounting in all to some 30, 000 words.

40   E.T. Cook, *The Life of John Ruskin* (London: George Allen, 1911).

41   *Latin Hymns, for the use of the Parish of St Hugh Letchworth* (Letchworth: Fortescue, 1913). This work would be reprinted by the Cambridge University Press in 1924.

42   E. Gill, Letter to *The Tablet* of 2 August, 1913.

43   Letter to *The Tablet* of 9 August, 1913.

44   E. Gill, Letter to *The Tablet* of 16 August, 1913.

LATIN HYMNS

SUNG AT THE CHURCH
OF SAINT HUGH LETCHWORTH
ARRANGED & TRANSLATED
BY A·F

PRINTED AT THE
UNIVERSITY PRESS·CAMBRIDGE
FOR THE CONGREGATION OF
ST·HUGH·M·CM·XXIV

Title page for Fortescue's *Latin Hymns* for liturgical use in his parish.

Gill writes very well, and some people admire his sculpture. On the strength of this he thinks he is competent to teach us all about everything, social questions, theology, economics, philology and everything else. You saw his paper in *Blackfriars*, in which he laid down that it is impossible to produce ornament till we have converted England. This is to drag in a question of metaphysics in which he is quite incompetent to have an opinion. The man is uneducated, and a bumptious little cad. In this matter of V or U he did not understand what the question is about. It is not one of artisticness, it is a matter of Latin philology — if one may use so big a word for so elementary a matter. . . . To distinguish between them is exactly the same blunder as to distinguish I and J in Latin.[45]

If Fortescue's multifarious interests and occupations became too pressing, there was always the possibility of holidays, intelligently pursued especially when on the Continent. Just as in the summer of 1909 he had taken John Mason Neale's *The Jansenist Church of Holland* on an expedition to Germany via the Netherlands,[46] stopping off at Utrecht to attend an Old Catholic Mass (after which a 'woman with a strident voice sang a piece of horrible secular music in the Dutch tongue'),[47] so when in Italy in 1913 he made a point of attending the Byzantine rite at Grottaferrata (on which he lavished praise) and visiting the Greek-Albanian seminary in Sicily (useful for his planned, but in the end posthumous, study of the Eastern Churches in union with Rome).

Renewed acquaintance with the city of Rome did not soften his heart towards the popes: rather the contrary. Recapitulating the lessons of the visit some few years later for the benefit of Stanley Morison who was planning to include Rome in a European tour:

Rome is . . . worse than ever now. Last time I was there was in 1913. I was struck by its general getting worse since I was a student there. They have made it into a huge noisy cocknified modern town, with Cinemas and hideous vulgar new buildings all over it. The old Papal Rome (not yet quite extinct in my time) had at least a certain rather debased picturesqueness. All that has gone now. There never were more than three really good things to see there, S. Maria in Cosmedin, the tower of

---

45 Cambridge University Library, MS Add. 9812/D/90, Letter to S. Morison of 1 September, 1920.

46 The full title was *A History of the So-called Jansenist Church of Holland: with a Sketch of its Earlier Annals, and some Account of the Brothers of the Common Life* (Oxford and London: J.H. and J. Parker, 1858).

47 Downside Archive, IX AF, Box E, 'Diary 1909–1910', entry for 22 August, 1909.

S. Giorgio in Vellabro (nothing else, the church is hideous), the plan and fragments of old work in S. Clemente. A catacomb may be worth looking at, and the inside of the Colosseum. There is nothing else to see in Rome at all. You can exhaust all worth notice in about three hours. Then take the train and go somewhere else. Above all do not go near either St Peter or St John Lateran; both are a repulsive nightmare. But there a lot of very fine things in the little cities around, the *Castelli romani*, especially Frascati, Marino, Lariccia, Castel Gandolfo, Genzano, Grottaferrata. What is left of the old Roman life is to be found in these. They represent still, more or less, what Rome would be if generations of Popes had not destroyed it, systematically, expensively, thoroughly.[48]

The restrictiveness of Fortescue's counsel is shown in the accompanying advice that at Florence there was nothing worth seeing at all. His artistic vision must have narrowed since his love-affair with Ruskin. By contrast, Charles Gore, at Florence to prepare his Bampton Lectures, had been in 'ecstasy over Fra Angelico's frescoes in San Marco, and the Della Robbia bambini and the Meeting of St. Francis and St. Dominic in the neighbouring Piazza'.[49]

In these years immediately prior to the Great War the diary entries, roughly made, often in pencil, are few, and the same is true for 1914 itself where he notes, a few days before England's declaration of war on Germany, *Horrenda audimus de Bello*, 'We hear things that should horrify us about war'.[50]

At Christmas 1914 Fortescue noted in his diary the many Belgians — refugees, like Agatha Christie's 'Hercule Poirot', from the German invasion of Belgium — who were present at Midnight Mass. Curiously, with all its disastrous, or at any rate far from wholly reassuring news, from the various Fronts, 1915 was a year when he reverted to keeping his diary in fine calligraphy — in ink, of course, thus strengthening the thesis that a beautiful chronicle of a far from perfect history played some apotropaic or compensatory function in his life.

Naturally, he was deeply engaged by the War. In *The Tablet's* opening number for 1915 he launched an appeal for practical assistance to the Belgian refugees. 'Now we have seen the crowds of tired men and ragged women, we have heard the children talk Flemish in our streets, and we

---

48   Cambridge University Library, MS Add. 9812/D/90, Letter to S. Morison of
     18 June, 1920.

49   G.L. Prestige, *The Life of Charles Gore. A Great Englishman* (London and
     Toronto: Heinemann, 1935), p. 134.

50   Downside Archive, IX AF, Box E, 'Diary 1914', entry for 31 July, 1914.

know what it all means'.[51] Writing to Mrs Crickmer, he was brutally frank (as well as surely, hyperbolic) about what it 'all meant' for the cultured inhabitants of Letchworth.[52]

> The town suffers from the Belgies all round. They are all drunk and fight among themselves in the street. When you go out you are almost sure to see a bleeding Belgie shrieking down the street, pursued by three others with blood-stained knives. Personally, I do not mind a Belgie bleeding a bit, but it looks messy in our once quiet streets. Mrs Allen was complaining bitterly about the town the other day. She says it has become simply a large and dirty manufacturing centre, and she wants to know what earthly advantage there is for herself to come and live here . . . . We are becoming a place rather like Bradford or some such hole. Where is the beautiful long-haired enthusiasm of Garden City now?

The flow of Fortescue's sympathies was obstructed not least by the habits of the young Belgian priest who shared his church.

> He thinks everything I tell him is English (it is not really; it is common decency). So he has his back up against it and says he prefers the Belgian customs. A filthy woman yells Gounod's *Nazareth* while he says low Mass, and they stink out (in this case my favourite expression is meant literally) the whole place.

To set this letter in proper perspective, it is necessary to be aware of Fortescue's delight in shocking. And it has to be balanced by recognition of the effort he put into learning Flemish so as to deal pastorally with the refugees (on major feasts he preached his Letchworth sermons in three languages, English, Flemish, and French),[53] and, of course, his initiative in arranging, through the columns of *The Tablet*, the appeal to assist them.

He also used *The Tablet*, owned as it was by Bourne as archbishop, to address patriotic anxieties over the silence of the Pope on where exactly war-guilt lay. The silence from Rome contrasted markedly with the enthusiastic support for recourse to arms offered by national churches in Germany and England. Thus, one study of the attitudes of Anglican church leaders to the Entente cause is significantly entitled 'The Last Crusade'.[54] Some Catholics in England were evidently embarrassed that their own 'supreme pastor' took no stand. But here the desire to retrench the scope of the

51 'Dr Adrian Fortescue's Appeal', *The Tablet*, 2 January 1915, p. 15.

52 Letter to Mrs Courtenay Crickmer of 25 April, 1917, quoted in J.R. McCarthy, *Adrian* , op. cit.

53 E. Cowell, 'Adrian Fortescue', art. cit., pp. 1029–1030.

54 A. Marrin, *The Last Crusade. The Church of England in the First World War* (Durham, NC: Duke University Press, 1974).

teaching authority of Pope and Church (I shall consider this in the context of reactions to Liberal Catholicism and Modernism in the last chapter of this book) stood Fortescue in good stead.

> In such a matter as this he [the Pope] has no commission from Christ to teach. His infallible authority extends only to questions of faith and morals, not to politics. Our Lord did not found the Church that she might teach us which side is in the right in a war between Christian nations . . . . If the Pope has an opinion on the war, it is only his private opinion.[55]

Fortescue defended British arms — the defence of Belgium was, he believed, a just cause for war. But, so the editor reported in the issue of 13 March 1915, many *Tablet* readers had written to express outrage at Fortescue's assertion that in some sense both Belgium and England were also aggressors, since they had chosen to resist German demands (Belgium) or German decisions (England) by military means. A letter signed 'A Temporary Clerk at the Admiralty' insinuated that Fortescue's long stay on the territory of the Central Powers (i.e. at Innsbruck) might have something to do with his opinions. 'We laymen all recognize that the Doctor (with his Austrian education) naturally holds the scales more evenly than we can', was the correspondent's somewhat sardonic comment.

A pamphlet by Fortescue on pacifism may have reassured him. Delivering a sharp 'word' to conscientious objectors, Fortescue declared:

> [W]e may put the argument for the lawfulness of just war simply like this: As a general principle, it is always lawful, it is often a duty, to inflict physical evil when this is the necessary mean for preventing greater evil, and when no obligation of natural or positive law is violated thereby. Neither philosophy nor the Christian faith teaches that physical evil does not exist or can cease to exist in this imperfect world.[56]

For the Christian, 'it does not matter so much how soon or how late he dies; what matters is that when he dies, he should save his soul'. To be sure, he agreed that:

> [h]uman life is so precious, so that certainly, only the very gravest cause can justify a man in taking it. That is not the issue between us and the Pacifist. The issue is whether it is the supreme good, so that nothing can ever be more valuable. To think so is his mistake. The good estate, peace, civilization of a whole country is a greater good than human life, or a number of human lives.

---

55 'Why does not the Church speak?', ibid., 16 January 1915, p. 73.

56 *Pacifism. A Word with Conscientious Objectors* (London: Catholic Truth Society, 1916), p. 5.

It may be difficult in each case to measure the balance, to say exactly how many men's lives are equal to a certain other good. But the Pacifist's general principle is obviously false.

Naturally, Fortescue accepted that not all wars are just. And yet 'there are good results which outweigh the evil of war, and so there are just wars'.[57] What he was combating was, he considered, a deleterious humanitarianism, 'centred on the good things of the earth, counting such benefits as earthly life supreme', and this he took to be 'characteristic of the vague unchristian philosophy so much in vogue among kindly people who have nothing better'.[58] He preferred to say, 'We must love our enemies, even while we fight them'.[59] And he added a poignant contemporary illustration.

> The French priest-soldier, who shoots Germans, without hatred, because he must do so to save France; and then goes out to kneel beside the man he has shot, to bring him to the ambulance, or hear his confession and pray with him till he dies — he understands our Lord's teaching better than the pacifist.[60]

In a letter of 18 May 1918 to his cousin Sir John Fortescue, reproduced in the posthumous *Memoir*, Adrian Fortescue made it plain that, though he totally disapproved of the Kaiser's policies, he found it impossible to dislike Germans (and especially German Catholics) as such. 'When I think about the war on big lines, I eat fire, as every Englishman does; and I want Mr. Hohenzollern (and especially Mr. Hohenzollern, Jun.) to be — hanged.'[61] He was, however, 'fetched [i.e. affected] enormously' when he had to administer the sacraments to German prisoners of war.

> They had made absurd bouquets of wild flowers, butter cups and dandelions and things, and put them in mugs. . . . They sang the old hymns I have not heard for years — all day since the tune of *Hier liegt vor deiner Majestät* has been sounding in my head . . . This evening, as they [his parishioners] were singing Compline, I heard the tune of *Hier liegt vor deiner Majestät* all the time, and the sound of cow-bells. I sat in my place by the altar, and looked out of the window at the evening light, and wondered if that light were shining with alp-glow in the Tirol Mountains as it used to. When I began to preach to my own people it was an effort not to start in German.[62]

---

57 Ibid., p. 4.

58 Ibid., p. 6.

59 Ibid., p. 8.

60 Ibid., pp. 8-9.

61 Cited J.A. Vance and J.W. Fortescue, *Adrian Fortescue. A Memoir*, op. cit., p. 41.

62 Ibid., p. 42.

Just so, a decade or more previously, writing (in French) to Harold Burton from Sankt Bonifatius Kirche in Whitechapel, the chattering of children in the 'Bavarian or Black Forest dialect' had brought back to him 'the great and distant fatherland, that ancient Germany, mother of peoples, [with its] tranquil villages, its vines, long and silent white roads, the majestic flow of the Rhine, and the eternal mountains'.[63]

The diary for 1915 highlights his close relation with the re-founder of the Catholic Truth Society, James Britten (1846–1924),[64] and its current organizer, George Eliott Anstruther.[65] In his latter years, the admirable Britten became rather a bore in the way he dominated the Catholic Truth Society's coordinating Committee. According to its Chairman, Mgr Cuthbert Collingwood, he tended to 'regard a question as a challenge, and an objection as something near an affront'.[66] Fortescue, who had been publishing with the Society a good deal, was not sympathetic. Indeed, his comments show him at his most pugnacious.

> Nearly all that committee sit like toothless fishes and just vomit up any silly consent that Britten demands for his pornographic proposals. They are dumb dogs and draggle-tailed tadpoles. Britten drives them before him as a wild dog would drive consumptive rabbits.[67]

He had earlier written to the Jesuit scholar Herbert Thurston (1856–1939), 'Will you join my new league for discouraging Britten and rendering him comparatively innocuous: I am hereditary President and Grand Master. Subscription 10/6 a year, to subsidize pamphlets exposing his offences'.[68]

---

63 Westminster Diocesan Archive, Series 20, Box 22, Letter of 1 July 1903 to Harold Burton.

64 Editor from 1879 onwards of the *Journal of Botany*, Britten re-founded the Catholic Truth Society in 1884; he recounted his conversion in *Why I Left the Church of England* (London: Catholic Truth Society, 1893).

65 Editor of *The Universe* 1906–1909, organising secretary of the Catholic Truth Society 1907-1920, assistant editor of *The Tablet* 1920–1936, author of *A Hundred Years of Catholic Progress: Being a Short Account of the Church's Fortunes in Great Britain since the Time of the Emancipation Act* (London: Burns, Oates and Washbourne, 1929). For these figures see C. Ralls, *The Catholic Truth Society. A New History* (London: Catholic Truth Society, 1993), pp. 3–5, 12–15 (Britten), 10–11 (Anstruther).

66 Cited ibid., p. 12.

67 Westminster Diocesan Archives, Series 20, Box 22, Letter of 11 October, 1911.

68 Westminster Diocesan Archives, Series 20, Box 22, Copy of Letter of 8 May, 1909.

Despite the Zeppelins over London in the September of 1915 (not much one could do about that), he worked on his 'book of ceremonies' (for generations of clergy before the Second Vatican Council this volume would be familiar as 'Fortescue' — no more explanation needed, or later 'Fortescue and O'Connell'), and the splendid Burns and Oates English-Latin Mass-book for the laity (to be known, through its multiple re-printings, as the 'Fortescue Missal'). The Ceremonial book, though beautifully done, with exquisitely drawn symbols to assist those involved in liturgical ceremonies, gave him rather a headache. The Missal was a fruit of his collaboration with one of the best book-designers of the century, Bernard Newdigate (1869–1944) of the Arden Press, and arguably the century's finest typographer, Stanley Morison (from 1925 on, he was typographical adviser to the Cambridge University Press, before moving to the *Times*). These men became firm friends.[69]

The Fortescue Missal (as it became known) was a long-matured labour of love: in a letter (in German) from a decade earlier he regrets there was no English translation of the Missal comparable in linguistic quality with the Anglican Prayer-book: 'a perfect model would be the German translation of P. Anselm Schott, OSB, — with splendid notes!'[70]. (This was the Missal on which Joseph Ratzinger, later Pope Benedict XVI, lavished high praise in his autobiographical memoir.)[71] As with his ceremonial book, Fortescue was keen to avoid or, in the case of the Missal, remove Latinisms. In effect, his Missal was a self-consciously Anglo-Saxon rendering of F.C. Husenbeth's *The Missal for the Use of the Laity*, first published in 1837 but re-printed a number of times till as late as 1898. Francis Meynell, son of the writers Wilfrid and Alice, was in charge of book design at Burns and Oates. Meynell was sufficiently impressed with the Missal to commission from Fortescue an introduction for *The Holy Week Book* and an essay on hymns to accompany the collection *Pange Lingua*, both published in 1916.

---

69 Accounts for the Fortescue-Morison collaboration can be found in J. Moran, *Stanley Morison* (London: Lund Humphries, 1971), pp. 40–41, and M. Barker, *Stanley Morison* (London: MacMillan, 1972), pp. 66–69; 86–93, 112–115, 150–151. Newdigate's son Charles became Fortescue's curate at Letchworth, ibid., p. 67. There is a good discussion of Fortescue's relations with both Newdigate and Morison in the context of his belief that calligraphy and typography were closely related in M. Davies (ed.), *The Wisdom of Adrian Fortescue*, op. cit., pp. 24–31.

70 Westminster Diocesan Archives, Box AGD, Letter to Hamilton Macdonald of 24 May, 1905.

71 J.Ratzinger, *Milestones. Memoirs 1927-1977* (Et San Francisco: Ignatius, 1998), pp. 19–20.

In 1915 the *Catholic Directory for England and Wales* reported him as being dean of the St Laurence of Canterbury deanery of the Westminster archdiocese, which took in Baldock, Hatfield, Hitchin, Royston and Stevenage as well as Letchworth and probably involved him in more pastoral as well as administrative duties. The appointment showed he was not by any means *persona non grata* in the local church, though he once told his cousin Lady Fortescue, 'I went to Westminster yesterday, but I smelt Bishops and fled away'.[72] Such diary entries as there are for the remaining years of the First World War suggest a concentration on relations with Anglicans, eirenic as well as controversial, and this is borne out by his occasional journalism. In July 1917, so the diary reports, he went to hear the Anglo-Papalist Henry Joy Fynes-Clinton (1872–1944),[73] co-founder of the Catholic League, who was speaking on reunion.[74] Evidently, not all his efforts were represented by the squib on Ritualism entitled 'Pretending' he had written in February of the previous year for *The Tablet*, though he certainly did not refrain from giving, in Samuel Butler's phrase, 'apostolic blows and knocks' when he thought them merited.

At New Year of 1917 he was able to congratulate his friend Edwin Burton, Vice-President of St Edmund's Ware, on his becoming a canon of Westminster, which missive turned, characteristically, into a diatribe against the 'prelates of honour to his Holiness' (an award that conveyed the title 'monsignor') instead.

---

72 W. Fortescue, *There's Rosemary, There's Rue* (Edinburgh and London: Blackwood, 1939), p. 226.

73 On Fynes-Clinton, see M. Yelton, *Anglican Papalism. An Illustrated History, 1900–1960* (Norwich: Canterbury Press, 2005), pp. 27–34. Yelton points out and this is useful context for Fortescue's approach, both positive and negative, to 'Anglo-Roman' issues, that 'The First World War was a period of growth for many Anglo-Catholic organisations, partly because of the popularity of requiem masses for the dead and of increased devotion to the Blessed Sacrament as the losses mounted, but also because the gaze of the episcopate was elsewhere', ibid., p. 31.

74 I cannot forebear from noting that ninety-five years later the office-holders of the Catholic League declared Pope Benedict XVI's Apostolic Constitution for Anglican Catholics, *Anglicanorum coetibus*, a or, rather, *the* Providential response to the foundation of their Society. 'As for the Catholic League itself, the Officers who form the Executive evenly composed of Anglican and Catholic members believe that with *Anglicanorum coetibus* the League has reached its time of consummation': thus The Catholic League, 'Statement on *Anglicanorum coetibus*', in *The Messenger of the Catholic League* 292 (2010), p. 12, a collection of materials brought together under the overall title *Anglicans and Catholics in Communion. Patrimony, Unity, Mission.*

[S]o far you have not had to add a filthy Italian prefix to a decent English name . . . for a man who fears the God of Israel, it must be an awful thing to be classed among the sweepings of the Italian gutters who lurk around the backyards and latrines of the Vatican, their greasy palms out-stretched for tips, their oily lips bubbling with servile lies in bad French.[75]

A sad little entry, added in the last year of the War to the diary from the first year of the century, recorded the ending, on 31 March 1918, of his eighteen years of friendship with Florence Fielding of Blake Hall, 'whom I deeply loved',[76] but with whom he had latterly had a painful correspondence — which does not survive, but a reference in a letter to her cousin, Harold Burton, makes it likely that what came between them was religion. Fortescue could suffer no more of her anti-Catholicism.[77]

After the Great War

On the level of the Church-institution, a significant moment for the life of the modern Catholic Church in England took place when, along with pastoral clergy up and down the country, Fortescue was called in by the archdiocese to recite the Creed of Pope Pius IV and take the anti-Modernist oath so as to be made a canonical *parochus* rather than a mere missionary rector (for Fortescue, the formalities took place on 9 December 1918). So far as the taking of the oath was concerned, this was not a happy moment, for, as he made plain in a letter to the Jesuit polymath Herbert Thurston, he shared the conviction of many priests by no means sympathetic to Modernism of the full fig variety that its terms of reference were too narrowing of the scope of scholarship. That must be investigated in the final chapter of this study.

1919 was a year rich in recognition. He was made a Consultor of the Congregation *Pro Ecclesia Orientali*[78]: an honour which might have played a part in his selection as preacher at a Mass in Westminster cathedral in the presence of the cardinal-archbishop, to mark the inauguration of the Kingdom of the Serbs,

75 Westminster Diocesan Archive, Series 20, Box 22, Letter to Edwin Burton of 1 January, 1917.

76 Downside Archive, AF IX, Box E, 'Diary 1901', entry for 28 August, 1901.

77 Westminster Diocesan Archives, Series 20, Box 22, Letter to Harold Burton of 25th Sunday after Pentecost 1907. Writing (in French) to Burton four years earlier, he regretted that someone he found so 'loveable' and 'charming' should have so obviously suffered from an upbringing 'in this dreadful milieu of Bible-reading, the Protestant Sunday, the heavy and banal English virtues', ibid., Letter to Harold Burton of 1 July, 1903.

78 The letter of appointment, signed by Benedict XVI's Cardinal Secretary of State, is dated 7 July 1919: Westminster Diocesan Archive, Series 20, Box 21.

Croats and Slovenes, later called 'Yugoslavia', as part of the post-War European settlement.79 He was also appointed Professor of Church History at St Edmund's Ware, the seminary of the archdiocese and successor with St Cuthbert's College, Ushaw, of the Douai College of Elizabethan (and priest-martyrs') fame. Thus his Oscottian disappointment was assuaged, indeed reversed, and in a setting which brought him admirably compatible colleagues, above all Ronald Knox (who, just received into the Church from Anglicanism, joined the staff at the same time) and the dogmatician George Smith (later to finish, at Fortescue's request, his edition of Boethius). Fortescue's appointment was a sign of confidence in him on the part of Cardinal Bourne, for St Edmund's Ware was Bourne's favoured — some said, spoiled — child. [P]rimarily concerned with the education of his future priests', Bourne chose to withdraw his students from other English seminaries at home and abroad, so as to concentrate on St Edmund's, whose 'gradual improvement . . . was his life-long preoccupation'. At the cardinal's own wish, it was there he would be buried.80

Three books of lecture-notes (in Latin) for Fortescue's courses on Church history at St Edmund's survive in the Westminster Diocesan Archives.81 They show intelligent attention to the position of the study of Church history in the cycle of the sacred sciences, to methodology (more briefly), and to the evaluative listing of secondary works as well as editions of their primary sources. In Fortescue's view, ecclesiastical history includes Christian origins, so considerable time was spent on Judaism in the time of Christ and the conditions of life and thought in the Greco-Roman world at the moment of the Incarnation. His firm intention that Church history should not be separated from dogma is apparent in his treatment of what he called the 'Pentecost event'. He asked, 'When did the Catholic Church *begin*?', and answered his own question, 'Immediately there were those who believed in Jesus Christ. Thus, not on the day of Pentecost, nor when the apostles were called, but already before: that is, as soon as Christ was born'.82 The course notes end with material on Baptism and the catechumenate, the Eucharistic liturgy and the discipline of penance and excommunication in the first three centuries — though doubtless had Fortescue lived he would have taken the story far beyond the ante-Nicene Church.

79 An example of the invitation card from the Legation of the Kingdom of the Serbs, Croats and Slovenes is held in the Downside Archives, IX AF Box B.

80 G. Wheeler, 'The Archdiocese of Westminster', in G.A. Beck, A.A. (ed.), *The English Catholics 1850–1950* (London: Burns and Oates, 1950), p. 173.

81 Westminster Diocesan Archives, Series 20, Box 19, 'Historia Ecclesiastica I', dated 22 September 1919 – 7 February 1921; 'Historia Ecclesiastica II', dated 15 February 1921 – 21 February 1922; Series 20, Box 20 'Historia ecclesiastica III', begun 22 February 1922, but never completed.

82 Ibid., 'Historia ecclesiastica I', p. 131.

Not that his seminary chair led him to neglect lecturing opportunities of a more rough-and-ready kind to the people of his own adopted town and its neighbours. Latin notes survive of five lectures on 'Religion and Philosophy in the Roman Empire', given in the Howard Hall at Letchworth in March-April 1921 ('The State Religion', 'The Mystery Religions', 'Philosophy', 'Marcus Aurelius Antoninus', 'The Lyons Martyrs'),[83] and of lectures on Dante in the same venue on the four Saturdays of June, 1921 ('Dante and his Time', 'On the Principles of Dante's Politics', 'On the Divine Comedy at Large, and the Inferno', 'On the Purgatorio and Paradiso'.)[84] There are also notes for a single lecture at Hitchin, to the Methodist Society, from October 1921, on 'Christ and Plato';[85] and a series of half a dozen lectures on 'The Death of the Gods' given in Letchworth's Howard Hall on Thursdays of February and March 1922 ('On Constantine the Great', 'On Christians and Pagans after the Edict of Milan', 'On the August Julian', 'On the Neo-Platonists', 'On Celsus', and 'On Origen').[86]

Though Fortescue's cancer was hidden, he evinced some of the behaviour of the elderly or those terminally ill – not in abbreviating his activities but in taking up opportunities to revisit familiar scenes. In 1913, he had gone back to his old room in the Scots College at Rome, writing kindly, even elegiacally to the unfortunate Campbell's successor as rector, Robert Fraser.

> The days when I wore a purpose cassock and red belt seem very remote to me. They were not altogether happy days, less so (if I may venture to say this) than if I had had the good fortune to be a student at a later period, in more favourable conditions. . . . Perhaps I may venture to say this too, that since the other day, when I saw again the old places and the uniform I once wore, I have already a much kindlier impression of my college at Rome, and am much more inclined, not only to remember with gratitude my German years, but also to count myself with pride a student of the Scots College.[87]

Now, after the War, in the last summer of his life (1922), he made a bee-line for Innsbruck, to find those of his old Jesuit teachers who were still living. On the way back he met up with his old friend Karel Mosterts at the Bavarian town of Dinkelsbühl and, enjoying it, stayed on for ten days. A letter he sent home to England struck an elegiac note.

83 Westminster Diocesan Archives, Series 20, Box 20, 'Libellus praelectionum I', pp. 9–87.

84 Ibid., pp. 89–133.

85 Ibid., pp. 135–145.

86 Ibid., pp. 147–169; 'Libellus praelectionum II', pp. 7–125..

87 Scots College Archive, Rome, 27/50, letter of 20 February 1913, cited in R. McCluskey, 'Tribulations, 1820–1922', art. cit., p. 90.

This evening at eight I was sitting down to dinner when I heard the distant sound of extraordinarily beautiful music. I asked the waiter what this might be. He told me it was the *Todtenklang* and explained; it is the custom in Dinkelsbühl since ever so long ago, when a citizen dies, the evening of the funeral to play a chorale from the church tower. I left my dinner to go cold and went out into the square. The sun had set, but there was still light. The sky in the west was that clear pure green you see after a very hot dry day. In the square, all grey and dark under its high gables, the people stood silent and bare-headed. The great church tower stood, a huge blue mass against the gleaming green sky; it became purple and rose-madder lower down where it sank into the church. And from high up, coming down into the dark square out of the sky, was music of trumpets. They were playing — Heavens! they were playing the most exquisite, poignant tune in the whole world, *O Haupt voll Blut und Wunden*, to Bach's heavenly setting, with the wailing chromatic chords and the strange, restless bass. Not a sound from the people below; I was just conscious of a silent crowd. The dark shadows, high gables, and above the clear emerald light, the blue mass soaring up into the sky cut in sharp outline agains the twilight, and that unspeakably sad, sweet tune, exquisitely played high up there over the silent little town. I wonder if I can make you see it, and hear it.[88]

Less than four months later, on 20 December, fatefully, he went to see his doctor.[89] An emergency appointment was made for him with a specialist for 21 December. On 22 December he wrote to Edward Myers, the President of St Edmund's, 'I have had what at first was a very great shock ... A week ago, as far as I knew I was in perfect health, except for what I took for a little indigestion'.[90] He had now been told that even if an immediate operation, which would leave him a 'horribly maimed and patched-up body', managed to succeed, he could not expect to live long. In the spring he had been walking all over south Cambridgeshire, west Suffolk, and a corner of Essex.

---

88 Letter of 29 August, 1922, as reproduced in C. B. Purdom, *Life over Again*, op. cit., pp. 248–249. The name of the recipient is not given.

89 Downside Archives, IX AF, Box A, Adrian Willson, hand-written notes for the benefit of Michael Davies, entitled at this point 'The Letchworth Guide'; cf. the chronology in M. Davies (ed.), *The Wisdom of Adrian Fortescue*, op. cit., p. 84.

90 Westminster Diocesan Archives, Series 20, Box 22, Letter to Edward Myers of 22 December, 1922.

On 3 January, after his last Christmas at Letchworth, he went up to London. He spent the day before going into hospital with the Dominicans at Haverstock Hill ('no Molinism for me, thank you', he told Myers in what turned out to be the farewell letter — the Jesuit theology of grace was too humanistic for what he called 'a soul that has no hope but in the mercy of God'). He would make a 'general confession' there, where his father's memorial chapel was situated.

> I think it silly to make a fuss about so inevitable a thing as death; nor do I want to work up an emotional crisis. I am spending these last days making my will, arranging things for my successor, sorting papers. I think I have already got over the pang of parting with work half done and the too many interests I had in life. Only let me say this: if I do not come back from Dollis Hill, if Azrael [the angel of death] has got me, I like to remember how very kind and nice you, Vance, Flynn, George Smith and everyone there were to me always.

On 5 January he wrote to Mrs Crickmer:

> It is coming quite soon now. I am waiting for it. They have done all sorts of queer things to me, including painting me a cheerful and elegant yellow. I am all right now, in peace and content and happy. The O.P.'s [Dominicans] were darlings. In Matins today I stuck on the psalm: *Et si ambulavero in medio umbrae mortis, non timebo mala, quia tu mecum es.* That is for me now. I look out over quiet green fields and bare purple inter trees, and I think that tomorrow is Epiphany. *Vidimus gloriam eius.*

Adrian Fortescue died of cancer in the Dollis Hill Hospital on 3 February 1923. He was forty-nine years young

Schloss Munot,
Schaffhausen.
10 aug. 1922.

The fortified castle of Munot in Schaffhausen, Switzerland: sketched by Foretescue on the last European tour of his life.

7. The Theory of the Liturgy: Encyclopaedias, and *The Mass*

If the Eastern churches were a lifelong passion for Fortescue so similarly were 'liturgics', the study of liturgical worship and the passion to celebrate it well. In this chapter I consider him not so much as practitioner — that will be the subject of the chapter that follows — but as theoretician, which must mean as *theologian-cum-historian of the rites*.

If not exactly easy (some of the subject-matter is inordinately complex), it was at any rate convenient for Fortescue to take on the writing of a series of articles on liturgical subjects for the great Anglo-American *Catholic Encyclopaedia* which began production in 1907, with multiple collaborators and an imprimatur from the archbishop of New York. According to its editors, the *Encyclopaedia* aimed to 'give its readers full and authoritative information on the entire cycle of Catholic interests, action and doctrine'.[1] The request to Fortescue was timely because he was at the time planning a book on the early history of the Mass.[2] Naturally there would be overlap. The editors of the *Encyclopaedia* wanted general articles on the nature of liturgy and rite. They also wanted particular articles on the Roman Liturgy, and notably on the various 'moments' in the liturgical action, from the preparatory prayers 'at the foot of the altar' to the Last Gospel, which follows the dismissal and blessing. These will be considered in connexion with Fortescue's handbook on the Mass of the Roman rite. Here we must consider first his wider view of the Liturgy and his contributions to the study of its Eastern Christian forms.

The Liturgy at large

Fortescue draws on the Septuagint text of the Old Testament and, within the New Testament, the Gospel of Luke and the Letter to the Hebrews, in order to support his claim that, in Christian usage, the term 'liturgy' always meant 'the offical public service of the Church', corresponding to

---

1   C.G. Herbermann et al. (ed.), *The Catholic Encyclopaedia I* (London: Caxton, and New York: Robert Appleton, 1907), p.v.

2   The invitation evidently came through the good offices of Herbert Thurston, S.J.: Westminster Diocesan Archives, Series 20, Box 22, Letter to Herbert Thurston of 20 June, 1906.

'the official service of the Temple in the Old Law'.[3] He points out that, as a consequence of the development of idiom, there can be some confusion nonetheless. 'Liturgy' can be taken to denote 'the whole complex of official services, all the rites, ceremonies, prayers, and sacraments of the Church, as opposed to private devotions'. And this is generally what is meant in the West. Alternatively, the word may be restricted, as is the case with Eastern Christians, to the 'Sacrifice of the Holy Eucharist, which in our rite we call the Mass'.[4]

I note in this connexion the strength of Fortescue's doctrine of the Eucharist as the 'sacrifice of the Mass', intimated most obviously in the introduction to the Fortescue Missal.

> Each Mass contains the slaying of the Victim, not repeated here in the West after centuries, made once only long ago in Palestine, yet part of the sacrifice offered throughout the world each morning. All Masses are one sacrifice, including the death of the cross, continuing through all time the act of offering then begun. . . . Every time we hear Mass we look across that gulf of time, we are again before the cross, with his mother and St. John; we offer still that victim then slain, present here under the forms of bread and wine.[5]

This statement is so marked by the Eucharistic sensibility of a Tridentine Catholic that we feel a certain sense of surprise when Fortescue, in the article 'Liturgy', declares his preference for the Oriental nomenclature. Counselling the universal adoption of the Eastern linguistic practice, by which the Mass is 'The Liturgy' and other public acts of worship must find some different name, Fortescue sees no reason why Latin Christians cannot simply describe the celebration of the Hours, for instance, as 'official' or 'canonical' rather than 'liturgical' prayer.

'The Liturgy' was Fortescue's preferred name for the Mass, though when addressing a Catholic readership he retained as normative the familiar term; by the same token, he was willing to give the liturgy of the Hours some less prestigious label. The reform of the Roman rite, carried out within half a century of Fortescue's death, did not follow this lead. It must be said that, had the Western Catholic Church taken Fortescue's

---

3   'Liturgy', *Catholic Encyclopaedia* IX (1910), pp. 306–313, and here at p. 306; the New Testament references are Luke 1:23, and Hebrews 8:6, the first of which concerns the last days of the Old Law and the second the fount of the Liturgy in the New.

4   'Liturgy', art. cit., p. 306.

5   *The Roman Missal*, compiled by lawful authority from the *Missale Romanum*, with an introduction by Adrian Fortescue, D.D.,(London: Burns and Oates, 1912), p. xiv.

advice, achieving an integrated approach to the worshipping day would be seriously handicapped. The Mass is the sun of each liturgical day, but around it, in a constellation, the planets of the other acts of divine worship always circle.

Fortescue's self-denying ordinance (the Liturgy is the Mass and that alone) meant that when he comes to speak about the origin and development of the Liturgy what he will actually describe is the origin and development of the ceremonial celebration of the Eucharist. His questions in this regard are: 'From what date was there a fixed and regulated service such as we can describe as a formal Liturgy? How far was this service uniform in various Churches? How far are we able to reconstruct its forms and arrangement?'[6]

Fortescue's approach does not diverge in any obvious fashion from the median position of scholars in his time. There was much fluidity, much variability, in the worship of the apostolic age, but there were also fixed reference points, both in the synagogue model for a liturgy of the Word (those writing on this subject after the work of the pioneering Methodist student of biblical worship-patterns Margaret Barker would have to note the absence of much 'Temple theology' in Fortescue's account)[7] and in the memory of what the Lord himself did at the Board on the first Holy Thursday when he instituted this continuing sign of his Sacrifice. Two features — the Eucharistic agape and the 'spiritual exercises' of prophesying in the Holy Spirit — dropped out quickly (their presence in the anonymous late first century text called the *Didache* or 'Teaching of the Twelve Apostles' shows that the latter 'in some ways lies apart from the general development').[8]

By the time of the Apostolic Fathers, forms are becoming set. The bishop has a certain right to improvise but this can only have been extremely restricted since the deacon and people had to know how and when to make their responses or acclamations. Moreover, the themes to be covered were more or less constant since the content of the divine blessings under the new and everlasting Covenant was always the same. And the conservative instinct, ever powerful in religion, would have served as a barrier against constant change. Daughter churches, for instance, would imitate a mother. Fortescue will not go so far as to say that all liturgies, Eastern and Western, derive ultimately from a single apostolic prototype but he writes nonetheless, 'The mediaeval idea that all are derived from one parent rite is not so absurd, if we remember that the parent was not a written or stereotyped Liturgy, but rather 'a general *type* of service'.[9] Here

---

6   'Liturgy', art. cit., p. 307.
7   M. Barker, *Temple Theology. An Introduction* (London: Society for the Promotion of Christian Knowledge, 2004).
8   'Liturgy', art. cit., p. 308.
9   Ibid.

Fortescue is coming close to the highly influential concept, put forward after his death by the Anglo-Catholic liturgical historian (and theologian) Dom Gregory Dix, that what is crucial in the origin and development of the Church's worship is the Liturgy's overall 'Shape' (typically, Dix kept the word in capitals), not, as was customarily thought by comparative liturgists, the detailed content of a Eucharistic Prayer.[10]

Comparing the account of the Mass in Justin's First Apology, the liturgical allusions in the First Letter of Clement of Rome and the liturgical rite laid out in the eighth book of the so-called *Apostolic Constitutions*, Fortescue thinks it is possible to construct that 'general type', at any rate up to a point. Here he intervenes in a controversy among, above all, German scholars. He follows the line of Paul Drews in the latter's *Untersuchungen über die sogennante clementinische Liturgie*.[11] Drews had sought to locate and defend a germ of truth in the complex but over-systematising proposal of an earlier liturgical historian, Ferdinand Probst. Probst's attempt to demonstrate that the Liturgy of the *Apostolic Constitutions* can be considered the universal primitive Liturgy of the Church Fortescue calls, in a memorable phrase, the 'monomania of a very learned man'.[12] For Fortescue, as for Drews, the Liturgy in the *Apostolic Constitutions* is a developed Syrian form of something much older and not absolutely tied to Syria at all.

Fortescue thought that the overall development of the liturgies resembled that of languages. A diversity arises, but then some particular strains within that diversity acquire a hegemony, and further, if regional, uniformities result. The key to the new regional uniformies is the emergence of the patriarchal centres, Rome, Alexandria, Antioch. 'As the other bishops accepted the jurisdiction of these three patriarchs, so did they imitate their services.'[13] By a natural progression, then, Fortescue was led

---

10 G. Dix, *The Shape of the Liturgy* (London: Adam and Charles Black, 1982 [1945]), p. 5. Dix stressed the way the 'Shape' was dictated by the fourfold nature of the Eucharistic action: the Offertory; the Prayer of Thanksgiving; the Fraction; the Communion. A more recent Anglican liturgiologist, Paul Bradshaw, has, however, set a question-mark against Dix's assumption that 'only what was common could be regarded as primitive': thus P.F. Bradshaw, *The Search for the Origins of Christian Worship. Sources and Methods for the Study of Early Liturgy* (London: Society for the Promotion of Christian Knowledge, 1992), p. 143.

11 P. Drews, *Untersuchungen über die sogennante clementinische Liturgie* (Tübingen: Mohr, 1906).

12 'Liturgy', art. cit., p. 309. The two principal works by Probst were his *Liturgie der drei ersten christlichen Jahrhunderte* (Tübingen: Laupp, 1870), and *Liturgie des vierten Jahrhunderts und deren Reform* (Münster: Aschendorff, 1893).

13 'Liturgy', art. cit., p. 310.

on to speak of the genesis of the principal liturgical families, Eastern and Western, on which he also provided more detailed accounts in essays for the *Encyclopaedia* on the great rites (and even some lesser ones).

The Eastern liturgies

Though the request for articles on the Eastern liturgies, and notably on the Byzantine Liturgy, was less germane to Fortescue's purposes in his forthcoming handbook, it too was grist to his mill. Like all the major historians of the early liturgies, he was aware that the Western and Eastern forms of Christian worship could not satisfactorily be studied in mutual isolation. And moreover, owing to his fascination with Orthodoxy, and its non-Byzantine estranged sisters, the (Nestorian) 'Church of the East' and the (Monophysite) non-Chalcedonian churches, he had an additional ground for wanting to take on the burden of the Oriental liturgical articles as well.

A yet further incentive was his conviction that the Catholic Church is not exclusively Roman or, more widely, Latin. She is made up of a number of ritual churches, of which the Latin church merely happens, for reasons of historical accident, to be the largest. As at the London Eucharistic Congress, it was important to him to show separated Western Christians that the Catholic Church was splendid in her internal variety, and this was manifested most persuasively in the diverse worshipping life of the 'Uniate' churches within her single communion.

Fortescue's first article for the *Encyclopaedia* was in fact on the Alexandrian (or, as he — or possibly his editors — preferred, 'Alexandrine') Liturgy. It gives us a good idea of his chosen approach. Though the forms of worship used for some centuries by the 'orthodox Melchites' as well as enduringly by Copts and Ethiopians would be of more interest to the Church historian or, for that matter, to the contemporary student of Christianity in Egypt and the Horn of Africa, he thought it desirable to begin with a speculative archaeological construction of the primitive (Greek) liturgy of Alexandria, the 'old use of the Church of Alexandria as it existed before the Monophysite schism and the Council of Chalcedon'.[14] It meant identifying what was common to these various (presumed) daughter rites and synthesizing it with occasional allusions in other relevant texts — such as, in this particular case, Athanasius of Alexandria's writings. This was very much in the manner of the comparative liturgists of Fortescue's day and later, though his version seems idiosyncratic in that it includes among the sources for pertinent allusions the *de Hierarchia ecclesiastica* of the Pseudo-Denys, whom he regards as a fourth (rather than sixth) century figure and not Syrian (as generally claimed) but Egyptian.

---

14 Ibid., p. 303. Fortescue was not consistent in his spelling of the word 'Melkite'/'Melchite'. Ouside of citations, I prefer to use here the first of these.

Firmer ground is reached with the Greek Liturgy of St Mark —
eventually abandoned by the (highly minoritarian) Orthodox in Alexandria
in favour of the worshipping template found at Constantinople. Here
there is a *textus receptus* (reproduced in the *Liturgies Eastern and Western* of
Fortescue's Oxford contact F.E. Brightman), largely based on a thirteenth
century manuscript in the Vatican Library. Though this rite has undergone
Byzantine influence, Fortescue draws attention to its most distinctive
feature: the 'Supplication' (for 'various causes and people') which in all
other liturgical traditions follows the Sanctus comes before it in what 'we'
(i.e. Latins) would call the Preface of the Mass.

> The Alexandrine Preface then is very long; interwoven into it
> are a series of prayers for the Church, the Emperor, the sick,
> the fruits of the earth, and so on. Again the priest prays God to
> "draw up the waters of the river [Nile] to their right measure"; he
> remembers various classes of Saints, especially St. Mark, says the
> first part of the Hail Mary, and then goes on aloud: "especially
> our all-holy, immaculate, and glorious Lady Mary, Mother of
> God and ever Virgin". The deacon here reads the diptychs of
> the dead; the priest continues his supplication for the patriarch,
> the bishop, and all the living; the deacon calls out to the people
> to stand and then to look towards the east; and so at last comes
> the Sanctus: "the many-eyed Cherubim and the six-winged
> Seraphim".[15]

This peculiarity emboldens Fortescue to float the hypothesis that in all the
liturgies of the Church it was originally the case that the deacon began to read
out the supplications as soon as the priest started the Preface. This would explain
why in some places (Alexandria) those supplications precede the Consecration;
in others (Antioch) they follow it; in yet others (Rome) they come partly before
and partly after. Fortescue finds the anaphora of the Greek Liturgy of St Mark
to bear some obvious resemblances to the Roman Canon. Following the much-
admired Louis Duchesne, it is 'with this Egyptian Liturgy that ours is generally
supposed to have had a common source'.[16]

He ends by describing much more briefly the Coptic and Ethiopic
liturgies. After the schism, the former added three anaphora (dedicated
to St Cyril, St Gregory Nazianzen, and St Basil) in the Coptic tongue, the
latter 'ten or fifteen' in the ancient predecessor of Amharic, though the
most commonly used Eucharistic Prayer is a Ge'ez translation of the Coptic
Anaphora of St Cyril. Again, the Vatican Library is the best place to look for
manuscripts, but Fortescue can also tell the reader how to get hold of the

---

15   Ibid., p. 304.
16   Ibid., p. 305.

texts used by Uniates in his own day: *Missale Coptice et Arabice* printed at Rome in 1736 for the Catholic Copts, and, for the Uniates a 1548 *Missale cum benedictione incensi, cerae, etc* (containing the *Ordo communis* and the *Anaphora of the Twelve Apostles* i.e. the Coptic St Cyril) for the Catholic Ethiopians. In reality, the latter were only just emerging, in their small numbers, from a Roman-rite regime based on the unavailability of printed liturgical texts suited to their needs. Fortescue wondered aloud whether among the Greek Orthodox in Egypt the current 'strongly anti-Phanariote' patriarch might not one day try to resume use of the Greek Liturgy of St Mark as a gesture of independence from Constantinople.

The other great family of Eastern liturgies took its name from the Syrian metropolis, Antioch. Fortescue's view of the origins and development of the Antiochene Liturgy turns on his account of the so-called *Apostolic Constitutions*, or more precisely, of the eighth and last book in that collection. The *Apostolic Constitutions* purport to be the work of St Clement of Rome, who died soon after the end of the first century. That they are a genuine Clementine product is hardly credible. On Fortescue's analysis: the first six books are a modified version of the early third century *Didascalia Apostolorum*, the seventh book is a variant on the *Didache*, or 'Teaching of the Twelve Apostles' (which, he thinks, could well be a first century work). But the eighth book, aside from 85 'Apostolic Canons', is a 'complete liturgy',[17] which Fortescue ascribes to a Syrian Christian, living in Antioch or near it, around the year 400. He thinks it the form of worship used at the anonymous compiler's time in the church of Antioch, but with modifications whose character is discernible from the changes he had made to the *Didascalia Apostolorum* (Fortescue draws a connexion here to the pseudonymous letters added at some point to the little epistolatory bundle left, at the start of the second century, by St Ignatius of Antioch).

This of course is all grist to the antiquarians' mill. Of more import to the reader interested in how later Christians worshipped is Fortescue's claim that the liturgy of the eighth book of the *Apostolic Constitutions* is 'obviously built up on the same lines as all the Syrian ones':[18] he means, up to the present day. Its structure consists of

> the Mass of the Catechumens and their dismissal; the litany; the Anaphora beginning with the words "Right and just" and interrupted by the Sanctus; the words of Institution; Anamnesis, Epiklesis and Supplication for all kinds of people at that place; the Elevation with the words "Holy things to the holy"; the Communion distributed by the bishop and deacon (the deacon having the chalice); and then the final prayer

---

17 'Antiochene Liturgy', ibid., pp. 571-574, and here at p. 571.
18 Ibid.

and dismissal — this order is characteristic of all the Syrian and Palestinian uses, and is followed in the derived Byzantine liturgies.[19]

That there is no mention of the name of the Mother of God Fortescue takes to be a sign of the antiquity of this rite (before the Council of Ephesus, 431, when Mary's status as *Theotokos* was formally confirmed); he can find no explanation for its omission of the Our Father which the *Didache* had enjoined to be prayed thrice daily.

The main features of the text whose provenance and content Fortescue has been discussing are reproduced in more elaborate form in the Greek Liturgy of St James used throughout Syria and Palestine, including at Jerusalem. The elaboration concerns chiefly the *Prothesis* or preparation of the Gifts prior to the Liturgy of the Word, and the way in which the entry of the sacred ministers for the reading of the Scriptures and the carrying of the Gifts from the *Prothesis* to the altar became solemn processions. The oldest extant manuscript of the Greek Liturgy of St James, so Fortescue tells us in passing, dates from the tenth century, and was formerly the property of the Greek monastery in the Sicilian city of Messina, in whose University library it could still be found. That is a flickering shadow of the 'Italo-Greek' church, once so glorious, whose fate he had described in *The Uniate Eastern Churches*.

The principal features of the Antiochene rite are likewise continued in its successor after the Monophysite schism, viz. the Syriac Liturgy of St James, used with variations by both Syrian Jacobites and their Uniate brethren, whether Syrian Catholic or Maronite. Fortescue is able to refer readers to Brightman's *Liturgies Eastern and Western* to get an idea of the basic development from the *Apostolic Constitutions* through the Greek to the Syriac Liturgy of St James. But the Jacobites went on to add — apart from the famous clause 'Holy Immortal One who wast crucified for us', stigmatized by the Orthodox (rightly or otherwise) as unacceptably Monophysite — a large number of supplementary Anaphoras (Fortescue can count sixty-four), ascribed to various saints and Monophysite bishops, as well as a shortened version of the Anaphora of St James. We read that the 'complete Jacobite texts are not published',[20] while an 1843 Roman *Missale syriacum iuxta ritum antiochenum Syrorum* has been superseded by liturgical books now published for Syrian Uniates at Beirut. That was the kind of information Fortescue's 1907 travels, with their Beirut base, would have enabled him to acquire with ease.

---

19 Ibid., p. 572. The 'Anamnesis' is when the celebrant makes memorial of the death and subsequent exaltation of Christ, the 'Epiklesis' when, on this basis, he asks for the coming of the Holy Spirit onto the Gifts or the people, or both, so that the sacrifice may be fruitful.

20 Ibid., p. 574.

The Orthodox of the patriarchates of Antioch and Jerusalem long ago abandoned their own use for that of Constantinople, 'one result of the extreme centralization towards Constantinople that followed the Arab conquests of Egypt, Palestine, and Syria',[21] though on the island of Zakynthos (better known to British visitors to Corfu by its Italian name of 'Zante'), the Greek Liturgy of St James has remained in use on one day of the year, 23 October, the feast of James the 'brother of God'. The text, so Fortescue tells us, was published locally in 1886. He reports that the patriarch Damianos I of Jerusalem revived the ancient Liturgy of his see in 1900 for use on 31 December, while commissioning an improved edition for the future.

Granted the inevitable stylistic constraints of encyclopaedias, Fortescue's account of the rite of Constantinople itself — the Byzantine Liturgy — has a detectible note of ardour, at any rate once we have got beyond the archaeological introduction. Though, historically, the Byzantine was 'not one of the original parent-rites',[22] Fortescue's love for it is palpable — though doubtless saying so is affected by awareness of the huge effort he made to arrange for its celebration in Westminster Cathedral during the Eucharistic Congress, as well as at Letchworth, and his own hankerings after transfer to the Melkite rite, the church of the Byzantine Liturgy in Arab dress.

He rehearses the pre-history as he sees it. An early form of the Greek Liturgy of St James was re-arranged and abbreviated by St Basil for the use of the church of Caesarea, the metropolitan church of Cappadocia. Though Constantinople was outside the exarchate of Caesarea, Basil's fame and the convenience of his reform may have meant this rite was in use in the capital before Chrysostom arrived from Antioch. As to Chrysostom: '[t]he Tradition of his Church says that during the time of his patriarchate he composed from the Basilian Liturgy a shorter form that is the one still in common use throughout the Orthodox Church'.[23] Though Fortescue writes 'still in common use', he makes it plain that much water has flowed under the bridge, for to reconstruct the worship Chrysostom knew we must take away from the present forms the preparation of the Offerings at the Liturgy's start, the Little and Great Entrances, and the Creed. (We find these rites in a transitional stage en route to their current form in a manuscript of the Barberini Library from c. 800: it is reproduced in the volumes of Fortescue's Oxford contact Brightman.) And as to the story of the Byzantine Office, Fortescue regards it as inherited from the Antiochene method of keeping the canonical Hours, with such great poets as Romanos

21 Ibid., p. 573.
22 'Constantinople, The Rite of', art. cit., p. 312.
23 Ibid., p. 313.

the Melodist, Cosmas the Melodist, John Damascene and Theodore of Studion intercalating a rich succession of 'canons' — by which term is meant 'unmetrical hymns'.[24]

After dealing with the topics of language, calendar, and service-books, Fortescue turns to investigate the altar, vestments and sacred vessels of the Byzantine rite as well as its music. He remarks on the latter: 'In Russia and lately, to some extent, in the metropolitan church of Athens they sing figured music in parts of a very stately and beautiful kind. It is probably the most beautiful and suitable church music in the world'.[25] But all this is only a preamble to Fortescue's describing the *déroulement* of the rite, confining himself to the Liturgy of St John Chrysostom, since, as he says, the older Liturgy of St Basil, apart from its restriction to a smaller number of feasts and vigils, differs only in a certain quantity of prayers. Modern Orthodox service-books sanctioned Fortescue's *modus operandi* by printing Chrysostom's Liturgy first and then the variant prayers of the Basilian rite (and those for the 'Liturgy of the Presanctified' ascribed, by a curious legend, to St Gregory the Great, who was the pope's envoy in Byzantium for six years in the 570's).

The 'first rubric' requires that the celebrant must be reconciled to all, his heart kept free from evil thoughts and his body fasting from midnight. At the time appointed, generally this is after None, he arrives in church with the deacon, says the preparatory prayers, kisses the icons and goes into the *diakonikon* (the equivalent of a Western sacristy, but fully joined to the body of the church on the south side) so as to vest. This may be as good a place as any to mention the serious study Fortescue put into the topic of iconophilia (and of the enemies of the icons, the Iconoclasts).[26] While conceding that among some Christians in the early centuries there was anxiety about the possible *entrée* images might offer to idolatrous attitudes,[27] Fortescue thinks the first Christians nevertheless developed a sacred art as soon as the conditions of their material culture allowed. 'They accepted the art of the time and used it, as well as a poor and persecuted community could, to express their religious ideas.'[28]

---

24 Ibid., p. 315.

25 Ibid., p. 316.

26 'Images, veneration of', *The Catholic Encyclopaedia* VII (1910), pp. 664–672; 'Iconoclasm', ibid., pp. 620–625.

27 'Iconoclasm', art. cit., p. 620. It should be noted that, somewhat confusingly, Fortescue wrote a further article, not substantially different from this, under the same title ('Iconoclasm'), for J. Hastings, *Encyclopaedia of Religion and Ethics, VII* (Edinburgh: T. and T. Clark, 1913), pp. 78–81.

28 'Images, veneration of', art. cit., p. 665.

The tradition of actually venerating images (by kissing, prostration, lights, incense and so forth) arose, for Fortescue, from 'decent reverence',[29] the conventions for which just happened to be more dramatic in the East than in the West. The honour to which the Second Council of Nicaea, the Seventh Ecumenical Council, in 787, gave the name 'relative' worship, since it passes through the image to its prototype, 'will be expressed in signs denoted by custom and etiquette'.[30] And this is the worship ('a general word denoting some more or less high degree of reverence and honour, an acknowledgement of worth, like the German *Verehrung*),[31] with which celebrant and deacon in the Byzantine Liturgy, 'are constantly told to pay reverence to the holy icons'.[32]

The first part of the Liturgy, the *Proskomidê* or preparation of the gifts now begins at the credence table (the *prothesis*). Using the holy lance the celebrant cuts out from five leavened rounds of bread portions marked with the initials of *Iêsous Christos, Nika* ('Jesus Christ, victory'), with the acclamation 'The Lamb of God is sacrificed', while other portions ('prosphora') are set aside in honour of the Mother of God and the saints, and for the bishop and others for whom he wishes to pray. All this is accompanied, explains Fortescue, by many prayers and much incensing. When finished, the celebrating clergy go to the altar, kiss the Gospel-book, and the deacon announces 'It is time to sacrifice to the Lord!'. That is the signal for the Litanies to begin as the deacon leaves the sanctuary through the north door and, standing before the Royal Doors (Fortescue has already explained their iconography) prays for all sorts and conditions of men. This is in turn the prelude for the 'Little Entrance', the deacon bearing the book of the Gospels, with acolytes carrying candles. Troparia (short hymns) are sung while the celebrant prays and a reader prepares to read the epistle. After a gradual, the deacon sings the Gospel and more prayers follow.

Once the catechumens (usually notional) have been dismissed, there comes the 'Great Entrance' whose drama is well brought out in Fortescue's account.

> The deacon covers his shoulders with the great veil and takes the diskos (paten) with the bread; the thurible hangs from his hand; the celebrant follows with the chalice. Acolytes go in front and form a solemn procession. Meanwhile the choir sings the Cherubic Hymn (*Kheroubikos hymnos*): "Let us, who mystically represent the Cherubim, and who sing to the Life-giving Trinity

---

29 Ibid., p. 669.
30 Ibid., p. 671.
31 Ibid., p. 670.
32 Ibid.

the thrice holy hymn, put away all earthly cares so as to receive the King of all things (here the procession comes out through the north door) escorted by the army of angels. Alleluia, alleluia, alleluia."

The procession goes meanwhile all round the church and enters the sanctuary by the royal doors.[33]

In the substantial essay on the hymn he wrote for the prestigious *Dictionnaire d'Archéologie chrétienne et de liturgie* (it is owing to his quartet of articles for this multi-volume work that I refer in the title of this chapter to 'Encyclopaedias' in the plural), Fortescue was inclined to agree with John Mason Neale that the *Cherubikon* was the 'least beautiful of the four liturgical hymns of the Byzantine rite'. But he thought the prayer the celebrant recited by way of accompaniment to it quite extraordinarily fine.[34] Praising the elaborately melismatic Greek music for the hymn, Fortescue finds the entire ceremony 'curious' in its anticipation of the Eucharistic consecration (in the *Dictionnaire* essay he noted the protest entered by Eutychius of Constantinople, in a homily of 582, against its, evidently recent, introduction).[35] Yet he also found this portion of the rite extremely moving. Now it is — or rather, after a few more prayers, and the deacon's cry, 'The doors, the doors!' — that the Anaphora, the Eucharistic Prayer, actually begins.

Consonant with the Orthodox insistence that the Words of Institution do not consecrate, the Euchologion to which Fortescue had access, published in Venice 'at the sign of the Phoenix' (he had already been told as a student in Rome visiting the Greek College that the Venice editions of the Orthodox service-books were the best), includes a rubric warning the sacred ministers not to make a reverence at this point but to wait until the Epiklesis, the prayer for the descent of the Holy Spirit. The Byzantine Uniates, on the other hand, 'make a profound reverence after each form'.[36] With the Orthodox, the deep prostration is reserved for after the Epiklesis which is also when 'the deacon waves the ripidion (fan) over the Blessed

---

33 'Constantinople, Rite of', art. cit., p. 317.

34 'Chéroubicon', *Dictionnaire d'Archéologie chrétienne et de liturgie* III/1 (Paris: Letouzey, 1913), cols. 1281–1286, and here at col. 1282.

35 Ibid., col. 1283. Fortescue notes the continuance of a controversy about it, among Greeks as well as Latin observers. For Germanus of Constantinople (in office 715–730), the procession, after all, signifies the entry of the saints and angels accompanying Christ as he draws near to accomplish his sacrifice, and the hymn makes sense in that context, ibid., cols. 1283–1284. Less piously: it is simply one of numerous examples of liturgical anticipation, 'to be found in all the rites', ibid. col. 1285.

36 'Constantinople, Rite of', art. cit., p. 317..

Sacrament. This ceremony, now interpreted mystically as a symbol of adoring angels, was certainly once a practical precaution. They have no pall over the chalice and there is a danger of flies.'[37]

Now comes the memorial of the saints and the diptychs of the dead and the living, whereupon, after a blessing of the people, the deacon re-emerges to stand before the iconostasis for a further litany asking for spiritual and temporal favours which climaxes in the Lord's Prayer. The curtains over the royal doors are drawn back, the Gifts are shown to the people, a Communion hymn is sung amd the distribution of Holy Communion begins. Fortescue draws attention to the beauty of the prayers made in preparation for receiving (especially the one that opens, 'I believe, Lord, and I confess'). There is some discussion, he says, as to whether the *prosphora*, particles of bread that have lain on the *diskos* since the preparation, have been consecrated. The Orthodox say no, Uniates yes. Fortescue comments sensibly that it depends on the intention of the celebrant concerned. The ceremony ends with the distribution of unconsecrated bread from the table of prothesis as 'antidoron', a substitute for communion for those who have not received.

Fortescue does not omit to describe the Byzantine office, and the way the Orthodox celebrate the remaining sacraments and sacramentals, though for a fuller account of these than that given in the *Catholic Encyclopaedia* he refers readers to *The Orthodox Eastern Church*. A major essay on the collections of odes in the Byzantine office appeared in the Cabrol *Dictionnaire* under the title 'Canon dans le rite byzantin'.[38]

The variety of Liturgies in union with Rome

Fortescue's concept of catholicity made him understandably concerned about the fate of the Eastern liturgies as practised by Oriental Catholics. He also felt an obligation to answer the question why the Roman rite in the course of its mediaeval and modern history had supplanted such a variety of Western liturgical usage beyond the City. He was sensitive to the charge — whether made by Orthodox, Anglicans, or simply by liturgical historians — that Rome tended to de-nature the Eastern rites through imposing its own preferences as well as eliminating other liturgical usages from its own patriarchate. Addressing the general issue of rites in the Catholic Church, he opined that 'supposing uniformity in essentials and in faith, the authority of the Church has never insisted on uniformity of rite; Rome has never resented the fact that other people have their own

37 Ibid., p. 318.
38 'Canon dans le rite byzantin', *Dictionnaire d'Archéologie chrétienne et de liturgie* II/2 (Paris: Letouzey, 1910), cols. 1905–1910.

expression of the same truths'.[39] That being so, he needed to explain why the Gallican rite had virtually vanished from the high mediaeval West; why the Holy See had intervened to modify the liturgical books of the Uniate churches; and why the later mediaeval usages, such as in England the Use of Sarum, had gone the way of all flesh.

Fortescue's line on the Gallican rites (within which he includes the Mozarabic) is that their disappearance was not the result of Roman fiat from above but of a groundswell of opinion from below, especially in the Frankish north. Led by the Carolingian emperors and their bishops, it flowed from a desire for a certain homogeneity of rite combined with admiration for the see of the apostles Peter and Paul. 'In the history of the substitution of the Roman Rite for the Gallican the popes appear as spectators, except perhaps in Spain and much later in Milan'.[40] He inferred from the general principle 'rite follows patriarchate' that a Romanization of the other Western liturgies would have happened in the natural course of things anyway – but somewhat spoils the neatness of his plan by conceding that in places where people really cared for their ancient liturgies, such as Milan and Toledo, they have kept them anyway. He would probably have been surprised to find that, in the wake of the Second Vatican Council, the Mozarabic Liturgy may now be celebrated not just in the cathedral of Toledo but anywhere in Spain.

He is more exercised about the Uniate question since, as he cites Duchesne in remarking, changes made by Roman correctors to the Oriental liturgies have sometimes smacked more of zeal than of knowledge.[41] The extent of the damage, says Fortescue, has been exaggerated. 'Despite the general prejudice that Uniat rites are mere mutilated hybrids, the strongest impression from the study of them is how little has been changed.'[42] There was never any question of possible false doctrine in the Byzantine Liturgy, so it was never tampered with in any way whatsoever. If the Ruthenians have elected to add the Filioque to the recitation of the Creed that was their choice uninfluenced or at any rate undetermined by Rome.[43]

---

39 'Rites', *Catholic Encyclopaedia* XIII (1912), pp. 64–72, and here at p. 64.

40 Ibid., p. 65.

41 L. Duchesne, *Les origines du Culte chrétien* (Paris: Fontemoing, 1898, 2nd edition), p. 69.

42 'Rites', art. cit., p. 65.

43 Fortescue was inclined to exculpate Rome from the charge of insisting on the inclusion of the Filioque in the profession of the Creed by Eastern Christians; but in fact from time to time pressure was exerted to this end if there was dubiety as to acceptance of the doctrine which underlies the credal insertion, or anxiety about the giving of scandal as candidly explained by Pope Benedict

The situation was rather different with those whose theological background was Nestorian, Monophysite or Monothelite. Rightly, their liturgies were keenly scanned for possible heretical expressions. Fortescue defends most but not all of the changes that were made. He thinks the Roman curia was correct to ask for the insertion of the Words of Institution into the Liturgy of Addai and Mari used by Chaldaeans. He would not have expected that, at the height of hopes for the final overcoming of the Nestorian schism around the turn of the bi-millennium, the Holy See told the Assyrians the insertion would not be insisted on in future, though it was still recommended. Fortescue also sought to justify the removal from the Trisagion, as used in rites of Monophysite lineage, of the celebrated words, 'Holy, Strong and Immortal One *who wast crucified for us*', though he signals the possible orthodoxy of the phrase when he writes, 'If only because of its associations this could not remain in a Catholic Liturgy'.[44] In other cases, however, Fortescue disassociated himself from demands he considered over-scrupulous. There was nothing to be objected to when the Armenian Liturgy anticipated the language used for the Consecrated Gifts when speaking about the *oblata* (the Byzantine Liturgy does the same — and so does, he could have pointed out, the Offertory rite of the Liturgy of St Pius V). Fortescue was shocked by the wholesale changes made by Latinisers in Portuguese India to the Syro-Malabar rite, though these had absolutely nothing to do with the Pope. In fact, in the later twentieth century strenuous efforts would be made to undo some of these changes, with Roman support. In the case of the Maronite and Armenian liturgies, some changes in the direction of Latin practice have been self-generated — as is clear in the case of the Armenians from the fact that the Gregorian (i.e. schismatic) Armenians embraced them as well. Fortescue had in mind such customs as the use of unleavened bread, the Roman prayers of preparation 'at the foot of the altar', the lavabo, and the reciting of the Johannine Prologue as the 'Last Gospel' — all adopted by Armenians during the time of the Crusades as badges, so Fortescue thinks, of Christian Armenia's defiantly non-Byzantine status.

Coming closer to home, what of the now defunct uses of Sarum and Hereford, York and Durham? Without, in the article 'Rites', mentioning the English usages by name, Fortescue is scathingly dismissive of the non-Tridentine variants. 'They are late, exuberant, and inferior variants, whose ornate additions and long interpolated tropes, sequences, and farcing destroy the dignified simplicity of the old liturgy'.[45] But one notes that

XIV in his 1755 letter *Allatae sunt*. I owe this information to A. Dragani, *Adrian Fortescue and the Eastern Christian Churches* op. cit., pp. 56–57.

44 'Rites', art. cit., p. 66.
45 Ibid.

the Uses that survived (the Use of Lyons, and those of Orders such as Carmelites, Dominicans, Carthusians) were not permitted to continue on the ground that they lacked the features Fortescue excoriates but because they could show a pedigree of at least two hundred years. It is not clear that the mediaeval English Uses failed that test.

In an essay on the liturgical book known as the *Rituale* Fortescue pointed out that, unlike the other books of the Roman rite, there has never been any question of imposing a single standard whereby to measure customs in vigour in different dioceses with regard to, for instance, marriage, or the visitation of the sick, or, again, processions, blessings, sacramentals.[46] If texts and rubrics for the prayers and ceremonies in question are not found in the Roman Missal and Breviary then they can exist perfectly well in a variety of local forms. Asked to contribute an article on the Use of Durham,[47] Fortescue gave, inter alia, a sympathetic account of a late Elizabethan work entitled *The Ancient Monuments, Rites and Customs of the Monastical Church of Durham before the Suppression*, which had recently been edited under the auspices of the Surtees Society from two seventeenth century manuscripts.[48] He noted elements of distinctive Durham ceremonial: on Good Friday, the crucifix for the Creeping to the Cross was brought by two monks from inside a statue of the Virgin Mother; the same day the Blessed Sacrament was enclosed in a figure of Christ on a side altar and candles kept burning before it till Easter; on Holy Saturday the monks sang the Miserere as they went towards the Paschal fire; between 3–4 o'clock on the morning of Easter Day the Sacrament was brought in procession to the high altar during the singing of the antiphon *Christus resurgens ex mortuis iam non moritur*, a statue of the risen Christ was kept on the same altar throughout the week of Easter.

Did Fortescue think of these as praiseworthy local variants of the ritual, or regrettable over-dramatic ornamentations of the Liturgy? It is hard to generalize. Judging by what he has to say about the Use of Sarum in *The Mass* (on which more below) he placed some variations in the one category, the rest in the other.

On the Mass of the Roman rite

Much of what Fortescue had to say about the early history of Christian Liturgy in general is comprised in his *Encyclopaedia* articles, and may largely be taken for granted in any account of *The Mass. A Study of the Roman Liturgy* where it occupies the opening two chapters which, between them,

---

46 'Ritual', *Catholic Encyclopaedia* XIII (1912), pp. 88–90, and here at p. 89.

47 'Durham Rite', *Catholic Encyclopaedia* V (1909), pp. 213–214.

48 *The Ancient Monuments, Rites and Customs of the Monastical Church of Durham before the Suppression*, Surtees Society, Volume CVII, (1903).

make up a quarter of the book's bulk.[49] On the model of his *Encylopaedia* articles, and following, no doubt, the demands of a sane methodology, Fortescue's attention to the Roman rite in its specificity is first engaged by the question of its origin and historical development.

The reader who, following the order of exposition of Fortescue's writings given here, begins reading *The Mass* at, accordingly, its third chapter, is in for an unpleasant surprise. There is nothing else in Fortescue's corpus so complicated and confusing — I do not say *unnecessarily complicated*, nor do I say *confused* — as that very section of this particular book. The reason concerns the extreme difficulty of the subject matter, namely discussion of a variety of theories of how the Roman Canon — which in its present form we know only as early as the Gelasian Sacramentary (dated somewhere between the sixth and eighth centuries) — came to have the form it does. It is probably best to begin with Fortescue's conclusion to the chapter — not simply the ultimate conclusion, to the effect that 'we have no certainty about the origin of our Canon',[50] but also the penultimate conclusion where, with inevitable simplification, he seeks to shake down the theories he has been describing into two more or less national forms.

On the one hand, there is the 'school of French Benedictines' (Dom Paul Cagin of Quarr and Abbot Fernand Cabrol of Farnborough are chiefly in mind), for whom the solution to the problem of the original structure of the Roman canon must be sought by way of a comparison with the Gallican rites — which these students regarded as proto-Roman.[51] The other is that of the 'school of most German scholars' for whom the proper comparison is, rather, with Eastern rites, whether Antiochene or Alexandrian.[52] (Actually, one at least of Fortescue's 'Germans', was Austrian, but Fortescue is following a common convention in describing German-Austrians in the period.)

Fortescue offers readers the following litmus test for deciding between these two schools. It consists in asking the question, where in the Roman Liturgy would a pre-Gelasian generation have expected to find the prayers he (and his fellow archeologists of the rite) lump together as 'the Intercession' — by which he means the Roman Canon's Memento of the Living, its Memento of the Dead, and the two prayers to which lists of the saints are attached, the *Communicantes* and the *Nobis quoque peccatoribus*. These are the prayers which in the *Encyclopaedia* articles, when describing the Eastern liturgies, he had called 'the Supplication'.

---

49 Unless otherwise stated, I shall be using the second edition, in its 1954 re-printing with a new introduction by the late Mgr J.D. Crichton.

50 Ibid., p. 171,

51 Ibid., p. 170; cf. pp. 144–146, 166–168.

52 Ibid., p. 170; cf. pp. 140–143; 148–166.

The decisive move in answering this question, so Fortescue believed, must be consultation of a letter of Pope Innocent I, written in 416 to Decentius, bishop of Gubbio, on matters liturgical.[53] Apparently, the bishop had been reading the diptychs (and hence, praying the prayers of 'the Intercession') before the Eucharistic Consecration. Innocent advises him that this is much better done after: '[T]hey should be named during the holy mysteries, not in the part that comes before, so that we may open the way for the prayers that follow by the mysteries themselves'.[54] If the French scholars are correct, the pope must have meant that prayers hitherto recited at the Offertory should be said during the canon, whereas if the 'Germans' are right what Innocent was counselling was the removal of these prayers from one place in the Canon to another, i.e. from before the Consecration to after it. It is because Fortescue finds this by far the more plausible interpretation of Innocent's text that he prefers the 'German' — the Austro-German — view.

But *which version* of that view? Is Rudolf Buchwald of the Weidenau seminary in Austrian Silesia right when he thinks that Rome borrowed much of its Canon from Alexandria and then re-arranged it? Or should one support Anton Baumstark of the Roman Campo Santo who thinks the Roman Canon originally had an Antiochene order which was modified from Ravenna which itself had borrowed elements from Alexandria? Or defer to Ferdinand Probst of Tübingen who thought the oldest Roman Canon Syrian, as in the *Apostolic Constitutions,* but radically altered by Pope Damasus who sought to have the changing feasts of the Calendar reflected throughout the rite? Or is one to place one's bet on Paul Drews of Halle for whom the original Roman liturgy resembled that of Jerusalem-Antioch such that its Canon must be reviewed from the angle of the Anaphora of the Greek Liturgy of St James? It is here that Fortescue washes his hands of the whole affair, and leaves the reader entirely to his own devices. As we shall see, he caused offence to some English Catholics by treating matters as so open, and irritated others by nudging the reader in at any rate one *general* direction.

Fortescue had already explained that the peculiarities which separate the Roman rite from all others (whether Gallican or Eastern) are fourfold: the absence of litanies of intercession and the consequent eclipse of the role of the deacon; the place of the kiss of peace immediately before the Communion; the lack of an explicit invocation of the Holy Spirit to consecrate the elements, and the order of the various elements of

---

53 Fortescue cites long extracts from the letter in ibid., pp. 132–133. It is to be found in the twentieth volume of Migne's *Patrologia Latina* at columns 551–561.

54 Quoted in *The Mass*, op. cit., p. 133.

the Canon. If in fact he has concentrated on the last of these, he has borne the other three peculiarities in mind throughout his discussion. After chapter three of *The Mass* he can leave aside the seemingly irresoluble controversies these points raise, and deal with much more straightforward matters: the story of the Roman Mass from Pope Gregory I to the present, and the significance of the Mass's different parts as they unfold.

The history of the Roman Mass

Let us take the history first. It is not that the Mass has been left unchanged since Gregory — who himself is credited with three changes: the adoption of the Kyrie, the prolongation of the *Hanc igitur* prayer which follows on the *Communicantes* in the Canon, and the insertion of the Lord's Prayer before Communion.[55] (The reader needs a copy of the historic Order of the Roman rite to follow Fortescue's account fully: the text was and is readily available.) However, '[a]ll later modifications were fitted into the old arrangements, and the most important parts were not touched'.[56] That is true even though, as Fortescue recognizes, the 'infiltration of Gallican elements' (as the Roman rite came south again from its journey north, it brought back new luggage) and the 'evolution of prolific mediaeval derived rites' (the 'Uses' on which comment has been made vis-à-vis the *Encyclopaedias*) can hardly be described as the mere addition of details.[57]

Fortescue would have appreciated, I think, for its elegance of analysis and expression Dix's neat comparison between the historical fate of the Eastern and Western liturgies.

> The present main Eastern type has developed from the fourth century rite of the Eastern "holy city", Jerusalem, as remodelled and expanded in the Eastern political centre, Constantinople. The present main Western type has developed from the fourth century rite of the Western "holy city", Rome, as remodelled and expanded in the Western political centre, the nucleus of Charlemagne's empire in Gaul and the Rhineland.[58]

Still, in describing in the form of a moving tableau the eighth century Roman rite set out in the *Ordo romanus primus* Fortescue can write nevertheless,

---

55 Ibid., p. 172.
56 Ibid., p. 173.
57 Ibid.
58 G. Dix, *The Shape of the Liturgy*, op. cit., pp. 10–11.

In picturing thus a Papal High Mass of the eighth century we realize chiefly how little has been changed since. An ordinary modern Catholic would find himself quite at home with the whole service and would understand what is going on all the time perfectly. We should miss the Creed, the Offertory prayers, elevation, blessing and last Gospel only. There are as yet no incensings of persons or things, no bell-ringing. These things are the later additions.[59]

We have already noted that Fortescue thought it perfectly normal and proper that the rite of the Roman patriarch should elbow out others in its own patriarchate. We know he admired what the English lay liturgiologist Edmund Bishop stressed as the typical sobriety of ancient Roman Christian worship.[60] Did he then regret the embellishments that accrued to the Roman rite from the influences it underwent north of the Alps in the age after the eighth century? Actually, no. As he writes,

> If one may venture a criticism of these additions from an aesthetic point of view, it is that they are exceedingly happy. The old Roman rite, in spite of its dignity and archaic simplicity, had the disadvantage of being dull. The Eastern and Gallican rites are too florid for our taste and too long. The few non-Roman elements in our Mass take nothing from its dignity and yet give it enough variety and reticent emotion to make it most beautiful.[61]

So much for what some have understood, rightly or otherwise, as Bishop's liturgical Puritanism.[62]

Then what? Well, the emergence of Low Mass, the abridged celebration, when it became normal for each priest to celebrate daily. 'The older system of assistance and communion or concelebration was replaced in the early middle ages by a separate Mass said apart by each priest.'[63] (In an interesting footnote, reporting on contemporary practice, Fortescue observes that

---

59 *The Mass*, op. cit., p. 177. Fortescue's vivid scene-painting of the 'First Roman Order' seems to have been inspired by S. Beissel, S.J., *Altchristliche Kunst und Liturgie in Italien* (Freiburg: Herder, 1899), pp. 296–328.

60 Fortescue several times refers, in *The Mass* and elsewhere, to Bishop's famous essay, 'The Genius of the Roman Rite', originally published in sections in *The Weekly Register* for 1899 and then in V. Staley (ed.), *Essays on Ceremonial, by various authors* (London: Moring, 1904), pp. 283–307.

61 *The Mass*, op. cit., p. 184.

62 For a discussion of the essay vis-à-vis Bishop's own mind, see N. Abercrombie, *The Life and Work of Edmund Bishop* (London: Longmans, Green, 1959), pp. 275–279. Bishop recognised that the ancient Roman rite was excessively austere, even marmoreal.

63 *The Mass*, op. cit., p. 187.

Uniates 'in most rites' have adopted this practice under Latin influence, but even without a deacon they still need two assistants, one for incense and one to be choir; and he also says that in small Orthodox churches it is possible to see a priest trying to manage without a deacon likewise.[64]) The theology of the Mass as propitiatory sacrifice helped on this development. Why be content with only one celebration if there could be two, thus doubling the salvific value?

The question of how to reckon the multiplicity of concelebrants at a single Mass, especially in regard to the issue of distinct 'intentions', with their stipendiary and hence financial implications, was not an easy one to answer in Eucharistic theology half a century after Fortescue's death, by which time the earlier practice he described had again become, at any rate in Religious houses, the statistical norm. Fortescue reports that, while the Missal of St Pius V made definitive provisions for how to celebrate a Low Mass, its mediaeval predecessors had long since given 'occasional directions as alternatives where there was no deacon or choir'.[65] The *Missa cantata* — sung like the High Mass but otherwise Low — Fortescue calls 'a compromise of a compromise', precisely by having the ceremonial of Low Mass combined with the music of High; it is 'only justifiable to enhance the dignity of Sunday Mass when a deacon and subdeacon cannot be had'.[66] Fortescue adds from his wealth of historical knowledge some very odd examples of alternative forms, of which the least objectionable is the *Missa nautica*, said at sea when the rocking of a boat could upset the chalice and consisting of the Liturgy of the Catechumens as far as the Gospel together with the prayers of dismissal.

So far as the local uses were concerned, Fortescue is at pains to scotch the idea that they constituted parallel rites with the Roman rite. 'They can indeed hardly be called derived rites; if one may take a parallel from philology one may describe them best as dialects of the Roman rite.'[67] Taking the example of the Use of Sarum (in which interest revived in England, first on the part of Anglican High Churchmen and then, in the later twentieth century, among Roman Catholics), Fortescue does not seem to have any objection to its insertion, in the prayers at the foot of the altar, of Kyrie, Pater, Ave and a versicle before an abbreviated Confiteor, nor to the kiss of peace given to the deacon and subdeacon before the ministers ascended the altar steps. The farced Kyrie, the shorter Offertory prayers, the single offering of bread and wine, the bowing rather than genuflecting at the elevation, the extension of the arms at the *Unde et memores*, the lack of a concluding blessing and the recitation of the Last Gospel on the way back

64 Ibid., fn 2.
65 Ibid., p. 189.
66 Ibid., p. 191.
67 Ibid., p. 201.

to the sacristy, these generate no negative comments. But the same is not true of the Holy Week customs, which included throwing unconsecrated hosts — 'singing breads' — at choirboys.[68]

More widely, Fortescue declares that, given the comparative superficiality of the differences in the Uses, it is 'quite accurate to say that from the time of the Synod of Cloveshoe in 747 to the Reformation, the Roman rite was used throughout England; though we may add the further detail that it was used in slightly modified local forms'.[69] This is, of course, a poke in the eye of Anglicans hostile to the 'Western Use' as 'un-English'. Fortescue was eminently supportive of Pius V's liturgical efforts, considering the reform over which he presided sensible and responsible, and productive of a rite that was 'essentially more archaic and venerable than the mediaeval development'.[70] What Fortescue objected to was what had happened after Trent: an 'endless addition of Masses for new feasts',[71] for which ever growing appendices had to be provided, as the Proper of Saints spread to cover the entire year and the work of identifying the correct Mass to be celebrated grew ever unwieldier. The most ancient offices are or were in danger of becoming marginal — Fortescue was able, before going to press, to insert a footnote to the effect that Pope Pius X's 1911 decree *Divino afflatu* began a very desirable process of restoring priority to the Proper of Time.

The order of the Mass

All that was now left to Fortescue was to take people through the order of the Roman Mass, section by section, thus arranging in a single narrative the materials he had scattered alphabetically in discreet sections of the *Catholic Encyclopaedia*. His account is sparkling with judgments and choc-à-bloc with historical information, engagingly offered after his personal style.

The Mass begins with the Introit, which is 'simply the processional psalm sung as those who are about to celebrate and assist come in'.[72] If early writers do not mention the *antiphona ad introitum* (the structure is antiphon, psalm, doxology, antiphon), that, says Fortescue coolly, is because they consider the service to begin at the altar. The First Roman Order already allows for most of the verses to be omitted if the pope has reached the altar and gives the choirmaster a sign. Since some fairly

---

68 H.J. Feasey, *Ancient English Holy Week Ceremonial* (London: Thomas Baker, 1897).

69 *The Mass*, op, cit., p. 205.

70 Ibid., p. 208.

71 Ibid., p. 211.

72 Ibid., p. 216.

primitive date (Pope Damasus?) the Introit like much in the Mass varies with the calendar. Who chose the Propers is one of 'the many unknown details of the origin of our rite',[73] but for the ancient feasts they were, often enough, chosen well. For other occasions, for example the Sundays after Pentecost, it is true of the Introit as of other variable parts of the Mass, that '[e]ach of them is a certainly an excellent prayer, its idea is most appropriate for any day, therefore also for this'.[74] Enough said. Anciently, the verse was always the opening words of a psalm; later compilers felt no need to adhere to this principle, and some introits are of ecclesiastical composition, rather than taken from Scripture. The Mass is often named for its Introit, as with the four Sundays of Lent: *Invocabit, Reminiscere, Oculi,* and *Laetare.*

The prayers at the foot of the altar were originally the celebrant's prayers before the procession moved off or as it moved up the church. The Tridentine reformers simply took one of the more widespread forms. Arriving at the altar the celebrant kisses it, an 'obvious reverence':[75] Fortescue noted that a bishop kept the older practice of kissing the Gospel as well. Then the altar is incensed, a custom whose advent Fortescue describes as 'inevitable' given not only the Old Testament background but also the incense offered Christ by the magi (Matthew 2:11) and the incense at the heavenly altar in the book of the Apocalypse (8:3–5). The Kyrie, granted that it is in Greek, the older liturgical tongue at Rome, might appear an old survival, but seemingly it is nothing of the kind. Rather is it a late (sixth century) import from the East. Fortescue interprets a letter of Pope Gregory I to John of Syracuse to imply it formed part of a litany, and he thinks this was some version of the Litany of the Saints, which has survived, introduced and followed by the Kyrie, in the Mass of the Vigils of Easter and Pentecost (and at Ordinations). About the ninth century the number of invocations was fixed at three triplets.

The *Gloria in excelsis Deo*, anciently translated from the Greek, first appears in the Gregorian Sacramentary, but is omitted on Sundays in Lent and Advent owing to their penitential character (though Fortescue thinks Advent only began to be considered a season of penance in about the thirteenth century). Seen as concluding the Kyrie, it serves the same role as the hymn which follows the first litany in the Greek Liturgy of St James (and there is something comparable in the Byzantine rite).

The collect, which Fortescue defines as 'the opening prayer by the celebrant after the common prayer (litany) and hymn (Gloria)', then follows.[76] It was

73 Ibid., p. 220.
74 Ibid., p. 221.
75 Ibid., p. 226.
76 Ibid., p. 245.

probably preceded by a longer invitation to prayer than our curt *Oremus*, 'Let us pray'. The oldest ones are in the Leonine Sacramentary and are typified by a marked 'logical order and style'. 'Nothing in the Missal is so redolent of the character of our rite, nothing so *Roman* as the old collects — and nothing, alas, so little Roman as the new ones.'[77] At one time the *Laudes regiae* (better known to modern Catholics as the *Christus vincit*) were sung after the collect on great feasts — possibly a borrowing from Gaul.

We come to the readings of the Mass or, as Fortescue prefers to write, the 'Lessons'. Fortescue explains the significance of the ancient *liber comitis* which gave all the lessons in order by recording their first and last words. He is inclined to doubt the mediaeval tradition that St Jerome arranged the Roman lections (the sermons of Augustine and Peter Chrysologus enable scholars to infer the choice in Africa and at Ravenna, and something similar can be done for Rome by using Leo I and Gregory I in the same way). Though in the Roman rite there are days with more than two lessons, the older trio of prophecy, epistle, Gospel was largely reduced to a duo of epistle and Gospel by the seventh century. Except for feasts, when the choice of texts is theologically perspicuous, the principles on which the Roman lectionary was devised are, claims Fortescue, opaque to us — despite the minute and exigent research of the the German Jesuit Stephan Beissel in his *Entstehung der Perikopen des Römischen Messbuchs*, which had just appeared in time for Fortescue to use.[78]

Yet the order *may* be as old as Pope Gregory I (c. 540–604) — or even as Pope Damasus (c. 304–384). Preachers must be content with the awareness that 'any part of Scripture may be read with profit on any day'.[79] This somewhat deflating pronouncement reduces what Fortescue can usefully say about epistle, gradual and alleluia, (sequence) and Gospel. But some helpful comments can still be made. He sees no reason why modern churches cannot be built with ambos, one on the north for the Gospel and perhaps on a higher step, the other on the south for the other lessons. The alleluia (or tract on days of fasting or mourning) he describes as, in effect, a substitute second psalm to the gradual psalm. For the mediaevals its *iubilus* (the highly melismatic setting of the actual word 'alleluia') is not just a 'place where the neums happen to be rather longer than usual. They see in the iubilus an inarticulate expression of joy, by which the mind is carried up to the unspeakable joy of the saints'. Here Fortescue refers readers to Pothier, whom he had read when at Whitechapel, for further discussion.[80]

77 Ibid., p. 249.

78 S. Beissel, S.J., *Entstehung der Perikopen des Römischen Messbuchs* (Freiburg: Herder, 1907).

79 *The Mass*, op. cit., p. 262.

80 Ibid., p. 269; J. Pothier, *Les Mélodies grégoriennes*, op. cit., pp. 170–179.

Fortescue felt Pius V had kept the best of the immediately pre-Gospel sequences (most were rather bad), though it was a pity a place had not been found for Venantius Fortunatus's Easter sequence *Salve festa dies* and for at least one example from the inventor of the genre, Notker Balbulus of Sankt Gallen (in Switzerland).[81] On the Gospel itself, Fortescue tended to think that at Rome the catechumens were dismissed before it was read. The First and Second Roman Orders already describe its ceremonial reading as a solemn affair. 'People who carried sticks laid them down, but the bishop holds his crozier.'[82] He speaks with great admiration of the care and craft with which the Byzantines (and how often in *The Mass* does he refer to them as well as to other Orientals!) embellished their Gospel-books.

Then come the homily and Creed — except that in 'most mediaeval uses' the homily followed the Creed which, joined as its content was to the understanding of any Gospel text, seemed its natural extension.[83] The use of the Creed at Mass (as distinct from Baptism) is rather late at Rome (in the eleventh century); Fortescue considers that everywhere in the West it was 'an addition borrowed from Constantinople'.[84]

The Prayers of the Faithful, which begin the Liturgy of the Sacrifice (Fortescue calls it, logically enough, the 'Mass of the Faithful') are represented in the Missal of St Pius V only by the single word, *Oremus* — though in France they are represented semi-liturgically by the *prone*, before the sermon, and in the England of the Sarum Use by the 'bidding prayers' said after the Gospel from altar or pulpit (in cathedrals and collegiate churches this was done at the Asperges, the celebrant standing before the rood-screen).

Then follows the Offertory which in Rome remained a simple procession with loaves (later, from about the eighth century, azymes) and wine, represented now by an offering of money since '[n]o doubt the offering of the actual gifts became difficult and cumbersome'.[85] An offertory chant accompanies the offering of the gifts, using, in the Tridentine liturgy, prayers adopted from those in the Fourteenth Roman Order (its date is easy to remember, since it is *fourteenth* century), most of them hailing from elsewhere than Rome itself. Fortescue notes the 'dramatic misplacement' whereby in the prayer *Suscipe sancta Pater* the consecration is anticipated

---

81 On whom his readers could consult a fellow Swiss: J. Werner, *Notkers Sequenzen. Beitrag zur Geschichte der lateinischen Sequenzdichtung* (Aarau: 1901). Only about 15 of the sequences in his *Liber Sequentiarum* are regarded as genuine.

82 *The Mass*, op. cit., p. 282.

83 Ibid., p. 285.

84 Ibid., p. 289.

85 Ibid., p. 300.

(there is talk already of *hanc immaculatam hostiam*). Anathema to the reformers of 1969 and the object of a sophisticated defence by Dr Catherine Pickstock of Emmanuel College, Cambridge,[86] Fortescue considers this something unexceptionable 'of which all liturgies have examples'.[87]

The mixing of water and wine in the chalice conforms to the custom of all ancient peoples practicing viniculture, and, accordingly, corresponds to what would have happened at the Last Supper. The symbolic interpretation, in terms of the uniting of the two natures of Christ, or of the union of the redeemed with the Redeemer, comes later, but Fortescue shows no sign of disprizing it on that ground.

Is the prayer *Veni Sanctificator* (again, the close reader will need a copy of the text of the Missal) the epiclesis of the rite of St Pius V? Hardly, or it would appear in the Canon, and yet it is 'one example of the many invocations of the Holy Ghost scattered throughout all liturgies, of which invocations the classical Epiklesis is only one among others'.[88] The incensing of gifts, altar, celebrant, ministers and people is the most elaborate in the Roman Liturgy, while the 'offertory act' ends with the ceremonial ablutions of the Lavabo (late mediaeval), the summing up of what has preceded in the (non-Roman) prayer *Suscipe sancta Trinitas*, and lastly the most ancient and authentic element in the whole, the Secret prayer which, in an 'often very ingenious' manner, brings together with the universal concept of oblation the particular motif of the feast being celebrated.[89] By ending with the clause *per omnia saecula saeculorum* sung aloud it warns choir and people that the Preface — and therefore the Canon of the Mass — is about to begin.

We have seen already that Fortescue makes rather heavy weather of the Roman Canon, following in this the numerous modern scholars who have found the puzzle of its arrangement a possible key to its origins. At any rate, the Preface belongs to it, for at the first Eucharist, in the Cenacle, the Lord gave thanks, which is what the Preface does. Only then, or rather, only after the Sanctus — a continuation of the Preface, but there is a 'dramatic touch of letting the people fill in the choral chant of the angels, in which (as the Preface says) we also wish to join',[90] does the celebrant move on to the Institution, which then puts him in mind of the Cross, Resurrection, Ascension, and Descent of the Holy Spirit, which (so Fortescue surmises — he admits he cannot find a reference to Pentecost in the Anamnesis of the historic liturgies) introduced the moment of the Epiklesis.

---

86 C. Pickstock, *After Writing. On the Liturgical Consummation of Philosophy* (Oxford: Blackwell, 1998).

87 *The Mass*, op. cit., p. 305.

88 Ibid., pp. 307–308.

89 Ibid., p. 313.

90 Ibid., pp. 320–321.

In Fortescue's day there were fifteen Prefaces (the Leonine Sacramentary had two-hundred and sixty-seven, some of them rather strange). But in the mediaeval and early modern period, and indeed until the liturgical reform that followed the Second Vatican Council, the principle Fortescue lays down about the Preface held more or less good: 'the preface was considered on the whole too sacred, too near the intangible Canon to be much altered'.[91]

Fortescue cannot resist the temptation to revisit the archaeological analyses of the Canon made earlier (in this we shall not follow him), but he also has nuggets of theological insight that can stand irrespective of literary reconstructions. Thus in the Commemoration of the Living he notes how three phrases: 'sacrifice of praise', 'for the redemption of souls; and 'for the hope of salvation and safety', sum up cumulatively the 'threefold idea of sacrifice — praise, atonement, petition'.[92] Again, in the phrase 'this excellent chalice' he highlights 'the dramatic identification of the chalice we actually hold with the one our Lord held' as 'a sign of Roman insistence on the words of Institution as the consecrating form'.[93]

The words *Mysterium fidei*, inserted into the Consecration formula, Fortescue takes to be (possibly) an exclamation said by (perhaps) the deacon — meaning that the Eucharistic elements, now consecrated, are 'only for the faithful, not for catechumens nor strangers'.[94] He anticipates the provision made in the Missal of Pope Paul VI when he draws a comparison with the Antiochene practice in which the people call out at this point 'We announce thy death, O Lord, and we confess thy resurrection': words he took from Brightman's text of the Greek Liturgy of St James.

Fortescue is a trifle off-hand about the elevation of the Host and chalice. It is more important, he says, for people to understand the Consecration and Communion. But of course to appreciate the elevation *is* to understand the Consecration. At least he appreciates the piety behind the traditional practices of either looking at the elements thus lifted up or of bowing low at those points. And just as Fortescue was unphased by dramatic anticipations of the Consecration in the Offertory, so likewise he considers prayers for the blessing of the *oblata* after the Consecration (the *Supra quae* and *Supplices*) as examples of 'dramatic postponement'. '[T]he celebrant cannot express everything in one instant.'[95] The final doxology makes a fine end to the Roman Canon, inspired, appropriately enough, by Paul's Letter to the Romans, 11:36.

---

91 Ibid., p. 319.
92 Ibid., p. 330.
93 Ibid., p. 336.
94 Ibid., p. 337.
95 Ibid., p. 347.

'Our Father' begins the rite of Communion (once called the *Canon communionis*, as distinct from *Canon consecrationis*). Owing to its dignity, the Lord's Prayer is preceded by a request that we be allowed to say it. It is also followed by a prayer, the 'Embolism', expanding on its last clause, 'Deliver us from evil'. This is customary in the liturgies, but Fortescue finds the Roman version especially admirable (one of the non-improvements of the rite of Paul VI when used in English was that the introductory invitation acquired supplementary alternatives less fine than itself, and indeed a suggestion that the celebrant might wish at this point to devise words of his own). The fraction and mixing of the consecrated Bread and Wine in the rite of St Pius V are, Fortescue explains, only a 'fragment' of the complicated ritual provided in the early Roman Orders. According to that ritual, particles from a previous celebration (the 'Sancta') were added to the chalice prior to the admixture of particles from the present celebration and the dispatch of other such particles (the 'fermentum') to the suburbicarian bishops and the Roman parish priests. 'As the Sancta were a symbol of the identity of the sacrifice from one Mass to another, so was the fermentum a sign of union between the bishop and his clergy . . . this particle of the Holy Eucharist unites the Church as leaven unites bread.'[96]

The kiss of peace follows, moved to this place by, it seems, Pope Innocent I: in other rites, except where, as at Milan, they have adopted the Roman sequence, it belongs with the beginning of the Offertory. As to the distribution of the consecrated elements: Fortescue discusses the evidence for the placing of Communion on the hand, and on the tongue (the shift seems to come between Bede and the Sixth Roman Order which is ninth century. He thinks that, until the mediaeval epoch, people generally received standing except on fast-days and stational days when, since they prayed kneeling, they made their Communion kneeling as well. Gradually Communion under one kind for the laity became, by the fourteenth century, the dominant practice after a range of strategies against spillage — intinction (common in England), or the use of a tube or a spoon — had been tried and set aside. Fortescue notes that,

> whereas, on the one hand, everyone who goes to Communion under any rite receives *ex opere operato* the same grace; on the other, the principle of doing what our Lord did at the Last Supper is saved at each Mass by at least one person, the celebrant, who receives both kinds.[97]

The recital of the Agnus Dei is a late-patristic addition to the Roman liturgy (the Communion chant is more primitive) but Fortescue finds 'the use of St. John the Baptist's greeting (John 1:29, 'Behold the Lamb of God!') at

---

96   Ibid., p. 369.
97   Ibid., p. 381.

the Communion time is natural'.[98] And then all comes very swiftly, even abruptly, to an end with the Postcommunion Prayer, its motifs those of thanksgiving and petition that the Communion be fruitful, sometimes an additional 'Prayer over the People', and the famous dismissal *Ite missa est*, replaced by *Benedicamus Domino* on days when people were expected to stay in church for penitential prayers or other rites.

Later times have incorporated into the Mass the Last Gospel about whose status, however, Fortescue is doubtful. In the Use of Sarum it is recited on the way back to the sacristy, and so it is likewise at a bishop's Mass in the Roman rite itself, but he admits that the text, the Prologue of St John's Gospel, 'was the object of special devotion from the time of the Fathers'.[99]

Critical reception

Fortescue produced in quick succession two editions of his book on the Mass in 1912 and 1914; by 1954 it had reached its eleventh impression. Not all readers had been altogether enamoured, however, notably when Fortescue touched on the heart of the Liturgy, the Eucharistic Prayer. For many devout laymen, and indeed priests, the Roman Canon was peculiarly sacrosanct. In his (1737) *The Catholic Christian*, the much venerated vicar-apostolic of the London District, Richard Challoner, had refused even to print the text of the Canon, resorting instead to paraphrase. To those who thought thus, speculation about the Canon's origins and (as scholars generally maintained) complex history, was offensive to pious ears. Fortescue had written about it in much the same terms as source-critics brought to historic literature in general, analyzing its putatively component parts and outlining different theories about how they might have come together in their present form. A controversy on this topic in *The Tablet* (the semi-official nature of which, as the property of Cardinal Bourne should be noted) lasted from May to July 1914.

On 23 May, Fortescue lamented that there were people with the 'absurd idea that my book is in some way derogatory to the dignity of the Roman Canon'. He reiterated the claim made more than once in *The Mass*.

> Everyone may (as every priest does) say the words of the Canon, in their plain meaning, as they stand, with entire devotion. He will be using a prayer which, for its antiquity, its intrinsic beauty and suitableness *as it stands*, has hardly a rival in the world.[100]

---

98 Ibid., p. 387.
99 Ibid., p. 393.
100 *The Tablet*, 23 May, 1914, p. 624. Italics original.

He had never spoken of the Canon as a 'patchwork' or used any term remotely suggesting the idea.[101]

However, as was soon pointed out, he *had* spoken of its 'dislocation'. Fortescue sought to make light of dislocation. There was no such thing as a 'dislocationist' school standing over against an 'integralist' school (which, it was insinuated, should, by the orthodox, be preferred). There was, however, he remarked with possibly unwise relish, 'a real distinction between serious students of the difficult problem [of the Canon's composition] and people who think they can settle the whole matter by guesses at mystic reasons for the order of the Canon as it now stands'.[102] 'Undoubtedly', so he wrote to *The Tablet* from Letchworth on 27 June, 1914, 'the Canon was composed by someone at some time. What can be the harm of explaining various theories as to how this may be supposed to have happened?'[103] And he went on to say,

> There are many theories in the field about the origin of the Roman Canon. I could not think any of them final, or devoid of difficulty. So I considered it best to explain those which seem most probable, which are defended by the best authorities, and then to leave the reader to form his own conclusion about them. If he thinks none of them probable, I have no objection to this conclusion either.[104]

This rather airy expression of generosity was, for the objectors, somewhat missing the point.

Writing in the *Downside Review* in the year of publication of *The Mass*, Dom Hugh Connolly, pupil of the formidable Edmund Bishop ('facts not theories'), came at the matter from another angle. For Connolly, while Fortescue had poked fun at Ferdinand Probst (1816–1899), influential professor of liturgy of the previous generation at Tübingen, to all intents and purposes he had swallowed Probstian theories whole.[105] That would not have mattered had the evidence in their favour been forthcoming. But Fortescue had reproduced some patent misinterpretations of the data, affecting not least the question raised in the succeeding *Tablet* discussion. Thus for instance, Probst had misconstrued the case, described by St Cyprian, of a demoniac child who 'could not endure' being present for the Eucharistic Prayer. The Tübingen scholar had mistaken the unfortunate sufferer for a young believer 'impatient' of the length of time that elapsed between Consecration and Communion.

---

101 Ibid.
102 Ibid., 20 June, 1914, p. 984.
103 Ibid., 4 July, 1914, p. 30.
104 Ibid.
105 H. Connolly, O.S.B., 'A Review', *Downside Review* N.S. 12 (1912), pp. 221–232.

Fortescue had blithely followed Probst, but, plainly, there was no ground here for Probst's claim that much of the Roman Canon that now precedes the Consecration of the elements was once prayed after that Consecration. The Cyprianic 'evidence' for an inversion of the content of the Canon was nothing of the kind. No doubt Fortescue *should* have noticed that in Cyprian's Latin *impatiens* was unlikely to mean 'impatient' in the modern sense. But the point was a rather limited one. And, in general, one could hardly complain that Fortescue's multi-choice presentation of diverse theories about the composition of the Roman Canon was doctrinaire.

More widely, Connolly pointed out how Fortescue had in effect adopted Probst's view that the liturgical proceedings outlined in the *Apostolic Constitutions* (dated by Connolly to the second half of the fourth century) constitute our best evidence for what Liturgy was like in the apostolic age — and had judged the history of the known rites of the Church on that (debatable) basis.[106] Connolly, linked to such leading Cambridge patristic scholars as J.A. Robinson and F.C. Burkitt, was deep into early Syrian Christianity. Fortescue's dating of the *Apostolic Constitutions* was deviant only by a few decades, but possibly this made all the difference if one were to argue, as Fortescue had done in his *Encyclopaedia* articles, that the compilers of the Greek Liturgy of St James, and thereafter the Liturgies of St Basil and St John Chrysostom, had started from here. However, Fortescue was clear in those same articles that Alexandria had been from the start a distinct tradition, so Connolly cannot have been correct in ascribing to him a 'one size fits all' view.

In Connolly's eyes, Fortescue had simply not realized the difficulty of the task he had set himself in such a 'Study of the Roman Liturgy'. Fortescue's tone was 'independent, and even judicial' (these terms are presumably intended as complimentary), but Connolly wondered about the degree of attention he had brought to the data at first hand.[107] Certainly, the most impressive feature in any Fortescue bibliography is his acquaintance with German scholarship on a wide variety of topics — and hence with secondary sources, albeit of the highest order. That is not to say that he never looked at primary sources — his diary jottings of reading at the British Museum would indicate the contrary, and one notes the care with which he traced the history of the editing of patristic texts in *The Greek Fathers*. True, he did not go round Europe comparing manuscripts in the way that the German 'Monumentists' had pioneered early in the nineteenth century; this became the *ne plus ultra* of Victorian scholarship, where discussion of texts from late antiquity up to the invention of printing

106 Ibid., pp. 222–223; 229–230.
107 Ibid., p. 232.

was concerned.[108] There was no organized version of this in England (the 'Rolls Series' was both geographically restricted and, at times, editorially hit-and-miss) but individual scholars, such as Edmund Bishop, did some of their finest research along these exigent lines.

What was feasible for a State subsidized corporate project in Germany, or for a full time private scholar in England, was obviously not possible to a pastoral priest in the Westminster diocese. That did not mean Fortescue was unserious. It was scarcely without reason that the leading Coptic scholar in England, based at the British Museum, should have recommended him for the task of bringing into publishable form the unfinished work of a French Byzantinist. One notes that the massive study *Missarum Sollemnia* by the Austrian Jesuit Josef Andreas Jungmann, which is generally regarded as the most comprehensive and 'scientific' twentieth century study of the Roman Mass, refers to Fortescue's opinions on no less than twenty-six occasions.[109] Connolly probably mistook the easy fluency, and touches of humour, in Fortescue's writing manner for *amateurisme*. Or perhaps he thought a parish priest with a dozen other interests could not have taken the pains that were necessary. The Westminster Diocesan Archives preserve a loose-leaf wallet with notes, taken in Latin, from both primary and secondary sources, for the two editions of Fortescue's book.[110]

In November 1912, Herbert Thurston uses the columns of *The Tablet* to register a protest about the tone of Connolly's review.[111] Fortescue went out of his way to correct any mistakes pointed out to him in the second edition of *The Mass*, which dates from 1914. A letter to Thurston in January of the previous year shows how thoroughly he proposed to apply himself. He explained,

> I do not like the idea of making some changes and not others; because, if readers see a second edition revised in places, they will naturally conclude that where I have left the old text, I, having

108 For an account of the Monumentists, see D. Knowles, *Great Historical Enterprises. Problems in Monastic History* (London: Nelson, 1963), pp. 63–97. In the seventeenth and eighteenth centuries, serious scholars had collated manuscripts, usually through correspondents. But it was advance in the technologies of transport in the nineteenth century which enabled work of this kind to progress with leaps and bounds.

109 J.A. Jungmann, S.J., *Missarum sollemnia. Eine genetische Erklärung der römischen Messe* (Freiburg: Herder, 1952, 2 vols., 3rd edition).

110 Westminster Diocesan Archives, Box 20. 18, 'Notata de liturgia romana in bonum libri mei: "The Mass, a Study of the Roman Liturgy"', Longmans (The Westminster Library), ed. I, 1912'. In fact the 'Notata' extend to the second edition as well.

111 *The Tablet*, 2 November 1912.

considered the matter, deliberately stand by it. Really I want very much to go through the whole book carefully. Putting together all the reviews I have, there are a great many passages which I ought to re-examine — not necessarily modify, but at any rate reconsider.[112]

Fortescue confided to Thurston that Dom Connolly had not, in his opinion, treated him fairly.

After Connolly's review appeared, he had, apparently, written to Fortescue in a friendly fashion. Connolly 'admitted entirely that at least the tone of his review was regrettable and unfair, and expressed himself anxious to do what he could to modify the impression it would produce'. The Downside monk suggested Fortescue should write to *The Tablet* 'in order to give him an opening to make amends'. But when Fortescue did so, no further word came from Connolly's side.

Now he answers that all he meant was that I might write to *The Tablet* to state my grievances, if I had any. This is absurd. I do not need his permission to write to *The Tablet,* and it is contradicted by his own earlier letters. I think really that he expected me to write a very meek and submissive letter, acknowledging all he wanted essentially. Then he would have paid me for that by a few general compliments.[113]

It was the sort of situation that gets *odium academicum* its bad name.

Fortescue's loves (and hates)

What Fortescue loved in the Western rite was the classical Roman Liturgy in its main lines, and the traditional calendar of the Latin church before its excessive complication by additional modern feasts.

As to the historic Western liturgy, he had little time for the demands for change made by the sixteenth century Reformers.

The Protestant rites are deliberate compositions made by the various Reformers to suit their theological positions, as new services were necessary for their prayer-meetings. No old liturgy could be used by people with their ideas. The old rites contain the plainest statements about the Real Presence, the Eucharistic Sacrifice, prayers to saints, and for the dead, which are denied by Protestants.[114]

---

112 Westminster Diocesan Archive, Series 20, Box 22, copy of letter to Herbert Thurston, S.J., of 8 January, 1913. The original is in Cambridge University Library, MS Add. 9812/D/90.

113 Ibid.

114 'Rites', art. cit., pp. 66-67.

Breach of continuity with earlier worship was inevitable. However, some of the Reformers wanted to make this breach as little apparent as possible: hence their practice of borrowing the more harmless elements of the ancient liturgical orders, re-arranging them, and evolving new ritual orders that carried nuggets from the old. Fortescue makes it plain he is thinking especially of Anglicans.

Fortescue calls the First Prayer Book of Edward VI (1549) 'Lutheran' in its Eucharistic Prayer, while the Second Prayer Book (1552) was of course more radically Protestant still (Fortescue avoids saying whether he thinks the final state of Cranmer's mind on the subject of Eucharistic theology was Calvinist or Zwinglian). He admits that the Scottish Prayer Book (1637, revised in 1764) is 'decidedly more High Church in tone', and elements of it were used in the making of the 1789 American book, thus guaranteeing it a further influence.[115] 'The Anglican service-books are now the least removed from Catholic liturgies of those used by any Protestant body. But this is saying very little.' Even those put together by the Non-Jurors suffer from being 'conscious and artifical arrangements of elements selected from the old rites, instead of natural developments'.[116]

It is in this aspect of Fortescue's thinking as a student of the Liturgy that the appeal to him by critics of Western liturgical revision after the Second Vatican Council seems most appropriate. It is difficult to think he would have warmed to the new Eucharistic Prayers of the Missal of Pope Paul VI. Fortescue admitted that the wider introduction of the vernacular would bring advantages of improved understanding (historically, in the Roman rite, it was confined to the Eastern coast of the Adriatic, in Slavonic, and to Rome itself when occasionally it was used in Greek). But 'the loss would probably be greater than the gain', since '[t]he use of Latin all over the Roman patriarchate is a very obvious and splendid witness of unity'.[117] Latin, at any rate Church Latin, is easy to learn, and for those who cannot or do not wish to learn it, 'the Missal in English is one of the easiest books to procure'.[118] Moreover, Fortescue thought insistence on the vernacular would spell the end of the chant, since its adaptation to other languages sounded hopelessly forced.

There was a wider aesthetic question as well.

> The rhythmical accent and terse style redolent of the great Latin Fathers, the strange beauty of the old Latin hymns, the sonorous majesty of the Vulgate, all these things that make the Roman Rite so dignified, so characteristic of the old Imperial City where the Prince of the Apostles set up his throne, would be lost altogether in modern English or French translations.[119]

---

115 Ibid., p. 68.
116 Ibid.
117 Ibid., p. 70.
118 Ibid.
119 Ibid.

As to the calendar, in the course of a letter to *The Tablet* complaining about the introduction of a feast of the 'Finding of the Child Jesus in the Temple' in the midst of the Epiphany Octave, he wrote,

> There must be many of us who regret the ever increasing novelties that have already destroyed the dignity, that are fast obliterating the very essence, of the old Roman Calendar. For my part I can never understand who it is who can prefer months to the ecclesiastical seasons, Fridays to Sundays, and this host of new feasts that swamp the old year of the Church, fill Lent with white Masses and Glorias and make the old Sunday offices (far the most splendid things we have) almost as strange to us as if we were some new sect.

And he asked for liturgical change in a conservative direction', pointing to the example of the 1570 reform. Pius V's commission 'did fine work by abolishing novelties and restoring, at least to some extent, the austere dignity of the old Roman rite. The same thing might perhaps happen again.[120]

In this dimension of Fortescue's thinking, much in the revised Missal of 1969 might have met with his approval.

Fortescue had no confidence in the officials entrusted with liturgical matters in the contemporary Roman curia. To his eyes, they were constantly tampering and tinkering in a way that suggested they lacked all understanding of the historic genius of the rites. He wrote to the typographer Stanley Morison: 'whatever beauty interest or historic value, or dignity, the Roman rite ever had has been utterly destroyed by the uneducated little cads who run that filthy congregation in Rome'[121] — a typical exaggeration when in heat, for if it were so, how was it still possible for him to write about the parts of the Mass *as celebrated in his own day* with such inspirational force? Fortescue's real target was rubricism, a disproportionate concern with the detail of how rites are orchestrated in matters of movement and gesture.

Rubricians, he declared in the same letter, are careless of the history of the rites.

> To them it is not the history nor the development of rites that matter a bit, it is the latest decision of the Congregation of Rites. These decisions are always made by a crowd of dirty little Monsignori at Rome in utter ignorance of the meaning or reason of anything. To the historian their decisions are simply

---

120 Letter to *The Tablet* 0f 14 January, 1911.
121 Cambridge University Library, MS Add. 9812/D/90, Letter to H. Morison of 24 November, 1919.

disgusting nonsense, that people of my kind want simply to ignore. It is a queer type of mind that actually is interested in knowing whether the deacon should stand at the right or the left of someone else at some moment.[122]

Fortescue was quite correct in his concern that intervention by those canonically empowered 'authentically' (as the Romans say) to interpret or indeed to modify the Liturgy can spoil an ancient pattern with a coherence of its own, but one suspects that some of his anger arose from the burden of letter-writing produced by the publication of his book on Ceremonial — to which, in the next chapter, we must give its place.

> Because I have written a book, it does not follow that I have turned myself into a society for giving free advice, and doing free research work for every unknown fool who may choose to write and ask for it. I could of course spend my few hours at the Museum by having out again Martinucci [an Italian expert on ceremonial] and his peers, verifying points, comparing authorities. I could ask for the whole collection of the decrees of the Stinking Congregation of Rites [the proper adjective was 'Sacred'], and pass three hours or so hunting for the date of a decree. But why cannot these impudent scoundrels do their own dirty work. Their cheek takes away my breath. . . . Why am I to be pestered without ceasing, by any fool in Cornwall, Scotland, Isle of Man? What makes me most furious is when they enclose a stamp for the answer. It is not the value of their beastly halfpenny, it is the hours, sometimes days, of work they have the infernal impudence to expect me to put at their service. . . . Do please tell anyone who threatens to fire off strings of questions at me that I am exceedingly busy, that I am not a society kept out of the rates for answering anyone's queries, that I have no time to write letters, that I wish for Goodness' sake they would leave me alone, so that I may have a little time to do my own work.[123]

And yet a major element in that 'work' was in fact the liturgical celebration for whose excellence he made the name of Letchworth a bye-word once upon a time. That must be our next theme.

---

122 Ibid.
123 Ibid.

8. The Practice of the Liturgy: *Rivalis Villa,* the Ceremonial, and the Chant

At 'Rivalis Villa'

Fortescue did not keep up the mock-Latin names of his cures of souls as assiduously at Letchworth as he did elsewhere — perhaps a sign that it is right to think of this verbal habit as more distancing than affectionate. But Letchworth gained a sobriquet nonetheless — via the Anglo-Saxon 'Lecha weorthing', it was *Rivalis Villa,* 'The Farm by the Rivulet'. The Liturgy at *Rivalis Villa* was Fortescue's pride and joy. A parishioner recorded after his death:

> His Mass was something to remember. It was slow; every word was perfect, and audible; every gesture was measured. All that was about the altar was exquisitely tended. He spent hours with his servers, before every great feast, practicing every detail of the ceremonies. The offices for Holy Week, for which he had a deep devotion, were carried out with every possible ceremony in St. Hugh. (How angry he was if you said St. Hugh's!) He laboured incessantly to teach the choir to sing *Tenebrae.* To be a member of the choir was to receive, in fact, a thorough education in liturgical music.[1]

Music first

So far as music was concerned he was extremely fortunate in his choirmaster, (Thomas) Wilfred Willson, who had an excellent musical, especially choral, formation from his Anglican background. With Willson's help (offered originally on condition he was not to be expected to become a Catholic, though he did so within the year),[2] Fortescue was able to bring into use on the great festivals at Letchworth not only the Chant but also the austere yet beautiful polyphony the Catholic Reformation had espoused

---

1   E. Cowell, 'Adrian Fortescue', art. cit., pp. 1030–1031.
2   M. Davies, 'Adrian Fortescue Priest and Scholar', in idem., *The Wisdom of Adrian Fortescue,* op. cit., p. 43.

after the Council of Trent. Here he favoured Palestrina, whose Masses recur in the diaries;[3] for instance, at Easter 1912, he noted of Palestrina's *Missa brevis*: 'excellently sung'.[4] The music of Gabrieli was also adopted — another *Missa brevis* (probably these relatively easy 'Short' Masses were best fitted to a modest choir), chosen this time for Easter 1916, though on that occasion Fortescue recorded that the choir was not at its best.[5] While the late seventeenth century Antonio Lotti puts in an appearance at Easter 1917,[6] this was a composer of polyphony who still used the *stila antiqua* and so was acceptable to purists, among whom Fortescue must surely be counted.[7]

In Fortescue's time as parish priest, *Rivalis villa* took its place, on a miniscule scale (this was hardly Downside, or even Corpus Christi, Bournemouth), in the revival of Renaissance polyphony which featured so highly in the late nineteenth and early twentieth century English Catholic world.[8] Though composers like Palestrina had written for royal chapels, papal basilicas, and aristocratic households, they now found themselves taken up by amateur choirs — partly owing to the favour bestowed on the form of harmonized music deemed by Church authority closest in ethos to plainchant, and partly through the fervent partisanship of such committed Church musicians as Sir Richard Terry, who moved from Downside to Westminster Cathedral in 1901, while the building was still under construction and the Liturgy celebrated in a hall.[9]

Unsurprisingly, Fortescue selected Palestrina's *Aeterna Christi munera* for the official blessing of his new church, St Hugh (he deplored the use of the partitive in church titles, so not 'St Hugh's').[10] Granted Fortescue's combination of international Catholicity with robust Englishness, it is perhaps surprising that the diaries mention no Letchworth version of Terry's rediscovery of the English polyphonic composers like Byrd and Tallis. The desirability of combining Catholicism with Englishness in music via such figures is the theme of Terry's *English Catholic Music* which appeared in 1907, perfectly timed for Fortescue's ministry at Letchworth, though maybe he

3   For example: Downside Archives, IX AF, Box E, 'Diary 1908', entry for 6 September 1908; 'Diary 1919', entry for 20 April.
4   Downside Archives, IX AF, Box E, 'Diary 1912', entry for 7 April, 1912.
5   Downside Archives, IX AF, Box E, 'Diary 1916', entry for 23 April, 1916.
6   Downside Archives, IX AF, Box E, 'Diary 1917', entry for 31 March, 1917.
7   T.E. Muir, *Roman Catholic Church Music in England, 1791–1914. A Handmaid of the Liturgy?* (Aldershot: Ashgate, 2008), p. 224.
8   For a sensitive discussion, see ibid., pp. 129–133, 224–246.
9   See for this important figure, H. Andrews, *Westminster Retrospect: A Memoir of Sir Richard Terry* (London: Oxford University Press, 1948).
10 Downside Archives, IX AF, Box E, 'Diary 1908', entry for 6 September 1908.

missed it owing to absence on the grand tour.[11] His notions of what sort of music was suited to the weekly round of a parochial church are best attested by a magnificently bound organ book 'dedicated in perpetuity to the use of the church of St Hugh Letchworth by Adrian Fortescue'. This book, now in the Westminster Archdiocesan Archives (but it would still be perfectly serviceable at Letchworth for the 'Extraordinary Form'), contains Fortescue's instructions for the organist at Sung Mass, for the organ at Vespers and Compline, and for the celebration of Sunday and weekday Benediction.

This may be a good point at which to interject a note on Fortescue's great keenness that the people should attend the Liturgy of the Hours and especially Vespers. Before the 1911 breviary reform of St Pius X, the Office of Vespers changed so often on the different feasts of the calendar that one needed a Vesperale to keep up with it. After that date, when for most of the year Sunday Vespers was, precisely, 'of the Sunday', it was nearly as easy to follow Vespers as it was Compline. Pointing out that 'in most Catholic countries Vespers on Sunday evening are almost as much a matter of course as Mass in the morning',[12] Fortescue saw no reason why, especially after 1911, English Catholics could not follow suit. The Pian reform 'removes the chief difficulty against celebrating Vespers as the normal Sunday evening service; it opens the way for a more general use of the official evening prayer of the Church'.[13] And he added that he wanted the laity to come to the Liturgy of the Hours above all for Matins of Christmas Night, for Tenebrae (on the last three days of Holy Week) and for Sunday Vespers, since then 'lay people will not altogether lose touch with what was originally meant for them, as much as for the clergy'.[14]

The bulk of the Letchworth organ book — to return to that important monument of Fortescue's period at St Hugh — is occupied by stave music, chiefly harmonisations of the chant for organ accompaniment, in his own hand. As its indications of source material show, it is an eclectic work. Its sources range from organ accompaniments for the Vatican edition of the chant from two Regensburg publishers, Pustet and Coppenrath,[15] as well as a book of similar character produced for Benediction and processions ('Les Saluts') at Solesmes;[16] the Oxford University Press's admirable *The Unison*

---

11 R.R. Terry, *Catholic Church Music* (London: Greening, 1907).

12 'Preface', in *Vespers for Sunday with an Introduction* (London: Catholic Truth Society, 1913), p. 12.

13 Ibid., p. 5.

14 Ibid., p. 13.

15 F.X. Mathias, *Organum comitans ad Vesperas et Compl[etorium] iuxta ed[itionem] Vaticanum* (Regensburg: Pustet, 1913); M. Springer, *Orgelbegleitung zum Kyriale Vaticanum* (Regensburg: Coppenrath, 1907).

16 *Chants usuels pour les Saluts ... éd. Par les Bénédictins de Solesmes ... avec*

St Hugh's exterior and surrounding countryside: much of the planned 'Garden City' was still virgin soil when Fortescue arrived. It was not his favourite landscape.

St Hugh's early interior. Fortescue's emphasis as a church designer lay on making a noble altar: site of the Eucharistic Sacrifice.

Chant Book;[17] *The English Hymnal with Tunes*, famously yet discreetly edited by Ralph Vaughan Williams;[18] Terry's less successful Catholic counterpart *The Westminster Hymnal*,[19] and such gems as *The Cowley Carol Book* of the Plainsong and Mediaeval Music Society collector G.R. Woodward,[20] and Massé and Scott's *A Book of Old Carols*.[21] (Recovering for use forgotten English carols became a Letchworth specialty.) The book, which a splendidly written title page in Latin and Greek declares to have been begun on the feast of St Cyril of Alexandria (9 February) 1916, is prefaced by a fading black and white photograph of the church — Ecclesia Sancti Hugonis apud Rivalem Villam — taken in 1916. [22]

The visual setting

Fortescue did his best to render worthy the visual context of this aural offering to almighty God. A parishioner noted:

> His church, dedicated to St Hugh of Lincoln, and built largely out of his own means and earnings, was a mere barn as he said, but made beautiful by the devotion he bestowed upon it. It is the only church worth looking at west of Constantinople, he would say with a mischievous smile.[23]

This gem was replaced in 1963 by a new building better able to accommodate an increased worshipping attendance, and downgraded to the status of a hall, but a contemporary description is available, incorporated in a tribute to Fortescue published by a Letchworth newspaper at the time of his death.

> In three short years, owing to the enthusiasm of our well-loved priest, Dr Adrian Fortescue, the church has become as nearly perfect as knowledge and love allied can make it. Built according to Byzantine ideas, of a type severe and dignified, its interior decorations are a running pattern with a Latin inscription,

Accompagnement d'orgue (Versailles, 1894).

17 *The Unison Chant Book* (Oxford: Oxford University Press, 1909).

18 *The English Hymnal with Tunes* (Oxford: Oxford University Press, 1907).

19 R.R. Terry (ed.), *The Westminster Hymnal* (London: R. and T. Washbourne 1912).

20 G.R. Woodward, *The Cowley Carol Book* (London: Mowbray, 1902). This is generally held to have been the best carol collection until the 1928 *Oxford Book of Carols.*

21 H.L.L.J. Massé and C.K. Scott, *A Book of Old Carols* (London: Fisher Unwin, 1910).

22 Westminster Archdiocesan Archives, Box MR.

23 C.B. Purdom, *Life Over Again*, op. cit., p. 245.

The Interior of St Hugh's decorated for the Paschaltide Notice; the altar crucifix, candlesticks and sanctuary lamp were all designed by Fortescue's cousin, C.S. Spooner.

picked out in black and white round three sides of the church, and one small stained glass window showing St Francis preaching to the birds. The dossal curtains are of Morris tapestry, and form a background to the chief architectural beauty of the scheme, which consists of a ciborium or canopy built right over the altar, standing on four pillars, and reaching half-way down the chancel. Its roof is solid gilt, and reflects gloriously; the rest is heavily patterned in gesso-work, while its inscription, at once so simple and so suitable, runs in the official language of the Church: "Blessed are they who are called unto the marriage supper of the Lamb".[24]

This was the church of which an obituarist wrote: 'Nothing was too much trouble, nothing was too good for the church he loved — the church he was seen to enter, by an unobserved spectator, for the last time to kiss passionately the altar at which he had said his Mass for fourteen years'.[25] An oaken pulpit and prie-dieu, made to Fortescue's designs, completed the ensemble. Fortunately, it proved possible to transfer to the post-Fortescue building the baldacchino of the old church, its best feature, evidently, along with the altar crucifix, candlesticks and sanctuary lamp, together with the alabaster font, all of which were designed by Spooner, and the statue of the Virgin sculpted by the architect's sister, Phoebe Stabler.[26] Recently, the baldacchino, a fine example (albeit in wood) of one of the most glorious innovations of liturgical architecture, has, regrettably, been dismantled. Perhaps it was surprising that it lasted so long in a Philistine phase of the life of the Western Catholic Church.

Mystagogy in Holy Week

At Easter 1910 — even before the erection of the baldacchino which set off the whole — Fortescue expressed his delight in the setting he had been able to provide for the Holy Week ceremonies and the way the ceremonies had been carried out.[27] He made a point of ensuring nothing was omitted in the ceremonies, not excluding the lengthy and musically demanding Office of Tenebrae (in this period, anticipated on the three evenings of Wednesday of Holy Week, Holy Thursday, and Good Friday).[28] In his introduction,

---

24 Cited M. Davies, 'Adrian Fortescue – Priest and Scholar', in idem., *The Wisdom of Adrian Fortescue*, op. cit., p. 36.

25 E. Cowell, 'Adrian Fortescue', art. cit., p. 1030.

26 M. Davies, 'Adrian Fortescue Priest and Scholar', in idem., *The Wisdom of Adrian Fortescue*, op. cit., p. 37.

27 Downside Archives IX AF, Box E, 'Diary 1910', entry for 24 March, 1910.

28 C.B. Purdom, *Life Over Again*, op. cit. p. 245.

'The Rites of Holy Week' to the finely printed 1916 *Holy Week Book* —
one of a series, 'Liturgy for Layfolk', on which he and Francis Meynell
were working for Burns and Oates — he explained the great importance of
the *paschalia solemnia* understood as stretching from Palm Sunday to Low
Sunday inclusive.[29] 'The reason why this Paschal feast is the greatest of all is
not so much because it is the remembrance of certain events in our Lord's
life, as that these events mean our Redemption'.[30]

The Sacrifice of Christ on the Cross, along with the Resurrection ('just
as much part of our redemption as his pain and death'),[31]makes this two-
week feast tower above the normal course of the year, such that 'five-sixths
of the year revolves around Easter; no wonder that these days are unlike
any other'.[32] Fortescue describes its main moments for the benefit of the
faithful using this little book to follow the ceremonies. He succeeds very
well in fusing an account of the meaning of the rites with an explanation
of their origins or history. It gives us a good idea both of what was done at
Letchworth and how Fortescue taught his people about the sense of what
was done there.

On Palm Sunday the procession, he notes, always ends where it began,
and this indicates its origin. It was a Jerusalem celebration whereby the
faithful went on to Bethany to relive Christ's solemn entry into that very
City from where they had started. Then pilgrims to Jerusalem took the
notion back with them, including to the West. 'Their friends could not
perhaps go to Jerusalem; but they could make a Jerusalem at home. Their
church was Jerusalem to them'.[33] He is inclined to think that the ceremony
of blessing of palms was originally itself a Mass. It begins, after all, with
several of the elements of a fore-Mass and continues, in the form with
which Fortescue was familiar, with its own Preface and even the Sanctus.
He thinks that at some earlier time a sort of interim Mass was said at
another church where the procession of the faithful called and the palm-
blessing carried out, prior to returning to the cathedral for the bishop's
more solemn celebration. Of the first Mass (perhaps a 'dry' Mass, without
the Consecration) only, in time, some fragments remained.

---

29 'The Rites of Holy Week', *The Holy Week Book. Complied by authority from the
    Roman Missal and Breviary as reformed by order of Pope Pius X* (London: Burns
    and Oates, 1916), pp. xi–xxxvii.

30 Ibid., p. xii.

31 Ibid.

32 Ibid., p. xiii. The 1969 calendrical reform of Paul VI reduced this proportion
    by suppressing the Sundays from Septuagesima to Quinquagesima and
    numbering Sundays after Pentecost as 'through the year' a year that begins
    with, rather, the feast of the Baptism of the Lord.

33 Ibid., p. xv.

Fortescue lingers lovingly over the ceremony of the entrance, where the subdeacon uses the processional cross to knock at the door. This takes place after the singing of the chant 'Lift up your gates, ye princes, and be ye lifted up, eternal gates, that the King of glory may come in' (Psalm 23:7). On a platform or in a gallery choirboys will have alternated verses of Theodulph of Orleans' hymn *Gloria laus* ('without question, one of the most splendid hymns we possess') with verses sung by those in the procession below, until the latter enters the church to the words of the responsory *Ingrediente Domino in sanctam civitatem.*

Fortescue favours the mediaeval custom of cutting fresh green branches (usually of willow or yew) for the palms rather than buying from abroad what he termed with a sniff 'dead vegetation', but in general he disapproves of the additional embellishments found in pre-Reformation England.

> In some churches they carried round a statue of our Lord on the ass; sometimes they turned the whole service into a kind of Corpus Christi procession, using white vestments, taking down the Lenten veil, bearing the Blessed Sacrament and strewing about singing cakes. This is a good example of that exuberant late mediaeval ceremonial which so often spoiled the functions, destroying their old meaning for the sake of more gorgeous ornament.[34]

It was a good thing that the reformed missal of 1570 swept all this away, so that 'we have now the simpler, infinitely more pregnant ceremonies, as they were received at Rome, though not originating there, long before these later additions'.[35]

The reading of the Passion on Palm Sunday (and Good Friday — and indeed, in the version of the ceremonies Fortescue knew, on Tuesday and Wednesday of Holy Week as well) is not, he explains, in itself something out of the ordinary, for the Passion text is simply the Gospel of the day, though a remarkably long one.

In a similar way, less out of the ordinary than might seem the case is the Office of Tenebrae, held on Wednesday, Thursday and Friday of Holy Week. In each case, this is anticipated Matins and Lauds of the next day. And yet it also differs from how those Hours are celebrated on other occasions. For one thing, the Offices have a more archaic form (no hymns, no Invitatory, no blessings), since people were less willing to alter the services of the more solemn days by adding extra items. For another, there is the ceremony of lighting (and then extinguishing) fifteen candles on a triangle, known as the 'hearse'. That word, so Fortescue explains, means a harrow for raking the ground. (In mediaeval

---

34 Ibid., p. xviii. The singing-cakes are rather a *bête noire* in Fortescue's criticism of Sarum.

35 Ibid.

funeral practice, a coffin would have been placed on a stand, with, over the coffin, spiked triangles for the holding of candles). The unbleached wax of the Tenebrae candles is undoubtedly a sign of mourning, but Fortescue inclines to a pragmatic rather than symbolic view of the candles themselves. They were needed to read the books with their somewhat atypical contents, even if he concedes that the hiding of the last candle and its restoration to the hearse may be a symbolic indicator of Christ's death and resurrection — for 'this ceremony is not originally Roman'.[36] Fortescue was keen on the idea that characteristically Roman ceremonial is always straightforward and practical.

Maundy Thursday is the only day in the year, he says, when Mass and Office do not correspond.

> The office is all mournful. Here the memory which seems most
> to fill the mind of the Church is the betrayal of Judas. But when
> Mass is said the Church cannot forget, although it is the middle
> of the week of mourning, that this is the day to which we owe
> the Holy Eucharist.[37]

The ringing of the bells at the Gloria of the Mass signals that they will not be used again till the first Mass of Easter. 'The Church is accustomed to do a thing solemnly for the last time before it ceases, as we say the "Alleluia" solemnly twice at the end of Vespers before Septuagesima.'[38] The procession with the *Sanctissimum*, the reserved Sacrament, to the altar of repose, unlike the Palm Sunday procession, actually goes somewhere, and hence Fortescue classifies it as 'a real Roman procession, having a definite object'.[39] He thinks the veneration of the Sacrament at the altar of repose is the beginning of the practice of Exposition of the Blessed Sacrament and the 'Forty Hours' devotion. When it had become normal to reserve the Sacrament in the tabernacle of every church, this 'watching' retained its old aura of special holiness nonetheless, and 'indeed, in this night of all nights, when our Lord was suffering his bitter torment, it is natural that people should spent part of the time with him in prayer, honouring the gift of that day'.[40]

In Fortescue's time, all this took place in the morning (for the Mass could only be celebrated then), not in the afternoon. But it was still followed immediately by Vespers. 'On all fast days Vespers are now said in the morning, from the old idea that one does not break one's fast till after Vespers'.[41] The stripping of the altar was, in ancient times, a daily event. Now it is restricted to Holy Thursday and Good Friday as a symbol

---

36 Ibid., p. xxii.
37 Ibid., p. xxiii.
38 Ibid.
39 Ibid., p. xxiv.
40 Ibid.
41 Ibid., pp. xxiv-xxv.

of desolation. There follows the Mandatum — the Washing of the Feet — which gives 'Maundy' Thursday its name. As Fortescue notes, 'Still in Catholic countries it is the custom for the Sovereign to wash the feet of thirteen poor men today [i.e. in 1916].'[42] The Eastern rites keep to twelve men, but the Latin West says thirteen (in the Pontifical, not the Missal which is silent on the point). The number perhaps indicates the inclusion of Matthias or Paul or even of Christ himself. Fortescue tells us that in the twelfth century, as witnessed by *Ordo romanus* XII, the Pope washed the feet of twelve sub-deacons after Mass and thirteen poor men after dinner.

He is quietly eloquent about Good Friday.

> The very strangeness of the rites, utterly unlike any others, gives us at once the feeling that this is a day different from any other day. That little procession coming to the altar in dead silence, the prostration before the altar, then the lessons, the series of collects with their strange chant, all this produces a sense of desolation, of mourning, such as no other service in the year approaches. Today the most ignorant observer who enters a Catholic church can see that the church mourns because her Lord is dead.[43]

The 'Creeping to the Cross' is the one element that is not especially ancient. Fortescue thinks it began because it was thought strange that, on Good Friday of all days, it was not possible to see the crucifix, all images having been veiled since Passion Sunday (or, in earlier centuries, the beginning of Lent). So 'they made this one exception and uncovered the crucifix'.[44] 'Not especially ancient' — yet Fortescue also tells us that a rite very like the Roman rite of his day (or indeed later) is found in the eighth century, north of the Alps, prior to its adoption at Rome. Then comes:

> the one gleam of light in the dark service, as we bring the Sanctissimum back to the altar, singing that superb hymn of the triumph of the cross. The gleam of light fades again; there follows the strange little Communion service that we call Mass of the Presanctified, then Vespers; again the altar is stripped, and now all the church is indeed desolate, waiting in gloom for the first light of the Easter sun next day.[45]

In Fortescue's time, before the reform of the ceremonies of Holy Week by Pius XII, Easter began in effect on the morning of Holy Saturday, rather than, as originally and, by the mid twentieth century once more, on the night between Saturday and Sunday. The Armenians too, Fortescue remarks,

42 Ibid., p. xxv.
43 Ibid.
44 Ibid., p. xxix.
45 Ibid., pp. xxvi-xxvii.

keep the Vigil, including the Eucharistic Liturgy, in the afternoon of Easter Eve; probably the Latins pushed the celebration yet further back since it seemed so odd to have the Mass after midday. Fortescue admits it takes a good deal of imagination to mistake mid-morning for the pitch of night. Still, the service remains deeply impressive in its perpetuation of the mind of antiquity, notably in its fusion of the themes of Easter and Baptism. The new fire symbolizes both, for the baptized are enlightened, while 'light, fire and warmth are obvious symbols of the glory of the Resurrection.'[46]

In Fortescue's day fire was borne up the church on a triple candle or torch (probably a guard against accidental extinction of the light) before the great Candle of Easter was lit as the deacon (in Easter white, the rest of the sacred ministers still in Lenten purple) sang the *Exsultet* — which he considers perhaps the most splendid example of 'emotional poetry' in the Roman rite, and, in the chant that carries the words, its most expressive music. The (twelve) prophecies — which can be rather tedious, Fortescue urged people to follow them in their books — may be the final instructions for the catechumens but he also draws attention to the theory of his friend Herbert Thurston that they are, rather, a relic of the ancient vigil service, when lessons and psalms alternated.[47] In either case, they 'form a wonderful account of God's dealings with his people before Christ came'.[48]

The blessing of the water of the font, so Fortescue thinks, has fascinating parallels with the Eucharistic Prayer (not least its Epiclesis, invoking the descent of the Holy Spirit). Fortescue underlines the relation of Baptism to the Death and Resurrection of the Lord, as is customary in the Latin West by, he thinks, a 'happier instinct' then that of the Byzantine East which links them to the Epiphany. [49] And then as:

> priest, deacon and subdeacon lie prostrate before the altar and the clauses of the Litany are chanted, the last edge of the great Lent cloud rolls away. For forty days the Church has been preparing for what will follow now. Liturgically, we have arrived at the end of the night watch; in the East already the first light of the grey dawn breaks, soon it will be sunrise, the rise of the Easter sun. Towards the end of the Litany they prepare the altar for Mass, for a festal Mass indeed — it will be the first Mass of Easter.

---

46 Ibid., p. xxxii.

47 H. Thurston, S.J., *Lent and Holy Week* (London: Longmans, 1904).

48 'The Rites of Holy Week', art. cit., p. xxxiv.

49 Ibid., p. xxxi. 'The Cathecumens, who during Lent, have become "Competentes", are baptized during the Easter vigil, they wear their white robes during the Easter octave, and make their first Communion, then laying aside the robes, on Low Sunday', ibid.

The ministers leave in purple and come back in white for the intoning of the Easter Gloria, 'the dramatic moment of the whole year',[50] after which alleluias will not cease for days to come (as Fortescue points out, their association with joy is Latin and Western — in the Greek East they are used in Lent and at funerals as well).

No deliberately composed pageant could be as effective, he thinks, as this gradually, organically, produced ritual form. And yet

> [t]he ceremonies of our churches are only the outer expression of the real religion of spirit and truth, the veil which covers without hiding the mysteries beyond. Beyond the white Mass of Thursday and the procession, the altar of repose, behind the desolation of Friday, with its sudden burst of splendour, behind all the old rites of the Paschal vigil, we still see after so many long centuries, the table of the Supper to which we owe our Lord's last gift to us, the hours of his pain, the silent grace in which the Paschal moon shone that night; the bells, the organ, the Alleluia tell us, each year again, of the glory of that Easter sun which never set.[51]

This conclusion gives a reminder of how some of the most memorable and moving passages in his extant letters are, in effect, paeans to the beauty of Catholic worship.

The adjuncts of the rites

Even the advertisements for the rites were a work of art. The memorial exhibition at the Letchworth Public Library which followed his death included as examples of his calligraphy not only Arabic inscriptions and book markers with the Syriac text of John 6:69 and the Latin text of John 17:3, but such everyday items as the 'choir notice' for the church of St Hugh, and the 'order for the week at the Catholic church of St Hugh'.[52] Excellence, including in ordinary things, was a Fortescue hallmark. Everything connected with the Liturgy had to be of the best.

In the memorial catalogue, J.G. Vance describes the trouble Fortescue took in designing fabrics, which included altar frontals and apparels for albs and amices, but focused particularly on the chasuble, the priestly garment par excellence, since its use was reserved to the Eucharistic Sacrifice.

---

50 Ibid., p. xxv.

51 Ibid., p. xxxviii.

52 From the catalogue in J.G. Vance, *Short Memoir of the Revd Dr Fortescue, with a catalog of the memorial exhibition* (Letchworth: The Book Club, 1923), items 81, 82, 74, 75, 65, 66, respectively.

In designing vestments, Dr Fortescue's desire was to get beauty in the garment itself apart from any added decoration, and this he felt could best be obtained by adopting a form which by reason of its shape and material would fall in beautiful and dignified folds. Hence the vestments he designed for use at his church in Letchworth were made much larger than those in general use.[53]

Vance gives as example the first set of Mass vestments Fortescue designed for St Hugh's, which were 'of purple silk lined with green linen and ornamented with black and white chequered braid. The lines of the braid followed those in the chasuble of St Thomas of Canterbury at Sens.'[54] But in every case the chasuble was 'designed to reach within about a foot from the ground and almost to the wrist when the arms were extended'.[55] It may seem strange that a man so given to pugilism (in the Levant but also, at any rate threatened, at the presbytery door) was also keen on designing vestments, but this is Fortescue's all-round Renaissance humanity again. We note the Puginesque aesthetic (decoration must be secondary to a form that fulfils function), the reference to native English hagiology (using as model a garment associated with Becket), and the decisive choice for 'Gothic' (though, as we shall see, Fortescue disapproved of the word in this context) rather than 'fiddleback' (indicated by the dimensions of the chasuble). That strongly expressed preference for the more voluminous kind of vestment is the clue to Fortescue's remark, cited in the Preface to this book, that if the great Latin fathers returned he *hoped* they would recognize on the shoulders of a modern Mass-priest the same garment they had worn when standing at the Table of the Lord.

He made the point with his accustomed acerbity in an address to the Westminster Cathedral Altar Society (in Cardinal Bourne's presence) in 1912. Having said that vestments should be so made as to correspond to liturgical law and not inhibit their users by their inconvenience, Fortescue turned to the congenial topic of their beauty.

> Large garments falling in massive folds are dignified and beautiful. Garments cut short, stiff, flay, of bad outline are ugly. A man in massive folds of rich material looks manly, dignified, and fine. A man in tights looks ridiculous. That is one chief reason why we see the only hope for beauty of vestments in a return to the older tradition, in which they were large and fell in fine folds.[56]

53 Ibid., p. 17.

54 Ibid.

55 Ibid., p. 18.

56 *The Vestments of the Roman Rite* (London: Catholic Truth Society, 1912), p. 21.

Alas, a wave of eighteenth century bad taste had swept over the Church, affecting not only vestments but art and music. 'We do not like Baroc [sic] vestments any more than Baroc architecture or Baroc music.'[57] And just as modern Rome has welcomed the Solesmes reform of the chant, giving us back 'the old full neums of plainsong, instead of the skimped, degraded forms we used to hear', so likewise, Fortescue predicts, she will return to the older vestments.[58]

It is not a question of Roman or Gothic, for the crux of the matter is time not place. 'These modern shapes are not specially Roman; they came in at the same time nearly everywhere. And the older shape was used at Rome just as much as everywhere else.'[59] Citing impressive Teutonic monographs, Fortescue declared no known historian of the Western Liturgy would disagree with his analysis or his programme.[60] Of course there is no need for absolute uniformity in design so long as there is good design, and Fortescue was inclined to think that, for the moment, though there was good workmanship in embroidery for vestments, there was not, in that respect, good design. The published form of his lecture showed photographs of what he considered exemplary vestments, made of fine, heavy silk, in good colours, generous in the quantity of their fabric and with hardly a touch of embroidery on them.

Fortescue expressed the hope that, starting from Westminster Cathedral, the excellence of whose practice was well-known,

> love of our liturgy and of its historic ornaments will make the service of the Catholic Church in this diocese worthy of its splendid past, worthy of Him to whom it is offered, and a not unworthy foretaste of the beauty of that other house of God, whose walls are of jasper and streets of fine gold, where there is a seven-branched candlestick, a golden thurible, and a great crowd in white garments who sing: *Salus Deo et Agno* ['Salvation to our God and to the Lamb].[61]

---

57 Ibid.

58 Ibid., pp. 21–22.

59 Ibid., p. 22.

60 J. Wilpert, *Die Gewandung der Christen in den ersten Jahrhunderten* (Cologne: Bachem, 1898); J. Braun, S.J., *Die priesterliche Gewänder des Abendlandes* (Freiburg: Herder, 1897); idem., *Die pontifikalen Gewänder des Abendlandes* (Freiburg: Herder, 1898); idem., *Die liturgische Gewandung im Occident und Orient* (Freiburg: Herder, 1907); idem.., *Handbuch der Paramentik* (Freiburg: Herder, 1912).

61 *The Vestments of the Roman Rite*, op. cit., p. 24.

The Fortescue and church servers at St Hugh's. Notice the 'English' surplices and the cope of Fortescue's own design.

The Ceremonial book

Fortescue embarked on his new version of a Ceremonial for the Roman rite in England not because he liked the idea of the project but because he thought it was needed. He considered the regnant book, a partial translation from the Italian, to be a monstrosity.[62] The Italian *ceremoniale* on which it was based was 'redolent [wrote Fortescue], not only of Rome, but of Rome in the palmy days of the Papal State'.[63] It assumed that a bishop was standing in for the Pope, and it more or less ignored the *Missa cantata,* since a 'solemn' Mass, with deacon and subdeacon, was so easy to organize anywhere in Rome. Naturally enough, it was ignorant

---

62 *Ceremonial according to the Roman Rite*, translated from the Italian of Joseph Baldeschi, by the Rev. J.D. Hilarius Dale (London: Burns and Oates, 1913, 11th edition).

63 *The Ceremonies of the Roman Rite Described, in accordance with the rubrics of liturgical books, the decrees of the Congregation of Sacred Rites, the Code of Canon Law, and approved authors, containing all such ceremonies as may occur in a parish church, the rules for pontifical functions and directions for the administration of the sacraments, with plans and diagrams by the author and with a preface by His Eminence Cardinal Bourne, archbishop of Westminster* (London: Burns and Oates, 1918), p. xiii.

of specifically English Catholic customs (and local liturgical legislation). Its translator had not troubled to include the lengthy section on the Low Mass which, as the most frequently encountered form of Eucharistic celebration, ought to have been basic. He had retained some errors of the original author, and conveyed the whole in a pompous pastiche of proper English whereby, for example, 'The M.C. [Master of Ceremonies] goes about apprizing people and comporting himself till he observes to perform the customary salutation'.[64]

For cathedral use, there were more comprehensive works than the Baldeschi ceremonial book from which the hapless Father Dale had started out. Holding that '[a] complete work would not be a book but a library',[65] Fortescue set himself the more modest task of producing a handbook serviceable by the secular clergy in English parishes (where, for example, it was unlikely that the pope would celebrate with the additions then proper when the Supreme Pontiff was presiding. Fortescue did not foresee that, some decades later, two popes would come in turn to England: admittedly they did not celebrate parish Masses).

To be useful to parish priests, and their curates, he included, therefore, the rites of sacraments (other than the Eucharist, he meant) and sacramentals, since

> It is a mistake to judge the importance of a rite by its elaboration. The manner of hearing confessions is less complicated, but considerably more important, than pontifical Vespers at the throne. In these shorter rites too the priest must do everything accurately, according to the rubrics, just as much as in the longer ones.[66]

Though Fortescue did not eschew all Latin words ('It is not strange that in the Roman rite some objects should have a technical name in the Roman language'),[67] he eliminated every last trace of Italian ones, and wherever possible introduced older English terms, even if they had fallen into disuse. He retained Latin for the recurring phrase 'the accustomed kisses', *solita oscula*. This referred to the kiss given ceremonially to various pieces of liturgical paraphernalia as well as the hand (and occasionally the cheek) of the celebrant: Fortescue's reason for keeping this in Latin turned on 'what Gibbon calls the decent obscurity of a dead language. The thing itself is not strange, as every deacon knows; but the constant repetition of the words kissing and kisses is not pretty'.[68]

---

64 Ibid., p. xv, footnote 2.
65 Ibid., p. xvi.
66 Ibid., p. xvii.
67 Ibid.
68 Ibid., p. xviii.

Fortescue pointed out that the actions described in a Ceremonial book are really a lot less complicated than they sound. 'If one had to write out in detail all the ceremonies of getting up in the morning or of eating one's dinner, these would seem exceedingly elaborate rites.'[69] Yet if doing is simpler than describing, then there is something to be said for being pernicketily precise.

> [T]he more exact details of direction are, the less complicated their performance becomes. . . . In many cases we may say that it does not so much matter, in itself, in which way a certain action is performed; but it does matter that all concerned should agree to do it in the same way. If only for the sake of this agreement, it becomes necessary to describe in detail some way of doing it. That being so, we may as well describe the right way, according to the rubrics and recognized authors.[70]

That does not rule out personal touches in the body of Fortescue's text not all of which are ironic. Thus Fortescue noted that at the elevation of Host and Chalice the celebrant is permitted to say a short mental prayer, for there are no liturgical prayers provided to be spoken at these points. He proposed two alternative sets of possibilities. One is from the Sarum rite, where a short text recited before the priest's Communion could, he thinks, appropriately be transferred to this point for silent prayer: *Ave in aeternum sanctissima caro Christi*, 'Hail for evermore, most holy Flesh of Christ' (at the elevation of the Host), and (at the elevation of the Chalice), *Ave in aeternum caelestis potus, mihi ante omnia et superomnia dulcedo*, 'Hail for evermore, Heavenly Drink, to me before all and above all the highest source of joy'.[71] The other, drawn from the Alexandrian Liturgy of St Basil, seems rather too prolix for the purpose Fortescue assigned to it.[72]

Fortescue also had fun. He noted, for instance, that at the offering of the chalice at Pontifical High Mass 'at the throne', the deacon pours a little of the wine and water for the sacristan to drink. 'This is the "praegustatio" ceremony, a curious relic of early times. It is obviously a precaution against poison. The ceremony is now often omitted'.[73] Or speaking of the use of a ladder when the monstrance used for Exposition of the Blessed Sacrament is to be enthroned high up in a building, he writes, 'It is impossible to genuflect on the top of a ladder, If a ladder is used, he must first come down, then genuflect on the ground'.[74]

---

69 Ibid.
70 Ibid., pp. xviii–xix.
71 I take these translations from A.H. Pearson's translation in *The Sarum Missal, in English* (London: The Church Press Company, 1908), p. 319.
72 *The Ceremonies of the Roman Rite Described*, op cit., p. 54, footnote 3.
73 Ibid., p. 178, footnote 1.
74 Ibid., p. 243, footnote 1.

The Fortescue ceremonial was not intended simply as an accurate guide to rubrics. It had elements of an agenda of its own. One way of subtly forwarding this agenda was by means of the carefully drawn illustrations in Fortescue's own hand. His diagrams for the proper placing of the choir in parish and cathedral churches are a case in point. The usual custom in the England of the Catholic revival was to situate choirs in galleries at the west-end of the building. Fortescue was against this. He placed the choir within the sanctuary, albeit in the area of the chancel closest to the nave. His aim was to unite more closely music with the Liturgy — though T.E. Muir suspects the arrangement was also intended to exclude women from choirs (a debated point from the mid nineteenth century on).[75] If so, he ignored his own preferences (on Muir's hypothesis) at Letchworth, where the choir was certainly mixed.

Fortescue was also keen that what he termed 'Romanizing' should be kept to a minimum.

> This book . . . will, it is hoped, give no encouragement to that excessive and uncanonical Romanizing, which, instead of going to legitimate sources of canon law, follows the easier path of ignorant copying of everything done in that city. When, as happens not infrequently, the local Roman custom differs from the rubrics of lawful liturgical books or the rules of lawful liturgical authority, far from abandoning the rules ourselves, we should rather regret that they are not always obeyed exactly in Rome.[76]

Despite his sensible remarks about how much better it is to have a formula for agreement on how a ceremony should be conducted before one starts[77] (and the present writer can testify what superfluous discussion attended this subject in connexion with the revised (post-1969) rites of the Latin Church before Father (now Bishop) Peter Elliott produced a small two-volume Ceremonial of his own),[78] Fortescue made plain in no uncertain terms his dislike for the office of a rubrician as such.

---

75 T.E. Muir, *Roman Catholic Church Music in England, 1791–1914*, op. cit., p. 46–47.

76 *The Ceremonies of the Roman Rite Described*, op. cit., p. xxi.

77 In the Middle Ages, he pointed out, no one bothered to say how exactly the celebrant should cense the altar at the start of High Mass. But, he added, 'We need not regret the minute exactness. Such increased definiteness was bound to come and, after all, you must incense an altar somehow; it does not hurt to be told how to do it', *The Mass*, op. cit., p. 230.

78 P.J. Elliott, *Ceremonies of the Modern Roman Rite* (San Francisco: Ignatius, 1995); idem., *Ceremonies of the Liturgical Year* (San Francisco: Ignatius, 1998).

He wrote to the President of St Edmund's: 'I do not think I have ever yet undertaken a task that I so hated carrying out'. As he explained,

> Try to imagine for one solid year of my life (and life in any case is scandalously short) I spent all day comparing Merati and Martinucci and Le Vavasseur, to find out where the thurifer ought to stand before the Magnificat, who takes off the bishop's left glove, what sort of bow you should make at the Asperges. . . . Conceive of man, said to be made in the image of God, spending his time over that kind of thing. Even now that the burden is over, it still fills me with rage to think of those days. I could have learned a new language easily in the time. I could have gone every day to the Cinema. I could have read the complete works of Maria Corelli [the author of popular if moralizing melodramas]. My cat was spending his time in sane and reasonable pursuits, chasing birds in the garden, climbing trees, or sleeping in his basket, while I was describing the conduct of the second M.C. at pontifical vespers not at the throne. And they affect to believe that we lead a nobler life than the beasts.[79]

Fortescue also reported that he had no patience with correspondents who wrote to him in the hope of engaging in discussion of this or that particular point.

> I neither know nor care one straw whether the celebrant should or should not have a hassock to kneel on, nor which sort of Monsignore may use a Bugia [hand-candle]. The obvious thing to me would seem to be that if it is possible to find a grown-up man who cares whether he has a Bugia or not, by all means let him have it; and envy him whose desire is so easily satisfied.[80]

The minutiae dear to professional rubricians that Fortescue so deplored are prominent in the review of the Ceremonial book published by its posthumous re-editor, the Dublin diocesan priest John B. O'Connell.[81] And in a companion review to Fortescue's second edition of his work, O'Connell commented

> The present edition of Fr Fortescue's book introduces itself as "Second and Revised Edition", and the author tells us, in an addendum to his original preface, that "he will always be grateful for corrections or suggestions". We must say that we cannot find much evidence of either any very thorough revision, or of the author's gratitude for corrections and suggestions, unless his

---

79 Westminster Diocesan Archive, Series 200, Box 22, Letter to Edward Myers of 27 May, 1918.

80 Ibid.

81 *The Irish Ecclesiastical Record* (1918), pp. 349–352

gratitude takes the form of ignoring the help which he professes to desire. In our notice of the first edition we offered some suggestions for securing greater fullness of treatment of certain points of practical importance, not one of these suggestions has been adopted.[82]

Clearly, Fortescue had abided by the mind-set in which he wrote to Morison in November 1919, rather than the more chastened temper exhibited in a letter to the same correspondent of 20 May 1920. In the latter, he declared that, after reading O'Connell's review of the first edition, he was 'quite prepared to look up the necessary muck in the debauched housebreakers aforesaid [earlier writers of ceremonial, q.v.], and change where he is right'. In the same letter he admitted he had not yet seen O'Connell's review of the second edition of his book, quoted above, which, had he done so, might have produced an act of contrition since, as he confessed,

> They [Burns, Oates and Washbourne] paid me quite well for the book. I cannot doubt that it is my job, as part of the work for which they had paid, to correct any mistakes which are my fault. So I will do this too. Only you cannot conceive how I loathe the idea of going into all that horrid business of the minutiae of tomfool modern ceremonies once again.[83]

Perhaps he would have been surprised to know that a fifteenth edition of his work would be published the best part of a century later, in 2009.[84]

Fortescue was in some danger of rubbishing his own book ('about as readable as a Bradshaw. I wish it could be as useful'[85]). He did not live long enough to appreciate the influence it had, even beyond his own Church. Dom Anselm Hughes of Nashdom (near Burnham in Buckinghamshire), of the Anglican Benedictine foundation, looking back from the vantage point of the early 1960s, considered the two dates that defined the 'turn of the tide' from 'Sarum Use' to 'Western Use' among English Anglo-Catholics to be the founding of the Society of SS. Peter and Paul in 1910,[86] and, in 1918,

---

82 Ibid. (1919), at pp. 262-263.

83 Cambridge University Library, MS Add. 9812/D/90, Letter to S. Morison of 20 May, 1920.

84 *The Ceremonies of the Roman Rite Described,* by A. Fortescue, J.B. O'Connell, and A. Reid (London and New York: Burns and Oates, 2009, 15th edition).

85 Westminster Diocesan Archive, Series 20, Box 22, Letter of 13 May 1918 to Herbert Thurston, S.J.

86 For an account of the work of this body, which combined encouragement of the full replication of the 'Western' (i.e. Roman) Rite, with advocacy of Baroque décor and a desire to annoy mainstream Anglicans, see P. Anson, *Fashions in Church Furnishing, 1840–1940,* op. cit., pp. 316–327.

the publication of Fortescue's *The Ceremonies of the Roman Rite described*. Fortescue's work, so Hughes reported, further encouraged 'those who desired authoritative instruction in the right way of attending to practical details, and were not afraid of the Roman bogey'.[87] Presumably he had (not least) the Nashdom Benedictines in mind, for, as Peter Anson observed,

> Every detail here is in strict conformity with the rubrics of the Roman Missal and with the decrees of the sacred Congregation of Rites. . . . Even the most captious critic would find it hard to detect faults in the rendering of the plain-chant or the minutiae of ceremonial.[88]

Fortescue would not, however, have approved of a Liturgy 'carried out with an impeccable Italian pronunciation of Latin',[89] to which he was implacably opposed, writing to *The Tablet*, in 1909, that readers should listen to

> a choir sing good Plainsong, according to the Solesmes rules, with Restored pronunciation (there are many such choirs abroad and at least one in England) and then judge if it does not sound more logical, clearer, simpler, enormously more beautiful than the slovenly hissing ('amitshitsia' [*amicitia*]) of the Italian way.[90]

Visitors to Letchworth who heard the one choir in England referred to in Fortescue's letter, sometimes came away regretting that, though the singers were good, it was a pity they had such strong Cockney accents (singing, for example, 'syecula syeculorum' for *saecula saeculorum*, in the doxologies).[91] This brings us conveniently to the topic of the Chant.

Protagonist of the Chant

Fortescue was keen to take part in the new movement of popularization of the Chant. Advertisements are extant for 'Two Lectures on Plainsong', offered by him at the Letchworth Arts Club in 1911, to be suitably illustrated with 'examples by singers from St Hugh'.[92] The programme of the lectures shows Fortescue's appeal for comparative purposes to the Byzantine chant (its eight mode system was the origin of the similar system adopted by the first codifiers of the chant in the West). It also makes plain his intention

---

87   A. Hughes, *The Rivers of the Flood. A Personal Account of the Catholic Revival in England in the Twentieth Century* (London: Faith Press, 1961), pp. 55–56.

88   P. Anson, *The Call of the Cloister*, op. cit., pp. 188, 189.

89   Ibid., p. 189.

90   *The Tablet*, Letter of 2 October, 1909.

91   E. Cowell, 'Adrian Fortescue', art. cit., p. 1032.

92   'Letchworth Arts Club, Two Lectures on Plainsong', Downside Archives, IX AF, Box B.

to use the new Solesmes *Graduale* (1909) which contained rhythmic signs devised, somewhat controversially, by Dom André Mocquereau in furtherance of his general interpretation of the chant. On Mocquereau's reading, strictly musical considerations (pitch, note duration, and musical dynamic at large) were more prominent than they had been for the more text-inclined Dom Pothier, whose study Fortescue had read a decade earlier. Fortescue made an exception for pieces from the *Kyriale*, which sets to music the *Ordinarium Missae*. For this, he continued to use the 'Vatican Edition' — the version based on Pothier's work, and supported by, among others, Terry at Westminster.

There was quite a rivalry between the two approaches in England, to where the Solesmes monks had transferred after their expulsion from France under the Third Republic, settling at Appledurcombe on the Isle of Wight. Gradually, the Mocquereau approach won out, ably abetted by Dame Laurentia McLachlan of Stanbrook, a Pothier trained convert to Mocquereau: witness her 1904 *Grammar of Plainsong*. Passions were aroused by this rivalry. Though McLachlan's *Grammar* had been produced at the request of the archbishop of Birmingham, the work of Mocquereau (which it represented) was banned in 1905 by the archbishop of Liverpool who proceeded to present fifty copies of the (Pothier-inspired) Vatican Gradual to his diocesan seminary.[93] Evidently, Fortescue was keeping a foot in both camps, admiring the revised *Graduale* yet conscious that what congregations had been learning was the version in the earlier Solesmes books.

In the wider context of life in the Latin church, Fortescue's musical policy at Letchworth, regarding both polyphony and the Chant, was not idiosyncratic. 'The Fourth Synod of Westminster, convened by Manning in 1873', writes the historian of the English Catholic music of this period,

> asserted the primacy of plainchant and Renaissance polyphony. At that time both had "Roman" connotations. Renaissance polyphony meant music by Palestrina or Victoria; plainchant meant the music found in the Ratisbon editions, which was based on the Medician Gradual of 1614–15 and supported by a papal grant of monopoly.[94]

Why Fortescue considered himself something of a protagonist in a musicological struggle was not, then, the lack of authoritative backing for plainsong and Renaissance polyphony, but the incidence of resistance in parishes and other institutions, where the preference was for more modern music.

---

93 T.E. Muir, *Roman Catholic Church Music in England, 1791–1914*, op. cit., pp. 209, 208.

94 Ibid., p. 28.

Investigation of surviving collections of Catholic church music shows that 'in the nineteenth century nearly half the repertoire was composed after 1750, and British composers contributed more than any other national group'.[95] Much of this music was in the style of the Classical Viennese school, or at least took the form of a hybrid, marrying Renaissance polyphony with the more operatic voices of Vienna. Such plainchant as was sung was typically of the slow, 'measured', kind, favoured as this had been by Early Modern composers and editors. The mystical élan (arguably) characteristic of the chant in its original versions whether late antique or mediaeval, was domesticised and largely lost.

Despite their internal disagreements, the work of the Solesmes school of monk-researchers, restored the integral musical text and re-introduced a contemplative quality to the chant.[96] They convinced the Holy See, which abrogated its contract with Pustet of Ratisbon — the last publisher of books of 'measured' chant — in 1901. They also had no difficulty in convincing Fortescue.

Fortescue was clearly aware that the history of the chant had not always been happy. But he also knew it was not particularly helpful to provide for parishes versions of the texts not yet adopted by the Church for public worship. Thus, though he deplored the re-writing of many of the patristic and mediaeval Latin hymns in the edition of the Breviary promulgated by Urban VIII in 1629, he realized there was little point in anticipating somewhere in Hertfordshire a properly universal restoration, for which he looked hopefully to the reform of the canonical hours begun by St Pius X. His *Latin Hymns: sung at the church of S Hugh Letchworth* was printed at the University Press in Cambridge, with translations all his own, except for the Christmas hymn *Veni, veni Emmanuel*, whose familiar English version was found in the *Arundel Hymnbook*, and *Te lucis*, the hymn for Compline, where he used the version of the Redemptorist translator Edward Caswall.

Even with the Urbanian changes, Fortescue could still wax lyrical about the contents.

> There is not and there is never likely to be any religious poetry in the world worthy to be compared with the hymns of the Latin Office. . . . Other religious bodies take all their best hymns in translation from us. It would be a disgrace if we Catholics were the only people who did not appreciate what is our property.[97]

---

95 Ibid., p. 29.

96 K. Bergeron, *Decadant Enchantments. The Revival of Gregorian Chant at Solesmes* (Berkeley, CA: University of California Press, 1998).

97 *Latin Hymns: sung at the church of S Hugh Letchworth*, arranged and translated by Adrian Fortescue (Cambridge: Cambridge University Press, 1923), 'Preface', pp. v–viii, and here at p. viii.

He was probably thinking of Anglicans. He admitted he could not rival the verse translations of John Mason Neale (1818–1866) — though he considered Neale's hymns from the Greek and Syriac to be in effect new compositions.[98] Hence his decision to offer a parallel translation in prose. There was one innovation. Putting on a composite evening service by joining together Eucharistic devotions with Compline was relatively common in parish life in Fortescue's period, and, granted the nearly invariable character of Roman-rite Compline, he recommended priests and people, during or after Benediction, to 'remember the feast or season' at such services by singing the Vespers hymn of the day, together with its accompanying versicle and collect.[99]

A concluding letter

No more winning statement of Fortescue's loving service of the Liturgy can be found, I think, than the letter of 29 December 1909 in which he expresses his delight in the Christmas celebration at *Rivalis Villa*.

> And I said the prayers before Mass — strange to be saying them in the evening. At eleven the church was lit up and warm and we began matins. All the singing was quite beautiful: the *Invitatorium* — *Christus natus est nobis: venite adoremus* — twined and curved and twisted like garlands of beautiful strange sound, in the IVth mode across the church. Then the glorious Christmas hymn — *Jesu redemptor omnium*; we sang . . . the first nocturn lessons to the old German chant with wonderful neums . . . You know — the Isaias lessons: *Puer natus est nobis et filius datus est nobis . . . et consurge, consurge Hierusalem . . . et ecce virgo concipiet et pariet filium et vocabitur nomen eius Emmanuel. . . .* And the second and third nocturn lessons, beautiful homilies of the old Fathers, Leo and Ambrose and Augustine and the Christmas psalms and the responsories to beautiful tunes I had made myself, and then just before midnight the *Te Deum*. Then we went to the sacristy and I vested and we came through the

---

98 A.G. Lough, *John Mason Neale: Priest Extraordinary* (Newton Abbot: Lough, 1975); Neale's Eastern interests are stressed in the fuller study by L. Litvack, *John Mason Neale and the Quest for Sobornost* (Oxford: Clarendon, 1994). Neale had produced his collection of verse translations of the Latin hymns, soon included in Thomas Helmore's *Hymnal Noted* (1852), for St Barnabas, Pimlico, in 1851.

99 *Latin Hymns: sung at the church of S Hugh Letchworth*, op. cit., p. 5. Fortescue's *Latin Hymns* was republished in facsimile by Roman Catholic Books at Harrison, New York, in 1994, with an afterword by Michael Davies.

garden and in at the big doors. In the garden I saw the blue cloud of the incense against the moonlight of the sky and the tall cross black outlines against the stars and the pale flames of the acolytes' candles burning clear in the cold still air. And we came up the church as they sang — quite beautifully — the Introit of midnight Mass, while the smoke of the incense and the black and silver cross moved slowly along. Then all that wonderful and strange Mass in the middle of the dark night. I sang the gospel about the shepherds and the crowd of the heavenly army, and the Christmas preface, under the dark garlands of holly and bay, while the thin white candles held up their flames among the lilies and the chrysanthema and shone on the white corporal and silver chalice. And the choir's *Sanctus* rang out across the silent night, and from the windows the light shone out into the dark outside. Then the silence and the bell and the Canon: "Communicating and remembering the most sacred night when the unspotted Mother gave birth to the Saviour of the world, and honouring the memory first of that same glorious Virgin Mary, mother of our God and Lord Jesus Christ, and of Thy blessed Apostles and Martyrs Peter and Paul, Andrew, James.". . . And the long rows of my nice little people kneeling at the altar rails while I gave them Communion. . . . And at half past one I went to bed and did not sleep for excitement and saw it all again, and our dear Lady laying Him in the manger — *haec sacratissima nox*. I said the dawn Mass at eight, as the grey winter light shone in the east, and the third Mass at ten; and then was utterly done and tired, but frightfully happy as I ate my tea and toast. I did remember you too . . . and everyone I love, when I stood before my altar all white and gold and gleaming under the tall candles in the holy night.[100]

---

100 Cited M. Davies, 'Adrian Fortescue Priest and Scholar', in idem., *The Wisdom of Adrian Fortescue*, op. cit., pp. 51–52.

9. Anglo-Roman Debates

The challenge of the High Church

Fortescue was well aware that Anglican Ritualism was taking to itself much of the best in Catholic liturgical practice and often outdoing the original owners in both zest for 'Catholic privileges' and perfectionism of performance. More widely, granted the competing claims of Rome's English disciples and Canterbury's Anglo-Catholic partisans — 'competing' since there could hardly be two 'Catholic Churches', non-recognisant one of the other, in the same country — there was something of a polemical war on. In the world before the Second Vatican Council, controversialists, though theologically and historically as literate as their blander successors, the ecumenists, tended to give as hard as they got. Fortescue chose to involve himself in Anglo-Roman debates, to which his book on the office of Peter in the early centuries may suitably be assimilated.[1]

Percy Dearmer and the Branch Theory

In *An Anglican on Reunion*, Fortescue considered the 1910 study *Reunion and Rome* by the well-known author of *The Parson's Handbook* Percy Dearmer (1867–1935), rector of St Mary's Primrose Hill,[2] where carefully orchestrated liturgies married the ceremonial of the Sarum Use to Cranmer's text from the Book of Common Prayer.[3] Actually, there was

---

1 *The Early Papacy. To the Synod of Chalcedon in 451* (London: Burns and Oates, 1920).

2 D. Gray, *Percy Dearmer. A Parson's Pilgrimage* (Norwich: Canterbury Press, 2000).

3 This was not new: John Purchas's *Directorium Anglicanum* of 1858 had as its aim to accommodate the rubrics of the Book of Common Prayer to the ceremonial of the Sarum rite. A revised edition published by Dr F.G. Lee of All Saints, Lambeth a founder of the Order of Corporate Reunion patronized by Adrian Fortescue's father was 'somewhat "higher" in tone', P. Anson, *Bishops at Large* (London: Faber and Faber, 1964), p. 63, fn 2. It remained for the Revd Orby Shipley, in his *The Ritual of the Altar: the order of the Holy Communion*

quite a lot in common between Fortescue and Dearmer (and between their parish congregations as well).[4] Dearmer shared Fortescue's admiration for the Arts and Crafts movement — though with a background in High Church social radicalism (the Guild of St Matthew and the Christian Social Union) he differed from Fortescue in applauding Morris's Socialism as well. Assiduous visits to the newly created Victoria and Albert Museum had trained his eye. His standards for the artifacts used in worship were demanding (for some years he held a chair of Ecclesiastical Art at King's College London).[5] A great devotee of the chant, his advocacy of Sarum Use ceremonial (justified, he argued, by the Prayer-Book's 'Ornaments rubric' which approved whatever liturgical adjuncts were recognised in the 'second year of Edward VI') drew on an instinctive Anglo-centric opposition to Roman Catholicism.

Dearmer regretted that 'many of those who had begun by taking their stand on the Ornaments rubric ended by denying it in favour of "the customs of a very hostile foreign church"',[6] a xenophobic remark which rather ignored the historic origins of the Sarum rite in the (Norman-French) Use of Rouen.[7] Fortescue was impressed by some of Dearmer's ceremonial

---

according to the use of the Church of England: together with rubrcal directions, secret prayers, ritual music, and general rubrics, illustrated (London: Longmans, Green, 1878, 2nd edition), to devise a way of celebrating the Prayer-Book liturgy to look as little different as possible from the 1570 *Ordo Missae* of Pope St Pius V.

4   The 'younger members' of the Primrose Hill congregation were said to evince an 'urge to live in Garden Cities or quaint little houses of the "Simple Life" style, designed by architects such as Annesley Voysey or M.H. Baillie Scott, with white rough-cast walls, low rooms, casements with leaded lights, rose pergolas and crazy paving. If possible, the furniture would be hand-made by Ernest Gimson or Ambrose Heal; the crockery '"leadless glaze"', P. Anson, *Fashions in Church Furnishing 1840–1940*, op. cit., p. 309. This sounds more than vaguely reminiscent of Letchworth Garden City with its well-attended Arts Club, Literary and Debating Society at the Howard Hall, etc.

5   Dearmer's 1908 *The Ornaments of the Minister* could well be compared with Fortescue's 1912 *The Vestments of the Roman Rite*.

6   D. Gray, *Percy Dearmer*, op. cit., p. 42.

7   In his study of Dearmer, Donald Gray, basing himself on *The Parson's Handbook*'s posthumous reviser, Cyril Pocknee, comments that the distinctive features of Sarum (vis-à-vis the rite of the Roman Curia at the end of the Middle Ages) are 'now' known to belong with a general trend in northern Europe, ibid., p. 44. But the link to Rouen was pointed out by J.B. Pearson, the translator of the Sarum Missal into English, as early as 1868: *The Sarum Missal in English*, op. cit., p. xi.

proposals in the *Parson's Handbook* ('there are many things about the artistic side of Ritual in the book that Catholics might read with profit'). And he was unstinting in his praise of Dearmer's work on the first edition of the *English Hymnal* ('the best English hymnbook of any kind, whose excellent hymns and translations as well as its beautiful tunes make us wish we had anything as good').[8] But Fortescue was at a loss to see anything worthy of commendation in Dearmer's effort at controversial theology,[9] which he judged 'one of the very poorest, shallowest, most confused examples of anti-Roman controversy that has appeared'.[10]

When Dearmer stuck to reproducing 'scraps' from Bishop Gore, or Hunt's *History of the English Church*, or the pamphlets of the Church Historical Society, he was, wrote Fortescue, at any rate saved from the embarrassment of showing the 'incompetence' betrayed by passages, all his own, which included egregious errors, like turning Döllinger into a bishop, and gratuitous assertions, like declaring St Leo I the 'founder of the Papacy'.[11] True, the 'Catholic theologian' may be inclined to excessive severity towards Anglicans owing to his own 'perfectly logical, clear-cut, definite system . . . a system that we all understand and that really works'. But by itself this does not suffice to explain the impression of 'exceeding confusion' that Anglican controversial literature conveys. 'On the negative side, these writers are clear enough: they will have no Pope. But when you look for their positive ideas you are amazed to find how little in the way of a rival theory they can produce'.[12] Thus in Dearmer's case, '[h]e knows that the Roman Communion is not the whole Church, but he has no idea what is; he has not yet even made up his mind as to which are the real general councils'.[13]

In drawing attention to Dearmer's lack of theological focus, Fortescue was perceptive: in his later years, if report may be credited, it was hard to say *what* Dearmer believed.[14] Why, then, we may ask — and Fortescue himself asks — is he writing about this book? The answer is, in part, it made a stir — the Archbishop of Canterbury had granted it a preface, High Church papers had noted it favourably. But Fortescue also wished to use the opportunity to make to Anglicans certain salient points from the other side.

---

8   *An Anglican on Reunion* (London: Catholic Truth Society, 1910), p. 2.

9   P. Dearmer, *Reunion and Rome* (London and Oxford: Mowbray, 1910).

10 *An Anglican on Reunion*, op. cit., p. 3.

11 Ibid., citing P. Dearmer, *Rome and Reunion*, op. cit., at pp. 27 and 10 respectively.

12 *An Anglican on Reunion*, op. cit., p. 5.

13 Ibid., p. 6.

14 D. Gray, *Percy Dearmer*, op. cit., p. 192.

First of all, he advised, logic is not to be sniffed at.

> [L]ogic, though not everything, though not even a certain guide
> to truth (since your premises may be false), is one absolutely
> necessary condition of truth. A true theory cannot contradict
> itself; an illogical, that is, self-contradictory theory cannot be
> true.[15]

Secondly, he counseled Anglican apologists not to be so 'absurd' as to
'inveigh against the papal theory of the Church before you have made up
your mind what theory you can oppose to it'.[16] Anglicans:

> talk glibly enough about the branches of the Church; one never
> finds one who can say which the branches are. The Anglicans,
> Romans and Orthodox are branches certainly, probably the
> Jansenists, Old Catholics, and Bulgars too. But what about the
> Nestorians, Copts, Armenians, Señor Cabrera's sect in Spain, the
> Mariavites in Poland, Swedish church, and Malabar Christians?
> It will make a considerable difference to our idea of Catholic
> consent if we include them and take their vote too.[17]

Thirdly, Fortescue asked that Anglicans look again at the English
Reformation. Dearmer had claimed that the schism from Rome was made
by Rome itself, in 1570, when Pope Pius V 'excommunicated all who took
part in our Church services'.[18] Fortescue suggested that, to the contrary, the
schism 'took place in 1558 when Elizabeth's government forcibly ejected
(with one exception) every single Catholic bishop in England, because,
true to the old faith, they all refused to accept her new Act of Uniformity
establishing the Reformed religion'.[19] The schismatical bishops introduced
in 1558 to 1561 'had no illusions about being in communion with their
predecessors'.[20]

Fourthly, Fortescue invited Anglicans not to take pleasure in the
demographic setbacks of the Church of Rome in its regions of historic
influence. Anglicans cannot necessarily crow (Fortescue cites a High
Anglican author who registers very low figures for Church of England
communicants considered as a proportion of the general population).[21]
And, more widely, they should recognize the gravity *also for them* of the
'great wave of free-thinking, agnosticism, secularism, and so on, passing

---

15 *An Anglican on Reunion*, op. cit., p. 10.

16 Ibid., p. 14.

17 Ibid., p. 13.

18 P. Dearmer, *Reunion and Rome*, op. cit., p. 8.

19 *An Anglican on Reunion*, op. cit., p. 15.

20 Ibid., p. 16.

21 D. Macleane, *Lancelot Andrewes* (London: George Allen, 1910), p. 11, note.

all over Europe'.[22] Citing approvingly the remark of the Anglo-Irish Jesuit George Tyrrell (1861–1909) that 'If Rome dies, other Churches may order their coffins', Fortescue comments, 'If this flood of rationalism were to overwhelm Rome, it would not be the graceful cloudiness of High Church Anglicanism that would stop it'.[23]

Fifthly, Fortescue reproved Anglicans for misrepresenting the Petrine claims. Dearmer had declared that all Catholics must practice 'complete submission' to the pope's 'dictation', but '*complete* submission', so Fortescue points out, would cover 'submission in all questions — of literature, art, politics. The Pope's authority as chief bishop and visible head of the Church affects only questions on faith and morals'.[24] And so far from enforcing uniformity in ritual and liturgy, as Dearmer claims, Rome has within her communion 'millions of Uniates' who use their own rites.[25]

Sixthly, he wanted Anglicans to cease presenting Eastern Orthodoxy as 'an ideal of peaceable federation'.[26] And giving as examples some of the more unfortunate conflicts, many recent or even contemporary, that were also chronicled in *The Orthodox Eastern Church*, Fortescue wrote, forthrightly enough,

> The Orthodox Church is not, like the Church of England, in a state of anarchy about what she believes, but in every other way she is infinitely less respectable. Her internal quarrels and schisms are the crying scandal of Christendom. Nowhere is the need of a central authority recognized by all — in short of a Pope — so obvious as in the East.[27]

The last chapter of this book will show Fortescue was certainly anxious about possible hyper-inflation of the papal office — but not to the point of reconsidering acceptance of the Petrine claims.

The vagaries of the 'branch theory' were a topic to which Fortescue returned in another context that same year.[28] The Anglican:

> looks out over the enormous number of churches and sects that divide Christendom and tells us that some of them are branches of the Catholic Church, others are schismatical sects. Surely it is not too much for us to expect him to tell us which are which?[29]

---

22 *An Anglican on Reunion*, op. cit., p. 20.

23 Ibid., p. 22.

24 Ibid., p. 22.

25 Ibd., p. 31.

26 Ibid., p. 29.

27 Ibid., p. 30.

28 Fortescue wrote on this in *The Tablet* for July 1910 in a text subsequently published as *The Branch Theory* (London: Catholic Truth Society, 1911).

29 Ibid., p. 5.

The Orthodox, Nestorians and Monophysites all anathematize each other as heretics. Yet some Anglicans claim the Armenians, who are Monophysites, as true branches (Fortescue does not mention that in the instance he has in mind, the author of *The Armenian Church* was his own half-brother).[30] Similarly, it was 'difficult to understand the conduct of the Archbishop of Canterbury's Mission to the Nestorians unless these gentlemen think the Nestorians a branch of the Church too,' for they 'protest continually that they do not wish to convert Nestorians, and are indignant with the Roman missionaries who do'.[31]

Fortescue asks, 'Would they do this for heretics and schismatics? Is it possible so to co-operate with schism? One can hardly imagine High Anglicans doing all this for Methodists and Calvinists.'[32] And after surveying other examples in East and West Fortescue asserted:

> The only possible basis for an answer to each particular case would be a consistent test, a criterion that one could apply to any body of Christians. What conditions are required to be a branch of the Catholic Church? And they have no such criterion. There is no test they can suggest that will apply to all and only the churches any one claims; all the conditions they propose either exclude some or admit too many. That is the fundamental impossibility of their theory. No wonder then that they cannot tell us which are the branches.[33]

Anglican overtures to the East

For Fortescue, anticipating critiques, both Anglican and Catholic, of a later period, the Church of England was a Noah's ark, sailing with a bewildering variety of inmates on board.

> It is not a religion; it is a conglomeration of half a dozen different religions, held together by the external bond of State establishment only. No one can speak for the Church of England, no one can say what she believes . . . Anglicans must first agree among themselves in some direction before they can approach anyone outside in any direction.[34]

As early as 1913 he noted what would strike some Catholic observers of the various 'bilateral' dialogues of the later twentieth century ecumenical movement: 'The most curious point about the various, and very varying,

---

30   E.F.K. Fortescue, *The Armenian Church*, op. cit.
31   *The Branch Theory*, op. cit., p. 7.
32   Ibid.
33   Ibid., p. 13.
34   'Fr Puller's Visit to Russia', *The Tablet* for 22 February, 1913, p. 282.

presentments of Anglicanism we see is the way in which in every case she appears to be, on the whole, very fairly in accord already with the people whose sympathy she solicits'.[35]

Talking to Catholics, it turned out that the Roman Primacy was unproblematic to Anglicans except for some comparative details about how *potestas* should be exercised or infallibility understood. But when 'Home Reunion' with Nonconformists was concerned, or an approach to Swedish Lutherans envisaged, the matter was very different. Then the Church of England was, it seems, cordially in agreement with Protestants in rejecting outright the 'intolerable yoke of the Papacy', and the associated superstitions of the mediaeval Church. In 1912 the 'Russian Society for Promoting Friendly Relations between the Churches of Russia and England' had invited Father Puller of the Society of St John the Evangelist to go to St Petersburg and deliver lectures on the Anglican Church before an audience of Russian ecclesiastics and theologians. Unsurprisingly in this context, the rights of the universal Primacy *iure divino*, so dear to Anglo-Catholics like the theologian Thomas Lacey and their premier layman Viscount Halifax,[36] went unmentioned.

Indeed, Puller, quoted by Fortescue, for the lectures had appeared in book form,[37] had appealed to his hearers, 'You, here in Russia, must surely sympathize with us in our determination to repudiate those Papal claims, which were really accepted in an age of ignorance, on the authority of documents now known to be forgeries', a reference, presumably, to the so-called Pseudo-Isidorian Decretals, which, possibly at the hand of supporters of ordinary bishops, downplayed the role of metropolitans in favour of that of the Pope.[38] 'One wonders', commented Fortescue naughtily, 'whether some day some Anglican enthusiast will not go to Etshmiadzin, and prove to the astonished Armenians that his Church believes and teaches Monophysism'.[39]

Fortescue noted that, in Father Puller's mouth, the English Church denied Transubstantiation as clearly as she affirmed it through the mouths of Lacey and Halifax. And slightly unfairly, perhaps, he reported that for Puller what she actually teaches about the Eucharistic change is *presushchetvlenie* (a word Fortescue left untranslated, to heighten the irony) 'which, by a most providential coincidence, happens to be just what the

---

35 Ibid., p. 283.

36 A reference to Lord Halifax's *Leo XIII and Anglican Orders* (London: Longmans, 1912).

37 F.W. Puller, S.S.J.E., *The Continuity of the Church of England* (London: Longmans, 1912).

38 Ibid., p. 14.

39 'Fr Puller's Visit to Russia', *The Tablet* for 22 February, 1913, p. 283.

Russians say'.[40] Puller protested, in a letter in the following issue of *The Tablet*. In using the Russian word he had not been seeking to put forward the Anglican doctrine of the Presence, but had simply cited the 'Longer Catechism' of the highly influential nineteenth century theologian-bishop Philaret of Moscow, who distinguished the referent of the term from the 'transubstantiation' of the Latins.[41] It was left to an anonymous Orthodox reader to claim that *presushchetvlenie* simply translates the Greek *metaousiôsis* which in turn translates the Latin *transsubstantiatio.*[42]

Aside from tail-pulling, Fortescue had some serious points to make. High Anglicans looked longingly to the Orthodox for confirmation of their position since they knew from experience they would find cold comfort from Rome. On the one hand, they held the Church to be 'both one and visible'. On the other, they regarded it as 'torn by glaring schisms'. Though, in Catholic eyes, this was a contradictory position to take up, Catholics could nevertheless admire their willingness to suffer any rebuff in pursuit of mending the 'Church's broken unity' (he had in mind the critical questions asked of Puller at Petersburg when the topic of the Thirty-Nine Articles surfaced). What was amazing and impressive was their 'unswerving faith in Christ' who, on High Anglican presuppositions, had not achieved the fulfillment of his high priestly prayer at the Last Supper that the Church founded on the apostles should remain essentially one.[43]

Fortescue returned to the topic of Anglican-Orthodox relations in 1914, by which time he had been able to catch up, through the bi-lingual pages of the *Russian Orthodox American Messenger*, with the Russian side of the same St Petersburg 'Society' addressed by Puller. A Petersburg theologian, I.P. Sokoloff, surveying recent (and disparate) Orthodox expressions of attitude to Anglican Orders, had judged the position little less negatively than had Leo XIII (in the bull *Apostolicae Curae* of 1897).[44] The Prayer-Book gives the impression Ordination is a sacrament. The Articles state firmly it is not. The Orthodox, for Sokoloff, cannot recognize Anglican Orders while this ambiguity persists.

In his reply to Dearmer, Fortescue had recorded that at the reception of a High Anglican cleric into the Orthodox Church at Constantinople in 1907, when Fortescue himself, on the Levantine grand tour, had been present, the Patriarch 'had him not only re-ordained but first re-baptized,

---

40   Ibid.
41   Letter in *The Tablet* of 1 March, 1913, p. 343.
42   Letter in *The Tablet* of 8 March, 1913, p. 386.
43   'Fr Puller's Visit to Russia', *The Tablet* for 22 February, 1913, p. 283.
44   'A Russian Theologian on Anglican Orders, I', *The Tablet* for 11 April, 1914, pp. 562–564; 'A Russian Theologian on Anglican Orders, II', ibid., for 18 April, 1914, pp. 601–603.

so entirely do the Orthodox authorities ignore Anglican sacraments'.[45] And though, as Fortescue notes, recognition of the sacramentality of Order, for the Russians, took pride of place over the idea of a sacrificing priesthood (uppermost, when considering the same question, in the mind of Leo XIII), Sokoloff makes it plain that the latter could not be dismissed as a bagatelle. The 'idea of the negative Anglican doctrine concerning the sacrifice of the Eucharist, reflected by their ordinals, making valid or non-valid Anglican ordinations, certainly deserves the full attention of the Orthodox also'.[46] Certain dogmatic errors deprive of its grace the laying on of hands. Sokoloff's conclusion, that only with the clarification of the Anglican mind, at any rate on the full status of Order as among the seven sacraments of the Church, could Orthodoxy, by the application of 'economy' subsequent to that change of mind, recognize, in the Church of England, a ministerial priesthood in the apostolic succession.

Sokoloff's conclusion, which turned on what Fortescue called 'the odd idea that an invalid hierarchy may become valid by a subsequent change of belief on the part of its members' (the 'economy' idea), was less interesting than the wider implications of the debate.[47] The Orthodox, Fortescue wrote,

> have nothing to lose, from any point of view, but rather much to gain, from alliance with a rich, cultured and progressive body like the Church of England. Many in Russia and the Levant turn envious eyes towards the more advanced civilization of the West; many regret the isolation of the Orthodox Church. . . . It does enormous credit to their unswerving fidelity to what they believe to be the faith that they can still look upon the question of reunion with Anglicans so impartially, with such caution not to compromise their principles.[48]

It is easy to see how the same mind-set is at work in what is positive in Fortescue's attitude to the Orthodox as to the High Anglicans. What he praises in both is unswervingness — the Orthodox for unswerving devotion to the Orthodox faith even when a fudge here or there would bring geo-political reward, High Anglicans for their unswerving loyalty to Christ whose claims the contradictions of their ecclesiology might well be thought to undermine.

Fortescue was led to ask, accordingly, How sympathetic should Catholics be to High Churchmen? His answer is 'as sympathetic as we can be'. He writes:

45 *An Anglican on Reunion*, op. cit., p. 18.
46 Russian Orthodox American Messenger XVII, 12–23, for 28 June 1913 to 14 December 1913, p. 324.
47 'A Russian Theologian on Anglican Orders, II', art. cit. p. 601.
48 Ibid.

> No one can know anything of High Churchmen without
> respecting their great earnestness, the heroically unselfish lives
> many of them lead, their pathetic desire for reunion. Nor do
> we forget that they are to a great extent accustoming people to
> Catholic ideas.

But he insisted that, nevertheless, in 'the thing that really matters', the
High Church movement is affecting people 'not at all'.[49] His reason for
saying so was that, in his judgment, the Catholic movement in the Church
of England has not improved the chances of unity in a single universal
Church. 'Ritualists attain no unity with us, and shatter it still more inside
their own communion.'[50] For:

> does any one imagine that all Anglicans will ever come round
> to Mr Dearmer's advanced way of thinking, or to the still more
> advanced ideas of the Caldey "Benedictines"? In her state of
> anarchy the only possible future for the Church of England is
> to accept the situation, to make the best of it, and open out
> her arms widely to contain every one. Such an attitude has
> advantages; generous toleration of sincere convictions appeals
> no doubt to very many people now. But such a body must give
> up all hope of reunion with Rome or the East. It would be wiser
> to look to the wider-minded foreign Protestants.[51]

This was prescient, in the light of the global ecumenical situation by the
beginning of the following century. So Fortescue's appeal was for 'return'.
In bald terms: 'All other Christian bodies left us at some period; they must
come back'. People may break away from the centre of unity but the result
is 'written plain over all their further quarrels and schisms'.[52] Only of the
Church of the origin, he concluded, is it written that the gates of hell shall
not prevail.

An unusual eirenicon

An engaging writer, presenting himself anonymously (though the
records of the Catholic Truth Society have transmitted his name as 'The
Revd Mr Boudier'), made in the following year a 'Statement' to which
Fortescue (writing equally anonymously) offered a 'Reply'. With undoubted
eirenicism of spirit Boudier had suggested that the restoration of the Roman
hierarchy in 1850 could be considered — in words Fortescue quoted in his

---

49   *An Anglican on Reunion*, op. cit. p. 32.
50   Ibid., p. 33.
51   Ibid., p. 35.
52   Ibid., p. 36.

Reply — an act of coming to the 'assistance of the Church of England, in her hour of weakness, in the work before her of recatholicizing the life of the English people'.[53] Fortescue commented,

> The author stands alone in his theory: it is by no means the attitude of the Hierarchy in question. Our object is rather to bring people out of the schism of the Church of England to the unity of the Church of Christ. Nor is it the view of the Anglican Hierarchy. They, quite rightly from their position, regard our bishops as schismatical intruders in their dioceses — as we should be, if they were Catholic bishops.[54]

For High Anglicans generally, the Church of England *was* the Catholic Church in England. But as Fortescue had pointed out in *The Branch Theory* surely then in logic (Roman) Catholics must be schismatics 'throughout the British Empire, in the United States, and wherever else may be Anglican bishops – otherwise, again, there would be two rival Catholic authorities in the same place'.[55]

Fortescue rubs the point in. On their theory,

> All Uniates and Latins in the Levant are schismatics. We are schismatics in Holland because of the Old Catholics, in France because of M. Loyson [of the 'Catholic Gallican Reformed Church']. Indeed, do not the Reformed branches [of Episcopalians] in Spain, Portugal, and Italy make us schismatics in these countries too? The authentic Roman branch of the Church sinks to small proportions. Or rather — if only the Anglicans were logical — the schism of one part of that Roman branch must make it all schismatical, wherever it is. This, too, follows from the contradictory nature of the terms. For all the Roman Church is in communion with us Romanists in England. So, if we are schismatics, all the other Romanists are too.[56]

He concludes, 'Each man is either inside the Church or out. Being in communion with Catholics means being inside; being a schismatic means being outside. The same man cannot be both at once.'[57] So, writing seven years later (in 1917), Fortescue would not accept that even so well-disposed a figure as Boudier could be regarded, morally speaking, as in communion

---

53 *Catholic because Roman Catholic: A Statement and a Reply* (London: Catholic Truth Society, 1917), p. 16.

54 Ibid.

55 *The Branch Theory,* op. cit., p. 24.

56 Ibid., p. 25.

57 Ibid.

with the Catholic Church since 'unhappily, every Anglican, whatever his own personal views may be, is excommunicate, *lata sententia*, because he is in Communion with heretics, because he receives sacraments from a Church publicly and officially committed to heresy',[58] in the shape, that is, of the Thirty-Nine Articles. Fortescue evidently had no truck with Newman's attempt as an Anglican to read the Articles in a sense compatible with Trent. The 'manliness' which observers so often noted in him and which he himself regarded as an intellectual virtue, comes to the fore when he writes, 'The test of all such declarations . . . is the plain meaning of the words, as understood by any ordinary person who reads them, as understood by those who compiled them, and the consent of those who use them'. Concluding, 'In this sense these Articles are utterly incompatible with the Council of Trent, with the Vatican Council, with the Catholic Faith as taught by the Holy See'.[59]

In another (but related) pamphlet, *The Date of the Anglican Schism*, Fortescue noted with surprise the increasing number of Anglo-Catholics who held that there had been, in England, no true schism from Rome, that the pope had never excommunicated the Anglican Church as such, and that, despite the absence of full visible communion, no real rupture in communion had ever eventuated.[60] For Fortescue, this 'latest theory . . . all rests on the extraordinarily childish idea that the only way a man can cease to be in communion with the Pope is by the Pope writing a special Bull to say so'.[61] He expressed amazement at the lack of canonical knowledge involved. In the overwhelming majority of instances, the excommunicate find themselves in this position since guilty of something that involves excommunication *ipso facto*, and asked, rather testily, 'Have these people really never heard of excommunication *latae sententiae*?'[62]

The 'Church of England' could not in any case be excommunicated because there *was* no 'Church of England' to excommunicate. Rather,

> [t]here were certain dioceses in this island; at any period, if anyone or any group of people in those dioceses publicly professed heresy, or communicated with those who did, they would thereby cease to be Catholics. This is exactly what happened at the Reformation.[63]

58 *Catholic because Roman Catholic*, op. cit., p. 15.
59 Ibid., pp. 13–14.
60 *The Date of the Anglican Schism* (London: Catholic Truth Society, 1917), reprinted from *The Tablet*.
61 *The Date of the Anglican Schism*, op. cit., p. 5.
62 Ibid.
63 Ibid.

Of course Anglo-Catholics cannot be told the date of the loss of communion by their ancestors if by 'the date' is meant the month and the day. But a process commenced with the Elizabethan Act of Uniformity. And 'as in all such cases, it was a gradual process, though in England it did not take long'. '[The Church of England's] members were never in communion with the Pope from the day the Government founded it. They are not in communion now.'[64] And he asked of High Anglicans:

> What argument will remain to them then, or what step will they take next? Will they find some new paradox or wild assertion, or will they not at least realize that there is only one way of not being in schism, and this is by being in real communion, communion admitted on both sides.[65]

T.A. Lacey and Donatism

Thomas Alexander Lacey, already mentioned in connexion with Fortescue's diaries, was the most eminent Anglican apologist with whom Fortescue engaged in debate — an erudite historical theologian and liturgical scholar, absolutely orthodox in all that concerned the principal dogmas of faith. The two men had crossed swords before the War when Lacey came to Dearmer's aid after Fortescue had published his (severely critical) *An Anglican on Reunion*. Fortescue dashed off a lengthy letter to *The Tablet* in reply to Lacey's seconding of the incumbent of Primrose Hill.[66] The question at issue on that occasion was Lacey's contention that the Marian bishops and the bishops intruded by Elizabeth I *were* in communion with each other, in such wise that the continuity of the Church could not be regarded as ruptured when the Marian bishops themselves passed from the scene. A proper answer required close knowledge of Tudor history. For this Fortescue felt he needed to call on a Catholic with the relevant expertise. He found the help he was looking for in Harold Burton's brother Edwin, who was Vice-President of St Edmund's College Ware (and subsequently President, from 1916 to 1918 in which year ill health forced his resignation).

Fortescue turned Burton's materials into an article, 'An Important Corner of History'.[67] Preparing his weapons, he wrote to Burton in September. With the copied extracts from historical documents sent across from Ware (a letter of Archbishop Matthew Parker of Canterbury to Elizabeth I's Secretary of State Robert Cecil and matter from the recusant Nicholas Sander's *Report* to Cardinal Giovanni Morone), Fortescue thought he could do the job.

---

64 Ibid., p. 11.
65 Ibid., pp. 11-12.
66 *The Tablet* for 17 June, 1911.
67 'An Important Corner of History,' *The Tablet*, 7 October 1911.

Of course I can smash Lacey now — smash him to bits. . . . I can lap his blood. Only — it would be — so to speak — with your spoon. You have done the whole thing and I have some qualm of conscience about affecting knowledge thus gleaned wholly from you.[68]

Accordingly, Fortescue proposed that Burton should write the article himself rather than let Fortescue take the credit. He added:

But, if you do, for goodness' sake put aside all thought of an Eirenikon. Eirenikon indeed! Lacey is the mis-born spawn of scrofulous swine, he is a verminous fool, a skin-diseased ape with yellow fever and an obsessing ring-tailed devil, he has yellow fever, water on the brain, kleptomania and homicidal lunacy. His mother was bought in the Cairo market and his father's tomb is a slaughter-house for diseased swine. All this must be expressed or at least plainly inferred in the *Tablet* article.[69]

Unsurprisingly, Burton took fright at this missive and indicated his happiness that Fortescue should administer the desirable coup de grâce himself. Perhaps this was the exchange Fortescue had in mind when he wrote to Mrs Crickmer, 'My dear, it isn't any good for Anglicans to fly at the Apostolick Throne because the more they do that, the more I get 2 guineas for saying they are skunkful swine'.[70]

When in 1917 Fortescue published *Donatism*, an account of the North African schism which had so exercised Augustine of Hippo, it was principally an excuse to take up the cudgels with Lacey again.[71] What Fortescue wanted to bring home to Lacey was the real significance of the Donatist schism in the Anglo-Roman debate. Fortescue provides a good run-down of the story of the schism's making on the basis of the latest edition of the relevant patristic texts from the 'Vienna edition' (*Corpus Scriptorum Ecclesiasticorum Latinorum*) as well as secondary literature in German and French. Essentially, the schism started (in the early fourth century) when North African Catholics rejected bishops tainted by temporization with the pagan civil power. Certain bishops, charged with forwarding an illicit religion, had handed over copies of the Scriptures, and other Christian books, along with liturgical vessels: an act of *traditio*, a word which means both conveying and betraying. Up to a point, Donatism

---

68 Westminster Diocesan Archive, Series 20, Box 22, Letter to Edwin Burton of 20 September, 1911.

69 Ibid.

70 Letter to Mrs Courtenay Crickmer of 27 February, 1912, cited in J.R. MacCarthy, *Adrian*, op. cit.

71 *Donatism* (London: Burns and Oates, 1917).

exemplified the notion of a schism without heresy. (The qualification 'up to a point' is needed because it is erroneous to hold that a sin against the virtue of faith on the part of the Church's minister entails the invalidation of the sacramental status of the bishop concerned.)

Fortescue stresses how Donatism in its homelands was a great success. Donatists may not have been a majority in *Africa Proconsularis* or at Carthage, the metropolitan see, but they were a substantial minority. They were the overwhelming majority in Numidia. And at some point they began to plant churches overseas, in Spain and, audaciously, at Rome itself. Like present-day historians, and the scholars who were his own contemporaries, Fortescue considered nationalism (it might be preferable to read 'ethnic particularity') as the key to Donatist victories.

> The Donatists are the national Church of Africa, or at least of Numidia. Almost everyone who had written about them sees behind the quarrel about *traditio* the cause of a national party against foreigners, against Catholic unity, against Rome.[72]

It is because the Donatists embody the protest of a national church against Rome (both ecclesial Rome and civil Rome) that what the Fathers made of them is instructive for later, parallel cases. Of those cases the Church of England provides the best example close to home. Or does it?

Fortescue thought the parallel holds, not between the Donatists and the Church of England as understood by all her theological parties, but between the Donatists and what High Anglicans claim for the national church. Donatists taught no grave heresies (unlike the Prayer-Book and Articles), and they had (unlike Anglicans) valid Orders. Yet if High Anglicans were right about all three of Prayer-Book, Articles and Orders — namely, that the first two were capable of a Catholic interpretation and the third were authentic — the position of the Church of England would be strictly comparable to that of the Donatist Church. This was the comparison Nicholas Wiseman, the first archbishop of Westminster (but at the time rector of the Venerable English College in Rome), had used against the still Anglican John Henry Newman in the pages of the *Dublin Review*, scoring thereby a palpable hit.[73]

Newman described in the *Apologia pro vita sua* how words of Augustine against the Donatists, as cited by Wiseman, echoed in his ears: 'The whole world [i.e. the universally extended rather than national Catholic Church] is

---

72 Ibid., p. 14.

73 Wiseman's essay, from the *Dublin Review* for 1839 was re-published as a free-standing work: *The Anglican Claim of Apostolic Succession* (London: Catholic Truth Society, 1905, 2nd edition).

a safe judge'.[74] But Anglicans had answers for Wiseman. In *Roman Catholic Claims* Gore made two key points. Whereas Donatists claimed to be the whole Church, Anglicans do nothing of the kind. And whereas Donatists re-baptised their ecclesial opponents, Anglicans do not presume to repeat the baptism of those — such as Roman Catholics — who disagree with them. Donatism was not a reform of a national church, as Anglicanism was in a perfectly laudable way, but, rather, a schism from the Church of its members' own 'country' — and therefore, unlike the Church of England, a theologically unlawful undertaking.[75]

But Lacey had now gone further that Gore had dared. In his 1914 study *Catholicity* Lacey argued that *Roman Catholics* were the true Donatists.[76] Like the Donatists, (Roman) Catholics make much of the purity of their Church; like them, they re-baptise; they too are given to excommunication as a penalty (some recent cases Mivart, Loisy, Tyrrell and his amanuensis Maude Petre, to be considered later in this study, would surely come to mind); and, above all, they claim that their Communion constitutes the entire Church. The latter, for Lacey, is the defining heresy of Roman Catholicism, and it is specifically a Donatist heresy.[77]

In his reply Fortescue points out that, in fact, not all Donatists considered they amounted, theologically speaking, to the whole Church. That should be accounted, rather, an extreme opinion within their ranks, if also, in Fortescue's judgment, an honourable one. Why honourable? Fortescue explains.

> [A]fter all, in claiming this they were at least maintaining the visible unity of the Church. It is the dilemma of all such local schisms. If they still hold the unity of the Church, they are forced to say that they are the whole Church; if they have not the courage to claim that, they must give up what is an essential note of the Church, her unity, and fall back on the absurdity of some sort of Branch theory.[78]

Moderate Donatists did not, however, make this claim, though they denied the counter-claim of the Catholics to be themselves more than a mere branch — as the Donatists (on the moderate view) *were* a branch. Fortescue

---

74   J.H. Newman, *Apologia pro Vita sua. A History of his Religious Opinions* (London: Longmans, Green, 1905), pp. 116–117.

75   C. Gore, *Roman Catholic Claims* (London: Longmans, 1900, 7th edition), pp. 128–129.

76   He was anticipated in this by the seventeenth century archbishop of Armagh, John Bramhall's 'Replication to the Bishop of Chalcedon's Survey' in *The Works of the most reverend father in God John Bramhall, D.D., II* ((Oxford: John Henry Parker, 1842), pp. 256–257.

77   T.A. Lacey, *Catholicity*, op. cit., pp. 135–149.

78   *Donatism*, op. cit., p. 20.

cites Augustine's treatise 'Against the Books of Petilian'. It is always possible, says Augustine, to distinguish between the Catholic Church and separated branches which (in Fortescue's paraphrase):

> lie where they fall. Each of them is local either in East or West; but the true Church is everywhere, where each of them is and everywhere else too. . . . If Mr Lacey is right, the Catholic Church has been schismatic from the time of the Apostles. Never has she admitted that people in schism with herself are nevertheless Catholics.'[79]

Fortescue continued:

> Mr Lacey says we are Donatists, and the *Church Times* adds that we are heretics in our Donatism. If so, then the Church in England before the Reformation was Donatist and heretical too. There is no doubt that the old Catholics of England, St Anselm, St Thomas of Canterbury, and the others, held our view. They did not admit that anyone in schism with themselves and the Pope could nevertheless be a Catholic.[80]

If High Anglicans are right, then the Church from which they claim to be lineally descended — the pre-Reformation *Ecclesia anglicana* — was itself an heretical and Donatist church.

Moreover, granted that the Eastern Orthodox *also* claim to be the whole Church, a very strange situation must pertain.

> There are three main communions of the Catholic Church — the Roman, the Eastern and Anglican. But the Roman and Eastern communions, because they claim to be the only true Church, are Donatists, therefore schismatics and no Catholics at all. The Anglican branch alone is unaffected by Donatist virus. So the Anglicans, just because they do not claim to be so, really are the whole Church.[81]

Fortescue admits that Augustine thought it worthwhile to cite against the Donatists the example of the apostolic sees of the East — and not just the lone apostolic see of the West. In Augustine's time, the Eastern churches of apostolic origin (Alexandria, Antioch, Jerusalem) were in full communion with the see of Peter in the West.

Yet at different times in the patristic epoch all the Oriental churches founded by apostles had fallen or would fall into heresy, and that is not surprising because there is 'no divine guarantee that every Apostolic see

---

79 Ibid., p. 24.

80 Ibid., p. 25.

81 Ibid, p. 26.

will always remain faithful'.[82] Fortescue was inclined to think that when Augustine or Optatus of Milevis (another of the anti-Donatist Fathers) cite the Eastern churches to Donatists, they are offering:

> an *argumentum ad hominem*, as if now we found an Anglican having special devotion to St. Ambrose, and pointed out that he is in schism with St. Ambrose's see. That would not mean that we think Milan can never fail, or that union with Milan is the final test of catholicity.[83]

Certainly Fortescue is on unassailable ground when he writes, '[I]f to be in communion with all the Apostolic Sees were a test of Catholicity, no one would be a Catholic now anywhere'.[84]

There is, however, he writes, 'one Apostolic See that can never fail, one with whom union is a final test'. It is of course the see of Rome, a point well made by Optatus to a Donatist addressee: 'The See of Peter is ours; through it the other gifts (*dotes*, dowries of the Church of Christ) are ours also'.[85] More widely, looking at the apologiae offered by High Anglicans in his own day, Fortescue was able to list the extraordinary number of similarities with Donatist strategies, in far more circumstantial a way than was possible to Wiseman in the 1830s.

> Here we have a national Church, out of communion with all others, yet claiming the name Catholic on other reasons, in schism itself yet blaming schism from itself [on the part of Dissenters], resenting the presence of the real Catholics in its sees and finding nicknames for them, denying that it was founded by anyone later than Christ himself, not judging Catholics abroad except in that they hold with the Catholic minority at home, pathetically seeking some sort of recognition from eastern Christians, denying to the great Church its title catholic because it is not in communion with other schismatics in the East.[86]

But, he remarked epigrammatically, 'A man does not become a Catholic because he calls himself one.'[87] Fortescue concludes by encouraging the somewhat embattled Catholic minority in England to stand fast.

> If we are pained to see the cathedrals built for our Mass in possession of Protestants, we may remember how the Donatists seized the basilica Constantine had built for Catholics. If we feel ourselves a small number here and regret that our bishops

---

82 Ibid., p. 32.
83 Ibid., p. 33.
84 Ibid., pp. 32-33.
85 Optatus, *De schismate donatista* II. 9, cited ibid., p. 34.
86 *Donatism*, op. cit., p. 48.
87 Ibid.

have not the civil prestige of Anglicans, we are comforted by knowing that St. Optatus, nay, the great Augustine himself, were missionary bishops surrounded by a Donatist majority. The Catholic bishop in England is proud to stand in a position so closely like his.[88]

Dr Orchard and 'Free Catholicism'

There was one such dialogue which was not with Anglicans. It concerned the Congregationalist minister William Edwin Orchard (1877–1955) whose 'Free Catholicism' seems to have been brought to Fortescue's attention by Stanley Morison.[89] Orchard had been brought up in the (newly formed) Presbyterian Church of England, which joined together various older English Presbyterian congregations along with Scottish implants south of the Border. After an evangelistic experience which led him to deepened conversion, Orchard studied part time at the University of London while working first as a railway clerk and then as a lay missionary in the Isle of Dogs. This hard-won education enabled him to begin training in 1901 as a Presbyterian ordinand at Westminster College, Cambridge — the institution founded (or re-founded from an earlier London base) two years earlier by the 'Sisters of Sinai', Mrs Agnes Lewis and Mrs Margaret Gibson, Janet Soskice's study of whom has inspired (as explained in my Preface) *The Latin Clerk*.[90]

In June 1904 Orchard was appointed Presbyterian minister at Enfield in Middlesex — coincidentally, it was a place the restless Fortescue, who was two years his senior, had abandoned for Witham a month previously. After flirtation with liberal theology, Orchard returned to an orthodox view of the principal Christian doctrines (he wondered for a while whether Modernism would provide a via media between Catholicism and Protestantism but decided that Tyrrell and others offered only 'Ritschlianism in Catholic dress', i.e. a religiously coloured ethics shorn of dogma).[91] Already touched by the modest liturgical revival in later nineteenth century Scottish Presbyterianism, Orchard began to introduce structured worship, a central Communion Table and the doctrine of the Church as the Body of Christ — thus entering on a trajectory which would take him between 1914 to 1931, the years of his second and increasingly celebrated charge as minister

---

88 Ibid., p. 51.

89 E. Kaye and R. Mackenzie, *W.E. Orchard. A Study in Christian Exploration* (Oxford: Education Services, 1990). Much of their account draws on Orchard's autobiography, *From Faith to Faith. An Autobiography of Religious Development* (London: Putnam, 1933).

90 E. Kaye and R. Mackenzie, *W.E. Orchard*, op. cit., p. 19.

91 Cited ibid., p. 40.

of King's Weigh House, a Congregationalist church in Mayfair, to ever-increasing approximations in Liturgy and doctrine to the practice and beliefs of the Catholic Church. (In his new charge he was affiliated not to the Presbyterian Church but to the Congregational Union.)

As fully reported in Nonconformist newspapers, Orchard's electrifying preaching was matched by the innovative character of his ministerial deportment and attire. Dressed in cassock, Roman collar, silk surplice, embroidered stole and sanctuary shoes to which a pair of John Wesley's silver buckles (a family heirloom) were attached, it was plain that this would be 'no ordinary, conventional Congregationalist ministery'.[92] Orchard made common cause with the author of the 1907 manifesto *A Free Catholic Church*, the Unitarian J. Lloyd Thomas, who proposed a coming together in a single body of Christians of all sorts on the basis of devotion and worship rather than dogma – though Orchard made plain he personally was joining the 'Society of Free Catholics' as a full-blooded Trinitarian.[93]

In his sermon 'The New Catholicism', Orchard explained that he wanted, among other things, to appropriate everything of spiritual value in historic Catholicism.[94] One way in which he acted out this aspiration he later regretted; in 1916 he was ordained priest in a private oratory in Lathbury Road, Oxford, by an *episcopus vagans,* Bishop Ulric Vernon Herford, who himself had received consecration from Mar Basilius Soares, a former Catholic, subsequently attached to a recently founded Indian church-body of the East Syrian liturgical type.[95] This information did not become public until 1922, when, in an attempt to embarrass Orchard, it was revealed by J.A. Kensit of the Protestant Truth Society.[96]

Fortescue asked Morison in a letter from Eastertide 1919: 'When are we going to meet Orchard?'[97] Orchard was by now quite a celebrity. His Mayfair church was crowded out for services based on his own compilation from

---

92 Ibid., p. 54.

93 Ibid., p. 57.

94 Reprinted in W.E. Orchard, *The New Catholicism, and Other Sermons* (London: Allen and Unwin, 1917).

95 For Herford's life and activities, see P. Anson, *Bishops at Large* (London: Faber and Faber, 1964), pp. 130–155. Herford was even more eclectic than Orchard in his liturgical samplings, though few (if any) were genuinely East Syrian (Chaldaean). Anson calls the Indian body from whom Herford received episcopal Orders 'neo-Nestorian', while the oddness of the whole thing is compounded by the fact that, in matters of theological doctrine, Herford seems to have remained a Unitarian throughout his life.

96 E. Kaye and R. Mackenzie, *W.E. Orchard,* op cit., p. 73.

97 Cambridge University Library, MS Add. 9812/D/90, Letter to S. Morison of Low Sunday, 1919.

Anglican, Roman and Eastern as well as Scots Presbyterian sources, *The Order of Divine Service for Public Worship*, published in the course of 1919 at the Oxford University Press. The same year he had become president of the Society of Free Catholics. He could build on the moral reputation he acquired during the First World War by his participation in international efforts for peace (he was extremely concerned that the churches would be compromised by jingoism).

By the time Fortescue wrote to Morison in the autumn of 1919 the meeting he wanted with Orchard had transpired. Fortescue was convinced it had not been a success. Orchard had written to Morison in its wake, calling Fortescue 'boisterous', a word which the latter — almost certainly correctly — interpreted as not altogether complementary. In a post-mortem on the encounter, he lamented to Morison:

> I am afraid I am not a success with such men ever. I know, of course, in theory, that he is thoroughly good, earnest, well-meaning and kindly, probably already well-disposed towards us, also that our right policy is to be very gentle and sympathetic with such as him.

But what Fortescue saw as Orchard's muddle-headedness drove such peaceable thoughts from his mind. They had been talking about the vision of God, taking the concept in its proper theological sense, when Orchard interjected the words, 'My heaven is being where God wants me to be'. Fortescue claimed to be outraged. He complained to Morison:

> You cannot argue reasonably about anything with people who think it an effective close to discussion to fire off a sparkle of rhetorical froth at you. Of course we know the young man who says that his heaven is in the lady's eyes; but then we do not understand that kind of high-flown metaphor as a contribution to theology. "My heaven is where God wants me to be." He might as well say that "his dinner is playing the piano".[98]

Fortescue admitted that

> for qualities of the heart and all that, I think very well of Orchard. It is all the more kind that, in spite of my bullying him (and I wish I had not done so), he has asked me to go and talk to his people in February. I am going to accept, and I must try and be so gentle and subtly flattering to Orchard that I shall make a better impression. That is what tells, I know, not the value of what you argue in itself. Only it is a rummy world where things are so.[99]

---

98 Cambridge University Library, MS Add. 9812/D/90, Letter to S. Morison of 24 November, 1919.

99 Ibid.

Not all Orchard's hearers were so unimpressed by his intellect. Herbert Asquith, the first of the war time prime ministers, noted in his diary for 22 December 1919: '[Orchard] is well worth hearing, as he knows what argument means and talks excellent English'. Asquith added, 'But his sermon would have shocked my Puritan forebears'.[100] Granted that by this date an evangelistic Sunday evening service at the King's Weigh House was followed by a celebration of Benediction of the Blessed Sacrament it is not hard to imagine why. So far as Letchworth is concerned, it may or may not have been known that plainchant, sacred polyphony, and the use of Johnston-inspired calligraphy and illumination for the production of the distinctive service books were salient features at Orchard's church. But similarities in externals would not by itself have impressed Fortescue's cool brain.

He picked out of an issue of *The Free Catholic* a statement by Orchard to the effect that Roman Catholics seek to drive other Christians by 'ruthless brutal logic'. This did not further endear Orchard, whom Fortescue put down as 'rather a poor creature as theologian or controversialist'.[101] He expected the 'people' at King's Weigh House to want from a visiting speaker a 'torrent of rhetoric that evades every real issue'.[102] But after his lecture there, which was followed by questions, Fortescue reported 'I am not at all pleased with my part in it'. Owing to excessive haste, he had missed important points, notably in what concerned qualifications to Catholic claims, such as:

> to what exactly is a Catholic committed, how far is he bound
> to agree with the Pope, how far do we admit that the Church
> may really need reform, why the Reformation was a failure, the
> development of doctrine, are laws infallible, how far the church
> has the right to make laws at all, and so on — heaps of points.[103]

Fortescue had been right, he found, in his prediction that questions from the floor would be 'silly'. But in retrospect he felt he should have taken the questioners themselves more seriously, rather than preferring to answer humorously instead. Nor did he appreciate the service-book, commenting to Morison,

> I think the habit of making up new liturgies could easily grow
> on a man, like dram drinking. It must be quite fun to spread out
> before one translations of all the best liturgies, and then to pick
> out and string together the prettiest snippets from each. Orchard

---

100 H.H. Asquith, *Memories and Reflections* [1852–1927], (London: Cassell, 1928), II., p. 177, cited E. Kaye and R. Mackenzie, *W.E. Orchard*, op. cit., p. 67.

101 Cambridge University Library, MS Add. 9812/D/90, Letter to S. Morison of 5 January, 1920.

102 Ibid., Letter to S. Morison of 7 February, 1920.

103 Ibid., Letter to S. Morison of 17 February, 1920.

has not the ghost of a sense of liturgical style. He understands nothing about the historic development of the inherent build of the rite he plunders. . . . I admire the dome of St Peter's and the windows of Chartres and the Propylaia at Athens and the columns of Karnak, but I should not like to see them all jammed together.[104]

Some might think these words rather too close for comfort to what de facto transpired in Western liturgical revision in later years.

Clearly, Fortescue did not rate Orchard's theological culture highly. Orchard had said, at King's Weigh House, that while he saw the advantages of the structure of the Catholic Church, Catholics overdid it in:

thinking there can be no grace outside the right organization. I answered that we do not think anything of the kind, that every Catholic admits that God can and does give many graces outside the Church. He said that this was very unlike what most of our theologians say, and to the end he seemed to think that it was some cranky Modernism of my own. You see this means simply that he is grossly ignorant of the Catholic position. What is one to do? Ought one to smile and say that one quite agrees with him?[105]

Whether Fortescue was unfair to Orchard's theological knowledge and gifts as well as his qualities as a constructive liturgist, readers of the four volumes of Orchard's *Foundations of Faith*, published between 1924 and 1927 (and thus after Fortescue's death) must judge.

In the third volume of *Foundations*, Orchard looked ahead, all unwittingly, to his own reception into the Catholic Church in 1932, indicating at the same time his hopes for a papacy that was less authoritarian in its manner of acting, and more welcoming to scholarly research.

It is . . . possible to hold that one day the form which the Roman Church has preserved will be found capable of a much wider and more generous interpretation; that with that interpretation the other churches will be brought into communion with Rome; that with the putting aside of temporal policy, of all attempts to lord it over the brethren, the historic claims of the Petrine see will be accepted by Christendom. But such a thing cannot come until the Roman Church has changed its spirit, not necessarily its form; interprets its doctrines more generously, Christianly

---

104 Ibid., Letter to S. Morison of 26 April, 1920.
105 Ibid., Letter to S. Morison of 24 November, 1919.

and humanly; and especially brings out to the forefront those wider conceptions of the Catholic church which are certainly to be found and taught by some of her expositors.[106]

The affinities with Fortescue's own hopes for the Church's future can hardly be gainsaid.

The case for the office of Peter

In 1920 Fortescue brought together in a handsomely produced paper-backed book, finely printed by The Pelican Press, a set of articles he had published in *The Tablet* by way of answer to a challenge. He was to show Anglicans the validity of the papal claims based on documents dating from before 451 — the date of the Council of Chalcedon.[107] As Fortescue explained, *The Early Papacy* was a response to the Anglican theologian N.P. Williams, author of *Our Case against Rome*.[108] Williams had said he 'found no particular difficulty against the papacy in practice'; his 'difficulty', so Fortescue reported, was its 'historical justification in the early Church'.[109] Fortescue claimed to be astonished (and with some reason, perhaps, since his own 'difficulties' with the *curia romana* were quite otherwise). He commented that

> [t]o the present writer the Papacy seems one of the clearest and easiest dogmas to prove from that early Church. Theology would be an easier subject if everything could be shown to be the belief of the Church of Christ from the beginning as plainly as the Papacy.[110]

Fortescue's apologia is highly acute (and pertinent to ecumenical discussion of the Petrine office in the period following the Second Vatican Council).

He begins by reminding his readers that, as a consequence of the Great War there is far more interest in schemes for Christian unity than before. At the Front, soldiers discovered the unnaturalness of being divided among their various denominational chaplains. Such schemes are chiefly inter-Protestant in character. Yet it is obvious that if they are to address the state of divided Christendom at large they cannot leave Catholics out of count. A remarkable development is that many High Church Anglicans are now

---

106 W.E. Orchard, *Foundations of Faith, III – Ecclesiological* (London: Allen and Unwin, 1926), p. 47.

107 *The Early Papacy. To the Synod of Chalcedon 451* (London: Burns, Oates and Washbourne, 1920).

108 N.P.Williams, *Our Case against Rome* (London: Longmans, 1918).

109 *The Early Papacy*, op. cit., p. 62.

110 Ibid.

willing to say they can accept the Papacy, which, according to Catholics, is the divinely provided centre of unity. Only what they are saying is, they can accept the Petrine office as it was exercised before 451 (when Orthodox and Catholics were still manifestly united in a 'Great Church'), and, they argue, this pre-Chalcedonian Papacy was a constitutional, not an absolute affair. They offer a compromise: they will accept a constitutional primacy for the pope if Catholics will abandon the claim to an absolute primacy for him. The two can meet half way.

Fortescue's response is nuanced — not, in the first instance, as to the content of the claim so much as to the method of approaching the subject it implies. He denies that demonstrating some disputed point of doctrine by demanding documentation be shown in support of it from a given period is *in principle* the right way to proceed in debates between divided Christians. 'Suppose a man said that what inspires him with confidence is the Church between the years 250–300; would we kindly prove that matrimony is a sacrament, by documents from that period only?'[111] Fortescue generalizes from that hypothetical case: 'All these methods of taking some early documents, whether the Bible or fathers, and making them your standard, mean simply a riot of private judgment on each point of religion'.[112] He considers the claim of Father Puller (he of the Petersburg lectures) in his critique of Catholic claims in *The Primitive Saints and the See of Rome* that antiquity is the only appropriate criterion for settling what is or is not the Christian faith, all other tests being rationalistic.[113] Fortescue agreed that was a 'special halo' around the 'venerable antiquity of the first centuries'. Yet he insisted that 'the Church was not more guided by our Lord then than she is now'.[114]

The appeal to antiquity as a *criterion of belief* is hopeless. 'Good and learned men of different sects disagree as to what early fathers believed, what exactly their words mean, as much as they disagree about the teaching of the Bible'.[115] The only genuine test, and it can scarcely be called 'rationalistic' is 'what the living Church, guided always by God, teaches today. This, and this alone, is a real, objective standard of belief, about which there neither is nor can be any doubt, once you know what the Church of Christ is'.[116]

Those who hold that the Church was once united, but is so no longer, believe in effect that the original Church no longer exists. Fortescue provides a contemporary parallel. The 'Austro-Hungarian State' is now represented,

---

111 Ibid., p. 8.

112 Ibid., p. 3.

113 F.W. Puller, *The Primitive Saints and the See of Rome* (London: Longmans, 1914, 3rd edition), pp. xxviii–xxix, 432–433.

114 *The Early Papacy*, op. cit, p. 6.

115 Ibid., p. 4, footnote 1.

116 Ibid.

de facto, by a variety of successor States. In other words, Austria-Hungary has ceased to exist. Contrastingly: Christendom is divided, but the Church Christ founded is not. Schisms from the Church do not affect her essential unity. 'Nothing can destroy that, because her founder is almighty and promised that she should last always, till the end of the world.'[117] The proper way to prove any dogma is, then, to show that it is taught here and now by the Church of Christ. This is the *principled* way to proceed, once one is convinced of the credibility of the claims made for Jesus and his founding a community on the rock of Peter's faith.

That does not exclude, however, 'another kind of argument':[118] an historical kind, requiring knowledge of ancient languages and serious scholarship, and aimed at showing the continuity of each distinct item within the dogmatic repertoire as a whole. It is, of course, impossible that from the Creator could issue a religion which required all human beings to follow this path before they could tell what divine revelation contained. And yet such historical argumentation for particular doctrines can constitute 'a most valuable confirmation, which we [i.e. Catholics] are always ready to offer, as long as it is understood that it is not the main reason of our belief'.[119] And it so happens that the documentation for the Petrine office from the first four and a half centuries is especially abundant and clear.

It follows from what Fortescue has said that his criterion for assessing the content of the Roman claims is what the Catholic Church currently (that is, in 1920) teaches about the papal office. He insists, *pace* Anglican controversialists for whom that office has 'morphed' over time into a caricature, that the contemporary teaching concerns precisely a 'constitutional' Papacy.

> The Pope is not an irresponsible tyrant who can do anything with the Church that he likes. He is bound on every side by the constitution of the Church. Some day a Catholic theologian ought to write a treatise on the limitations of the Papacy. This would do much good among Protestants, who are accustomed to think of us as putting the whole system of our religion at the mercy of one man, and of such a man as Rodrigo Borgia.[120]

---

117 Ibid., p. 5.

118 Ibid., p. 7.

119 Ibid.

120 Ibid., pp. 10–11. One might be forgiven for thinking that from this passage was drawn the title of P. Granfield, *The Limits of the Papacy. Authority and Autonomy in the Church* (London: Darton, Longman and Todd, 1982). An especially balanced account of ths subject is found in W. Henn, O.F.M. Cap., *The Honor of my Brothers. A Brief History of the Relationship between the Pope and the Bishops* (New York: Crossroad, 2000).

Fortescue lists the things the pope cannot do. He cannot change the nature of the sacraments, or add to or subtract from the Scriptures. He has no gifts of inspiration (like the sacred writers) or revelation (like the apostles). In extraordinary circumstances (Fortescue has in mind the 1801 Concordat between Napoleon and Pius VII) he can re-arrange dioceses but he cannot 'abolish the universal episcopate'.[121] 'Each Catholic bishop receives his jurisdiction from God; though he must use it in the union of his fellow bishops, and in canonical obedience to the Bishop of Rome, who is his chief'.[122]

Anglicans should not be frightened by the phrase 'the vicar of Christ'. True, Catholics claim for the pope 'authority delegate' from Christ for the Church at large, but then they also say other bishops enjoy the same for their particular churches. If the position of the pope is awesome, that, suggests Fortescue, is owing to the 'awful responsibility he bears before his Master, to maintain the traditional faith unaltered, to discharge loyally the stewardship of which he will have to give a stern account, to set a good example to his brother bishops'.[123] Yes, the bishops call him their 'father' — but he addresses them as his 'brethren' (likewise, nuns call their abbess 'mother', she calls them her 'sisters').

But is Fortescue arguing, then, that the Papacy has not 'grown' in any sense at all? By clarificatory definition of its significance, the primacy has grown, yes, just as the dogma of the Trinity has. By increasing use of the pope's authority, the ministry of Peter has become amplified, yes, in the matter of Church governance. There has taken place a process of centralization 'about the opportuneness of which each man may form his own opinion'.[124] Drawing a parallel (again) with civil affairs, some people will prefer many matters to be decided in the municipalities; others will think it more rational to deal with them via central government. Both kinds of citizen retain their allegiance to their country. We know from Fortescue's private papers that, actually, he took a dim view of much in the Church's centralizing process. But in *The Early Papacy* he insisted nonetheless that 'nothing essential is altered by such modification. The essence of the Papacy to-day is what it has always been'.[125] The faith of Catholics about the office of Peter remains the same. What, then, pray, does that 'faith' amount to?

---

121 *The Early Papacy*, op. cit., p. 12.

122 Ibid. Influential theologians and canonists had considered that the entire juridical authority of the bishops (unlike their sacramental powers) stemmed from the pope. The teaching of *Lumen gentium,* the Dogmatic Constitution of the Second Vatican Council on the Church, notably in sections 21 and 27 as modified by the appended 'Nota praevia', corresponds better to Fortescue's opinion as given here.

123 *The Early Papacy*, op. cit., p. 12.

124 Ibid., p. 15.

125 Ibid.

He offers a statement as succinct as any that could be constructed. First, the pope is the chief bishop: that is, 'primate and leader of the whole Church of Christ on earth'. Secondly he has a jurisdiction of an 'episcopal' kind over all the Church's members. Thirdly, to be a member of the Catholic Church it is necessary to be in communion with the pope. Fourthly, divine Providence will 'see to it that the Pope shall never commit the Church to error in any matter of religion'.[126] Of course, the modern canon law of the Church of Rome has more to say on the subject than this. But, claims Fortescue, what it has to say, over and above the bare statement of this quartet of principles, is *either* a consequence of those principles *or* a matter of de facto historical arrangement where the question of 'Divine right' status does not arise.[127] These stipulations simplify his task, which is to show that the four principles concerned can be found attested in writers of the pre-Chalcedonian era. And indeed, the remaining four chapters of his book furnish a discussion of texts suggestive of each in turn. I do not propose to follow Fortescue through his catena of ancient authorities, though it is worth noting the range he adduces, including the Syrian Narses of Nisibis and a set of pseudonymous 'Canons of Nicaea' in Arabic, which he dates to the fifth century, as found in the lesser Eastern churches, both Nestorian and Monophysite. It will be more instructive to note how he spells out in greater detail the principles themselves.

To assert, firstly, that the pope is 'leader of the whole Church of Christ on earth' is to assert that 'the Bishop of Rome is the right person to take the lead in any common action of the whole Church' — at, Fortescue means, a general council.[128] Not that, in point of historical fact he has always done so. 'To say that a man has a right does not mean that he has always used his right'.[129] Councils that were ecumenical neither in their manner of summons nor in their composition (Fortescue is thinking especially of the Second Ecumenical Council in 381) can be rendered so through ratification by the universal primate. Drawing a comparison from civil history near to home, an English king 'can ratify anything done by Parliament without his consent hitherto, as Charles II did (to some extent) in 1660)'.[130] And indeed, 'Where is the consent of all, if the first Patriarch does not agree?'[131]

Then secondly, to affirm that the pope has an episcopal jurisdiction over all members of the Church is to claim for him a pastoral surveillance over people in the Church 'of every rite and rank' — including, most importantly

---

126 Ibid., p. 16.
127 Ibid.
128 Ibid., p. 17.
129 Ibid.
130 Ibid., p. 18.
131 Ibid.

for Fortescue, Orientals and their patriarchs.[132] Anglicans object that, surely, all bishops are equal. As to sacramental order they are correct. 'The Bishop of Rome, as far as order goes, is no more a bishop than the Bishop of Kishnagur'.[133] (In a footnote, Fortescue conciliates that worthy, should be he reading. He could not resist taking his title as illustration since 'the name of his see [is], to us, an odd looking one and little known. But there can be no real disrespect in saying that he is as good a bishop as his great brother at Rome'.)[134] Yet not all bishops are equal in the sense of one not holding authority over another.

The entire practice of the Church of antiquity, with its metropolitans, exarches and patriarchs indicates the contrary. The local bishop, who is the vicar of Christ for his church, must recognize that the pope is the vicar of Christ for the whole Church — and vice versa.

> Both Florence and Vatican [i.e. the First Vatican Council] are careful to state that this supreme jurisdiction of the Pope is not meant in any way to diminish the Divine right by which each bishop rules his own flock, placed by the Holy Ghost over his see, as real pastor and successor of the Apostles.[135]

Such a theoretical statement hardly resolves all the possible practical tensions that could arise through this duality of agencies. Yet Fortescue's principal point is that the case is no different, so far as the principle goes, between a bishop and a patriarch or any regional, as distinct from universal, primate.

The third of Fortescue's four principles states that to be a member of the Catholic Church one must be in communion with the pope. Behind and beneath this principle there lies an axiom that is even more foundational, and that is the 'necessity of communion between all members of the Catholic Church'.[136] Fortescue calls this 'the fundamental point on which every Anglican, however High he may be, must and does differ from us'.[137]

> All idea of Divinely given authority, Divinely guided teaching, depends on the first concept of all, namely, one united Church in communion with herself throughout the world. Unhappily, here the extreme High Anglican is as remote from us as any other Protestant. That is why his whole position is wrong and impossible. He copies our rites, he adopts most points of our faith, he uses our language. But he has not got the foundation on which all these things rest. He is not nearer to us really,

132 Ibid.
133 Ibid., p. 20.
134 Ibid., footnote 1.
135 Ibid., p. 19.
136 Ibid., p. 44.
137 Ibid.

not one whit more Catholic, than the Evangelical or the frank Protestant. We can leave all the rest as of secondary importance till we have convinced him of the one vital issue, the visible unity of the Church.[138]

Not surprisingly, then, a number of Fortescue's patristic citations under the heading of 'Communion with Rome' concern this wider claim. 'According to the present Anglican theory every Catholic is in schism with other Catholics.'[139]

That cannot be right, granted the *concept* of a 'Catholic' Church. In terms of that concept, it might suffice not to mention the pope directly at all. It should be enough to say one must be in communion with 'the first poor Irishwoman you may find saying her prayers in the corner of a London church'.[140] That is all right so long as the the poor Irishwoman perseveres in her Catholicity, her communion with the episcopal reference point of the unity of the visible Church. But like any member of the Church, she may fall away. By contrast, '[t]he Pope as supreme teacher cannot fall away from the Church, if his primacy is of Divine institution, as we believe (this does suppose the primacy)'.[141]

That brings Fortescue to the fourth and last of his claims, which concerns the protection the pope enjoys from committing the Church to error. Fortescue was probably aware of mediaeval and later discussion of the possibility of a heretical pope. The axiom that 'the first see is judged by no-one' did not hold in the case of 'deviation from the faith'.[142] In such a case, the pope, considered as a private theologian, could be deemed to have fallen into heresy, removed from his ministry, even judged excommunicate. By writing 'the Pope *as supreme teacher* cannot fall away' Fortescue rather avoids discussion of this point. And indeed it is not likely that those who looked into the *papa haereticus* question had in mind a pope *in the act* of making an *ex cathedra* definition of the faith, committing to some falsehood in Christian doctrine the entire Church.

Distortions of the Papacy

Of course Fortescue knew well that not all forms of papal claim to leadership were feasible or even admirable. In his little study of Gregory VII, he notes the sometimes 'very curious' grounds Hildebrand alleged for his claim to authority over kingdoms — sometimes the so-called Donation of Constantine, sometimes an act of homage paid to a former

---

138 Ibid., p. 45.

139 Ibid.

140 Ibid., p. 21.

141 Ibid., p. 22.

142 See, for instance, G. Dejaifve, 'La collegialità nella tradizione latina', in G. Baraúna (ed.), *La Chiesa del Vaticano II* (Florence: Vallecchi, 1965), p. 843.

pope, sometimes a crown sent to a king from Rome. Behind Gregory's pretensions lay the 'dream of a united Europe as one great commonwealth under the only authority that could exist over all'.[143] It was not ignoble but neither was it foreordained. As late as 1828 the Office of St Gregory was inhibited in France, Fortescue points out, interestingly, and so it was as late as 1848 in Austria. But the element of hubris in Gregory's policy does not lead him to doubt that nonetheless Gregory was raised up by God as his collect (25 May) affirms, *pro tuenda Ecclesiae libertate*, 'for the safeguarding of the freedom of the Church'. By wrong methods at times, the true Gospel was still communicated from the Rock. That is not to say, however, that Catholic enthusiasm for the Petrine centre of unity could not become unbalanced, or that particular voices, emanating from Rome itself, might not sometimes be (as indeed with Hildebrand) 'off-message'. The next chapter will show how, in his own period, considerations of this kind left Fortescue angered and worried.

143 *Gregory VII (1073-1085)* (London: Catholic Truth Society, 1909), p. 29.

10. Liberal Catholicism, Catholic Modernism, and the Posthumous *Boethius*

Irritation with the Neo-Ultramontanes

Fortescue was not enamoured of Neo-Ultramontanism — a phrase I use to distinguish the mid-nineteenth century movement of maximalising papal interventions in doctrine and Church government from its mediaeval predecessor, represented, for instance, by Thomas Aquinas. Various comments already cited, ranging from the jocular to the jaundiced, show how little inclined Fortescue was to take up an enlarged view of papal claims, whether these concerned the pope's primacy of jurisdiction or his teaching office, both of which had been defined in moderate terms at the First Vatican Council. (Indeed, this was how his family entered the Catholic Church, through his father's change of heart and allegiance.)

Fortescue was inevitably struck, therefore, by the asperities of Roman policy, especially in matters of scholarship, in the last decades of the nineteenth century and the opening decades of its successor.

Liberal Catholicism — or Catholic Modernism?

In the summer of 1924 a snippet of correspondence between Canon George Smith, Fortescue's friend at St Edmund's whom he commissioned to finish his Boethius work, and Ethel Elmes, Fortescue's literary executrix, raises the question of Fortescue's attitude to Modernism. The London Catholic publishing house, Burns and Oates, had accepted a translation, by Edith Cowell, of a book by the Italian Modernist, Ernesto Buonaiuti (1881–1946), on the understanding that her work — and thus Buonaiuti's — had Fortescue's approval. Actually, all Buonaiuti's works were on the *Index Librorum Prohibitorum*.[1] Smith pointed out, sensibly enough, that such global 'coverage' in the *Index* was often only a prudential indicator, alerting readers to the typical caste of mind of the author in question. It did not necessarily imply that, say, a largely historical work (the book in

---

1   A. Donini, *Ernesto Buonaiuti e il modernismo* (Bari: Cressati, 1961).

question was a study of Gnosticism),[2] exemplified errors found elsewhere in a writer's corpus. And he assured the — evidently somewhat uncomfortable Elmes — that

> the fact always remains that even in the amateurish translation presented by the lady in question, the Censor Deputatus of this diocese [Westminster] saw nothing to which exception could be taken. There is about as much reason for calling the Westminster Curia Modernist, as the holy man [Fortescue himself].[3]

In point of fact, Fortescue's diaries show that he read as much of the French Modernists as he could lay his hand on, notably the principal architect of Catholic Modernist thinking, Alfred Firmin Loisy,[4] who was excommunicated in 1908, and his friend (and, later, biographer) the ecclesiastical historian Albert Houtin, a priest of the diocese of Angers, reduced to the lay state in 1912.[5] He wanted to inform himself about the huge intellectual crisis brought on in the Church by the combination of post-metaphysical modern thought with radical historical-critical scholarship, as applied to the Bible, and the character of the resistance thereto by Church authority.[6] So likewise he had read, even in his student days, the Liberal Catholic historian Ignaz von Döllinger, the mighty opponent of the First Vatican Council's decree on the office of Peter.[7]

Döllinger's work had been made known in England, even among those who did not read German, thanks to Lord Acton (1834–1902), whom Gladstone made Regius Professor of History at Cambridge.[8] Döllinger's

---

2   *Gnostic Fragments edited, with an introduction and notes, by Ernesto Buonaiuti, and done into English by Edith Cowell* (London: Williams and Norgate, 1924).

3   Downside Archives, IX AF, Box C, Letter to Ms Elmes, written at St Edmund's Ware, 4 June 1924.

4   F. Heiler, *Der Vater des katholischen Modernismus: Alfred Loisy (1857–1940)* (Munich: Erasmus, 1947); E. Guichot, *Alfred Loisy et ses amis* (Paris: Cerf, 2002).

5   A. Houtin, *Une vie de prêtre: Mon experience, 1867–1912* (Paris: Rider, 1926); idem., *Mon experience II: Ma vie laïque, 1912–1926* (Paris: Rieder, 1928).

6   Considered as a response to critical scholarship, Catholic Modernism has its forebears in Liberal Catholicism: see W.J. Schoenl, *The Intellectual Crisis in English Catholicism: Liberal Catholics, Modernists, and the Vatican in the Late Nineteenth and Early Twentieth Centuries* (New York and London: Garland, 1982)

7   Downside Archives, IX AF, Box D, 'Diary 1899', note of reading in September 1899. For this figure, see J. Fisterhölzl, *Ignaz von Döllinger* (Graz: Styria, 1969).

8   Given his wide acquaintance with German-speaking scholarship, Fortescue

spirited defence of the role of critical scholarship in the Church divided Catholic opinion in England in the years immediately preceding the First Vatican Council.[9] Liberal Catholicism on his model survived his excommunication. Some commonality existed between such Liberal Catholicism and subsequent Catholic Modernism, though, typically, Liberal Catholics had no philosophical axes to grind, only scholarly ones. It would be too easy to assume Fortescue was reading works by Loisy and Houtin only to refute. Concerned with and for scholarly standards, he was sympathetic to Liberal Catholicism (of the mid to late nineteenth century variety), though such sympathy could — but need not — be translated into tolerance for Modernism proper. There can be no *assumption* of sympathy for both since the early twentieth century movement was readily distinguishable, or at any rate significantly different, from its predecessor.

The evidence for Fortescue's intellectual affinity with Liberal Catholicism is found in the first place in his diaries. In 1900, perusing the London journals, he was struck by some pieces by Jackson St George Mivart (1827–1900), considered the leading Catholic natural scientist in England, who had come a cropper over what Church authority judged to be audacities. Already a marked man in some quarters for his quasi-Darwinian defence of the development of the human body (he accepted evolution, but not natural selection), a trio of articles on eschatology, in which he sought to reduce to less alarming dimensions the notion of the horror of Hell, was placed on the Index of Prohibited Books in 1899. Refused an answer to his request to know which particular propositions had caused this action to be taken, Mivart denounced the Roman Congregation of the Index and, for good measure, sought an apology from Cardinal Vaughan for remarks about him in *The Tablet* (of which Vaughan was proprietor). Instead, Vaughan sent him a profession of faith for his signature, but this was not forthcoming.[10]

---

did not need English-language mediators, but Döllinger was in fact chiefly known in England through Lord Acton who surveyed his Church-historical writing in 'Döllinger's Historical Work', *English Historical Review* 5 (1890), pp. 700–744. (References to Döllinger's inspiration abound in R. Hill, *Lord Acton* [Yale University Press: New Haven and London, 2000].)

9   For the background in mid-Victorian controversies, see J.L. Altholz, *The Liberal Catholic Movement in England: the 'Rambler' and its Contributors, 1848–1864* (London: Burns and Oates, 1962); J.R. Altholtz and D. McElrath (ed.), *The Correspondence of Lord Acton and Richard Simpson* (Cambridge: Cambridge University Press, 1971–1975), 3 vols.

10 Mivart would die excommunicated. See on this figure J.W. Gruber, *A Conscience in Conflict. The Life of St George Jackson Mivart* (New York: Columbia University Press, 1960).

Mivart had not long to live and the question arose of whether he could receive Catholic burial. Vaughan did not feel able to license the use of Church rites, but his successor took the charitable view that the balance of Mivart's mind had been disturbed. Archbishop Bourne allowed the exhumation of the remains and their re-burial to the accompaniment of liturgical prayers. So this was a serious affair. Fortescue responded to Mivart's essay 'Some Recent Catholic Apologists',[11] by confiding to his diary, '[A]lmost all he says seems to me true'.[12] What was it that Mivart had asserted?

After a retrospect, for the benefit of readers of *The Fortnightly Review*, on his contributions to discussion of Church matters (including the eschatological essays that elicited the canonical penalties under which he was labouring), Mivart turned his fire on two named figures in particular. These were: the biographer of Newman, historian of the Catholic revival and religious philosopher Wilfrid Ward (1856–1916) who had sought to justify — up to a point — the papal sanctions against Galileo, and a more obscure writer, Robert Francis Clarke, a priest-contributor to *The Tablet*, whose offence in Mivart's eyes lay in seeking to defend (against Gore, as it happened) Leo XIII's 1893 encyclical on biblical inspiration, *Providentissimus Deus*. Among other things, Leo had reiterated the traditional teaching on the inerrancy of Scripture.

Mivart considered the Galileo case to have

> taught us, through history, that it is not to ecclesiastical congregations, but to men of science, that [God] has committed the elucidation of scientific questions, whether such questions are or are not treated of by Scripture, the Fathers, the Church's common teaching or special congregations or tribunals of ecclesiastics actually summoned for the purpose. This [Mivart went on] also applies to all science — to Scripture criticism, to biology, and to all questions concerning evolution, the antiquity of man and the origin of either his body or his soul, or both. For all ecclesiastics who know nothing of natural science, it is an act necessarily as futile as impertinent to express any opinion on such subjects.[13]

And he added in a footnote that unless 'some ignorant men of the *Curia* are not quickly muzzled' in their views of evolutionary theory, Rome would soon become the 'laughing-stock of the civilized world'.[14]

---

11 St G. Jackson Mivart, 'Some Recent Catholic Apologists', *The Fortnightly Review* LVII, New Series (1900), pp. 24–44.

12 Downside Archives, IX AF, Box D, 'Diary 1900', entry for 18 January, 1900.

13 St G. Jackson Mivart, 'Some Recent Catholic Apologists', art. cit., pp. 33–34.

14 Ibid., p. 34, footnote 2. Mivart had in mind the sanctions imposed on two priest-biologists who had written in favour of an evolutionary view of the

Moving on to Clarke's defence of Pope Leo, Mivart accepted that, if Leo had been obliged to speak on biblical inerrancy, his hands were tied, in what he might say, by the doctrinal constraints of Trent and the First Vatican Council. But he went on to deplore the fact that Leo had said anything on the topic at all. Far better would have been to let the indefensible thesis of biblical inerrancy quietly fade away, as, in the early Christian centuries, had befallen belief in the temporal imminence of the Parousia. Clarke had taken the view that the traditional teaching on the total inerrancy of the Bible could be maintained if one ascribed truth-value to statements contained in Scripture *when taken in the manner the biblical authors intended* in this or that given case. Mivart, whose sense of hermeneutics was not exactly subtle, replied that only those statements are true that correspond with objective fact, 'quite apart from harmony with the intention of him who makes them'.[15]

In the essay, Mivart confessed he had no patience with the elaborate idea of doctrinal development conceived by Newman. Nor was he any better disposed to those who held that, while in a given context it might not be easy intelligibly to represent certain historic formulations of doctrine, we could rest assured that the real meaning of those formulations was nevertheless continuously housed in the corporate mind of the Church. Such people, thought Mivart, had surrendered to a fiction: 'non-existent meanings, deposited in the non-existent mind of an hypostatized Church'.[16] In sum, he agreed with the remarks of an anonymous contributor, 'Romanus', writing on 'Liberal Catholicism' in *The Contemporary Review* for 1899: the cause of the God of truth could never be well served by 'clever dodges, studiously ambiguous utterances, hushing up unpleasant truths, and misrepresenting and minimizing their significance'.[17]

Fortescue's diaries do not indicate the limits of his agreement with Mivart ('almost all he says'), so it would be unfair to ascribe to him the whole Mivartian package. In some ways, Mivart was a prime example of the default position of modern English culture: a positivism of 'hard fact' combined with a belief in the epistemic primacy of science. If the agreement were indeed quasi-total, one is led to suspect that Fortescue had not done much to take further the

---

human body, as discussed in the semi-offical Curial journal, *Civiltà cattolica* in its issue of 7 January of the previous year, 1899.

15   St G. Jackson Mivart, 'Some Recent Catholic Apologists', art. cit., p. 39, where Mivart expressed the wish to know if Clarke thought the Tower of Babel to correspond to facts, such that 'the diversity of tongues really arose as there represented', adding sardonically that '[i]f he does, he differs from the overwhelming majority of competent philologists'.

16   Ibid., p. 30.

17   Cited ibid., p. 42.

basic education in speculative or systematic thinking he had received in Rome and Innsbruck. Questions of the kind broadly termed 'hermeneutical' could well be asked about the sufficiency of Mivart's approach. Clarke, for instance, was surely correct to think that we have to establish the meaning of a truth-claim before we can decide what might count as verifying or refuting it. And if on a variety of complementary grounds one has decided on the superiority of a given world-view, particular facts may well take on a different coloration (which is not to deny that a massive aggregation of relatively indigestible facts cannot in the end sweep a world view away).

But a letter of 1900 to Hamilton Macdonald showed Fortescue's serious irritation with ecclesiastical Rome.

> Think of what Rome used to be — the Rome of Gregory and Leo, the Rome that sent John the Archchanter to teach us in England how to sing: Rome strong, simple, manly, the glory and pride of the churches — and think of Rome now — so small, Italian, meddling: interfering in the dioceses of all our bishops in every absurd detail, down to the shape of a monstrance. The home of that lowest and basest of all creatures, the Italian Monsignore: making every year some declaration about politicks, history, astronomy, botany — and always ludicrously wrong. And so terribly forgetful of elementary Catholic morals — wanting above all things to be a trumpery state again, toadying Russia. Shuffling, dodging, diplomatising — a very very sad sight — all typified in the pink calico splendour of a Roman festa — or such a gross indecency as a fat man with a treble voice yelling the Miserere to a Polka tune.

He added, though, that 'no essential element of the Holy Catholic Church is lost in this. My Lord Pope is of course always Christ's Vicar'. And he spoke highly of Leo's personal holiness. Still, the

> special pleading of Catholics, who are so inclined to take things as they are, without history or dogma, and to try frantically to defend them — is the death of all Reform, and makes us try to defend what we know is bad, against our own better conscience.

He concluded on a more optimistic note, or, better, a note of theological hope.

> Rome has been so glorious once that it may become so again. What we should do is to go on begging our dear Lord to bless his church', ending his sentence with a citation from a Latin collect, 'that all adversities and errors destroyed, she may serve Thee securely in freedom.[18]

18 Westminster Diocesan Archives, Box AGD, Letter to Hamilton Macdonald of

As the reference to the Polka tune suggests, Fortescue's very real impatience with the steering-room of the Barque of Peter was lightened by humour. Michael Davies reports from an undeclared source 'an occasion when Fr. Fortescue was being shown one of the early automobiles. Gingerly he pressed the klaxon horn, and jumped back at its raucous noise. "Good heavens!" he exclaimed. "It sounds like the canons of St Peter's singing Terce"'.[19]

A further Mivart article, 'The Continuity of Catholicism', this time in *The Nineteenth Century*, drew from Fortescue a milder remark: Mivart 'shows the great difficulties about historicity at many places in the Old Testament'.[20] Mivart's principal concern was with developments — some might call them ruptures — in the self-understanding of Catholicism since its emergence in fully organized form at (so he suggested, diffidently enough) the end of the third century.[21] Disclaiming any status as a theologian, Mivart prudently warned his readers that 'I am by no means to be supposed to myself adopt all the novel views to which I may call attention'.[22] After rehearsing the usual suspects — geocentrism, the necessity of the Church for salvation, usury — Mivart comes to his preferred topic in this essay, which is the historical veracity of Scripture. For the most part, he leans on comments from an Irish theologian, the first President of St John's Seminary, Boston, who:

> very candidly admits that "work has been done on the Bible in recent times with results which are no longer seriously questioned. Theologians have to acknowledge, however reluctantly, that henceforth much less can be built on the Bible than in the past".[23]

As cited by Mivart, John Baptist Hogan (1829–1901) applied this maxim, whose wording is distinctly — and doubtless diplomatically — vague, to the plagues of Egypt (rather ordinary events) and Joshua's miracle of the

---

15 February, 1900.

19 M. Davies, 'Adrian Fortescue Priest and Scholar', *The Latin Mass* 3.5 (1994), pp. 26–33, and here at p. 31. This article must be distinguished from the later essay of the same name included in Davies's anthology of Fortescue's liturgical articles, *The Wisdom of Adrian Fortescue*, op. cit.

20 Downside Archives, IX AF, Box D, 'Diary 1900', entry for 29 January, 1900.

21 St George Mivart, 'The Continuity of Catholicism', *The Nineteenth Century* XLVII (1900), pp. 51–72.

22 Ibid., p. 53.

23 Ibid., p. 60, citing from J.B. Hogan, *Clerical Studies* (Boston, MA: Marlier, 1898). See on this influential book, E.J.T. Talar, 'Seminary Reform and Theological Method on the Eve of the Modernist Crisis: Transatlantic Reception of J.B. Hogan's *Clerical Studies* (1898)', *U.S. Catholic Historian* 25.3 (2010), pp. 1–17.

sun (poetic description of a natural phenomenon). But Mivart includes in the same category of de-supernaturalisation the messianic interpretation of Isaiah 7:14–16, a key text for the Christian use of the Old Testament since it includes words highly pertinent to the Nativity of Christ — 'a virgin shall conceive, and bear a son, and call his name Immanuel'. '[T]here is probably no well-informed Catholic now', wrote Mivart, 'who would deny that what Isaiah said was intended to calm the dread which Ahaz (King of Judah) felt with respect to Pekah (King of Israel) and Rezin (King of Syria) by assuring him that before a young woman's newly born child should be old enough to know right from wrong, the two kings so dreaded should have disappeared.

No one would fail to see the absurdity of supposing that King Ahaz could be comforted by being told of an abnormal birth to take place five hundred years after his death'.[24] And Mivart went on from there to the heart of the New Testament faith, raising the question of the historicity of the empty tomb of which disparate accounts are given in the Gospels and none, explicitly at any rate, by St Paul. Advised by an unnamed theologian that the decomposition of Christ's earthly remains would not affect the doctrine of the Resurrection — on the grounds that we do not know in what the 'essence' of a body consists, Mivart extended learned agnosticism to the virginal conception and birth of Jesus likewise.

> This doctrine relating to the termination of Christ's earthly career naturally brings to our mind what the New Testament tells us as to its commencement. . . . The possibility that the Scriptural account of what concerns the former doctrine may be an unhistorical interpolation, can hardly fail to suggest (as it has suggested) the speculation whether St. Luke's account of what concerns the second dogma may not be similarly explained.[25]

Mivart adds the information (as if this were conclusive) that 'in the last volume of T. and T. Clark's Dictionary it is quite admitted that the account in Luke belongs to a later structure of the synoptic narrative and was not known to the first generation of Christians'.[26] Fortescue's diary entry makes plain, by confining its agreement to comments on the Old Testament, that here at least he could not follow.

Continued reading

In late September 1901 we find Fortescue reading the former Catholic priest Ernest Renan's (1823–1892) *Vie de Jésus*, sceptical study of Christian origins from the previous generation — the original edition was published in 1863, and exactly a month later the Lutheran historian of dogma Adolf

---

24 St George Mivart, 'The Continuity of Catholicism', art. cit., p. 61.
25 Ibid., p. 68.
26 Ibid.

von Harnack's (1851–1930) much more contemporary (1900) *Das Wesen des Christentums* — the work which would stimulate the writing of *L'Evangile et l'Eglise*, the Abbé Loisy's ill-conceived apologia for Catholicism, itself the true beginning of the Catholic Modernist crisis. He found Harnack's work, though 'inimical to us orthodox Christians and especially to Catholics', nevertheless to contain 'many things worthy of note', even if he forbore to identify which they were.[27]

In the last months of 1902, Fortescue seems to have enjoyed Houtin's *La Question biblique chez les catholiques de France au xixe siècle* ('magnificently ironic'),[28] and in the first quarter of 1903 (the diaries are not more specific) tackled Loisy's reply to Harnack in *L'Evangile et l'Eglise*,[29] on which his comments are remarkably mild, given the splenetic nature of reactions elsewhere. Loisy's 'doubts about the authenticity of some texts will', Fortescue predicted, 'displease many, what he says about the evolution in the mind of the Lord and the evolution of Christianity more still'.[30] One's impression from this note is not of sympathy with Loisy so much as uncertainty. How should one deal with the questions *L'Evangile et l'Eglise* raises? Unlike the Liberal Catholicism which Fortescue evidently favoured — at any rate in the broad lines of its concern for historical scholarship and the liberty of the natural sciences, Modernism was not a movement to which, judging by the evidence at our disposal, Fortescue actually *warmed*. Rather (this at least would be my suggestion), he was bemused by it.

A recent historian of this period of English Catholic life has commented sharply on *Loisysme*. Loisy 'viewed Christ as a limited first century Jew who, by great good fortune, had inadvertently founded the Catholic Church. . . . No orthodox Church could tolerate Loisy's views'.[31] This judgment owes something to hindsight, based on Loisy's subsequent publications and (especially) the reminiscences that describe his (at first, publicly concealed) state of mind. In his memoir of the crisis, *Choses passées*, Loisy admitted that his relations with the Church had been founded on 'une equivoque énorme'.[32] But any alert reader of the first 'little red book' should have seen

---

27   Downside Archives IX AF, Box D, 'Diary 1901', entry for 20 October, 1901.

28   A. Houtin, *La Question biblique chez les catholiques de France au xixe siècle* Paris: Picard, 1902, 2nd edition); Downside Archives, IX AF, Box D, 'Diary 1902', note of reading for October to December.

29   A. Loisy, *L'Evangile et l'Eglise* (Paris: Picard, 1902).

30   Downside Archives, IX AF, Box D, 'Diary 1903', note of reading for January to April, 1903.

31   S. Gilley, 'The Years of Equipoise, 1892–1942', in V.A. McClelland and M. Hodgetts (ed.), *From within the Flaminian Gate. 150 Years of Catholicism in England and Wales* (London: Darton, Longman and Todd, 1999), p. 37.

32   A.F. Loisy, *Choses passées* (Paris: Nourry, 1913), p. 90. Loisy's mature

there would be a considerable price to pay, in terms of classical Christology (not to mention ecclesiology), for combating Harnack in Loisy's fashion. The liturgical historian Edmund Bishop commented, 'Loisy is good apologetic for the present R.C. Church; but there seems enough *Gospel* still in Petrine Rome to reject — and damn — such apologetics'.[33]

It should be added that when there were (correct) rumours of Loisy's imminent excommunication, Bishop took a less sanguine view of the Roman condemnations.

> Whilst every one else among us Catholics was helpless and so would in fact (though not in will) have left intelligent young Catholics to the influence of Harnack's book, — would have left the 'wolf' to ravage the 'fold', — Loisy, Loisy alone, stood up and did the work of a Shepherd of the flock: and so effectively that even Harnack or Harnack's friends recognized and allowed the force and power of the defence.[34]

And Bishop spoke of a consequent 'duty of gratitude to one who (it would seem to my mind, whatever be the mixture of human weakness in his work and workings) has in fact laid down his (spiritual) life for the sheep — has become anathema for our sake'.[35] By his choice of words Bishop was making Loisy not only a new Jesus but a new Paul.

In March 1908 Fortescue took up Loisy again. This time it was Loisy's privately printed *Simples Réflexions* which concerned, as the rest of their title indicated, the Roman response to Modernism, Pius X's encyclical *Pascendi*, promulgated in September 1907, and the decree of the Holy Office *Lamentabili*, issued in the previous July. This was the third celebrated (or infamous) 'little red book' — Fortescue seems to have missed the intermediate book, *Autour d'un petit Livre*.[36] To this he added in May Loisy's *Quelques letters sur des Questions actuelles* and Houtin's *La Crise du clergé*.[37] The 1908 diary leaves no comment on these works, unless we are

autobiography makes as plain as could be the dichotomy between his views and the *sensus fidei* of the Church: idem., *Mémoires pour servir à l'histoire religieuse de notre temps* (Paris: Nourry, 1930–1931, 3 vols.).

33   N. Abercrombie, *The Life and Work of Edmund Bishop* (London: Longmans, Green, 1959), p. 345.

34   Ibid., p. 355.

35   Ibid.

36   A. Loisy, *Simples Réflexions sur le décret du Saint-Office 'Lamentabili sane exitu' et sur l'Encyclique "Pascendi dominici gregis"* (Ceffonds: Loisy, 1908); idem., *Autour d'un petit Livre* (Paris: Picard, 1903).

37   Idem., *Quelques letters sur des Questions actuelles et sur des evénéments récents* (Ceffonds: privately printed, 1908); A. Houtin, *La Crise du clergé* (Paris: Nourry, 1908, 2nd edition).

to take as such the entry for the end of May, expressing concern that he had written imprudently to 'Mrs Trotter' about 'my religious ideas'.[38] But Loisy was excommunicated using the severest form known to the canon law of the time (the category *vitandus*) in March 1908. *Pace* Bishop, the self-immolation of Loisy, if such it were, did him no harm in worldly terms. A year later he was appointed to the chair of the History of Religions at the Collège de France. However, the manner in which Pius X proposed to deal with the 'Loisyste' challenge left Fortescue profoundly disturbed.

After Loisy and Houtin, Fortescue turned his attention to Tyrrell. The Jesuit George Tyrrell was the most prominent Catholic Modernist in England, or at any rate (if one is inclined to give the title 'Modernist' to Friedrich von Hügel (1852–1925), despite the latter's opposition to 'immanentism') the only one to suffer excommunication.[39] The final stages of Tyrrell's publishing history — which coincided with the last months of his life — can be traced in Fortescue's diaries for 1909 when he read Tyrrell's *Mediaevalism*,[40] and 1910 when he read his final work, *Christianity at the Crossroads*.[41]

Fortescue was evidently seeking to gain a wide-angled view, reading *Lendemains d'encyclique* by an anonymous group of writers, 'Catholici', in June 1908, and an Anglican equivalent, A.L. Lilley's *Modernism*, in August,[42] with Johannes Kübel's *Geschichte der katholischen Modernismus* following in March 1909,[43] and Paul Sabatier's *Les Modernistes* in April of that same year.[44] In and of itself, a reading list is not evidence for a response, though it is symptomatic of a concern. But, to repeat: I wonder whether Fortescue had so immersed himself in the facticity of empirical history, as well as of art and culture, that he had come somewhat to lack what his philosophical and theological formation was intended, at least, to equip him with: a speculative intelligence that could be brought to bear on broad issues, such as those that Modernism raised.

Instinctively, he disliked the way Protestants were supporting the Catholic Modernists on the basis of prejudices of their own. On his return from the Levant in 1907 he wrote to Burton,

---

38 Downside Archives, IX AF, Box D, 'Diary 1908', entry for 30 May.

39 N. Sagovsky, *'On God's Side': A Life of George Tyrrell* (Oxford: Clarendon Press, 1990).

40 G. Tyrrell, *Mediaevalism: A Reply to Cardinal Mercier* (London: Longmans, Green, 1908).

41 Idem., *Christianity at the Crossroads* (London: Longmans, Green, 1909).

42 A.L. Lilley, *Modernism: a record and a review* (New York: Scribner, 1908).

43 J. Kübel, *Geschichte der katholischen Modernismus* (Tübingen: Mohr, 1909).

44 P. Sabatier, *Les Modernistes. Notes d'histoire contemporaine, avec le texte intégral de l'Encyclique 'Pascendi', du Syllabus 'Lamentabili' et de la Supplique d'un groupe de Catholiques français au pape Pie X* (Paris: Fischbacher, 1909).

> Mrs Fielding [Burton's cousin] was very keen about what she
> called the courageous letter from certain Italian priests against the
> Pope. I hear about poor Tyrrell and Modernism from everybody I
> speak to now. It occurs to me that most of these people start from
> a fundamental principle that, if the Pope is down on any mortal
> thing, that thing must be right. I believe that if Rome condemned
> highway robbery or wholesale adultery, pious Protestants would
> begin to think that there is a good deal to be said for them.[45]

But he could not agree with some Roman policies of the anti-Modernist reaction.

The problem of the anti-Modernist oath

Fortescue considered the terms of the anti-Modernist oath *Sacrorum antistitum*, promulgated from Rome on 1 September, 1910, to be far too narrowly set. The only way available to us to determine the heads of his opposition must be the references in the diaries and letters to his difficulties with the positions of the later nineteenth and early twentieth century Papacy. As we have seen, these concern the intersection of magisterial teaching with the sciences, both historical and natural. Questioning the central truth claims of classical Christian doctrine (I include there those elements of doctrine which house a distinctively [Roman] Catholic ecclesiology) does not seem to have entered the picture. Looking in this perspective at the terms of the anti-Modernist oath, at what did he jib? My general estimate of his intellectual situation and a letter to Thurston (to be discussed below) which concentrated on exegesis of the phrase 'I submit myself with due respect and adhere with all my heart' point us towards the second paragraph of the Oath's fifth section.

Writing on 5 November 1910 to Herbert Thurston, Fortescue sought to find a way to 'take the oath without perjury'.[46] The subscribing cleric had to express his assent to the 'declarations, condemnations, etc' of Modernist errors in terms of 'subjection' and 'wholehearted adhesion'. Thurston had suggested to Fortescue that the Latin phrase *me subicio* ('I subject myself') could reasonably be understood as a promise not to mount resistance, in deed or word. Fortescue accepted the interpretation but had more difficulty about an analogous reading of *ac toto animo adhaereo* ('I adhere with my whole soul'), or, rather, of the verb *adhaereo* since the adverbial phase was, he thought, 'only an emphasis' and meant, in effect, 'thoroughly'. Still, he could think of ways of softening the verb's force. After all:

---

45 Westminster Diocesan Archives, Series 20, Box 22, Letter to Harold Burton of
    25th Sunday after Pentecost 1907.

46 Westminster Diocesan Archives, Series 20, Box 22, Copy of Letter to Herbert
    Thurston, S.J., of 5 November, 1910.

> You adhere to things in many ways, not only by interior assent
> to statements. You may adhere by a loyal and respectful hearing
> of what authority says by accepting it for what it is — a grave
> pronouncement of the Pope against which you would say nothing
> contemptuous or disrespectful, even if you cannot see that all he
> says is objectively correct. One adheres to the laws of one's country,
> even if one does not think them all perfect; one adheres to one's
> breviary because one recites it, even if one does not agree to all
> the second nocturn lessons [sometimes lacking in historicity, q.v.].

On inspection, the object of the solemnly worded phrase over which
Fortescue was agonizing turns out to be: 'all the condemnations, declarations
and prescriptions contained in the encyclical *Pascendi* and the decree
Lamentabili', to which is added the qualifier 'particularly in so far as they
concern the so-called history of dogma'.[47] Granted that the main principles
of the theology of revelation laid down by Pius X's letter *Pascendi Dominici
gregis* in its effort to reiterate classical doctrine are themselves re-stated in
the body of the Oath, it seems likely that it is among the more detailed
condemned propositions of the companion Curial document, *Lamentabili
sine exitu*, that the source of Fortescue's difficulty must be sought.

And when we turn to that text, we find indeed some statements that,
granted his earlier expressions of agreement with Mivart, he might well
have considered more true than false. These would include, I suggest,
the first of the condemned propositions, which was to the effect that 'the
Church law which requires writings that concern the divine books to be
submitted to a previous censorship does not extend to representatives of the
higher criticism (*cultores critices*) nor to scientific exegetes of the books of
the Old and New Testaments'.[48] Closely connected therewith is the second
condemned proposition for which 'while the ecclesial interpretation of
the sacred books is not to be disprized, it is however subject to the more
accurate judgment and correction of exegetes'.[49] So far as the freedom of
historical scholarship was concerned, these were *Lamentabili*'s two crucial
passages: nowhere did the knife of scholarly criticism cut more deeply than
in study of the history of Israel and of Christian origins.

---

47 For a translation of the Oath, see (K. Rahner, S.J., ed.), J. Neuner, S.J., and H.
    Roos, S.J., *The Teaching of the Catholic Church as Contained in her Documents*
    (Cork: The Mercier Press, 1966), pp. 41–44.

48 *Lamentabili*, 1. The text appeared initially in *Acta Sanctae Sedis* 40 (1907),
    pp. 470–478; it can also be found in the most recent edition of the standard
    collection of doctrinal statements: H. Denzinger, *Enchiridion symbolorum,
    definitionum at declarationum de rebus fidei et morum*, ed. P. Hünermann
    (Freiburg: Herder, 1991, 37th edition), pp. 932–939.

49 *Lamentabili*, 2.

Of wider pertinence, and raising issues of cosmology (especially human anthropology) discussed by Mivart, is the censure *Lamentabili* passes on the claim that 'since only revealed truths are contained in the deposit of faith, the Church is in no wise authorized to make judgments of assertions that fall within the remit of the human sciences (*assertiones discipinarum humanarum*)'.[50] Given Fortescue's lack of confidence in the workings of the Roman curia, he may well have jibbed at the rejection of the further, omnium-gatherum statement: 'Those are without fault who regard as nugatory reprobations issued by the Sacred Congregation of the Index or other Sacred Roman Congregations'.[51] In what touches the inspiration and inerrancy of Scripture, Fortescue's expression of sympathy with Mivart's articles is not readily compatible with the condemnation of the thesis by which: 'Divine inspiration does not so extend to the entirety of Holy Scripture as to preserve from all error each and every one of its individual parts'.[52]

Contrastingly, his unwillingness to follow Mivart beyond the realm of the Old Testament in this regard suggests he would have found less problematic the hedge *Lamentabili* sought to plant around the teaching of Jesus and the apostles, compared with the restrictiveness its authors wished to impose on the critical study of the Hebrew Bible. The tenth of the condemned propositions censures those who say that 'the inspiration of the books of the Old Testament consists in this: that Israelite authors transmitted in an especial way religious teachings which were either unknown to pagans or little known by them'.[53] So far as the Gospels and the New Testament writings generally were concerned, Fortescue's studies of the Church of the Fathers show that his Christology was fundamentally Cyrilline. Fortescue expressly states that he considered the Chalcedonian Definition the only possible way of making sense of the New Testament witness. Yet his lecture notes on Church history for students at St Edmund's Ware show he was keen to contextualize the ministry of Jesus in its Roman, Hellenistic and Jewish environment.

His approach to the New Testament was not exclusively, then, patristically mediated. So he may have had a difficulty with the Curial rejection of the claim that 'Christian doctrine was in its beginnings Jewish, but then through subsequent development became first Pauline, then Johannine and finally Hellenic and universal'.[54] My reconstruction of Fortescue's difficulties over Pius X's anti-Modernist policy is necessarily tentative, but it is, I think, congruent with his reactions to Mivart and his — admittedly,

50 Ibid., 5.
51 Ibid., 8.
52 Ibid., 11.
53 Ibid., 10.
54 Ibid., 60.

sparse — comments on his reading of Modernist writers. In the absence of more specific evidence, no higher status for these juxtapositions can reasonably be claimed.

There can be no doubt that subscription to the Oath entailed a real crisis for him. His discomfort was the more acute owing to the value he put on straightforwardness — in which his point of reference was Newman's elaborate over-interpretations of the Thirty-Nine Articles in Tract 90. 'Of course I realize the humour of all this. It is Romish doctrine of Purgatory and "Sacrifices of Masses" all over again.' He had, so he told Thurston, considered non-subscription and accepting the suspension that would inevitably follow. But

> [a] suspended priest who still believes things is in about the most hideous position you can imagine. I meant not to do it, and then had a vision of myself in a Bloomsbury lodging. How long should I go on saying my office and wearing a Roman collar? And all my friends would look upon it as much the same thing as if I had gone off with a lady.

He ascribed the dilemma to the way an over-centralization of the Church on Rome had conspired with the personality of Pius X, about whom he was less than flattering.

> Centralization grows and goes madder every century. Even at Trent they hardly foresaw this kind of thing. Does it really mean that one cannot be a member of the Church of Christ without being, as we are, absolutely at the mercy of an Italian Lunatic?

Yet, he reflected, '[a]fter all, it is still the Church of the Fathers that we stand by and spend our lives defending'.

> [B]ad as things are, nothing else is possible. I think that when I look at Rome, I see powerful arguments against us, but when I look at the Church of England or Mathew [the Old Catholic archbishop in England[55]] or anyone else, I see still more powerful arguments for us. But of course, saving a total collapse, things are as bad as they can be. Give us back the Xth century Johns and Stephen, or a Borgia! They were less disastrous than this deplorable person.

Just as Newman had hoped Pius IX might die before Neo-Ultramontanism did too much harm, so Fortescue allowed himself to hope Pius X's life would not be greatly prolonged. On 27 February, 1912, he wrote to Mrs Crickmer:

---

55   See on this figure, the Old Catholic 'Archbishop of London', P. Anson, *Bishops at Large*, op. cit., pp. 156–215.

> Our Apostolick Lord is going to die this year, which is really the
> best thing he can do. A holy nun has had a revelation, saw all the
> heavenly host crying, "Come long [sic], Pius Puss, Puss Pius". So
> he's got to go. When I am Pope I shall canonize the nun.

He had, it seems, forgotten the enthusiasm with which he had greeted Pius
X's espousal of the Solesmes chant, and his reform of the Roman Breviary.
In fact, Pius X did not die until 1914. One wonders what Fortescue would
have made of his canonization in 1954.

Some of the pronouncements of the Pontifical Biblical Commission
were, to Fortescue's mind, no better than the Oath which itself, indeed,
through its internal reference to *Lamentabili* was intended in part to erect
a fence around the sacred text. He wrote to Burton:

> Time was when I was young and had no sense, *regnante Leone*, that
> I meant to read the Bible. The various decisions of the Pontifical
> Biblical Commission have long shown me that Christians had
> better leave that interesting volume altogether alone. Apparently
> there is very little you are allowed to say at all and what there is is
> not *tutum* [safe]. So — do you know the advice L. de Vinci gave
> to the hopelessly ugly man — *Lasciare le donne et* [sic] *studiare la
> Matematica* [Leave the ladies and study mathematics].[56]

Once again, this strongly suggests it was questions of apparent factual mistakes
in the scriptural record, difficulties for the verbal inerrancy of the Bible, that
exercised Fortescue — not the wider philosophico-theological issues about
the God–world relationship that occupied the more speculative moments
of Catholic Modernist writers. The death of Pius X and the accession of
Benedict XV (who as Cardinal della Chiesa was himself supposedly suspected
of Modernism in the previous pontificate) made no difference at all in
this respect. The Commission continued to maintain its robust line about
questions of the historical value of the biblical text in all its particulars.

The problem, as Fortescue now saw it — and, in reality, had seen it since
reading Mivart in 1900 — lay with Leo XIII's encyclical on the standing of
Scripture, *Providentissimus Deus*. On 22 July, 1920, he wrote to Stanley Morison:

> Leo XIII commits himself to the historicity of every statement,
> not obviously a quotation, in the Old Testament. That is
> absolutely and finally hopeless. If we are really committed to
> that there is nothing more to be done with the Bible but to let it
> alone and ignore it. . . . The Old Testament is full of statements
> that are not true, that are proved as not true as certainly as you
> can prove anything in physical science or history. To maintain

---

56 Westminster Diocesan Archives, Series 20, Box 22, Letter to Edwin Burton of
12 October, 1911.

that the first eleven chapters of Genesis represent what really happened is to expose oneself to the derision of any educated modern person.

Fortescue continues, that when he heard a Catholic take that line he knew what it meant. 'I do not want to hear any more of his views and I only hope that some intelligent Protestant will not get hold of what he writes'.

Here Fortescue appealed specifically to Loisy, though the problem that vexed him had been identified well before *Loisysme*, with Mivart. Of course, in principle, Fortescue writes, it would be far better if one could back Leo XIII in his remarks about the unblemished truth of the Scriptural record. But 'in such matters as this one simply cannot refuse to be convinced by the evidence'. He adds, 'The absurdity is that these Encyclicals and the decisions of the Biblical Commission are not *ex cathedra*, they are admittedly not infallible, yet we are not allowed publicly to say anything contradicting them. I wish to goodness that the Pope would never speak at all except when he means to define *ex cathedra*.' And in the same spirit, Fortescue also wished that the Biblical Commission did not exist or at least that, if it had to exist, it would say nothing.

Though the formulation of the anti-Modernist oath could certainly have been improved, and the asseverations of the Commission more nuanced, this was not altogether an intelligent comment. Magisterial teaching is often more a matter of a trajectory than a declaration at one point. And as to the Commission: shifting styles, not to say fluctuating fashions, in biblical exegesis counsel caution where the academic study of the Church's foundational Scriptures are concerned. In matters biblical, not all modern erudition is subversive of the historical value of Scripture, as the strong tradition of Conservative Evangelical scholarship attests. At the time of my writing this book, the present Pope, Benedict XVI, has certainly learned a great deal from the modern critical study of Scripture, yet in the 'apostolic exhortation' *Verbum Domini*, issued in the wake of the 2008 Synod of Bishops which met to consider the 'Word of God in the life and mission of the Church', he could still refer positively to *Providentissimus Deus*: 'Pope Leo XIII's intervention had the merit of protecting the Catholic interpretation of the Bible from the inroads of rationalism, without, however, seeking refuge in a spiritual meaning detached from history'.[57] Doubtless there is much more that needs to be said by way of addressing criticism, and in orchestrating theologically this recent claim on the part of one of Leo's successors.[58]

---

57 Benedict XVI, *Verbum Domini* 43.

58 Ibid., 19. See for an example of helpful work by a monk-writer who is both theologian and exegete: D. Farkasfalvy, O. Cist., *Inspiration and Interpretation. A Theological Introduction to Sacred Scripture* (Washington, D.C.: Catholic University of America Press, 2010).

Fortescue was discontented with much that was taken for granted in modern Catholic practice. In the letter he wrote to Stanley Morison while the latter was preparing a descent on Rome in 1920, he asked,

> By the way, will you give a message from me to the Roman Ordinary? Tell him to look after his own diocese and not to write any more Encyclicals. Also, that there were twelve apostles and that all bishops are their successors. Also, to read the works of St Paul, also to open his front door and walk out, also that the faith handed to our fathers is more important than either the Sacred Heart or certain alleged happenings at Lourdes.[59]

This does not indicate much enthusiasm for either the official or the devotional culture of contemporary Western Catholicism.

Fortescue's quarrel with the contemporary Church

Taken overall, Fortescue's principal *gravamina* concerned Roman centralization, on the one hand, and the liberty of historical scholarship on the other. On the first, the invitation to contribute an article on Febronianism to the Hastings *Encyclopaedia* would have been a suitable opportunity to set forth, at any rate tacitly, an opinion about Church governance.[60] 'Febronius', the pseudonym of Johann Nicholas von Hontheim (1701–1790), who, as auxiliary to successive Prince-Electors of the church-state in Trier, was effectively Trier's bishop, had proposed that the Catholic princes should see to it that the power of the pope be reduced, that of the bishops augmented. Fortescue sets out very fairly the content of Hontheim's major work.[61] Among other things, his book was a plea for restoration of the ancient powers of metropolitans vis-à-vis local churches.

Quite possibly Fortescue was sympathetic to this (it was a widespread concern in the great sees in Austria-Hungary at the time of the definition of papal primacy of jurisdiction in 1870, and he is unlikely not to have encountered its residue while at Innsbruck). But Hontheim, who combined

---

59 Cambridge University Library, MS Add. 9812/D/90, Letter to S. Morison of 18 June, 1920.

60 'Febronianism', in J. Hastings, *Encyclopaedia of Religion and Ethics, V* (Edinburgh: T. and T. Clark, 1912), pp. 807–809.

61 *Justini Febronii Jurisconsulti de Statu Ecclesiae et legitima potestate Romani Pontificis liber singularis ad reuniendos dissidentes in religione Christianos compositus* (Frankfurt: Esslinger, 1763). The place of publication and name of publisher as given on the original title page 'Bullioni, apud Guillelmum Evrardi', are fictitious. Fortescue's summary is found in 'Febronianism', art. cit., p. 808.

the office of canonist with the aspirations of a proto-ecumenist, also taught the subordination of the pope to a General Council of the Church. Fortescue's loyalty to the *de facto* conciliar tradition, including the teaching on the role of the bishop of Rome offered by the First Vatican Council, would not allow him to go down this road. As a consequence, the tone of his essay is ambivalent. He speaks of Febronianism as if it were a dangerous virus 'not finally expelled' until the 1870 Council,[62] but he also writes as though it were a victim: 'The final blow to Febronianism' was given by the Council in question.[63]

Significantly, he stresses the sentence Hontheim erased from the retractation forced upon him: 'Rightly the government of the Church is called monarchic by Catholic doctors'.[64] Equally significantly, Fortescue records that the nuncio to the Elector agreed to the deletion of these words. We should not be far wrong if we took Fortescue's position to be something along these lines: the non-monarchical nature of Petrine authority obliges the pope to self-restraint in the use of his doctrinal and juridical powers. Pius X was a 'lunatic' in Fortescue's eyes insofar as he threw such necessary restraint to the winds.

On the question of the freedom of theologians and other scholars: that Fortescue's anxieties were principally focussed on historical facts about the scriptural record saved him from the more radical questioning of the great dogmas of Catholic Christianity, dogmas which those in the Roman communion shared with the Orthodox and with Catholic-minded Anglicans. As the examples of Loisy (and even Tyrrell) served to show, the classical doctrines were not safe in Modernist hands. What G.L. Prestige said of the author of *Roman Catholic Claims*: 'In spite of his Biblical criticism and his liberal view of evolution, neither then, nor at any other time, had Gore the remotest intention of abandoning the creeds',[65] could equally well be said of Fortescue. Positively, that was owing to the quality of his assent to the revelation carried by the Church. His Christian faith was ecclesial and therefore it was traditional. One might add that negatively, he was not especially well prepared for speculative reconstructions of doctrine.

In another contribution to 'Hastings', this time an essay on the rational theological system, influenced by both Kant and Fichte, of the early nineteenth century Bonn theologian Georg Hermes (1775–1831), Fortescue ends an account of Hermes' life and work and the Roman condemnation of his teaching by writing, rather lamely, 'The subject has now only a historical

---

62   Ibid., p. 807.
63   Ibid., p. 808.
64   Cited ibid., p. 809.
65   G.L. Prestige, *The Life of Charles Gore*, op. cit., p. 49.

interest'.[66] This, one finds, is rarely the case with adventures in ideas.[67]

Some consciousness of Fortescue's unpreparedness to deal with the philosophical issues Modernism raised may perhaps be implied in John Gabriel Vance's *Short Memoir of the Revd Dr Adrian Fortescue*, published immediately after his death. Vance comments that, after his Roman studies, Fortescue reacted against metaphysics in favour of historical facts. But,

> later he began again to read St Thomas for the light which the Summae of that doctor cast upon Dante. Later still his study of Boethius led him back across the fascinating heights of the history of philosophy. He was developing an undoubted love for just this kind of history at the end.[68]

Was it simply a spontaneous love, borne of sheer intellectual interest? Or might it have been, rather, the recognition of an ecclesial need?

Whatever the answer to this question, doctrinal troubles were to come once again, and close to home. In September 1921 he was shocked by the news, given by the President of St Edmund's, Edward Myers (1875–1956, later co-adjutor archbishop of Westminster, 1951–1956), that a work by Vance, his Old Hall colleague, friend, and (as we have just seen, memorialist) had suffered a Roman condemnation,[69] and Vance himself sent away ('he narrates horrific things of John Vance').[70] The cause is likely to have been Vance's study *Reality and Truth. A Critical and Constructive Essay concerning Knowledge, Certainty, and Truth*, for the Holy Office of this period was increasingly concerned about the influence of (arguably) relativist epistemologies.[71] But since Vance's year of enforced absence was

---

66 'Hermesianism', in J. Hastings, *Encyclopaedia of Religion and Ethics, IV* (Edinburgh: T. and T. Clark, 1913), pp. 624–626, and here at p. 626.

67 For an alternative account of this figure, see A. Nichols., O.P., *From Hermes to Benedict XVI. Faith and Reason in Modern Catholic Thought* (Leominster: Gracewing, 2009), pp. 25–47. I should say I wish I had been aware of Fortescue's article at the time of writing the book just mentioned; the bibliography mentions several nineteenth century studies of the reception of Hermesianism which appear to have fallen out of such lists, even in Germany.

68 J.G. Vance, *Short Memoir of the Revd Dr Adrian Fortescue*, op. cit., p. 21.

69 Idem., *Reality and Truth. A Critical and Constructive Essay concerning Knowledge, Certainty, and Truth* (London: Longmans, Green, 1917).

70 Downside Archive, IX AF, Box E, 'Diary 1919, entry for 22 September.

71 The fifth of twelve propositions condemned by the Holy Office on 1 December 1924 ran: 'Truth is not found in any particular act of the intellect wherein conformity with the object would be had, as the Scholastics say, but rather truth is always is a state of becoming, and consists in a progressive alignment of the understanding with life, indeed a certain perpetual process, by which the intellect strives to develop and explain that which experience presents or

spent in Prague, the finest Baroque capital in Europe, the penance was perhaps not so severe. In the event, the episode did not prevent Vance becoming a prelate of honour to the Pope and preaching the sermon at Archbishop Myers' requiem.[72]

Concluding remarks on the Liberal-Modernist question

Fortescue wanted liberty of thought and expression in the Church, but at the same time he also insisted on high standards of doctrinal clarity. It does not seem to have occurred to him that these might be competing desiderata. In November 1919 he told Morison that the entire system of submitting books to prior scrutiny by ecclesiastical censors should be abolished.

> The whole business, the shameless admission on our books that we have only a gagged and controlled literature, is degrading, and most injurious to our cause, in these days when everyone accepts the principle of seeing and judging for yourself as a matter of course.[73]

He agreed that in the Westminster of his day the obligation to submit manuscripts was not in practice onerous. '[T]o do our Cardinal justice, I think he is very liberal and tolerant in his passing of things (I expect in his heart he sees the odiousness and injury to us of the whole thing as clearly as I do).'[74] But less than three months later, addressing the same correspondent, Fortescue deplored what he considered the collapse of standards in Christian discourse, at any rate of an apologetic kind. 'It seems as if religious controversy were becoming, not a grave discussion of serious issues on reasonable lines, but a kind of chess game where you score by throwing out the smartest phrase'.[75]

It should be added that, while he had in mind chiefly Anglican and Free Church writers, he did not exonerate two Catholic writers of much contemporary renown in England, Robert Hugh Benson (1871–1914) and Ronald Knox (1888–1957). (Perhaps it was at the back of his mind that both were Anglican converts who had never had the Scholastic philosophical and theological formation from which he had benefited.)

---

action requires: by which principle, moreover, as in all progression, nothing is ever determined or fixed': *Monitore ecclesiastico* 1 (1925), p. 194.

72 *A Tribute to Archbishop Edward Myers … spoken at the Solemn Requiem Mass* (Cambridge: 1956).

73 Cambridge University Library, MS Add. 9812/D/90, Letter to S. Morison of 27 November, 1919.

74 Ibid.

75 Cambridge University Library, MS Add. 9812/D/90, Letter to S. Morison of 5 January, 1920.

What is certainly true is that while the censorial system could maintain a minimum level of doctrinal coherence, it was impotent to guarantee intellectual excellence.

Fortescue turned from what he considered the muddle of much contemporary writing, with its conceptual vagueness and reliance on often misplaced metaphor, to a classic text, at once philosophical and theological, a harbinger of the high Scholastics.

The last act: the Boethius book

Boethius, the late antique Christian Roman philosopher and statesman Anicius Manlius Torquatus Severinus Boethius (c. 480–524/5), had suffered a worse fate than John Vance at the hands of the Ostrogothic king of Italy, Theodoric. That was owing to the ecclesiastico-political vortex in which he had been swirled around. He was caught between his ultimate overlord, the Byzantine emperor Justin, on the one side, and, on the other, a regional Arian ruler at Ravenna. With his rational yet poetic intelligence, and his influence on both Thomas and Dante, Boethius was a good subject for Fortescue to choose.

> By common consent this remains one of the high masterpieces of European literature, translated since early mediaeval times into many languages; a work whose English translators alone include King Alfred, Geoffrey Chaucer, and Queen Elizabeth I; a dominant force (with Thomas Aquinas) in the making of Dante's mind. The *Consolation* is the work of a refined humanist scholar with a richly stocked memory, delighting in lyrical poetry and elegant prose, fascinated by logical problems almost to the point of obsession.[76]

And though Fortescue's cancer prevented him from finishing the work, when he picked his fellow Westminster priest George Smith, despite the latter's comparative youth, to finish off the book, he made a good choice for *Boethius* likewise.

While a dogmatic theologian rather than an historian, or even a philosopher for that matter (his best known work would be a judicious discussion of the Mother of the Lord as 'co-redemptrix'),[77] Smith proved himself, in his latter years, a responsible commissioner and co-ordinator of other men's work.[78] Having seen *Boethius* through the press, he wrote to Miss Elmes,

---

76 H. Chadwick, *Boethius. The Consolations of Music, Logic, Theology and Philosophy* (Oxford: Clarendon Press, 1981), p. 223.

77 G.D. Smith, *Mary's Part in our Redemption* (London: Burns, Oates and Washbourne, 1954, 2nd edition).

78 Notably in G.D. Smith, (ed.), *The Teaching of the Catholic Church* (London: Burns, Oates and Washbourne, 1955, 2nd edition).

> I must confess that much as I enjoyed doing the book, it is a great relief to have it done. I feel at the same time a certain nervousness as to whether it is all right, as to whether (as I have expressed it in the preface): *operi quae addidi non obfuere* [what I added to the work has not damaged it]. One thing I am certain of is that I have omitted none of the information contained in his own notes. I have added a certain amount of my own — but only what I think the Holy Man would have added had he lived to complete the book.[79]

If in one sense the book is, within these limits and in regard to its content, a collaborative effort by Fortescue and Smith, in another — the aspect of its physical appearance — it was the fruit of cooperation between Fortescue and Morison.

Fortescue had discovered, incredulously, that the Latin text of the *De consolatione philosophiae* was no longer available. He intended not only to remedy the want but to do so in a way worthy of its author, by an edition that would be a typographical masterpiece. In Morison he had the perfect candidate for the job, and was fortunate in communicating his own enthusiasm to him, as their correspondence, preserved in the Cambridge University Library, attests. The book proclaimed the qualities of its visual appearance and literary content by a title of over forty words.[80]

Writing in February 1919 to Morison's then employer, Francis Meynell of Burns and Oates, Fortescue explained,

> The book will be edited some day by August Engelbrecht in the Vienna Corpus; but Heaven only knows when it will appear. Meanwhile H.F. Stewart has just edited the Latin text, with an English crib on the opposite pages in the Loeb series (Heinemann). But I hate those Loeb texts, with the crib staring at you on the opposite page. They are nasty cram books for people too lazy to read a text properly. I cannot see for what class of person they are meant. If a man cannot read Latin, of course he must get a good translation. If he can, he does not want the crib. They are meant for lazy people who want to pretend they are reading a foreign

---

79 Downside Archives, IX AF, Box C, Letter to Miss Elmes, written at St Edmund's Ware, 26 March, 1924.

80 *Anici Manli Seuerini Boethii De consolatione philosophiae libri quinque quos denuo recognouit adnotationibus illustrauit adiectis apparatus critico biliographia indicibus biblico et Alageriano Adrianus a Forti Scuto; opus mortuo auctore appositis ad mentem ipsius praeuia dissertatione, appendicibus, indice generali &c. edendum curauit Georgius D. Smith* (London: Burns-Oates and Washbourne, 1925).

language when they are not. Also, I think there must be a number of people who would like a well printed edition of a most famous classic without the annoyance of a crib on the opposite page.[81]

And thinking of Morison more than himself, Fortescue went on to say that the exclusive use of Latin should be a joy to the printer, since 'Latin does much more justice to your type, and looks so much better on the page than English, with its short spiky words'.[82]

Though Morison's letters to Fortescue do not survive, the priest surely infected the typographer with his own enthusiasm.

> I want to see you very much. I want to talk about Boethius. I think of nothing but Boethius day and night. I want that edition (beautiful but elegant) more than anything else in the world. I am bubbling over with ideas, plans, schemes, intentions, proposals, all of which turn around the honoured name of Boethius.[83]

And again, in another letter from April 1919:

> I have practically given up every other work to devote myself to this. It absorbs me. I think it one of the greatest, most important and best books ever written by anyone. The glorious soul of that illustrious martyr shines on me all the day as I work at his book. I have now finished the entire revision of the text, with the readings of Peiper, Obbarius, Engelbrecht, Sitzmann and Renatus Vallinus. . . . Now I am at my notes.[84]

But precisely the notes were what went uncompleted by the time of his death.

From the correspondence with Morison it is clear that, toward the premature end of his life, Fortescue's mind was moving — as Vance rightly claimed — towards the largest questions of religious philosophy. He wrote in late November 1919:

> At present, I am much more interested in what Plato thought about ideas, and the relation of Proclus to Christianity, how far Neoplatonism is Platonism at all. I never cared a tinker's curse for what the Congregation of Rites may have decided about the order in which the acolyte should put out the candles after Vespers.[85]

81 Cambridge University Library, MS Add. 9812/D/90, Letter to F. Meynell of 7 February, 1919.

82 Ibid.

83 Ibid., Letter to S. Morison of 4 April, 1919,

84 Ibid., Letter to S. Morison of Low Sunday, 1919. The local calendar of the church of Pavia commemorated Boethius as a martyr on 23 October. The cult was formally approved at Rome by a decree of the Congregation of Rites, subsequently confirmed by Leo XIII, in December 1883.

85 Ibid., Letter to S. Morison of 24 November, 1919. The importance for

The contrast between, on the one hand, concern for ceremonial order and, on the other, the preoccupations of the author of the *De consolatione* with the problem of evil, the nature of perfection, the quest for the One, the relation of providence and fate, or of divine foreknowledge and human free will, could scarcely be more sharply expressed.

As Fortescue rightly saw, Boethius' treatise is 'a work written by a Platonist who is also a Christian',[86] though when Henry Chadwick (the author of the words just cited) goes on to deny it is a Christian work, he qualifies the judgment by adding that it is, though, 'an essay in natural theology apart from revelation; and the very possibility of that rests on Christian assumptions', concluding '[t]he Christianizing readers have not been absolutely wrong.'[87] At the same time, Proclus, of the enlightening power of whose metaphysic Fortescue evidently had high hopes, himself had an exalted view of the significance of (pagan) liturgy. Order may be multivalent. If there is cosmic order, should it not have — even for a Christian — ritual embodiment?

It is one of the bizarre flukes in authorial reception-history in twentieth century Catholicism that it was precisely for his shouldering the 'hateful burden of verifying in Merati, Martinucci, Le Vavasseur, Van der Stappen, what each person does in the course of these interminable ceremonies' that Adrian Fortescue's name lingered in the presbyteries of the English-speaking world.[88] But the clarity of his rubrical writing, the elegance of his diction, the fineness of the typography, the simple beauty of his self-devised symbols, all aided the execution of the older Roman rite at its best, as the present writer, when a youthful convert to Catholicism remembers it at, for example, Ampleforth Abbey or Westminster Cathedral. And 'at its best' means, precisely, *pace* Boethius, in the Liturgy's signalling of the divine order, which is at once the order of creation and the order of redemption in Jesus Christ.

Boethius of Proclus, the most systematic of the Neo-platonist thinkers, is clearly signalled in H. Chadwick, *Boethius*, op. cit., notably at pp. 203–211, where the topic under discussion is the third of Boethius's *opuscula sacra*, concerning the nature of the good, which later (so it seems) was given a title, 'De hebdomadibus', about whose meaning much ink has flowed.

86 Ibid., p. 249.

87 Ibid., pp. 251–252.

88 Cambridge University Library, MS Add. 9812/D/90, Letter to S. Morison of 24 November, 1919.

Conclusion

In her obituary of Adrian Fortescue in the Catholic Truth Society's bulletin, his parishioner Edith Cowell wrote, 'Don Adrian was a mass of inconsistencies, and the greatest of all was that between the arrogant being he often appeared to be and the humble priest he really was'.[1] Cowell herself is described as 'well-educated, artistic, musical', 'an enthusiastic member of the choir at St Hugh'.[2] She was well-placed to offer a judgment. And she developed her comments with a degree of psychological plausibility. For Cowell, it was Fortescue's reticence which led to his 'curious theory that it is just as ill-bred to show your love of your Church in public as it is to make love to your wife at a dinner-party'. Fertile source of misunderstanding and affront, the same reticence explained his cordial dislike of much in turn-of-the-century devotional practice, as expressed in lyrics, images, fabrics, conceived and executed in poor taste. The word 'kitsch' had not yet been invented but what it denotes was evidently already in mind. Sharp criticism in these areas, so Cowell points out, was understandably 'disedifying to muddle-headed people who were under the impression that he was attacking the object of the devotion and paining to those for whom such devotions had sacred memories'.[3]

Certainly, there were such incidents. A few days before Christmas 1909 Fortescue had written to *The Tablet*, 'inveighing' (his own word) against a popular hymn with the opening words, 'Sweet Heart of Jesus', and a not especially seasonal dispute was opened up.[4] C.B. Purdom, Letchworthian,

---

1   E. Cowell, 'Adrian Fortescue', in *Catholic Truth*, September 1923, pp. 136–137, and here at p. 137. This must be distinguished from the earlier obituary from the same hand published in the Dominican journal *Blackfriars* and cited earlier.

2   Downside Archive, IX AF, Box A, Adrian Willson, 'Edith Cowell'.

3   E. Cowell, 'Adrian Fortescue', art. cit., p. 136.

4   Downside Archive, IX AF, Box D, 'Diary 1909', entry for 20 December, 1909. To be fair, Fortescue's objection was not to Sacred Heart devotion entering into hymnography but to the words 'Sweet heart, may thy own Heart ever

town planner, writer on the theatre, and editor of *Everyman*,[5] was of the opinion that his 'constant outbursts of apparent irreverence and unrestrained hilarity especially directed against the hierarchy . . . were expressive of his deep love and reverence for what he would have died for.'[6] The latter part of that comment (but hardly the first!) chimes with some transparently simple words of Adrian Willson, the son of his choirmaster-organist, named for him in Baptism. 'He always kept up his parishioners' spirits and standards. He always showed us the best in Catholic traditions and our wonderful heritage.' And Willson added: 'But he never despised our Separated Brethren — and they always welcomed and respected him'.[7] This is the voice of a youthful hero-worshipper, but an intelligent one. Personally, I think he would have been nice to know: in 1953, looking back on their acquaintance at St Edmund's Ware, Ronald Knox wrote to John R. McCarthy (thus early, evidently, researching Fortescue's life), 'Perhaps he had too much sense of humour to be altogether a great man; he lacked pomposity'.[8]

Purdom, whom Fortescue 'instructed' but who, through a scruple about the political attitudes of the hierarchy, later regretted, was never received into the Church, offers an intriguing retrospective which at one and the same time seeks to sum up the man and to evoke the scene at Fortescue's extraordinarily well-attended funeral (presided over by Cardinal Bourne, the procession of mourners, according to one participant, took over an hour to pass through Letchworth from church to cemetery).[9]

> He was intensely proud, an aristocrat in mind and habit, a scholar unchallengeable in his own wide historical fields, a man bearing the unmistakable signs of genius; but he died of cancer

---

blessed be' which words, on the grounds that a heart cannot have a heart, he considered 'sheer nonsense'.

5   Charles Benjamin Purdom (1883–1965) became after Fortescue's death a disciple of the Indian mystic Merwan Sheriar Irani (1894–1969), who took the title 'Meher Baba'. Curiously, Meher Baba's mingled Muslim and Hindu inspiration is reminiscent of one of Fortescue's Eastern interests, 'Babism'.

6   C.B. Purdom, *Life over Again*, op. cit., p. 252.

7   Downside Archive IX AF, Box A, Adrian Willson, 'What I remember of Adrian Fortescue', no pagination.

8   Westminster Diocesan Archive, Series 20, Box 22, Letter of 4 March 1963 from Ronald Knox to John R. McCarthy.

9   'It was a striking scene in an English provincial landscape ... All Letchworth turned out to watch the procession pass by': Westminster Diocesan Archive, Series 20, Box 22, Letter of 17 February 1923 from J.J. Dwyer of St Thomas's Historical Society, to Harold Burton. It is pleasing for the present author to note the presence, recorded by Dwyer, of Father Fabian Dix, O.P., the then prior of St Dominic's Priory, Haverstock Hill.

at the height of his powers, and with a vast programme of work to be done. Why? As I stood in his Church at the mass for the dead, the tears running down my face, while outside there was an enormous crowd of people, which followed in silence as his coffin was carried to the cemetery at Wilbury Hill, passing through the town and finishing on the ancient Icknield Way, the question was insistent. Why had he died? My conclusion was that contrary to all seeming, in the situation in which he found the world, the Church, and himself, life had no more to offer.[10]

These words need some interpreting.

One possible view of them might run, not altogether implausibly: Fortescue's work at Letchworth demonstrated his rejection of a dichotomy between high culture and the culture of the *demos*, the great mass of the people. His was an act of resistance that, on the scale of English society as a whole, could reasonably be thought fore-doomed. That was already true in the 1920s. In the first half of the twentieth century the Catholic Church in England, by the complexity of its worship and theology, and the demands of its catechism and casuistry, had stood out against the coarsening of mass culture and its typical discourse (though, to be sure, it had certain asperities of its own). Had Fortescue lived into his 90s, he would have seen how in the Church the cultural revolution of the 1960s, seeping in, made that contrast with democratization's levelling effects far less possible for the future. Though one can hardly ascribe to Purdom a prophetic glimpse of the post-conciliar crisis in Western Catholicism, it is difficult to imagine Fortescue in a Church where 'dumbing down' was the order of the day.

And yet, *pace* Purdom, it must be said that the struggle in which Fortescue was engaged is not one the Church of all ages can ever relinquish. The French patrologist and theologian Henri de Lubac warned,

> There is nothing more demanding than the taste for mediocrity. Beneath its ever moderate appearance there is nothing more intemperate; nothing surer in its instinct; nothing more pitiless in its refusals. It suffers no greatness, shows beauty no mercy.[11]

It is fatal both to the *humanum* and to the Gospel.

An alternative possible interpretation of Purdom's comments inclines me to invoke another and very different point of reference. There are certain affinities between Fortescue and his fellow collegian Frederick William Rolfe's portrait of the unexpectedly elevated English pope in

---

10 C.B. Purdom, *Life over Again*, op. cit., pp. 252–253.

11 H. de Lubac, *Paradoxes of Faith* (Et San Francisco: Ignatus, 1987), p. 137.

The funeral procession for Adrian Fortescue, which took over an hour to pass throught Letchworth from church to cemetery.

Hadrian VII (and this is at the same time Rolfe's — idealized — portrait of himself, the artist). A.J. Symons's description of Rolfe's novelistic portrait in *The Quest for Corvo* ascribes to Hadrian the following qualities: 'his ready command over words, the breadth of his vision, the noble unworldliness of his beliefs and bearing, his mixture of pride and humility, of gentle charity and ruthless reproof for error, his sensitiveness to form and hatred of ugliness'.[12] All of these — by sheerest serendipity — are reminiscent of Fortescue.

Rolfe's recipe for reform of the Petrine office would also have appealed to Fortescue: simplification of tasks, with no reduction in grandiloquence of style. In real life, both men, Fortescue and Rolfe, were photographers, painters, calligraphers. There is no suggestion that Fortescue's emotional life paralleled the abnormalcy on which Rolfe suffered shipwreck. Far from it. Yet at least the comparison allows for another 'take' on Purdom's meaning. Fortescue had been astoundingly energetic, in work and at play. Was there an element of exhaustion in his falling victim to his disease? Rolfe finished his life of the prematurely dying Pope (aged 53, to Fortescue's 49) with the valedictory words: 'Pray for the repose of his soul. He was so tired.'

The new church at Letchworth was furnished with a memorial tablet carved in Roman stone. Its Latin text had a calligraphed English translation on a varnished panel. Done by a fellow student of Fortescue's in Edward Johnston's master class, it reads:

---

12 A.J.A. Symons, *The Quest for Corvo*, op. cit., p. 25.

Entreat the gracious mercy of God for the well-loved soul of Adrian Fortescue, D.D., first Rector of this church. Born on the 14th of January, 1874, he studied with no little success at London, Rome, and Innsbruck. After ordination to the priesthood he travelled widely in the East, gaining an intimate knowledge of the Oriental Rites, of which he was later nominated a consultor to the Holy See. Returning to England he cast his lot in this place, where he might duly build a church, with himself as a guide and pattern to his flock, might duly raise and adorn to the Lord a temple of living stones. He gave lavishly of his unusual talents of intellect and learning, gladly devoting all in the simplicity of his heart to God and to his brethren. His ministry discharged, undismayed either by the severest bodily pain or by premature death, he fell asleep very peacefully in the Lord on 11th February 1923. It was his wish to lie buried among his own people in the neighbouring cemetery, and there he awaits the blessed hope and the coming in the glory of our Lord Jesus Christ. May he rest in peace.

DORMIT IN PACE
ADRIANVS A FORTI SCVTO
PRESBYTER
WESTMONASTERIENSIS
QVI NATVS DIE XIV
IANVARII MDCCCLXXIV
ANIMARVM SALV·TI
SEDVLO INSERVIENS
AMPLISSIMIS TAMEN
DISCIPLINIS EGREGIE
VACAVIT
OBIIT DIE XI FEBRVARII
MCMXXIII

Quaerens me sedisti lassus
Redemisti crucem passus
Tantus labor non sit cassus

ORA PRO EO

Memorial inscription on the tomb of Adrian Fortescue.

Bibliography

Primary sources

Unpublished

Cambridge University Library, MS Addit. 9812 /D/90
Downside Abbey Archives, [Series] IX, A[drian] F[ortescue]
Westminster Diocesan Archives, Series 20

Books

An Anglican on Reunion (London: Catholic Truth Society, 1910)
The Branch Theory (London: Catholic Truth Society, 1911)
Catholic because Roman Catholic (London: Catholic Truth Society, 1917)
The Ceremonies of the Roman Rite Described (London: Burns and Oates, 1918; *The Ceremonies of the Roman Rite Described,* by A. Fortescue, J.B. O'Connell, and A. Reid (London and New York: Burns and Oates, 2009, 15th edition).)
The Date of the Anglican Schism (London: Catholic Truth Society, 1917)
The Divine Liturgy of Our Father among the Saints, John Chrysostom, translated by Adrian Fortescue (London: Catholic Truth Society, 1908)
Donatism (London: Burns and Oates, 1917)
The Early Papacy. To the Synod of Chalcedon in 451 (London: Burns and Oates, 1920; revised edition, Southampton: The Saint Austin Press, 1997, by S.M.P. Reid)
The Formula of Hormisdas (London: Catholic Truth Society, 1914)
The Greek Fathers. Their Lives and Writings (London: Catholic Truth Society, 1908; revised edition: San Francisco, Ignatius Press, 2007, by A. Reid)
How to Pronounce Latin (Letchworth: Fortescue, 1908)
Latin Hymns (Letchworth: Fortescue, 1913; reprinted Cambridge: Cambridge University Press, 1924; Harrison, NY: Roman Catholic Books, 1994).
The Lesser Eastern Churches London: Catholic Truth Society, 1913;

reprinted Piscataway, NJ: Gorgias Press, 2001)
The Mass. A Study of the Roman Liturgy (London: Longmans, Green, 1912; 2nd edition, 1914; 11th impression, 1955)
The Orthodox Eastern Church (London: Catholic Truth Society, 1907; reprinted Piscataway, NJ: Gorgias Press, 2001)
Rome and Constantinople London: Catholic Truth Society, 1908)
Russia and the Catholic Church (London: Catholic Truth Society, 1915)
The Uniate Eastern Churches (London: Burns and Oates, 1923; reprinted Piscataway, NJ: Gorgias Press, 2001)
The Vestments of the Roman Rite (London: Catholic Truth Society, 1908)

Articles

'Alexandrine Liturgy', in C.G. Hebermann, *The Catholic Encyclopaedia* 1 (New York: Encyclopaedia Press, 1907), pp. 303–306
'Americanism', in W.H. Cologan (ed.), *Folia fugitiva* (London: R. and T. Washbourne, 1907), pp. 265–290
'Antiochene Liturgy', in C.G. Hebermann, *The Catholic Encyclopaedia* 1 (New York: Encyclopaedia Press, 1907), pp. 571–74
'Apollinarism', in J. Hastings (ed.), *Encyclopaedia of Religion and Ethics* 1 (New York: Charles Scribner's Sons, 1908), pp. 606–608
'Aquileian Rite', in C.G. Hebermann, *The Catholic Encyclopaedia* 16 (New York: Encyclopaedia Press, 1913), pp. 3–4
'The Armenians', *Studies* V (1916), pp. 351–370
'The Balkan Peoples', *Studies* IV (195), pp. 527–544
'Canon, 2. Rit byzantin', in F. Cabrol–H. Leclerq (ed.), *Dictionnaire d'Archéologie et liturgie chrétienne* II/2 (Paris: Letaugey et Ané), cols. 1905–1910
'Canon of the Mass', in C.G. Hebermann, *The Catholic Encyclopaedia* 3 (New York: Encyclopaedia Press, 1908), pp. 255–267
'Canonarche', in F. Cabrol–H. Leclerq (ed.), *Dictionnaire d'Archéologie et liturgie chrétienne* II/2 (Paris: Letaugey et Ané, 1911), col. 1954
'Chartophylax', in F. Cabrol–H. Leclerq (ed.), *Dictionnaire d'Archéologie et liturgie chrétienne*, III/1 (Paris: Letaugey et Ané, 1912), cols. 1014–1019
'Chéroubicon', in ibid., cols. 1281–1286
'Christianity in the Balkans', *Studies* V (1916), pp. 1–21
'Collect', in C.G. Hebermann, *The Catholic Encyclopaedia* 4 (New York: Encyclopaedia Press, 1908), pp. 103–104
'Communion Antiphon', in ibid., pp. 169–170
'Concelebration', in ibid., p. 190
'Confiteor', in ibid., pp. 222–223
'Constantinople, Rite of', in ibid., pp. 312–320

'Cowl', in ibid., p. 463

'Denzinger', in ibid., pp. 736–737

'Docetism', in ibid., 4 (New York: Charles Scribner's Sons, 1912), pp. 842–835.

'Doxology', in C.G. Hebermann, *The Catholic Encyclopaedia* 5 (New York: Encyclopaedia Press, 1909), pp. 150–151

'Durandus, William', in ibid., p. 207

'Durandus, William, the Younger', ibid.

'Durham Rite', in ibid., pp. 213–214.

'Eastern Churches', in ibid., pp. 230–240

'The Eastern Schism', in W.H. Cologan (ed)., *Folia fugitiva* (London: R. and T. Washbourne, 1907), pp. 135–162

'Elias of Jerusalem', in C.G. Hebermann, *The Catholic Encyclopaedia* 5 (New York: Encyclopaedia Press, 1909), p. 385.

'Eparchy', in ibid., p. 494

'Ephesus, the Seven Sleepers of', in ibid., pp. 496–497

'Ephraim of Antioch', in ibid., p. 500

'Epiklesis', in ibid., pp. 502–503

'Epiphanius of Constantinople', in ibid., p. 504

'Etherianus, Hugh and Leo', in ibid., pp. 555–556

'Euchologion', in ibid., pp. 595–596

'Eudocia', in ibid., p. 597

'Euphemius of Constantinople', in ibid., p. 606

'Eusebius of Laodicea', in ibid., p. 623

'Eustathius of Sebaste', in ibid., pp. 628–629

'Eutychius I (Patriarch of Constantinople; in ibid., pp. 638–639

'Eutychius (Melchite Patriarch of Constantinople)', in ibid., p. 639

'Exarch', in ibid., pp. 676–677

'Febronianism', in J. Hastings (ed.), *Encyclopaedia of Religion and Ethics* 5 (New York: Charles Scribner's Sons, 1908), pp. 807–809

'Gennadius II, Patriarch of Constantinople', in C.G. Hebermann, *The Catholic Encyclopaedia* 6 (New York: Encyclopaedia Press, 1909), pp. 416–417

'Gennadius of Marseilles', in ibid., pp. 417–418

'George Hamartolus', in ibid., pp. 455–456

'Georgius Syncellus', in ibid., pp. 463–464

'Gloria in excelsis Deo', in ibid., pp. 583–585

'Gradual', in ibid., pp. 715–718

'Greece', in ibid., pp. 735–744

'Greek Rites', in ibid., pp. 774–776

'Gregory the Illuminator', in C.G. Hebermann, *The Catholic Encyclopaedia* 7 (New York: Encyclopaedia Press, 1910), ibid., pp. 23–25

'Henoticon', in ibid., pp. 218–219

'Hermesianism', in J. Hastings (ed.), *Encyclopaedia of Religion and Ethics* 6 (New York: Charles Scribner's Sons, 1914), pp. 624–626

'Hesychasm' in C.G. Hebermann, *The Catholic Encyclopaedia* 7 (New York: Encyclopaedia Press, 1910), pp. 301–303

'Holy Synod' in ibid., pp. 408–432

'Iconoclasm', in ibid., pp. 620–625

'Iconoclasm', in J. Hastings (ed.), *Encyclopaedia of Religion and Ethics* 7 ((New York: Charles Scribner's Sons, 1915), pp. 78–81.

'Images, Veneration of', in C.G. Hebermann, *The Catholic Encyclopaedia* 7 (New York: Encyclopaedia Press, 1910), pp. 664–672

'Introduction', *The Holy Week Book* (London: Catholic Truth Society, 1916)

'Introduction', in C.D. Cobham (ed.), *The Patriarchs of Constantinople* (Cambridge: Cambridge University Press, 1911)

'Introit' in C.G. Hebermann, *The Catholic Encyclopaedia* 8 (New York: Encyclopaedia Press, 1910), pp. 81–82

'Isidore of Thessalonica', in ibid., pp. 188–189

'Ite missa est', in ibid., pp. 253–254

'Jerusalem, II. From A.D. 71 to A.D. 1099', in ibid., pp. 355–361

'Jerusalem II. From the end of the Latin kingdom to the present time', in ibid., pp. 364–371

'Jerusalem, Liturgy of', in ibid., pp. 371–372

'John of Antioch', in ibid., p. 469

'John Scholasticus', in ibid., p. 484

'John Talaia', in ibid., pp. 485–486

'John the Faster', in ibid., pp. 493–495

'Julius Africanus', in ibid., pp. 565–566

'Justinian I', in ibid., pp. 578–580

'Kyrie eleison', in ibid., pp. 714–716

'Latin Church', in C.G. Hebermann, *The Catholic Encyclopaedia* 9 (New York: Encyclopaedia Press, 1910), pp. 22–23.

'The Latin Church in Russia', *Dublin Review* 162 (1918), pp. 41–70

'Lavabo', in C.G. Hebermann, *The Catholic Encyclopaedia* 9 (New York: Encyclopaedia Press, 1910), pp. 44–45

'Law (Christian, Western; Christian, Eastern)', in J. Hastings (ed.), *Encyclopaedia of Religion and Ethics* 7 (New York: Charles Scribner's Sons, 1915), pp. 832–840

'Lector', in C.G. Hebermann, *The Catholic Encyclopaedia* 9 (New York: Encyclopaedia Press, 1910), p. 111.

'Leo Diaconus', in ibid., pp. 180–181

'Lessons in the Liturgy', in ibid., pp. 193–199

'Libera me', in ibid., p. 214

'Liberatus of Carthage', in ibid., p. 215

'Liturgical Books', in ibid., pp. 296–304

'Liturgy', in ibid., pp. 306–313

'Lumen Christi', in ibid., p. 430

'Marcellinus Comes', in ibid., p. 639

'Marcian', in ibid., pp. 644–645

'Marcus Diadochus', in ibid., p. 650

'Marcus Eremita', in ibid., p. 650

'Mass, Chapter and Conventual', in ibid., p. 790

'Mass, Liturgy of the', in ibid., pp. 790–800

'Mass, Nuptial', in C.G. Hebermann, *The Catholic Encyclopaedia* 10 (New York: Encyclopaedia Press, 1911), pp. 5–6

'Maurice, Roman emperor', in ibid., p. 69

'Menaion', in ibid., pp. 177–178

'Metaphrastes, Symeon', in ibid., pp. 225–226

'Methodius I', in ibid., pp. 242–243

'Metrophanes of Smyrna', in ibid., p. 244

'Michael Cerularius', in ibid., pp. 273–274

'Monasticism, III. Eastern Monasticism', in ibid., pp. 467–472

'Nectarius, Patriarch of Constantinople', in ibid., p. 737

'Nikon, Patriarch of Moscow', in C.G. Hebermann, *The Catholic Encyclopaedia* 11 (New York: Encyclopaedia Press, 1911), pp. 77–78

'Nilus, saint', in ibid., pp. 79–80

'Nilus the Younger', in ibid., p. 80

'Nonnus', in ibid., p. 100

'Oecumenius', in ibid., p. 214

'Offertory', in ibid., pp. 217–219

'Orate fratres', in ibid., pp. 269–270

'Oremus', in ibid., p. 295

'Orientius', in ibid., pp. 305–306

'Orsisius', in ibid., p. 328

'Orthodox Church', in ibid., pp. 329–330

'Orthodoxy, feast of', in ibid., p. 330

'Palladius', in ibid., pp. 425–426

'Patriarch and Patriarchate', in ibid., pp. 549–553

'Paulicians', in ibid., pp. 583–585

'Peter Mongus', in ibid., p. 770

'Photius of Constantinople' in C.G. Hebermann, *The Catholic Encyclopaedia* 12 (New York: Encyclopaedia Press, 1911), pp. 43–46

'Postcommunion', in ibid., pp. 318–319

'Preface', in ibid., pp. 384–386

'Preface', *Vespers for Sundays with an Introduction* (London: Catholic Truth
    Society, 1915), pp. 2–6.
'Preface', *The Missal*. Compiled by lawful authority from the *Missale
    Romanum*. A new edition agreeable with the Vatican Typical Edition
    and with a preface by Adrian Fortescue. Together with a supplement
    containing the Additional Masses used in English-speaking countries
    and those for the greater feasts of the Principal Religious Orders
    (London: Burns and Oates, 1912), pp. I–xix.
'Protopope', in C.G. Hebermann, *The Catholic Encyclopaedia* 12 (New
    York: Encyclopaedia Press, 1911), pp. 503–504
'Psellus, Michael', in ibid., p. 545
'The Rite of Consecration in the East', in Bergh (ed.), *The Official
    Handbook of the Consecration of Westminster Cathedral* (London: Burns
    and Oates, 1910), pp. 68–78
'Rites' in C.G. Hebermann, *The Catholic Encyclopaedia* 13 (New York:
    Encyclopaedia Press, 1912), pp. 64–72
'Ritual', in ibid., pp. 88–89
'Roman Rite, The', in ibid., pp. 155–156
'Russia and the Catholic Church', *Studies* IV (1915), pp. 184–205
'Sanctus', in C.G. Hebermann, *The Catholic Encyclopaedia* 13 (New York:
    Encyclopaedia Press, 1912), pp. 432–434
'Schism, Eastern', in ibid., pp. 535–539
'Secret', in ibid., pp. 673–674
'A Slav Bishop: Joseph Georg Strossmayer', *Dublin Review* 163 (1919),
    pp. 234–257
'Suidas', in C.G. Hebermann, *The Catholic Encyclopaedia* 14 (New York:
    Encyclopaedia Press, 1912), p. 328
'Synaxarion', in ibid., pp. 382–383
'Syrian Rite, West', in ibid., pp. 417–419
'Theodosius I', in ibid., pp. 577–578
'Ticonius', in ibid., p. 721
'The Uniate Church in Poland and Russia', *Dublin Review* 161 (1917),
    pp. 215–243
'Votive Mass', in C.G. Hebermann, *The Catholic Encyclopaedia* 14 (New
    York: Encyclopaedia Press, 1912), pp. 508–509

Editorial work

Jean Maspero, *Histoire des patriarches d'Alexandrie depuis la mort de
    l'empereur Anastase jusqu'à la reconciliation des Eglises jacobites (518–610)*
    (Paris: Champion, 1923 [with Gaston Wiet])
Thomas a Kempis, *De imitatione Christi. Libri quattuor* (London:
    Methuen, 1909)

Anicius Manlius Severinus Boethius, *De consolatione philosophiae. Libri quinque* (London: Burns, Oates and Washbourne, 1925; reprinted Hildesheim: Gregor Olms Verlag, 1976)

Secondary works

E. Cowell, 'Adrian Fortescue', in *Catholic Truth*, September 1923, pp. 136–137

Idem., 'Adrian Fortescue', *Blackfriars* IV. 41 (1923), pp. 1029–1034.

M. Davies, 'Adrian Fortescue – Priest and Scholar', in *The Latin Mass* 3, 5 (September–October 1994), pp. 26–33.

M. Davies, 'Adrian Fortescue — Priest and Scholar', in idem. (ed.) *The Wisdom of Adrian Fortescue* (Fort Collins, CO: Roman Catholic Books, 1999), pp. 17–77.

A. Dragani, *Adrian Fortescue and the Eastern Christian Churches* (Piscataway, NJ: Gorgias Press, 2007)

J.R. McCarthy, *Adrian* (East Cleveland, OH: McCarthy, 1999)

J.G. Vance, *Short Memoir of the Revd Dr Adrian Fortescue, with a catalog of the memorial exhibition* (Letchworth: The Book Club, 1923)

J.G. Vance–J.W. Fortescue, *Adrian Fortescue. A Memoir* (London: Burns, Oates and Washbourne, 1924)

Index